SHOSTAKOVICH AND HIS WORLD

SHOSTAKOVICH

AND HIS WORLD

EDITED BY LAUREL E. FAY

PRINCETON UNIVERSITY PRESS
PRINCETON AND OXFORD

Copyright © 2004 by Princeton University Press

Published by Princeton University Press, 41 William Street,
Princeton, New Jersey 08540
In the United Kingdom: Princeton University Press,
3 Market Place, Woodstock, Oxfordshire OX20 1SY

For permissions information, see page xiii.

Library of Congress Control Number 2004104803

ISBN 0-691-12068-4 (cloth)
ISBN 0-691-12069-2 (paperback)

British Library Cataloging-in-Publication Data is available

This publication has been produced by the Bard College Publications Office:

Ginger Shore, Director

Francie Soosman, Cover design

Natalie Kelly, Design

Text edited by Paul De Angelis

Music typeset by Don Giller

Printed on acid-free paper. ∞

pup.princeton.edu

Printed in the United States of America

1 3 5 7 9 10 8 6 4 2

In memory of two dear friends,

Olya Kazakova
and
Alik Kovnatsky

Contents

PART II
ESSAYS

Preface and Acknowledgments

Dmitrii Shostakovich needs no introduction. Widely recognized by the end of the twentieth century as the most poignant and "meaningful" musical chronicler of his appalling era and an inspirational symbol of the resilience of art, his music has never enjoyed greater popularity, his immense accomplishments greater esteem. And yet, despite a burgeoning literature about the composer, a true-to-life, fully-dimensional portrait of the creative artist, the private man, and the public figure eludes our grasp. How could it be otherwise? It has been less than thirty years since Shostakovich's death. The Soviet Union, which both coddled and crippled him, has been gone less than fifteen.

Much about Shostakovich and his music remains to be learned. Much remains buried in archives, public and private. To be sure, much is now finally surfacing, but those who do not read Russian are disadvantaged by the dearth of translations. At this stage, no single volume can hope to fill all the gaps and answer all the questions. The format of the Bard Music Festival series, with its mixture of documentary materials and scholarly essays, offers a timely opportunity to address some of them.

The documents selected for translation here offer key insights into different facets of Shostakovich's world, the personal, the professional, and the political.

Throughout his life, Shostakovich was a prolific letter writer, yet only a small fraction of the letters known to survive has been translated into English. The letters young Mitia wrote to family and friends in the 1920s and early 1930s, before he recognized the imperative to guard his thoughts, are especially revealing. The volume opens with a selection of letters written to his mother between the ages of seventeen and twenty, when Shostakovich began to travel away from home for the first time. The confidence and determination, triumphs and setbacks of the young musician at the outset of his career come across vividly, together with a sense of just how difficult the day-to-day struggle to survive must have been for his family after the sudden death of his father in 1922.

Shostakovich's response to the questionnaire on the psychology of the creative process, a fascinating document only recently discovered in the archives, dates from shortly after the last letter to his mother included here. In the course of elaborating the working method and sources of inspiration of the young composer, the answers pinpoint his tastes in music and the other arts at the moment when he had just embarked on the composition of his first opera, *The Nose*. This merits close study. Mahler, for instance, already figures in the list of Shostakovich's favorite composers, just a few months after he had made the acquaintance of Ivan Sollertinsky, which suggests that the credit he attributed in later life to Sollertinsky for having opened his eyes to Mahler may have been somewhat exaggerated. Similarly, the presence of Stravinsky's *Oedipus Rex* in the list of his favorite works, only three months after it received its first performance in Paris, provides a striking illustration of how close the ties were between the new music communities of Leningrad and the rest of Europe.

The contrast between the style of the four preserved letters written by Shostakovich to Stalin in the late 1940s and early 1950s and the letters written to his mother twenty years earlier could not be sharper. Analyzing these and other documents he has recently uncovered in Russian archives, Leonid Maximenkov sheds light on Shostakovich's position within the highest echelon of the Soviet artistic nomenklatura and offers provocative new interpretations of the artistic crises of 1936 and 1948.

The post-World War II eclipse of Shostakovich's music in the West was an unfortunate by-product of the Cold War. Christopher Gibbs's documentary survey of the early reception of Shostakovich's Seventh ("Leningrad") Symphony in 1940s America recaptures what today seems like an inconceivable time when a piece of serious symphonic music by a composer from halfway around the globe could become the stuff of an all-out media blitz and the cover story of *Time* magazine, a fraught time when Shostakovich's music was propelled into virtually every American home.

The essays in this volume, contributed by both established and young scholars from North America, England and Russia, deal predominantly with aspects of the composer's legacy that have been neglected in the literature.

It is hard to believe that there is a major, full-length stage work by Shostakovich that to this day has received only a single public performance. And yet, after its premiere in April 1931, Shostakovich's ballet on the theme of industrial sabotage, *The Bolt*, was never performed again, even though some of its most appealing music became popular in a concert suite. (As I write, the Bolshoi Theatre has just announced plans to mount a production of this long-forgotten ballet in the coming season, following the success of their 2003 production of Shostakovich's third ballet, *The Limpid Stream*.) Employing a wide range of resources, Simon Morrison reconstructs the "scenario" behind the creation of the original ballet, how the music, dance, décor and costumes were designed (and reimagined years later), and how they fell afoul of shifting political and cultural realities.

The distance between Shostakovich's early and late works is more than just a matter of years. It is no secret that Shostakovich's evolution as a composer was anything but natural. This makes all the more paradoxical and intriguing the parallels Levon Hakobian draws between two masterpieces at opposite ends of Shostakovich's career, his manic first opera, *The Nose*, and his harrowing penultimate symphony, the Fourteenth.

In her essay on four case studies from the Russian literary tradition—the composer's two completed operas and two of his song cycles—Caryl Emerson peels back the inherited layers of significance and illuminates how Shostakovich played on the expectations of his audience in dealing with familiar texts in unexpected ways. Shostakovich belonged to a culture that knew its literature well.

His audience also knew its Russian musical heritage well, from the nineteenth-century classics to a rich array of folk and popular staples. In his essay on another lesser-known theatrical work, the 1959 operetta *Moscow, Cheryomushki*, Gerard McBurney homes in on the wide range of parodies, quotations, and allusions it contains and how its initial audiences might have appreciated them.

Shostakovich was highly impressionable, a keen "student" of music, new and old. In his survey of Shostakovich's activity as a pedagogue and mentor, David Fanning finds instances of influence extending in both directions, from teacher to student and vice versa. The example of the next generation may also have played a role in the composer's unexpected adoption of twelve-tone techniques in a number of his late works. Profiling the spread of dodecaphony in both the official and unofficial spheres of Soviet music in the 1960s, Peter Schmelz provides indispensable context for understanding Shostakovich's personal approach.

Issues of interpretation are inevitable in studies of Shostakovich; they inform the approaches of a number of the authors in this volume. In the concluding essay Leon Botstein confronts the pivotal issue of interpretation head-on, reflecting on the reasons listeners extract different meanings from his music and why it continues to captivate us.

* * *

I am indebted, first and foremost, to the authors and translators who contributed to this volume. Without their enthusiasm and active cooperation you would not be holding this book in your hands. I owe a special debt of gratitude to Caryl Emerson for her expert advice on questions of translation. Finally, I extend my heartfelt thanks to the members of the experienced editorial/production team with whom I have had the good fortune to collaborate: Paul De Angelis, Natalie Kelly, Irene Zedlacher, Don Giller, and Ginger Shore.

Laurel E. Fay
April 2004

Permissions

The following copyright holders have graciously given their permission to reprint musical excerpts from copyrighted works.

Works of Shostakovich

Antiformalist Rayok. © 1991 by G. Schirmer, Inc. (ASCAP). International Copyright secured. All Rights Reserved. Reprinted by Permission. a) At rehearsal no. 5; b) rehearsal no. 36–37.

The Bolt. © 1987 by G. Schirmer, Inc. (ASCAP). International Copyright secured. All Rights Reserved. Reprinted by Permission. a) "The Conformist," act 3, rehearsal no. 619, m. 4 to rehearsal no. 621, m. 9; b) "Lazy Idler," act 1, rehearsal no. 35, mm 1–17; c) "The Saboteurs (Intermezzo)" (no. 10), from act 1, 5 mm., after rehearsal no. 84 to no. 86.

Cello Concerto No. 1 in E-flat Major, op. 107. © 1960 (renewed) by G. Schirmer, Inc. (ASCAP). International Copyright secured. All Rights Reserved. Reprinted by Permission. First mvt., mm. 96–102, piano reduction.

Counterplan, op. 33. (Film Score) © 1932 (renewed) by G. Schirmer, Inc. (ASCAP). International Copyright secured. All Rights Reserved. Reprinted by Permission. "Song of the Counterplan."

Hypothetically Murdered, op. 31 *(Declared Dead)*. © 1986 by G. Schirmer, Inc. (ASCAP). International Copyright secured. All Rights Reserved. Reprinted by Permission. "Twelve Apostles," mm. 79–118.

Limpid Stream, op. 39. © 1987 by G. Schirmer, Inc. (ASCAP). International Copyright secured. All Rights Reserved. Reprinted by Permission. "Russian Dance" (no. 9), from act 1, mm. 5–24.

Moscow, Cheryomushki, op. 105. © 1959 (renewed) by G. Schirmer, Inc. (ASCAP). International Copyright secured. All Rights Reserved. Reprinted by Permission. a) Act 1 finale, "Song about Cheryomushki" (no. 17), mm. 1–38; b) "Boris's aria" (no. 4), from act 1, mm. 52–56; c) "Boris's song-serenade" (no. 5), from act 1, mm. 37–44; d) "Intermezzo" (no. 28) from act 2, mm. 114–33, piano reduction; e) "Lidochka and Boris's Duet" (no. 19), from act 2, mm. 1–8, piano reduction; f) ibid., from act 2, mm. 164–219; g) "Masha and Bubentsov's duet" (no. 19), from act 2, mm. 164–219; h) "Overture-Prologue" from act 1, mm. 119–26, piano reduction; i) ibid., mm. 181–83, piano reduction; j) "Pantomime" (no. 3) from act 1, mm. 78–88, piano reduction; k) "Vava and Drebednev's duet" (no. 8), from act 1, mm. 1–6, piano reduction.

The Nose. © 1962 Universal Edition, A. G. Wien, © renewed. All Rights Reserved. Used by permission of European American Music Distributors LLC, U.S. and Canadian agent for Universal Edition, A. G. Wien. a) Act 1, scene 2, from rehearsal no. 59 + 3mm.; b) act 2, orchestral interlude between scenes 5 and 6, rehearsal no. 238; c) act 3, scene 7, from rehearsal no. 346 + 4mm.; d) act 3, scene 8, from rehearsal no. 416 + 5mm.; e) act 3, scene 8, rehearsal no. 436 to 437; f) act 3, scene 8, ending.

Seven Verses of A. Blok, op. 127. © 1969 (renewed) by G. Schirmer, Inc. (ASCAP). International Copyright secured. All Rights Reserved. Reprinted by Permission. a) No. 6, "Mysterious Signs," mm. 1–9; b) ibid., m. 82 to end.

String Quartet No. 5 in B-flat Major, op. 92. © 1953 (renewed) by G. Schirmer, Inc. (ASCAP). International Copyright secured. All Rights Reserved. Reprinted by Permission. a) First mvt., mm. 261–66; b) third mvt., mm. 337–43.

String Quartet No. 12 in D-flat Major, op. 133. © 1968 by G. Schirmer, Inc. (ASCAP). International Copyright secured. All Rights Reserved. Reprinted by Permission. a) First mvt., mm. 1–4; b) first mvt., 1 m. before rehearsal no. 4; c) rehearsal no. 8; d) rehearsal no. 10; e) 1 m. before rehearsal no. 12.

String Quartet No. 13 in B-flat Minor, op. 138. © 1969 (renewed) by G. Schirmer, Inc. (ASCAP). International Copyright secured. All Rights Reserved. Reprinted by Permission. 3 mm. before rehearsal no. 18 to no. 20.

Symphony No. 8 in C Minor, op. 65. © 1946 (renewed) by G. Schirmer, Inc. (ASCAP). International Copyright secured. All Rights Reserved. Reprinted by Permission. First mvt., mm. 18–22, first and second violins and violas.

Symphony No. 10 in E Minor, op. 93. © 1954 (renewed) by G. Schirmer, Inc. (ASCAP). International Copyright secured. All Rights Reserved. Reprinted by Permission. Third mvt., mm. 492–97.

Symphony No. 11, op. 103. © 1958 (renewed) by G. Schirmer, Inc. (ASCAP). International Copyright secured. All Rights Reserved. Reprinted by Permission. Fourth mvt., mm. 347–54.

Symphony No. 14, op. 135. © 1969 (renewed) by G. Schirmer, Inc. (ASCAP). International Copyright secured. All Rights Reserved. Reprinted by Permission. a) Second mvt., after rehearsal no. 10; b) ibid., after rehearsal no. 11; c) third mvt., after rehearsal no. 32; d) third mvt., "Lorelei," 3 mm. before rehearsal no. 46 to end; e) fifth mvt., the refrain; f) ibid., after rehearsal no. 71; g) seventh mvt., after rehearsal no. 91; h) first mvt., beginning; i) third mvt., after rehearsal no. 26; j) ibid., after rehearsal no. 50; k) fourth mvt., after rehearsal no. 60; l) ibid., after rehearsal no. 62; m) fifth mvt., after rehearsal no. 70; n) seventh mvt., "In the Santé Jail," beginning; o) ibid., rehearsal no. 91 to 2 mm. after no. 93; p) ibid., after rehearsal no. 96; q) ibid., after rehearsal no. 103.

Violin Concerto No. 2 in C-sharp Minor, op. 129. © 1967 (renewed) by G. Schirmer, Inc. (ASCAP). International Copyright secured. All Rights Reserved. Reprinted by Permission. Third mvt., mm. 1–14.

Works of Other Composers

Symphony No. 4. By Akhmed Gadzhiev. © by G. Schirmer, Inc. (ASCAP). International Copyright secured. All Rights Reserved. Reprinted by Permission. First mvt., mm. 29–38, first and second violins and violas.

Concerto No. 1 for Piano and Orchestra. By German Galynin. © by G. Schirmer, Inc. (ASCAP). International Copyright secured. All Rights Reserved. Reprinted by Permission. Third mvt., mm. 88–92.

Symphony No. 3. By Kara Karaev. © by G. Schirmer, Inc. (ASCAP). International Copyright secured. All Rights Reserved. Reprinted by Permission. First mvt., mm. 1–16.

Note on Transliteration

With a few exceptions for names already familiar to the Western reader in anglicized spellings, the transliteration used in the text and discursive notes of this book follows the simplified Library of Congress system. Bibliographic citations and italicized Russian words supplied in the text for elucidation follow the system strictly, without concessions to common use, retaining the soft and hard signs of the original Cyrillic alphabet.

What this means, in practical terms, is that in a few instances slight discrepancies will be encountered between the spelling of a name or title found in the text and one in a bibliographic citation.

SHOSTAKOVICH AND HIS WORLD

PART I
DOCUMENTS

❖

Shostakovich:

Letters to His Mother, 1923–1927

SELECTED BY DMITRII FREDERIKS AND ROSA SADYKHOVA

INTRODUCED, AND WITH COMMENTARY, BY ROSA SADYKHOVA

TRANSLATED BY ROLANDA NORTON

From their first parting in 1923, Dmitrii Shostakovich corresponded with his mother for almost thirty years. Sofia Vasilevna Shostakovich kept her son's letters and even the short postcards he sent her from here and there on his travels. After her death in 1955, Sofia Vasilevna's personal archive remained in the family of her eldest daughter, Mariia Dmitrievna Shostakovich, and then of Mariia's son, Dmitrii Vsevolodovich Frederiks.

In 1981, an exhibition was organized by the Leningrad Philharmonic with the participation of the Leningrad Museum of Theatre and Music to mark Shostakovich's seventy-fifth birthday; during the creation of this exhibition Dmitrii Frederiks established a partnership with the museum. A few years later Sofia Vasilevna's personal archive—containing albums of family and theater photographs, several documents and musical autographs, and also letters—was handed over to the museum; the letters, however, were placed under the conditions of a private archive.

Several of the letters, dating from 1923 to 1927, were published in a somewhat abridged form in the journal *Neva* (1986, no. 9). Dmitrii Frederiks and I then chose the letters that we considered necessary to introduce into academic circles and that, it seemed to us, would be of interest to the general public. These letters are published here in their unabridged form for the first time.

The period of 1923–27 was one of unusually intense spiritual and creative growth for Shostakovich. Let us recall: in 1923 Shostakovich was seventeen; he was studying in two classes at the Petrograd Conservatory (piano and composition); he was a favored pupil, arousing the boldest predictions for his future; and he was already the author of several works that were striking in their originality, freshness, and clearly outlined individuality. By 1927 he was a famous composer and the diplomate of an international piano competition; his name was at the center of the most interesting musical discussions of the 1920s; and he was the author of the famous First Symphony and First Piano Sonata in which his not insignificant spiritual experience was already formed. In a few years he had traveled an enormous distance. Only a few of these events are reflected in these published letters. Of particular interest to researchers will be the letters in which Shostakovich tells of his links with composers in Moscow during those years. His letters both embellish and clarify existing factual material.

Because these letters are addressed to the composer's mother, they contain many domestic details that give a flavor of the family's daily life and the relationships therein. In 1922, when the composer's father, Dmitrii Boleslavovich Shostakovich, died, the family was left with no income. Sofia Vasilevna attempted to work; her eldest daughter Mariia, also a student at the conservatory, started giving music lessons; the youngest daughter, fourteen-year-old Zoya, was still at school. In 1924, while continuing his study at the conservatory, Dmitrii Shostakovich started working as a piano accompanist in the cinema, which had a bad effect on his health. As is apparent from his letters, both his friends and the teachers at the conservatory tried to help him. It is well-known, for example, that the rector of the Petrograd Conservatory, Aleksandr Glazunov, obtained a personal stipend for Shostakovich and additional rations. However, the family was always desperately short of money.

Shostakovich was particularly close to his mother at this time. He thought of himself as her principal support and shared the family's concerns with her. Directed by Sofia Vasilevna's advice he began to conduct his affairs with the seriousness of an adult. "Mitka is displaying great efficiency in administrative affairs and does not allow himself to be swindled," the composer Mikhail Kvadri wrote to her from Moscow. "Everywhere he goes he talks with self-respect and above all he is adored by everyone" (17 January 1927).

It must be said that Shostakovich's relationship with his mother was never idyllic. Sofia Vasilevna had a powerful and difficult nature. Loving her son as she did unreservedly and believing absolutely in his genius, she tried to be his "leader" in life, and, as often happens with frenzied parents, was somewhat overbearing. As a result their relationship sometimes had dramatic moments, but even in his young years, when they were closest, Shostakovich both missed his home and was constantly striving to leave it. Yet whenever he did go away, he wrote tender letters home, giving detailed, diary-like accounts, warmly sharing the joys of his first successes—so sacred to a musician who is just starting his career—knowing how his mother looked forward to receiving them. Shostakovich's letters to his mother are so sincere and contain so much direct perception of life that they give us a sufficiently full picture of the character of the young composer.

Koreiz,[1] 3 September 1923

Dearest Mother,

I am terribly bored here so far from *Piter*[2] and can't wait till we get home. I never thought I would be so homesick. My darlings, one day I will see you and embrace you again. Little Zoya—she's so good, so lovely. What is she up to? I guess her lessons have already begun in school? Really, Zoya is a wonderful person. Here I spend all my time in the sanatorium and I get terribly bored. I suppose it is fall in Petrograd now. I expect it's drizzling and the wind is bracing. Oh, dear Petrograd weather! Here all the really splendid people have gone their separate ways; there remain only rather dry, erudite fellows. The weather is still fine, thank goodness. It's as if the sun senses that it has to heal my lump and it is shining with all its might. Recently I caught sight of myself—it's terrible how I have tanned—I'm so brown. Incidentally, there are often big fires at the moment between Alupka and Simeiz. Fire is even threatening Ai-Petri. It is a huge natural disaster. The day before yesterday a singer, Epaneshnikova, gave a recital. She is amazing. Her voice is crystal clear. I'm not much of a fan of the voice and chamber singing, but she sang so well that I thoroughly enjoyed it. But I just can't tell you how I'm longing to go to the Mariinsky Theatre and hear *Kitezh, The Queen of Spades, Coppelia,* and *The Nutcracker.* On the whole it's awfully boring here. I don't suppose you've seen Maksimilian Oseevich?[3] What's up with him? Why hasn't he replied to my letter? And Leonid Nikolaev[4] too. It's pig-headed of them. I warned both of them that I cannot and do not enjoy writing letters, yet when I left they still both asked for a letter from me and now they haven't replied. I just don't know what's the matter with them. Epaneshnikova has just arrived; she's going to sing. She sang well. Mariia, Oleg, Galia, and I went off to the tower (we have a tower here in Gaspra) to look at the fire. It's a terrible sight, but beautiful. Purple smoke is rising above Ai-Petri and has surrounded all of the left-hand side. I didn't like Alupka much. True, where it flattens out down at the bottom it is very beautiful, but in the town it's horrible. Mother dear, don't send us any more money as we have easily enough. I've just come back from the sea: there were some people there with a life belt. I put it on, you know, but although I didn't sink I couldn't swim. I couldn't even move! So I suppose learning to swim will just have to remain a dream. But for the moment I just can't wait till I get to Petrograd and see you and our apartment, and the dog. . . . Oh yes! In your last letter you said the kitten has been given away. That's a real pity—he was so splendid. Well, good-bye. All the best. It won't be long now till we see each other.

D. Shostakovich.

1. In the spring of 1923 Shostakovich was diagnosed with tuberculosis of the lymph glands. After an operation the doctors insistently recommended spending his convalescence in the Crimea. Sofia Vasilevna sold certain items, even a grand piano, leaving her children without an instrument, in order to send Dmitrii and Mariia there for the summer. This was Shostakovich's first reasonably prolonged separation from his family.

2. *Piter* is a nickname for St. Petersburg/ Petrograd/Leningrad. *Trans*.

3. Maksimilian Oseevich Shteinberg (1883–1946), composer, professor at the Petrograd Conservatory. Shostakovich studied composition in Shteinberg's class from 1919 to 1925.

4. Leonid Vladimirovich Nikolaev (1878–1942), pianist, professor at the Petrograd Conservatory. Shostakovich completed Nikolaev's piano class in 1923.

Koreiz, 3 August 1923

Dearest Mother,

I have just read your seventh letter. My health, thank goodness, is now good. The lump is almost completely gone. Well, it's very tiny. I've had my thirtieth injection of arsenic and (don't tell Anna Vladimirovna) it doesn't hurt at all. There is a nurse in the sanatorium, Liubov Sergeevna, and she makes a fine art of administering injections. What's more, the day before yesterday Elena Nikolaevna, the doctor here, prescribed sunbathing for me. Yesterday I sunbathed for twenty minutes. Before I was only exposing my lump to the sun but now I can expose my whole body. I really didn't expect it to disappear so quickly. I have written to Viktor Grigorevich,[1] Maks. Oseev., and Leon. Vlad.[2]—all on the twenty-ninth. Moreover, I also wrote to you and Zoya and Val. Mikh.[3] on that day. You write that I should be careful and not throw myself into the whirlpool.[4] I would like to philosophize a little about this. Sheer bestial love (as when a man experiences desire for love—you can't even call it love—and he goes to a brothel and pays for a woman, etc.) is so disgusting that it's not even worth talking about. I presume you don't think I am like that. That kind of man is no different from an animal. Now, if, let us suppose, a married woman falls out of love with her husband and gives herself to another man whom she loves, and without regard for social prejudices they begin to live openly together, there is nothing wrong with that. On the contrary, it is even good when Love is truly free. Promises made at the altar are the worst thing about religion. Love can't last forever. Of course the best thing imaginable would be a total abolition of <u>marriage</u>, of all fetters and duties in the face of love. But that is utopian, of course. Without marriage there can be no family, and that really does spell disaster. But at any rate that love should be free—that much is indisputable. And Mother dear, I want to warn you that if I ever fall in love, maybe I won't want to marry. But if I did get married and if my wife ever fell in love with another man, I wouldn't say a word; and if she wanted a divorce I would give her one and I would blame only myself. (If that didn't seem right, for example, if the man she loved was married and his wife had prejudices, then I would handle the situation differently; and if she was afraid of social prejudice she would have to keep living at my address.) But at the same time there exists the sacred calling of a mother and father. So you see, when I really start thinking about it my head starts spinning. Anyhow, love is free!

Forgive me, Mother, for writing to you in this way. I am talking to you about all this not as your son, but as if we were two philosophers. I have wanted to talk to you about it for a long time but I was held back by some kind of false shame. Dearest Mother, I am completely pure and I expect I will remain so for a long time yet. If I fall in love I will do so in a way that I consider pure. There is no such thing as impure love, but there is filthy debauchery. I would like it very much if you would write a few words to me about it all. Debauchery is when a man buys a woman for money. But apart from that there is free love and depraved violation.

A big hug,
Your loving son, Mitia.

1. Viktor Grigorevich Valter (1865–1935), violinist, prominent figure in music. From 1918 he was secretary for the State Opera Council and other musical and concert organizations.

2. Maksimilian Shteinberg and Leonid Nikolaev, see notes 3 and 4 in preceding letter.

3. Valerian Mikhailovich Bogdanov-Berezovsky (1903–1971), composer, musicologist, prominent figure in music. In the 1920s he was one of the leading music critics in Leningrad and a close friend of Shostakovich.

4. In a letter from the Crimea, Mariia Shostakovich writes to Sofia Vasilevna about her brother: "He has grown up, got a tan, is happy and in love. This is quite clear. She is a strange girl, coquettish, I don't like her, but then it is so hard to please one's sisters." The girl in question was Tania Glivenko, with whom Shostakovich began a youthful romance in the Crimea which later became very serious for them both. His anxious mother began to warn her son of the dangers that come with relationships and of the difficulties of family life that destroy talent.

Moscow, 22 September 1923

Dearest Mother,

I am writing in case Misha[1] visits you. If he doesn't come he will post the letter in any case. I was in the Academicians' Club yesterday and was talking to him about Uzkoe.[2] As a result I am going there today at four o'clock in the TsKUBU[3] car. I'm taking a pillow and two changes of underwear. The Kostrikins[4]—what angels—have bought me a pair of lace-up shoes as my boots were starting to pinch. I left them the boots for Vitia or Mitia. Yesterday I met M. O. Shteinberg. We were full of mutual admiration. His friend Schmuller, a professor at the Amsterdam Conservatory, was coming to Petrograd and is now giving concerts in Moscow. As they hadn't seen each other for ages Schmuller brought Shteinberg along to Moscow, too. He said I had put on weight and looked in much better health. The lump, strange though it seems, has gone down greatly. The air in Moscow probably does it good. M. O. doesn't know where to stay yet. I am very glad he's here and I think he may even somehow call on me in Uzkoe. You can get to Uzkoe by tram from Moscow, so the Kostrikins will visit me a lot. TsKUBU is getting me a ticket for the return journey. How was Marusia's journey? Did she get there all right? Give her a big hug from me. She was so lovely and kind in the Crimea. Give Zoya a hug, too. I think of her often and miss her so much. She is a wonderful person. I went with Misha to see one of his friends, Oborin. He's a really splendid boy and a talented composer. On the whole I am really enjoying it here in Moscow. Yesterday I went to the Cathedral of Christ the Savior and I prayed for you all. Hold on, Mother dear. I'll come home soon, I will give concerts and make money and think how we'll live then! If only we have our health. Would you give Misha the manuscript of my Suite, the score and the arrangement for two pianos of the Scherzo (op. 1), and the score for the Variations? I would like to show them to the musicians here in Moscow. Tell Marusia that I met Lev Tseitlin.[5] He sends her his regards. Well, good-bye. My best wishes to you all, my own and dearest,

Your Mitia.

1. Mikhail Vladimirovich Kvadri (1897–1929), composer, at this time a student of the Moscow Conservatory and organizer of a circle of young musicians including Lev Oborin, Mikhail Starokadomsky, Iurii Nikolsky, Mikhail Cheremukhin, and Vissarion Shebalin. Kvadri was a "real musical knight" as defined by Oborin; he was infatuated with Shostakovich's work and began to take an active part in it, helping Shostakovich to enter quickly into Moscow's musical circle.

2. Uzkoe: a vacation village near Moscow where Shostakovich convalesced in the TsKUBU Sanatorium.

3. TsKUBU: Central Commission for the Improvement of Academic Welfare.

4. The Kostrikins were relatives of the Shostakovich family. The younger genera-tion of the Shostakovich and Kostrikin families were just as friendly toward one another as the older generation.

5. Lev Moiseevich Tseitlin (1881–1952), violinist, professor at the Moscow Con-servatory.

Moscow, 4 April 1924

Dearest Mother,

It's no good your sending me five rubles. Shor[1] is looking after me here. I sent *you* twenty rubles. I did it all as you're supposed to—I got a receipt, so I hope it will get to you. Now I am waiting to receive the instructions about my transfer[2] from you. This is how things stand: I went to see Shor and he gave me thirty rubles to start off with (twenty I sent to you, five I have put aside for my journey, and five I have kept to spend). Then he promised to get me a piano from Muzpred.[3] Moreover, he has arranged for me to join the Moscow KUBU. Yesterday I went to the conservatory and spoke to Igumnov.[4] He is taking me straight into his class without question. By the way, I heard him practicing and was pleased with what I heard. I spent three hours practicing today at Kvadri's. He was out and I had an excellent session. So. Should I ask Shor to get me a grand piano, or should I refuse his offer? Write and tell me what you think of my trans-fer in light of Shor's money. Should I transfer to the Moscow Conservatory or shouldn't I? Judging by your letter to Aunt Marusia,[5] it seems you have decided that I should not transfer. It seems to me that it would be bet-ter to think about it and not to decide against the transfer, especially as the material side of things has worked out so well—even better than we could have imagined. Moreover, when Shor promised me a steady income here I took action straight away: I went with Kvadri to see prorector Briusova, agreed to everything with her and immediately wrote a request for enrollment as a student of MGK.[6] Kvadri is taking care of the final formalities today. The motivation for all this is my health. I would not have set the ball rolling if I hadn't agreed to with you before I left. You said to settle the financial side first and then the conservatory. That is what I've done. Financially, I have arranged it so that I have some pocket money, some money for my journey, and the twenty rubles I sent to you. So, on the one hand, everything is coming along very well. And on the other hand, I must say that musical Moscow has welcomed me more than hospitably. In three weeks' time the professors are going to meet to get to know my compositions. In a word it's all going very well. I look forward to receiving a letter from you. You may say to hell with it all and let me become a student at the Leningrad Conservatory again, but it will be hard for me to do that. I am coming to Petrograd in a week, of course. But I will already be calling myself a student at the Moscow State Conservatory. Besides, I am enrolled for the Lunacharsky stipend, which amounts to eighteen rubles a month.

With much love,
Your Mitia.

1. David Solomonovich Shor (1867–1942), pianist, professor at the Moscow Conservatory.

2. In April 1924, owing to his "youth and immaturity," the council of the Leningrad Conservatory refused to let Shostakovich stay on in the academic course for piano studies (i.e., as a graduate student) and his composition classes with Shteinberg were postponed for a year or two. It was at this time that Shostakovich made an attempt to transfer to the Moscow Conservatory. This letter and the next tell about this little-known moment in the composer's life.

As the correspondence explains, Shostakovich had a number of reasons to make such a transfer. Financially it concerned him, since if he curtailed his studies at the Leningrad Conservatory, he would not have a stipend to rely on. Moreover, in Moscow he had acquired a close social circle of friends, and Tania Glivenko lived in Moscow. Nevertheless, the main reason was that certain creative disagreements had arisen in his relationship with his beloved and respected teacher Maksimilian Shteinberg. As a composer Shostakovich was developing fast, but Shteinberg pedantically put him through all the steps of an academic education, warned of "leftist tendencies" in his music and that he was "departing further and further from the essence of his gift." All of this strengthened the doubts that Shostakovich had acquired in his youth about his vocation as a composer.

Shostakovich's success in Moscow had a stimulating effect on him. However, primarily because of Sofia Vasilevna's antipathy, the transfer was not to be. That fall, thanks to Nikolaev's and Shteinberg's pleading, Shostakovich resumed his studies at the conservatory in Leningrad. At the time the composer was very hurt, but years later he evaluated the situation differently. In addition to his famous words in "Thoughts About the Path Traversed" (1956), something else from his published archive is worth noting here: "In 1925 I graduated from the composers' faculty. . . . I must honestly confess that at the time I was not all that taken with the conservatory education. There is among young people the opinion that talent alone is enough, and study is unnecessary. Later I understood what my conservatory education had given me—precisely a systematic education. . . . I know how to orchestrate, how to do certain modulations. Now I remember those years with love and I thank the conservatory for the knowledge it gave me." (Excerpted from a shorthand copy of a speech given by the composer to a teachers' collective at the music school in the town of Kuibyshev, 1942).

3. Muzpred: Association of Musical Enterprises of Narkompros (People's Commissariat of Enlightenment).

4. Konstantin Nikolaevich Igumnov (1873–1948), pianist, professor, and from 1924 to 1928 rector of the Moscow Conservatory.

5. Marusia B. Kostrikina.

6. MGK: Moscow State Conservatory.

Moscow, 8 April 1924

Darling Mother,

At the conservatory yesterday I was set something resembling an exam. Professors Miaskovsky, Vasilenko, G. Konius,[1] prorector Briusova, etc., were all there. I played the three cello pieces and the Trio. I played the cello pieces myself and the Trio was played by Vlasov on the violin and Klevensky on the cello. They played appallingly (worse than Valter and Pozen)[2] but the result was completely unexpected. I could never have guessed. They passed my Trio for Sonata Form and have taken me straight on to Free Composition. It turned out so well. Konuis—such an official old man—went up to Miaskovsky and asked: "Are you going to have him in your class?" Miaskovsky replied: "There is no question about that." Konius: "Are you entering him for the class on Form?" (that's the one I had with Ovesych this year). Miaskovsky: "Why enroll him for Form when he has already mastered form to perfection. He will go straight to Free Composition. What he has just played will count as his Sonata Form exam." Konius: "Yes, of course. I was thinking exactly the same myself!" I went red with pleasure just listening to them. Mishka[3] was in absolute rapture. They wouldn't have counted my Trio for Sonata Form in Leningrad. Stupid formalists. How was I supposed to pass Form if I wrote the Trio when I wasn't in the class on Form? Now this is the situation: if I manage to write a symphony by spring then I will have completed Theory of Composition at the Moscow Conservatory. However, I doubt that I shall finish a symphony by spring, more likely by autumn as certain ideas are beginning to stir in my head. So there you are. That's enough about the nice things. Now to business.

I have been accepted by the conservatory. There remain only the formalities. I have to get my marks and all the papers from the Leningrad Conservatory. I am writing a declaration to the rector saying that because of my health it is not possible for me to remain in Leningrad and therefore would he please send me my papers to the Moscow Conservatory. Let Marusia take this declaration officially to Ossovsky[4] and let him deal with it.

In a few days I will have the same exam in pianoforte. I am practicing a lot now at Misha's in the conservatory. On Wednesday I have a lesson with Igumnov. It is all going incredibly well. I am living splendidly at the Kostrikins'. I eat, drink, sleep, etc. Soon I will have a grand piano, only I need a memorandum from the Leningrad Muzpred to the Moscow Muzpred saying that I was getting a grand piano free of charge from the Leningrad Muzpred. Send the memo to me. I will give it to Shor and he will see to everything. There is a concert of Alpers[5] today in the

Small Hall of the conservatory. I met his sister and she gave me a double ticket. Misha isn't going, nor is Leva, and I don't feel I can ask Tania[6] to come as the tickets were complimentary and they are not assigned seats. I wrote a postcard to M. K. Alekseev to tell him to call or send someone for his parcel. I am in no condition to deliver it to him. By the way, I will have to pass elementary courses in political education and social science. Misha, Leva, Shebalin, Nikolsky, Starokadomsky, and I are going to study for these exams together. We'll get through them somehow or other. Well, Mother dear, don't worry now, and keep calm.

Don't send me money. I have money put aside both for the journey and for my expenses. Moreover, I have just sent you twenty rubles. I expect you have got it by now. Send my love to Marusia and Zoya. Say thank you to Marusia for her letter. Send my regards to everybody—Uncle Yasha, Aunt Zina, Tania, Vera, and Olia. How is Tania Frei? Say hello to Olga Aleksandrovna. If Volodia[7] and Val. Mikh. call, ask them to write to me. Well—good-bye, Mother dear. See you soon. And by then I will be a student of the MGK.

With much love,
D. Shostakovich.

P.S. I enclose my declaration to the Leningrad Conservatory. Mother dear, if you go to Nikolaev's, do stress that it has to do with my health. I already have one foot in the door of the Moscow Conservatory and the other one is up in the air, waiting to be set down in the same. I don't want to set foot in the Leningrad Conservatory anymore.

1. Nikolai Iakovlevich Miaskovsky (1881–1950), Sergei Nikiforovich Vasilenko (1872–1956), and Georgii Eduardovich Konius (1862–1933) of the Moscow Conservatory were leading professors of composition.

2. The name of the cellist, Pozen, is uncertain because it is almost illegible.

3. Mishka/Misha is Mikhail Kvadri.

4. Aleksandr Viacheslavovich Ossovsky (1871–1957), professor of the Leningrad Conservatory whose lectures on the history of music Shostakovich attended. In this instance Shostakovich is dealing with him as prorector of the conservatory.

5. Boris Alpers, a pianist Shostakovich met at concerts given by the circle of young composers at the Leningrad Conservatory.

6. Mikhail Kvadri, Lev Oborin, Tania Glivenko.

7. Vladimir Ivanovich Kurchavov (?–1925), poet, close friend of Shostakovich and Bogdanov-Berezovsky.

Moscow, 8 March 1925

Darling Mother,

I am sorry I haven't written to you clearly about anything, but I hadn't found out anything clearly myself until now. I am a little better informed now. There will be a concert on 20 March of compositions by Shebalin and myself.[1] I have just been to see G. A. Glazarin and he wants to organize a private concert. There's been a silly mix-up over his address. It turns out it's not Dannikovskaia Street, but Dominkovskaia. That's why I have only just found him today. I liked him very much. And I talked to him frankly about many things. Don't worry about money. I didn't tell you that I found eight rubles in the road, and Shchukin has given me ten rubles for the return journey. Moreover, Muztorg (under MONO)[2] are taking my Fantastic Dances and Trio, and I will get about two hundred rubles for them. I will send this to you as soon as I get it. I am living well here. The Kvadris are feeding me up. They won't take any money, and Nadezhda Nikolaevna[3] was even hurt when I made some mention of paying them. I saw all the Kostrikins—except for Iura and Maxim. I eat airan[4] every day, morning and evening. I am going to see Shor tomorrow. Maybe he will fork over some cash, too. This evening I am invited to a banquet at Yavorsky's;[5] he's a local musician. If the trip to Irkutsk works out, and if the concert there is going to be at the end of March, I will leave straight from Moscow on the twenty-first so as not to waste money traveling to Leningrad. Don't you worry, Mother. We are going to have a good life. I am glad that V. M.'s concert[6] went well. Please send him and Volodia my very best wishes and say sorry that I have not written to them. I am very busy here and just can't spare the time to write. I am practicing the piano. I have learned Schumann's *Fantasiestuce*.[7] I have orchestrated the first part of my Symphony here and I will try out the Scherzo on Thursday. I go to concerts and to the theater—always without paying and always in the front rows. Arnshtam[8] gets me into the Meyerhold; Fere[9] gets me into the Arts Theatre and Krasin[10] to the opera. Depending on how much time there is I would like to go to the circus. You are doing the right thing about Irkutsk. What a reply there'll be from Uncle Volodia. In which case, send a telegram saying that I can leave only on the twenty-first as I have a concert on the twentieth. I am very glad that my pieces have been accepted for publication and that my concerts are making something of a name for me in Moscow.

With much love,
D. Shostakovich.

1. At the concert in question—which took place in the Small Hall of the Moscow Conservatory—the Trio, Three Fantastic Dances, Three Pieces for Cello and Piano, and the Suite for Two Pianos were given their first performances before the wider public. For Shostakovich this was a very important debut as a composer.

2. Muztorg (under MONO): Musical Commerce under the Moscow branch of People's Education.

3. Nadezhda Nikolaevna, wife of Mikhail Kvadri.

4. Airan: Turkish buttermilk drink made from water, yogurt, and salt. *Trans.*

5. Boleslav Leopoldovich Yavorsky (1877–1942), musicologist, theorist, pianist, and teacher. In the 1920s he worked under the direct leadership of A. V. Lunacharsky; in 1925, he was head of the music education section of Glavprofobr, the Narkompros department for technical education.

6. V. M. Bogdanov-Berezovsky's first concert as a composer took place in the Hall of the Circle of the Friends of Chamber Music in Leningrad on 5 March 1925.

7. Misspelled, in Roman letters, in the original.

8. Leo Oskarovich Arnshtam (1905–1980), director and screenwriter. In the 1920s he studied with Shostakovich at the Petrograd Conservatory; in 1925 he was working at the Meyerhold Theatre.

9. Vladimir Georgievich Fere (1902–1971), composer; in 1925 he was a student at the Moscow Conservatory, in close contact with Mikhail Kvadri's circle.

10. Boris Borisovich Krasin (1884–1936), music activist, head of AKMUZO (Center for Musical Issues) of Narkompros RSFSR (Russian Soviet Federated Socialist Republic).

Moscow, 21 March 1925

My own, dear Mother,

I am in a state of some anxiety. If Narimanov's funeral[1] takes place tomorrow then the concert that Vera Ivanovna is organizing[2] will be on Monday; then I will be home on Wednesday. If the funeral is on Monday, I will be home on Thursday. I ask you one thing—do not worry, do not be upset. Yesterday there was a concert[3] of works by Shebalin and myself. It went very well: a huge success. Everyone liked everything except the Suite. And some people even liked the Suite. When I arrive I will need to have a detailed, calm, businesslike discussion with you about many things. I wish I had gone to Vera Ivanovna sooner. She sold a lot of tickets for the concert and as a result I got 109 rubles. I have already sent you twenty rubles. I have kept thirty myself just in case. What's more, she has organized a concert for me today as well. I don't know the exact results yet. And there will be another concert on Monday or Tuesday. I will get at least 150 rubles. So far, then, our dreams are coming true. I won't bring the money, I'll send it by mail. Otherwise, so they say, it will get stolen on the train. The only thing that makes me slightly sad is that the Fantastic Dances have not been accepted for publication. They haven't been accepted: to hell with them. There's no use whining. Here people are saying that the publisher doesn't deserve my particular confidence. I have tried several times to call on Shor, but each time he was either not at home or he was unable to receive me. At last I have made an appointment to see him tomorrow. He is very kind and accommodating. I am terribly pleased to have met Vera Ivanovna. After all, she took such an interest in me. Without her my visit would have been pretty useless: I am refused a state stipend, I am refused publication. Dear Mother, be as cheerful as you can and be sure to wear your rose-tinted glasses! Just you wait. Our time has not yet come. And we will start living. The main thing in life is good cheer, joy, energy, creativity, art, and soul. We are rich in soul. Our spiritual life is second to none. I haven't had a letter from you for ages. What's happened? Although there's no need to write now, we will see each other soon. Hold on, Mother dear, to all that is joyful. For there is so much joy that sometimes we don't see it. Joy must be everywhere. For example, I gave a concert and got at least twenty rubles—joy! I took the tram without a ticket—joy! Everywhere there is joy—all over the place. Don't be cross with me for such silly musings. I am just so happy to be able to send a little money home. I am sending it to you with my letter and a concert program. I will bring the poster with me. It will be interesting to see the reviews. I expect they will be insulting. Again there is no point in taking offense no matter what they say. Let them write that Shostakovich has no talent, that his compositions are dog shit (excuse the expression). Let them. We'll show them! Well—good-bye. It is quite late. Good night, dearest Mother.

> With ever so much love to you, and love to Marusia and Zoya.
>
> D. Shostakovich.

P.S. Liuba Nebolsina[4] was at my concert; she was upset with Marusia for not writing to tell her that I was in Moscow.

---

1. Nariman Kerbalii Nadzhav-ogly Narimanov (1870–1925), Soviet state and Party activist, writer, and publicist. From 1922, one of the chairmen of the Central Executive Committee of the USSR. At the Twelfth Congress of the RKP(b)—Russian Communist Party (of Bolsheviks)—he was chosen as a candidate member of the Central Committee. He is buried in Red Square in Moscow.

2. Beginning in the academic year 1923–24, the Moscow Conservatory conducted both private and public evening concerts of work by its student composers and performers in the Small Hall. Of concern here is the organization of concerts featuring Shostakovich.

3. Shostakovich was actually very upset after the concert. Many criticized his work as immature and contrived. At the same time some authoritative listeners remarked on his talent.

4. Liuba Nebolsina was probably the daughter of Vasilii Vasilevich Nebolsin (1898–1958), conductor at the Bolshoi Theatre.

Slaviansk,[1] 26 August 1925

My dear Mother,

I received your letter yesterday with notification that you are sending me a coat. Thank you very much—it will be very useful. I am very glad that you do not have anything against my staying here a little longer. The Sass-Tisovskys[2] are very kind and they are trying all ways to get me to stay. Boria wants to take a trip to Leningrad with me but says he hasn't any money. Yesterday I also got a postcard from Kvadri in which he begged me all ways to get stuck in Moscow, but I can see this happening only in the future. C'est la vie, as they say. Recently the Sass-Tisovskys ran out of money and they borrowed three rubles from me. I was very willing to give it to them. Yesterday Lid. I. took it upon herself to give me back the money but I would not take it. I told her that my meals and my stay with them were worth far more than three rubles. She was terribly upset and said that I am a guest, for goodness sake . . . I played Fools[3] once with Aunt Zhenia and cheated completely. At the end of the game she realized that something was amiss and started checking her takings. She noticed my dirty trick and was terribly angry with me. She wouldn't speak to me all day. Peace is restored now. Boria and I somehow came up with the idea of playing twenty-one. We played for about an hour and the result was stunning: 155 kopecks to me and 185 to him. I don't get bored living here. I have made friends with all the young people from the factory. I am taking part in their theatrical work. And on Friday I am going to play a non-speaking part as a waiter in their play *Warm Company*. I have made one or two solid friends. It seems my concert will take place soon, in some sort of club. I have no idea how it will go. Perhaps I will get 100 rubles, or perhaps just one ruble. Did you get my forty rubles? How did you celebrate Marusia's nameday and Zoya's birthday? I forgot to congratulate them. I congratulate them now. No doubt they will forgive my absentmindedness. And Marusia must be enjoying life and Frederiks's company[4] in Oranienbaum. I am very pleased for her. I too am enjoying life and excellent company. All the same I miss home and want to come back soon. It is nice to be a guest, but it is even better to be at home. I hope I will also be able to earn money at home. Perhaps the trip to Orel will come off. We'll pull through somehow and one day we will start living without being in need. Don't send me any music. I can't be bothered to write out any parts. I will leave rehearsals till I get home.

With all good wishes to everyone, and much love,

D. Shostakovich.

P.S. Yesterday I weighed myself at the resort. Three poods thirty pounds.[5]

1. Shostakovich was on vacation in Slaviansk after an intense bout of nervous exhaustion caused by both intellectual and physical overwork.

2. The Sass-Tissovskys, old friends of the Shostakovich family, had invited Dmitrii to stay with them in Slaviansk.

3. Fools: popular Russian card game. *Trans.*

4. Vsevolod Konstantinovich Frederiks (1885–1943), physicist and academic, future husband of Mariia D. Shostakovich.

5. Approximately 138 lbs. *Trans.*

Moscow, 8 February 1926

My Dearest Mother,

Forgive me for my long silence. All this time I have been well and truly swept off my feet. I have been given a hearty welcome in Moscow and am being accepted with great affection, which I find incredibly touching. People are very interested in me here. I feel almost as well-known here as I am in Leningrad. Yesterday and the day before I went to the conservatory and could hear all kinds of people whispering: "Look, there's Shostakovich." Yesterday was an out-and-out triumph for me. The introduction to the works, which was the whole reason for my coming here, took place in the conservatory. I played my Symphony. Everyone asked to hear it again, but I categorically refused as I still had to play, four hands, Goga's Symphony and Mikhailov's Variations.[1] The Association of Contemporary Music's[2] bigwigs Miaskovsky, Lamm,[3] Zhiliaev,[4] and Derzhanovsky[5] assured me that my Symphony would be included in a program of concerts in March and that I must give Malko[6] the score as soon as possible. Miaskovsky is concerned to get my Dances and the Trio published by Gosizdat.[7] I am always moved by the attitude taken toward me in Moscow. They are all terribly distressed that I have to play in the cinema,[8] and they want to put pressure on the Leningrad musicians to give me some other kind of work. Zhiliaev, Yavorsky, and Miaskovsky are going to write to Asafiev[9] about it. Frankly, I must say that I have never had such a successful trip to Moscow as this one. With regard to money there has been an unexpected surprise. When I got off the train at the station Gorodansky said to me: "Shostakovich, I forgot to give you your twenty rubles." The money is from the conservatory for living expenses. I had already taken some money from Nikolaev in vain. I keep meaning to send it to him by mail, but I literally haven't the time to get to the post office. I will certainly give it to him as soon as I arrive. My thirty rubles is now with Kvadri under lock and key. Fifteen is for Nikolaev. So for the time being I won't have to spend anything. Probably I won't have to spend much at all. Tomorrow I am going visiting. I will go to see the Kostrikins and

Sliva, and if I have time I will visit someone else as well. Today I am having a rest. Oh, and Tukhachevsky[10] has found me a room and a job. "You can move if you like," he said. I didn't give him any definite reply.

D. Shostakovich.

1. Goga is Georgii Mikhailovich Rimsky-Korsakov (1901–1965), grandson of Nikolai Rimsky-Korsakov. A composer, he studied in Shteinberg's class at the same time as Shostakovich.

Mikhail Kesarevich Mikhailov (1904–1983), musicologist, completed Shteinberg's class at the Leningrad Conservatory in 1927.

2. The Association of Contemporary Music, a creative and social organization, was founded in 1924 in Moscow as part of the International Society for Contemporary Music. Its aims included the propagation of contemporary Soviet and foreign music. Many important Soviet composers and music activists were members.

3. Pavel Aleksandrovich Lamm (1882–1951), musicologist, textual critic, pianist.

4. Nikolai Sergeevich Zhiliaev (1881–1938), music theorist, composer, textual critic, teacher.

5. Vladimir Vladimirovich Derzhanovsky (1881–1942), music critic, propagator of contemporary music, editor of the periodical *Contemporary Music,* published by the Association of Contemporary Music.

6. Nikolai Andreevich Malko (1883–1961), principal conductor of the Leningrad Philharmonic from 1925 to 1928.

7. Gosizdat: state publishing house.

8. Shostakovich played the piano accompanying silent films in cinemas. This exhausting and poorly paid work took up much of his time and energy.

9. Boris Vladimirovich Asafiev (1884–1949), musicologist and composer. People turned to him as the member of the Association of Contemporary Music in Leningrad most devoted to contemporary music trends.

10. Mikhail Nikolaevich Tukhachevsky (1893–1937), Soviet Marshal, was an amateur musician and close friend and pupil of Nikolai Zhiliaev. He had a great liking for Shostakovich.

Moscow, 11 February 1926

My Darling Mother,

I went to see Vera Sliva this morning. She has a five-month-old son. She has put on weight, grown plump, and become impossibly ugly. Before going there I called in at the station and got a ticket for Monday for the fast train. So I will be home on Tuesday. I had enough money. I haven't spent a kopeck of Nikolaev's fifteen rubles. And what's more, I still have ten rubles left from the conservatory's travel allowance. On Tuesday I played my Symphony, Octet, and Fantastic Dances at the Music Division of Gosizdat. They have all been accepted for publication! I cannot tell you how pleased I am about it. Three times was I mistaken if I ever imagined that I was badly thought of in Moscow. They accepted all my pieces—the Octet and Dances for immediate publication and the Symphony for publication after the first performance.[1] The first performance is going to be in March at the Association of Contemporary Music. So little by little—or rather not little by little but all at once—I am starting to get out into the public eye. The jury who listened to my work consisted of Miaskovsky, Zhiliaev, and some others. Everything was accepted unanimously, which pleases me immensely. And also I am so glad that this has happened in Russia rather than in some foreign country. Conditions are worse abroad. There they pay you in royalties—that is, for every copy sold I would get a certain predetermined percentage. But here, even though we are paid in installments, I will definitely get about 1,500. This evening I am going to see Miaskovsky and he will tell me what I need to do next. When I arrive I will write out a fair copy of the Octet and send it, but the Fantastic Dances will stay where they are in the Music Division. I expect they will come out in spring or summer. So it is such a good thing that I came to Moscow. I have met a lot of interesting musicians. I have played to a lot of people. Everywhere I have been given a very warm and hearty welcome. Now I only care about one thing—to get by until the first payment comes through. Then I will get 100–150 rubles a month, which I think will be a great help to us. I have just been to see the Kostrikins. I saw Aunt Marusia, Katia, and Natasha. I'm off again now. I'm going to have lunch and see the others. And from them to Miaskovsky. I have to do a lot of rushing around. It has been below freezing all the time I've been here. Today it is a little warmer. It seems as if it will stay warmer. I really am all right, and I am very well.

With much love to everyone,

D. Shostakovich.

1. After long discussions, the highly successful first performance of Shostakovich's First Symphony took place on 12 May 1926 at the Leningrad Philharmonic, conducted by Nikolai Malko.

Kharkov,[1] 6 July 1926

My own, darling Mother,

I got your letter just before leaving for the concert. I will describe it all to you in detail. When I arrived in Kharkov I went to the State Opera, and then went to look for Malko. Malko and I are living on Monastery Street, no. 6, apt. 1. If you have time to write again, then write to me here at this address: D. Shostakovich, c/o Professor Malko, 6 Monastery Street, apt. 1, Kharkov. I found Malko; we had some tea and went straight to rehearsal. I listened and immediately fell into a depression: instead of three trumpets there were two, instead of three timpani there were two, and instead of a grand piano was a vile jangling upright. I felt very grieved by all this. In addition the solo violinist was no good. In spite of Malko's efforts at the second rehearsal they did very little, I thought, or rather— nothing. Malko told me he was very pleased. I didn't distract him by trying to say anything. The third rehearsal was yesterday morning. It went better than the second and the musicians gave me an ovation. At last it was time for the concert. Malko came out (the thing took place in the garden. The acoustic was an outdoor one, the strings could be heard only weakly, the piano not at all, and the percussion completely drowned out all other sound). Malko took his position on the podium, and somewhere nearby some dogs started barking loudly. They barked for a terribly long time and so loudly, and the longer it went on, the more they barked, on and on. The audience roared with laughter. Malko stood motionless on the stage. Eventually the dogs stopped barking. Malko began. One of the trumpets (at the concert there were three) messed up his phrase straightaway. The bassoonist, who was unusually bad, followed with some nonsense (the way he played the Scherzo passes all understanding). After about ten bars the dogs started barking again. And thus throughout the whole of the first movement the dogs kept joining in with their own solo. The orchestra only just held together till the end of the first movement. They began movement two. In spite of all Malko's struggles during rehearsals, the cellos and double basses made a complete hash of the first two bars. The clarinet started playing slower than the strings. However much Malko tried to move him on the clarinetist played his solo slowly and carefully. After the clarinet solo the strings started to play by themselves. At this point I was somewhat surprised by what followed: with an immense effort Malko managed to even out the tempo, but in so doing he forgot about the dynamics. Instead of piano the violins played forte, and Malko somehow didn't quieten them. The bassoon solo began. I'm not even going to write about this. Let's just say that that the bassoonist grieved me to my limit. And do you remember how the bassoon played at the Philharmonic? They somehow strung the middle section together, but then it became a huge embarrassment. I nearly burst into tears then and there. Instead of good, strong wallops, there sounded something pathetic, weak, broken, and deranged. And the timbre wasn't that of a piano, but rather like a cross between cymbals and an old-fashioned harpsichord. I sat there thinking: "The thing is rubbish." They finished. There was a round of applause. A few people clapped, a few voices shouted: "Encore." Malko bowed, then continued. I will tell you now that they played the third and fourth movements significantly better than the first and second. The oboist was good and played both his solos uncommonly well. There were no misunderstandings in the third movement. It was played fairly correctly (Malko said it was better than at the Philharmonic, which made me all the more distressed about movements one and two). In the fourth movement noise and nonsense began again. The timpanist, incidentally, played his solo well. Although there were only two timpani instead of three he managed to get all three notes out of them. How he did it is an inventor's secret. The cellist played his solo very well. The end was too hurried. The percussionists were making such a din that it was impossible to make out anything. They finished. People started clapping and calling for the composer. I didn't want to take a bow, but Malko, coming out to bow himself, started clapping in my direction (I was sitting in the front row). It was uncomfortable, so I got up and took a bow. Then a second time; then, getting right up on the stage, I bowed again. Outwardly it was a success, but of course the audience had no idea and was clapping out of inertia. There were no whistles. Afterward I went to see Malko. He was pleased and radiant. The musicians came to the dressing room and shook my hand, etc. The ritual was observed. Then the violinist Blinder played the Tchaikovsky Concerto. He played very well. It was a success though not a huge one. After all, a garden has a terrible acoustic. I could hear everything from the front row, but I don't know about the back rows. Then Malko gave a stunning performance of the Variations from Tchaikovsky's Third Suite. Everyone said the concert was very good. But I say that the concert was partially good. The first part (my Symphony) was bad and the second part (Tchaikovsky) was not bad. Tchaikovsky's orchestral music is familiar and they played it better than mine. They did make a nonsense of it too, however. The bassoon particularly stood out. You couldn't find a worse bassoonist if you tried. Afterward we had dinner in the open-air restaurant. None of the Sass-Tissovskys were there. I'm not going to hide it from you. Not one. So I will tell you quite frankly that I am not at all pleased with yesterday's performance of my Symphony.

When we got home Malko said it was good all the same that my Symphony had been played. Good—well, good, but it wasn't good at all. What is good is that I will be paid a commission and, in addition, on the twelfth I will play the Tchaikovsky at a symphonic concert. In other words I have earned some money. But the fact that the local orchestra poured filth all over my Symphony—that cannot be described as good.

I am living very comfortably here. I have good dinners and breakfasts, etc. It is very hot, though. I spoke to you on the phone. Klopotov is a bit of a bigwig in Kharkov and he arranged it for free. I couldn't hear very well. I was very irritable so Klopotov spoke to you himself. I guess you grasped what it was all about as your telegram has arrived, saying: "I have sent it." I need the Trio and Octet here. Thank you for sending them. I am leaving here on the thirteenth. Perhaps I will stop for a day in Slaviansk. I am sending you another two articles about me. One is from *Moscow News,* the other was written by Malko and it has been published in Ukrainian in the paper *News*. I think my letter will distress you. Don't be upset. Outwardly it was a success, and as for my own worries and grievances—to hell with them. I am probably too fussy, as Malko found it all okay. I saw Yavorsky and Zhiliaev in Moscow. I sent you a postcard in Serpukhov. In Kharkov, too. I wrote Marusia and Irina a postcard and posted it in Serpukhov. A big hug for you. Write to me at the address above. Don't worry. All the same I am glad I came to Kharkov and heard my Symphony, even if it was a bad performance. The performance was not Malko's fault, it was the orchestra's. Again—a big hug. Give my love to Zoya, Tasia, Raia, Marusia, and Irina.

D. Shostakovich.

P.S. I will send the poster and whatever reviews there are.

1. When Malko was invited to take part in the summer symphonic season in Kharkov he included Shostakovich's First Symphony (in its second performance) in his program. He also managed to arrange for Shostakovich to be invited as a soloist. As Shostakovich was still completely unknown in Kharkov, they had to agree to a very low fee and Shostakovich was not provided with a hotel room. This was Shostakovich's first big concert tour, and he regarded it with a particular sense of responsibility and excitement.

Moscow, 10 January 1927

My Darling Mother,

The concert yesterday was a success. Everyone very much liked the sound of my Octet and Sonata. The Octet really did sound good. Especially the second movement. I played the Sonata twice. Judging from how it was received, the audience really seemed to get the taste of it.[1] In Moscow it is fairly cold now, but I don't notice it as I am usually sitting at home practicing. I am still pretty anxious. I haven't played the whole program to Yavorsky yet.[2] But those who happened to hear it were encouraging. The day before yesterday I sent you seventy-five rubles. Write to me when you get the money so that I am sure it has arrived. Yavorsky doesn't know for certain whether I have a stipend appointed to me or not, as it is a long time since he has been to GUS.[3] He is almost sure that one of the stipends that have been sent is for me. I recommend that when you get my letter you telephone Aleksander Ossovsky (home tel: 148-30, work: 618-17) and ask him if any instruction has come from Moscow concerning money. If the money is allocated to me, send it to me as it will pay for my journey to Vienna and Berlin. I have plenty for everything else. I have seen the third proofs of the Sonata. I will definitely send you a copy as soon as it is published. There were hardly any mistakes. Zhiliaev has done a good job of erasing them. Yesterday I had lunch with Tukhachevsky. He is a dear and after the fourteenth I will go and see him again. He fetched me for the concert yesterday in a very stylish automobile. In short, thank Marusia for the report she obtained from Ginzburg.[4] I am sending a corresponding application to the Technical School right now. I am enclosing in it a warrant for the receipt of my salary. I am writing the warrant in Marusia's name. Let her witness my signature at Mertsalova's, just in case.

Much love to you all.
Your loving D. Shostakovich.

P.S. Phone Nikolaev and tell him that I don't know anything yet so I still haven't sent a telegram.

1. The concert in question was the Moscow premiere of Shostakovich's Octet and Piano Sonata, which took place in the Mozart Hall. On the very same day the Association of Contemporary Music was organizing a concert for the Moscow musical public in the Bolshoi Theatre's Beethoven Hall. Written at a time of strong interest in, and assimilation of, the contemporary Western composers Stravinsky, Schoenberg, Krenek, and even Prokofiev, these works signified a sharp turn in the composer's creative work. After the Leningrad premiere the musicologist M. Grinberg wrote: "After the huge self-control, moderation and 'academic' loyalty characteristic of the Symphony, the Sonata, in its naked passion and uncontrollable elemental force, comes across as an explo-sion, a protest, a liberation and a break with the past." The musical language of the sonata was new and complex; many found it hard to understand, many did not understand it at all. So at the Bolshoi Theatre concert Shostakovich played the sonata twice, "for the sake of a better mastering of the music."

2. It was on Boleslav Yavorsky's initiative that Shostakovich was put forward to take part in the International Chopin Piano Competition.

3. GUS: State Academic Council of Narkompros RSFSR.

4. Possible reference to Semyon Lvovich Ginzburg (1901–1978), musicologist, pupil of Boris Asafiev, teacher of history and music theory at the Leningrad Conservatory from 1925.

Moscow, 15 January 1927

Well, Mother—a victory!!! But I will tell you from the beginning. The day before yesterday at two o'clock at Rosphil there was a casting of lots.[1] I met Malko at Rosphil—he has come for two days on Philharmonic business. I was very glad to see him. It was good to come across him at this difficult moment in my life. We had a chat. Then, when everyone except Shvarts had gathered, the lots were drawn. We drew them alphabetically. First Briushkov. He drew out number three. Second Ginzburg—number one. Third Oborin—number four. Next Malko picked one for Shvarts— number five. Last for me: number two. At last yesterday arrived. Before the concert, which was to start at seven o'clock, I went to see Raisky,[2] he lives in the conservatory and I played on a wonderful Bechstein there. So I didn't have to travel to the conservatory in the cold. I got warm at Raisky's, practiced, and went to the dressing room to hear Ginzburg. I had heard that he is a first-class virtuoso, etc. However, that is Moscow's patriotism. Ginzburg played very poorly. Not only that, but there wasn't a jot of Chopin in his playing. He mushed it like Professor Maikapar's worst pupil. Sinner that I am, I took heart. In that case, I thought, at least I won't be the worst player. Ginzburg finished playing. There was a ten-minute interval. There was an interval after each player. Then it was my turn. At first it was nerve-racking, and then I forgot about everything and started to play. Straight after the Polonaise, which I played first, applause sounded. They clapped after both Nocturnes, the Etudes, and the Mazurkas. In the Preludes I made a mess. I finished with the Ballade. My success was such as I had not expected. I went to bow, had a smoke in the dressing room, finished smoking, and again went to bow, etc. Yavorsky ran into the dressing room and said that it was great and he was glad (he whispered this in my ear) that I had not let him down. Then, so I was told, he went around the hall telling everyone that "Shostakovich is my protégé" and "you should all be thanking me for Shostakovich as it was I who discovered him," etc. Everyone congratulated me in earnest. Igumnov, Goldenveizer,[3] and the other Moscow musicians. They were all in rapture. Even Iura Kostrikin liked it. I will visit him today. After me it was Briushkov's turn; he began very well indeed. But then he made such a nonsense of the Preludes that after that he played most unimpressively. Oborin played wonderfully. I myself hadn't expected such liveliness from him. He has acquired artistry and great technique. He played the B-flat Minor Prelude astoundingly well, getting an ovation from the whole hall. I left as Shvarts started playing because he didn't start until midnight. The biggest success fell to me and to Oborin, as one might have expected. Well, that is all for now. I am going to the All-Union Society for Cultural Links with Foreign Countries to talk about passports and about my trip. The day after tomorrow we are playing for the Polish embassy in the Academy of Arts. The trip is finally settled for the twenty-first.

Much love to you all.
D. Shostakovich.

P.S. I got your letters. It would be good if Liuba Nebolsina did not find me at home. I am in an extraordinary mood. Did you receive the poster?

---

1. Rosphil: Russian Philharmonic. On 14 January 1927 in the Great Hall of the Moscow Conservatory a concert was given by the five pianists entered in the International Chopin Piano Competition. They were, from Moscow: Iu. V. Briushkov, G. R. Ginzburg, and L. N. Oborin; from Leningrad: I. Z. Shvarts and D. D. Shostakovich.

2. Nazarii Grigorevich Raisky (1876–1958), singer, professor at the conservatory. He accompanied the group of Soviet pianists to Warsaw.

3. Aleksandr Borisovich Goldenveizer (1875–1961), pianist, composer, teacher, music activist.

Warsaw,[1] 24 January 1927

My dearest Mother,

I got here quite safely and am living in tremendous comfort. I will have to play on Wednesday or Thursday. Oborin played today and he played very well. On Sunday the twenty-third they let through four people. They all played indifferently. But I will write about the competition in more detail when it is all over. I am in a really nervous state, but I am philosophical. The jury is made up exclusively of <u>Poles</u>. There are seventeen Poles taking part in the competition and about fourteen foreigners. Many didn't turn up. A lot of them just chickened out.

Warsaw is a splendid city. When I have finished playing I will devote a day especially to sightseeing. Living here is cheap and of course I have enough money both for Vienna and for Berlin, where Oborin and I are definitely planning to go.

The embassy is treating us wonderfully. Take, for example, the instance of my indigestion.[2] We go to the ambassador's to practice. He has a marvelous Bechstein, and he is very well disposed toward us himself and offers us the use of the piano from 10 AM till 10 PM. The journey itself was great. We went as far as Stolbtsy in an international carriage. You can't imagine how comfortable it was. We slept wonderfully and best of all you can wash with hot, cold, or warm water. Everything was clean and very plush. At the station we were met by some Polish representatives, who took us to the hotel by car. The four of us take up two hotel rooms. I share one with Oborin; Briushkov and Ginzburg are in the other. The rooms are very good. Lunches, breakfasts, tea, coffee, a bath, and other such comforts. There is just one unpleasantness: the cigarettes are much worse here than in Russia. Everything else is good. And the embassy, I repeat, has an exceedingly sympathetic attitude toward us. Inside the embassy I feel as if I am in my own country. The people are all excellent. For the concert they got me a dinner jacket at the embassy's expense with a soft shirt and collar to match.

At the moment I still have my confidence. My success in Moscow has cheered me up immensely. But of course anything could happen and I advise you not to be at all distressed, whatever failure happens.

With much love to you all,
Your loving D. Shostakovich.

1. Shostakovich was in Warsaw for the competition from 24 January until 5 February.

2. On the eve of his appearance in Warsaw, Shostakovich fell ill; he was diagnosed with appendicitis. In a letter to Yavorsky of 27 January 1927, Shostakovich begged: "For God's sake, don't tell anyone that I have appendicitis. Otherwise it might reach my mother and she will go out of her mind with worry." *Muzykal'naia akademiia* 4 (1997): 39.

Warsaw, 1 February 1927

My dearest Mother,

Well, the competition is over. The results: first prize: Oborin, second: Szpinalski,[1] third: Etkina,[2] fourth: Ginzburg. I got left out. I am not in the least bitter about it, as, after all, what's done is done. I played my program well and made a big success of it. I was included in the group of eight chosen to play their concerto with the orchestra. I played the concerto exceptionally well and had the greatest success of all eight. My success was even greater than in Moscow. I came on to a lively ovation and left to an even livelier one. Everyone congratulated me and said that there were two contenders for the first prize: Oborin and I. Moreover, it was both said and written that the Soviet pianists were the best of all. And if they had had to give all four prizes to one nationality it would have been us. Nevertheless, with a "pain in their heart," the jury decided to give the first prize to a Russian and they conferred this on Lev. The distribution of the remaining prizes aroused disbelief among the audience. I was awarded an honorary diploma. Maliszewski,[3] who read the list of awards, forgot to read my name. You could hear voices in the audience saying: "Shostakovich! Shostakovich!" and they broke into applause. Then Maliszewski read my name and the audience gave me a pretty demonstrative ovation. So don't you go upsetting yourself. Right now an entrepreneur is sitting here leading a discussion about concerts. I am leaving for Berlin this week: I will be giving a concert on Saturday.

With much love,
Your Mitia.

1. Stanislaw Szpinalski.
2. Róża Etkin-Moszkowska.

3. Witold Maliszewski (1873–1939), Polish composer and teacher.

Berlin, 8 February 1927

My darling Mother,

Even from this distance I can sense how you are suffering for your luckless son. And, more important, I can sense how completely unnecessary it is. I am now going to write to you about the whole competition and my impressions of it. Of course, I will write mainly about myself. On the way to the competition I didn't even expect to be among the eight people selected. When I did land among them I started thinking about the third prize. You see how precise my calculations were. One member of the jury, who had developed a great sympathy for me, told me the following: the prizes should have been awarded according to the number of points received by each pianist. Oborin got 166 points, Ginzburg 165, and I got 163. True, this annoyed me a bit as I played better than Ginzburg, but not to worry, I thought. At first the completely unexpected result depressed me. As I discovered, they had decided it was impossible to give all three prizes to Russians, so they gave the second prize to the Pole Szpinalski (149 points) and the third to the Polish girl Etkina (141 points) and then, so that it would not be altogether shameful, they invented a fourth prize, which they awarded to Ginzburg. Both the audience and the press had singled out us, the Russians, too much. But don't tell anyone, because I am bound by my word.

On Saturday Oborin and I gave a concert. I played the *Appassionata*, my Sonata, three Etudes, and the third Ballade by Chopin. It was a colossal success. Incidentally, they clapped hard after my Sonata. My fee was 1,000 zloty, or 111 dollars. From my previous money I still have forty dollars, so I decided to go to Berlin. I persuaded Oborin to come, too. He can speak the language, albeit not too well. Berlin is an enchanting city. I couldn't imagine anywhere like it. I will tell you about it in detail when I come. I will arrive, I hope, on the sixteenth. I would like to go to Vienna as well. If I manage to get a visa then I will go there. We will see each other soon. I miss home and all of you unbelievably. How is Zoya's health? I will see everyone soon. I will stop now as I am going out to see more of Berlin. But I repeat—it is an unusual city.

With much love to everyone,
Your loving Mitia.

P.S. I left Warsaw with: one—a huge success with the audience, and two—a mountain of all kinds of reviews. Above all I beg you all not to be upset. I am pleased and content and I am not a failure.

Responses of Shostakovich to a

Questionnaire on the Psychology of

the Creative Process

PREPARED BY ROMAN ILICH GRUBER

EDITED AND ANNOTATED BY STAFF
RESEARCHERS OF THE GLINKA STATE CENTRAL MUSEUM
OF MUSICAL CULTURE, MOSCOW

TRANSLATED, WITH ADDITIONAL NOTES,
BY MALCOLM HAMRICK BROWN

This document records the responses of the twenty-year-old Dmitrii Shostakovich to a questionnaire prepared by Roman Ilich Gruber.[1] For clarity in identifying Gruber's questions, they appear underlined in the text. Shostakovich responded orally to the questions, and Gruber wrote his answers down. Subsequently, Shostakovich reviewed his answers as recorded by Gruber and made numerous additions in his own hand; these are identified in the printed text by italic type. Underscores in the responses have been retained. Information in square brackets has been provided by the translator. Finally, the three spaced periods often encountered at the ends of answers are Gruber's; he evidently used them to mean *et cetera*.

Gruber conducted his survey in 1927–28 while working in the department of the theory and history of the arts at the State Institute of Arts History in Leningrad. The participants included several teachers at the Leningrad Conservatory, as well as students who had completed the conservatory and become members of the Leningrad Association of Contemporary Music (LASM), among them D. D. Shostakovich, Georgii Mikhailovich Rimsky-Korsakov, Khristofor Stepanovich Kushnarev, Nikolai Aleksandrovich

Malakhovsky, Iosif Moiseevich Shillinger, Gavriil Nikolaevich Popov, Vladimir Vladimirovich Shcherbachev, and Andrei Filippovich Pashchenko.[2]

1. Name, patronymic, family name and age.
   Dmitrii Dmitrievich Shostakovich, age twenty-one.

2. Your relationship to music (professional or non-professional).
   Professional.

3. Shaping of your personality.
   a. The areas of musical activity in which you have been involved.
      (1) During childhood.
         As a child I heard a great deal of music: my father sang (as an amateur, although he had some understanding of musical theory), and my mother played the piano (as an amateur). Acquaintances (on the other side of the wall) often convened an amateur string quartet; I loved to listen (age seven or eight), but had no desire myself to study music. My attitude toward studying was even rather negative. When I was nine, my mother insisted that I start piano lessons; up until that age I didn't even go near a piano. My sister started piano lessons somewhat earlier than I (when I was seven or eight). The musical repertoire that surrounded us was gypsy songs, duets (Villebois, Varlamov . . .), Tchaikovsky's songs . . . I don't remember my mother's repertoire or the neighboring quartet's. I didn't go at all to concerts or the theater (until age ten). The first opera I heard was *The Tale of Tsar Saltan* (the fanfares before the start of each act engraved themselves on my memory . . : but no particular impression otherwise).[3] My second opera, *Ruslan* (when I was eleven) made an enormous impression (most of all, Ratmir's aria, and other parts as well, in a purely musical sense, independent of the action on stage).[4] I was at a symphony concert for the first time at the age of twelve (in 1918): a Beethoven cycle conducted by Koussevitzky which made no particular impression on me (I hadn't yet learned to love Beethoven at that time, but more than anyone else—I loved Glinka!). I entered the conservatory in 1919.[5]

      (2) During the years following.
         From 1919 to 1920 I was engrossed by the ordinary musical life of Petrograd (the strongest impression from the period was Strauss's *Ein Heldenleben*). In 1920, Tchaikovsky was my biggest passion (as conducted by Emil Cooper): Symphony No. 6 and the symphonic poems . . .[6]

b. <u>Level of general education</u>.
Secondary education (high school).

c. <u>Musical</u>:
(1) <u>General</u>.

(2) <u>Specialized</u>.
I started piano at age nine (during the summer of 1916). My mother began teaching me the notes, but it didn't take; chance came to my aid—Streabog's six-hand works.[7] I asked mother to point out the repeated figure in the bass; then, more or less mechanically, I taught myself the notes. In the autumn I entered Gliasser's music school.[8] There, I remember, I went through the Burgmüller piano studies . . . To pass the class at the end of the year, I played Tchaikovsky's complete *Children's Album* (from memory); the next year, I played a Mozart sonata. In 1918–19 I took private lessons from Professor A. A. Rozanova and in 1919 entered her class in piano at the conservatory, and also the class in Theory of Composition (harmony) with M. O. Shteinberg; after preparing myself in elementary theory for a month, I took the first and second classes in solf[eggio] with Professor A. A. Petrov. Starting in 1920, piano with L. V. Nikolaev (with whom I finished in 1923); harmony, instrumentation, and form with Shteinberg; counterpoint, fugue, and also form with N. A. Sokolov.[9] I finished in Theory of Composition with Shteinberg in 1925; I am now a graduate student in the Composition Department of the conservatory.

d. <u>Your attitude toward the education you received</u>.
During the time I was going through the course in Theory of Composition at the conservatory, I looked on it as an "unavoidable evil," to which I submitted passively, to some extent. On finishing the course, I felt it impossible to compose freely, spontaneously; I was obliged somehow to "squeeze out" a series of works (in the summer of 1925, a symphony and two movements of a string octet . . .); starting in the fall of 1925 through December 1926, I kept trying to compose, but unsuccessfully (during that early period after finishing the conservatory, I had turned into too narrow a "professional," putting matters of technical fluency above everything else, unwittingly trying to make everything I wrote turn out "correctly" and fluently): my creative consciousness could not escape the bounds inculcated by academic canons. From the fall of 1926, I turned to the study of contemporary Western composers (Schoenberg, Béla Bartók, Hindemith, Krenek), which apparently provided the immediate stimulus for "liberating" my musical faculties: my first compositions from

this new period were composed in white heat (from the end of 1926 through 1927): the Piano Sonata, "Aphorisms" for piano, the "Symphonic Poem for the Tenth Anniversary of the October Revolution," and the first act of the opera based on Gogol's story *The Nose* (August 1927).[10]

Remembering it now, my attitude toward the academic canon was not entirely passive. Examples: in 1922, I composed a suite for two pianos. Prof. M. O. Shteinberg's opinion of it was rather negative and he ordered me to revise it. I did not. Then he insisted a second time that it be revised, and I reworked it according to his instructions. In the latter version, it was performed on one of the student concerts at the LGK.[11] After the concert, I destroyed the corrected version and set about restoring the original. M. O. was not pleased with this state of affairs. This was one of my many attempts to "revolt" against the dictatorship of "rules." Later on, the same sort of thing happened when I was composing the Trio, the Octet, and the Symphony, in which I kept everything as I wanted it and wouldn't accept M. O.'s corrections.[12] After I had composed the Sonata op. 12 and showed it to M. O. Shteinberg, I heard the following comment from him: "I can't say anything about this muSIC" (with the accent on the -SIC).[13] The same thing should be said about musical form. At the conservatory, they taught me "scheme," not "form." In the class on sonata form, I was told the following, before I was assigned to compose a symphony: "Sonata form consists of (a) an exposition, (b) a development, and (c) a recapitulation. The exposition consists of (a) a principal theme, (b) a subordinate theme, and (c) a closing theme," etc., etc. "For next class, come up with some sort of principal theme and write it down. If it doesn't work out, write another one. This way, once you've composed several principal and subordinate themes, we'll pick the best principal theme and make a transition to the best subordinate theme; and this way, we'll have an exposition." To my question, "What is a development?" came the answer, "Well, in the development the principal and the subordinate themes are 'developed' and 'interwoven.'" Not a word was uttered about the expressive character of the musical line, about relaxation, tension, and dialectical development.[14] In my opinion, the development was the hardest part (the thought had already crossed my mind that form ought to be dialectical and not architectonic). But the following answer came: given a principal and a subordinate theme, and if you have a tonic and know how to manage modulation and voice-leading, then the development will come very easily. I am now convinced that the development is indeed the hardest part of sonata form. Given the two themes (or theme groups), the exposition always has something of an architectonic structure, but the development must absolutely be dynamic and dialectical. Even then, all this was generating in my brain. What I said about relating passively to my academic studies is not quite accurate. It's another matter that on finishing the conservatory, I was defeated in an unequal struggle with the glorious traditions of Nikolai Andreevich.[15] It may have been unequal, but it was a struggle all the same. I often spoke about this with L. V. Nikolaev, who responded, "You know, everything you're going through now is nothing more than ABC's, which by itself, mechanically, will be forgotten." But he's mistaken about this. It's not right to cripple people. Some people are more weak-willed than I am, and they can be crippled for life, or anyway for a very long time. One example is the very gifted composer A. V. Grigorev (who is blind, and as a consequence, with less will to resist than I have), at one time he composed a great deal.[16] Now he's experiencing a "lack of inspiration," and this has continued for a long time up to the present day.

4. <u>Your attitude toward the other arts (level of professionalism, degree of interest and so on).</u>

I am not a professional in the other arts.

Above all a preference for prose literature (I don't understand poetry in the least and do not value it; but of the poets, I like Derzhavin and Mayakovsky, relatively speaking). Dostoevsky's *Demons, The Brothers Karamazov*—Dostoevsky generally. Alongside him, Saltykov-Shchedrin; in a different category, Gogol (*Evenings on a Farm near Dikanka, Mirgorod, Dead Souls* . . . but I don't like *The Portrait* and *The Terrible Vengeance* . . .). I also like Chekhov. As an artist, Tolstoy is rather alien (as a theorist of art, much of what he says is convincing). I have a sharp antipathy for Turgenev and Goncharov . . . and I don't much like Ostrovsky . . . Among those from the West: I can't appreciate Shakespeare (then again, I've not seen a single work of his on stage). Maupassant in first place. And I adore Goethe (*Faust, Dichtung und Wahrheit*), Heine, Stefan Zweig. For Schiller my feelings are about the same as for Ostrovsky (not much . . .). I adore Voltaire, but I detest Anatole France. From the "classics," I will single out Homer, Dante . . .

In second place—ballet: classical ballet (Lev Ivanov, for instance, *Nutcracker*; Petipa), Fokine, Goleizovsky . . .[17]

In third place, sculpture and architecture: St. Isaac's Cathedral, Falconet's monument to Peter the Great; the Kremlin and St. Basil's in Moscow.[18] I especially love the sculpture of antiquity (although I know little of it, I "thirst" for enlightenment in this area).

Painting doesn't speak to me, and I consider it a meaningless activity; I've tried to learn something in the museums of Leningrad and Moscow, but without success; what puts me off mainly is the static quality.

About painting: For a long time I couldn't understand why painting didn't speak to me. I gained some understanding after reading about an incident described by Leo Tolstoy: An artist is painting a "landscape." A peasant approaches and asks, "What are you doing?" "Painting." "What are you painting?" "That birch tree over there." "Why? The birch tree's already there. So why are you painting it?" I have something of the same attitude toward painting as Tolstoy's peasant. When I was living in the Crimea, I got great pleasure from contemplating Crimean nature, and Ai-Petri.[19] *The artist Kustodiev, who was also living there, up and painted Ai-Petri, and he painted the view very well.*[20] *But when I looked at Ai-Petri and at the copy of Ai-Petri, much became clear to me. Why do I receive such enormous satisfaction from the genuine Ai-Petri, but not from the painted scene? Quite simple. In the painting, everything is frozen. Everything is dead, static. In nature, there is no "stagnant" moment. The clouds are always shifting, the sea roaring, the wind blowing, now less, now more, the trees swaying. Everything is living, everything is moving. Art without motion is not art for me, no matter how closely the semblance has been captured and so on. Despite this, I must say that I enjoy the drawings of Iurii Annenkov and also successful caricatures by various artists.*[21] *To some degree, caricatures synthesize, and this is what gives me pleasure. Anything humorous and witty I always like.*

9 September 1927, Detskoe selo.

/signed/ *D. Shostakovich*

To opera as a scenic-theatrical event (independent of its musical worth) in its contemporary state I react in a sharply negative fashion (especially after getting to know *Vampuka*).[22] *Wozzeck* is the exception (I like it very much). Wagner as a reformer of opera does not satisfy me at all. I can listen to opera only with eyes closed. I've yet to find musical drama in the true sense anywhere (*Carmen* has some profoundly dramatic moments, for example in the fourth act) . . .

I love the art of theater very much and am strongly attracted to it (for example, *The Inspector General* as presented in Meyerhold's Theatre. In general, I consider Meyerhold to be a genius as a stage director). I value his Theatre most of all. Next, the Chamber Theatre and Vakhtangov's Theatre. I haven't seen anything on the first stage at MKhAT![23]

I love the circus very much and often attend (the gymnastic performances especially attract me, and the jugglers . . .).

5. <u>The scope of your musical interests.</u>
   a. <u>Favorite composers.</u>
     J. S. Bach, Mozart, Haydn, Gluck, Handel, Beethoven, Schubert, Chopin, Liszt, Mendelssohn, Schumann, Brahms, Mahler, Schoenberg, Hindemith, Krenek, A. Berg, Verdi (*Aida*), Béla Bartók, Richard Strauss, Richard Wagner . . .

Among the Russians, in first place Tchaikovsky and Stravinsky; then, Glinka, Dargomyzhsky (*The Stone Guest*), Musorgsky (everything), Borodin (everything), Rimsky-Korsakov (*Kitezh* and *The Golden Cockerel*), Rachmaninoff, Prokofiev, Shebalin . . .

I have a sharply negative attitude toward Scriabin (him first of all, and from the outset!), Bruckner, Miaskovsky, Medtner, and Feinberg . . .[24]

   b. Favorite types of compositions.
      Hard to answer this.

   c. Favorite individual works.
      (Besides those listed under 5. a.) Hindemith's Concerto for Orchestra and his Trio for strings; Schubert's Sixth, Seventh, and Eighth symphonies; *Wozzeck*; Bach's B Minor Mass; the Second and Fourth symphonies of Brahms; Strauss's *Salome*; Wagner's *Die Meistersinger* and *Tristan* . . .
      Russian works: Tchaikovsky's Fourth, Fifth, and Sixth symphonies (there's also much good in the First, Second, and Third symphonies), as well as his symphonic poems and the First Piano Concerto; Stravinsky's *Les Noces,* the Serenade for piano, *L'Histoire du soldat,* and *Oedipus Rex*; Prokofiev's "Ala and Lolly," and his Second and Third Piano Concertos . . .[25]

   d. Musical medium (instrumental, vocal).

   e. Style.

   f. Period.
      d, e, and f: hard to answer.

6. Particularities of life situation.

7. Particularities of personality.

8. Particularities of outer appearance.
   (no answers to questions 6, 7, and 8)

9. The creative process.
   The impulse to create (the first appearance of the creative urge).
   a. When.

   b. The immediate reasons and the attendant circumstances.
      (a & b) I started composing as soon as I started studying piano. One motivation (there were many of them) came from reading Andersen's *The Little Mermaid* (an attempt at a ballet); an epic poem on military themes in connection with the World War (*The Soldier* . . .); a funeral march in

memory of the victims of revolution (generally speaking, I composed a lot under the influence of external events). My method of composing was improvising at the piano and then attempting to write it down.

The next stage was studying with Georgii Bruni. He encouraged improvisation (he would give me a theme, for instance, "In the forest": (1) In the forest; (2) In the glade; (3) The little stream) . . .

    c. The earliest instances.

    d. The first record of the creative process.
       Simultaneously with the attempt at improvisation.

10. In your life since then, the constancy or the sporadic nature of creative moods.
    a. If the creative mood recurs sporadically, then what are the time periods.
  ADDENDUM. Creative mood is understood to include also the time actually involved in composing the work.

    b. Are you aware of periods of greatest creative urgency.
       The urge to compose is constant (with the exception of the period 1925–26). My period of greatest creative urgency was during the spring and summer of 1927.

11. Has there been a particular period of your creative life when your music reflected the influence of the musical procedures or the more general characteristic sound of any other composers; who in particular.
    a. Direct influence on your musical works.
       During my studies at the conservatory, I felt the influence of Rimsky-Korsakov and Glazunov.

    b. Influence from specific musical-theoretical views.

    c. Influences on your works from overall artistic, philosophical, scientific, social or other factors of any sort.
       (b and c): I don't know.

    d. Influence on your creative direction, generally speaking, of all aspects enumerated above.

12. <u>Which work do you consider the most successful</u>.
The Piano Sonata, "Aphorisms," and the opera *The Nose*.

13. <u>What external form is your favorite</u>.
Hard to say.

14. <u>Do you feel an attraction for techniques of form-building that you haven't yet made use of</u>.
For opera (before that, an attraction for the solo piano style).

15. <u>Is your creative activity associated with any externally unhealthy states of the organism (narcotics)</u>.
During a creative period I always experience insomnia; I smoke more than usual, take long walks (which helps me think things through), pace the room, jot things down while standing, and in general I can't remain at peace . . .

16. <u>The creative act</u>.
<u>The impulse to create: Does it originate outside yourself or inside, is it fortuitous or the result of preliminary mental effort (i.e., is it an organic directionality or a directedness of attention). Your attitude toward the impulse. [As opposed to] weighing options consciously. The evolution of the impulse before the initial appearance of form</u>.
The impulse is always internal. The preparatory stage lasts from several hours up to several days (no more than a week), with the exception of the opera *The Nose*, where the preliminary stage lasted nearly two years . . .
Examples of the preparatory stage:
Piano Sonata. The preparatory stage lasted several minutes. During these several minutes I was already able to imagine rather clearly the entire future composition. "Aphorisms" for piano. I conceived them in Berlin, at the beginning of February, as I was going to bed. At the time, I was thinking a great deal about one of the laws of nature, and this gave me the impetus to compose "Aphorisms," which are seized by a single idea. The nature of this idea I do not at the moment wish to say. At the beginning of March, already back in Leningrad, I started to compose and finished all ten pieces in one fell swoop. The preparatory stage lasted a month.

17. <u>The phase of internal embodiment</u>.
<u>The advent of the initial internal form. The characteristic features of the initial form and the delimitation of the idea of your work</u>.
I <u>always</u> feel the "initial form." It is always completely clear to me

what should be the beginning, the middle, and the end of a composition, and where the moments of tension and release belong. The work does not yet manifest itself aurally, but somehow in its "timbral" aspect . . .

I also sense the "complete intrinsic form," independent of its embodiment . . .

18. The process of internal embodiment.
 a. Does the process of bringing the initial form to fulfillment proceed without interruption and in order, or section by section; which compositional elements come first of all into your creative consciousness (harmony, melody, rhythm, dynamics).

  The filling out for the most part proceeds in order, from beginning to end. The timbre comes to me before anything else, then melody and rhythm, and afterwards the rest . . .

 b. Are you conscious of the principal structural points and how to establish connections between them.

 c. Is the process of the internal embodiment of a composition accompanied, entirely or partially, by the process of external embodiment, or is the latter independent of the former.

  The external embodiment of a work occurs only after it has been completely conceived and worked out mentally, although the latter process may comprise a series of comparatively independent links . . .

  Examples: *Difficult to cite them, although this certainly occurs, always.*

19. The process of external embodiment.
 a. Does it begin before the attainment of a fully conceived intrinsic form.

 b. How does it proceed.

  (a and b). The external embodiment always moves along more quickly than the process of mental formulation and often suggests new possibilities for treating the material. The reverse, i.e., the impossibility of embodying that which has been thought through in me, doesn't happen . . .

  I never return to a composition once it has been written out (*this is always the case, so there's no point in giving an example*).

  On completion of the external embodiment of a work, I experience complete satisfaction (*always*).

  Examples: *In composing "Aphorisms," that is, in embodying them externally, I changed almost completely the ending of the whole suite.*

20. <u>Is the full external form of a work, altogether or in part, revealed to</u> <u>you unexpectedly (a) before the creative process begins or (b) during the</u> <u>process (in a flash of insight)</u>.

I haven't experienced a flash of insight.

21. <u>What is the correlation between the conscious and the unconscious</u> <u>realms during your creative process (which one predominates, in what</u> <u>order do they alternate, and at what stage in the creative process are you</u> <u>aware of one or the other)</u>.

I often am aware of subconscious musical activity while occupied with routine daily matters . . .

During the creative process, rational treatment of the material predominates, to all appearances, although there are occasional instances of unconscious "finalizations" of musical aspects not subject to a "rational" treatment. Generally speaking, the "irrational" predominates at the beginning of the creative process and the rational during the later stages . . .
Examples: *Difficult to offer any.*

22. <u>Is the creative musical process accompanied by a more or less intense</u> <u>emotional high. Is this expressed in any outward movements; is it accom-</u> <u>panied by any change in physiological functions and, if so, which</u>.

I am aware of an emotional high, which is accompanied by insomnia and the other symptoms mentioned in item 15. I haven't noticed any disruption of physiological functions.

23. <u>How do you behave outwardly just before you begin to compose or</u> <u>while you are composing (do you use a piano or other instruments when</u> <u>writing the music down)</u>.

As per item 15, I compose with the help of an instrument, although I can do without it, too . . .

24. <u>How much is your capacity for work enhanced by such an emotional</u> <u>high and how long does the creative high last</u>.

The duration of an emotional high is generally significant (an entire night or twenty-four hours . . .).
Examples: *While composing "Aphorisms," my emotional high lasted an entire month, without breaks.*

25. <u>At what time do you usually notice an increase in creative activity</u>:
   a. <u>Day or night</u>.
      More often at night, but sometimes also during the day.

b. <u>Time of year</u>.

Most often spring, summer, and fall; less often the winter (this is mostly due, it seems, to the fact that winter responsibilities distract).

c. <u>Do you notice any periodicity in the high peaks</u>.

I don't notice any.

26. <u>What sort of reaction do you experience following a creative high (satisfaction, a neutral state, a letdown)</u>.

I have never experienced complete satisfaction; the expectation that I'll be satisfied, which is typically present while I'm working, is far from ever completely realized when the composition is finished (there's no "honeymoon"); there arises a need for more creative work . . .

I don't experience a letdown, however, and much less any aversion to work.

27. <u>During the musical creative process, do you struggle, with greater or lesser difficulty, to overcome the resistance of the material, or does the shaping move along involuntarily, without difficulty (the so-called agony of creation)</u>.

I experience not only "the agony of creation" (in connection with handling the most diverse elements in the compositional process), but also a state of "exhilaration" once I've overcome impediments that had seemed so recently insurmountable . . .

It helps considerably, when confronting such impediments, to play through what has already been composed, from the beginning and "for real," that is to say, getting to feel completely at home with the work and not thinking about the problems ahead . . .

Sometimes it's necessary to "skip over" a measure that isn't turning out; its music will be found later . . .

Examples: (none)

28. <u>Have you been aware of the process of improvisation, that is, of the parallel flow of internal and external embodiments, whether acknowledged or unacknowledged</u>.

29. <u>Do you make use of moments of improvisation as source material for the creative process</u>.

28, 29. Improvisation takes place often, almost always even at the stage of external embodiment; generally it is precisely improvisation that helps overcome the impediments in bringing a creative idea to realization . . .

30. <u>Heritage</u>.

Genetic information. *On my father's side:*

My grandfather, a Pole, was exiled to Siberia in 1863 for participating in the Polish uprising. He was a man who had a great passion for gardening. His brother was a restless sort. He couldn't live in the same city for more than half a year. My father never studied music. He taught himself to read music and, possessing a tenor voice, often sang. He sight-read superbly and played piano four-hand. He was an entirely normal human being.[26] *Not one of his brothers or sisters was in the least musical. The same applies to their progeny (my male and female first cousins).*

On my mother's side:

Both my grandfather and grandmother loved music, but they did not teach it to their children. All of my uncles and aunts are very musical. All of them played piano, and one uncle sang in a chorus. A deceased uncle (who died at age fourteen) had an enormous aptitude for painting, and in the opinion of experts at the time he might have become an important artist if he hadn't died. He was awfully religious and died raving about Christ, as though conversing with him. Not one of my male first cousins was notable for musicality. All are normal people. One female first cousin sings, another dances. Normal people.

The information contained in this questionnaire was dictated by me to R. I. Gruber and verified. 2–10 September 1927.

Detskoe selo.

D. *Shostakovich*

NOTES

1. The original manuscript document on which this publication is based is held by the Glinka State Central Museum of Musical Culture in Moscow (hereafter GTsMMK) f[ond] 285, ed[initsa] khr[aneniia] 21, ll[isty] 30–34. This translation is in turn based on the document's annotated publication in *Dmitrii Shostakovich v pis'makh i dokumentakh*, ed. I. A. Bobykina (Moscow: Glinka State Central Museum of Musical Culture, 2000), pp. 470–82. Additional annotations by the translator are either identified as such or in brackets in the notes which follow. Gruber's dates are 1895–1962. *Trans.*

2. Georgii Mikhailovich Rimsky-Korsakov (1901–65) was the grandson of the noted composer; Kushnarev's dates are 1890–1960; Malakhovsky's dates are 1892–1942; Iosif Moiseevich Shillinger (1895–1943) became known as Joseph Schillinger after becoming a naturalized U.S. citizen in 1936; Popov's dates are 1904–72; Shcherbachev's dates are 1889–1952; and Pashchenko's dates are 1883–1972. *Trans.*

3. *The Tale of Tsar Saltan* was composed by Nikolai Rimsky-Korsakov. *Trans.*

4. *Ruslan and Liudmila* was composed by Mikhail Glinka. *Trans.*

5. Koussevitzky is Sergei Aleksandrovich Kusevitsky (1872–1951), known in the West as Serge Koussevitzky. He conducted the State Symphony Orchestra (the former Court

Orchestra) in Petrograd during the years 1917–20. His "Beethoven cycle" comprised a series of concerts devoted entirely to the symphonic and chamber music works of Beethoven. Koussevitzky invited distinguished performers to participate in the cycle. See, for example, the program of a concert in Moscow on 7 April 1919, at which Antonina Vasilevna Nezhdanova [1873–1950] gave the first performance in Russia of "Adelaide" [op. 46], along with the First and Ninth symphonies (GTsMMK, f. 303, ed. khr. 418). A special program booklet was prepared for each concert providing detailed information about the works performed. [The conservatory Shostakovich refers to is the St. Petersburg Conservatory.]

6. Emil Albertovich Kuper [Cooper; 1877–1960] was principal conductor of the Petrograd Theatre of Opera and Ballet, 1919–24, where symphonic concerts were also given. Cooper was one of the most renowned conductors of Tchaikovsky's music.

7. Streabog is written in Roman letters in the original. *Trans.*

8. Ignatii Albertovich Gliasser (1850–1925) was the leading piano teacher in St. Petersburg at the turn of the twentieth century. *Trans.*

9. A. A. Rozanova is Aleksandra Aleksandrovna Rozanova-Nechaeva (1876–1942); M. O. Shteinberg is Maksimilian Oseevich Shteinberg (1883–1946); A. A. Petrov is Aleksei Alekseevich Petrov (1859–1919); L. V. Nikolaev is Leonid Vladimirovich Nikolaev (1878–1942); N. A. Sokolov is Nikolai Aleksandrovich Sokolov (1859–1922). *Trans.*

10. The "Piano Sonata" is no. 1, op. 12 (1926); "Aphorisms" is op. 13 (1927); the "Symphonic Poem for the Tenth Anniversary of the October Revolution" was subsequently renamed Symphony no. 2, "Dedication to October," op. 14 (1927); *The Nose* is op. 15. *Trans.*

11. Leningrad State Conservatory. *Trans.*

12. The "Trio" is no. 1, op. 8 (1923); the "Octet" is op. 11 (1924–25); the "Symphony" is no. 1, op. 10 (1924–25). *Trans.*

13. Shteinberg would have said, "*muZYka,*" an obsolete pronunciation that gives his answer an ironic twist. *Trans.*

14. Shostakovich's actual terms are *statika, dinamika,* and *dialektika*. His use of *dialektika* invokes the Hegelian principle of thesis and antithesis in confrontation, resulting in resolution through synthesis, i.e., a kind of transformational development. In some sense it can be said to have manifested itself in music in the same period in the nineteenth century, characterized by the theoretical term "thematic transformation." *Trans.*

15. Rimsky-Korsakov (1844–1908). *Trans.*

16. Andrei Vasilevich Grigorev (b. 1905), a composer, pianist, and also a student of L. V. Nikolaev.

17. Lev Ivanovich Ivanov (1834–1901) was a ballet artist and choreographer. He choreographed the first performance of *Nutcracker* to Tchaikovsky's music in 1892, a production that had a great influence on the subsequent development of the ballet theater. Marius [Ivanovich] Petipa (1818–1910) was a ballet artist and choreographer of the Russian classical ballet. Mikhail Mikhailovich Fokin or Fokine (1880–1942) was a ballet artist, choreographer, teacher, and active participant in the seasons produced by Sergei Pavlovich Diagilev [known in the West as Serge Diaghilev] (1872–1929). Kasian Yaroslavovich (Karlovich) Goleizovsky (1892–1970) was a ballet artist and choreographer who in his creations paid particular attention to the plastic expressiveness of the human body.

18. Étienne-Maurice Falconet (1716–91), a French sculptor who worked in Russia between 1766 and 1778, was the creator of the well-known equestrian statue to Peter the First in St. Petersburg, known as the "Bronze Horseman."

19. The name "Ai Petri" (The Rocks) derives from the Greek. This famous precipice drops down dramatically from a scenic outlook to the Black Sea. *Trans.*

20. Boris Mikhailovich Kustodiev (1878–1927) was a genre painter and portraitist who also did book illustration and stage design. During the summer of 1923, Shostakovich vacationed with the Kustodiev family in Gaspra, on the Crimean peninsula.

21. Iurii Pavlovich Annenkov (1889–1974), a Russian graphic artist and painter who lived abroad after 1924, provided the illustrations for Blok's poem, *The Twelve* (1918).

22. Vladimir Georgievich Erenberg's (1875–1923) opera-parody, *Vampuka, the African Bride,* "a model opera in all respects," based on a libretto by Mikhail Nikolaevich Volkonsky (1860–1917). Performed in St. Petersburg from 1909 to 1927, the work poked fun at every absurd coincidence and routine encountered in grand opera, especially Italian grand opera. *Trans.*

23. MKhAT is the Moscow Art Theatre. *Trans.*

24. Samuil Evgenevich Feinberg (1890–1962) was a pianist and composer whose music was influenced by Scriabin. *Trans.*

25. By "Ala and Lolly" Shostakovich means Prokofiev's *Scythian Suite,* op. 20. *Trans.*

26. Problems arising from some inadequacy, from the "abnormality" of a talented and brilliant personality, and the influence of heredity concerned many researchers—musicians, psychologists, sociologists. For Gruber, these questions had a very personal significance, because almost immediately after his birth his mother lost her mind and spent the rest of her life in a psychiatric clinic in Kiev.

Stalin and Shostakovich:

Letters to a "Friend"

Leonid Maximenkov

When, in 1993, Leningrad musicologist Isaak Glikman published the letters Dmitrii Shostakovich had written to him, he observed that the composer "did not keep letters that were sent to him, and urged others to follow his example."[1] By contrast, the main addressee of the Soviet nation, Iosif Stalin, preserved many letters sent to him, marking them with the notation, "for my archive." Among these were letters from Shostakovich.

> Dear Iosif Vissarionovich,
>
> Today I spoke by telephone with com[rade] L. P. Beriia. He told me that he had spoken to you about my affairs, about which I had written to him.
>
> Lavrentii Pavlovich told me that you regarded my situation very considerately. All of my affairs are sorting themselves out splendidly. In June I will receive a five-room apartment. In July I will receive a dacha in Kratovo and, in addition, I will receive 60,000 rubles for fittings. All of this made me extraordinarily happy.
>
> I ask you to accept my most heartfelt gratitude for the attention and concern. I wish you happiness, health and many years of life for the good of our beloved Motherland, our great people.
>
> Composer D. Shostakovich
> 27 May 1946[2]

On 1 February 1947, Shostakovich reported to the leader about his new Moscow home:

> To the Chairman of the Council of Ministers of the USSR
> com.[rade] Stalin I. V.
>
> Iosif Vissarionovich!
>
> A few days ago I moved with my family to a new apartment. The apartment turned out to be a very good one and it is very pleasant to live in. With all my heart I thank you for your concern about me. The main thing I very much want now is to justify—if only to a small degree—the attention you have shown me. I will apply all my strength toward that.
>
> I wish you many years of health and energy for the good of our Motherland, our Great People.
>
> Yours, D. Shostakovich
> 31 January 1947
>
> Moscow, Mozhaiskoe shosse no. 37/45, apt. 87. Tel. G 1-22-56.[3]

In terms of genre, these two brief letters are classic "receipts" acknowledging material blessings, with the expression of gratitude for the signs of the monarch's favor and the pledge "to justify the attention" shown by the leader. The documents are noteworthy because of their precise arithmetic tally; such and such sum of money received, such and such an apartment, a dacha in Kratovo, "fittings." In the numerous letters sent to Stalin by other authors, requests are frequently to be found, even entreaties for favors, for apartments, subsidies, trips abroad for medical reasons. The letters of Shostakovich stand apart in this respect: they express gratitude for largesse already bestowed.

Skeptics may retort that in February 1948 the thunderbolt of the Zhdanov resolution "About V. Muradeli's opera *The Great Friendship*" struck. What kind of Stalinist "concern" could compare with the humiliation and persecution that ensued? The Party's resolution certified that the music of Shostakovich, Sergei Prokofiev, Aram Khachaturian, Vissarion Shebalin, Gavriil Popov, Nikolai Miaskovsky, and others "displays most strikingly these formalist perversions and undemocratic tendencies so alien to the Soviet people and their artistic tastes."

According to the commonly accepted thesis of the history of Soviet culture, Shostakovich was subjected twice to public civic censure: in 1936, for formalism in his opera *Lady Macbeth of the Mtsensk District*, and in 1948, for the same formalism, but now in conjunction with an opera by a composer born of Armenian parents in Stalin's hometown and raised in Soviet Georgia, Vano Muradeli. The result of the first working over was that Shostakovich never again completed a single opera. As a consequence of the second, Shostakovich's Tenth Symphony, though contemplated several years earlier, did not see the light of day until after Stalin's death.

Documents from the archives allow us to reconstruct a somewhat different picture of these two pivotal events. The most complete and detailed survey of Stalin's views on music are to be found in the notes left by his deputy in charge of cinema, Boris Shumiatsky. As head of the Soviet film industry from November 1930 until his firing, arrest, and execution in 1938, Shumiatsky took notes on the Kremlin screenings of sound and silent movies attended by Stalin and his entourage. The documentation that follows is drawn from Shumiatsky's transcripts.[4]

By way of background, the first real blockbuster Soviet sound film, *Counterplan*, directed by Fridrikh Ermler and Sergei Iutkevich and made for the fifteenth anniversary of the October Revolution in 1932, contained a hit song written by Shostakovich, "Song of the Counterplan" ("The morning greets us with a chill"). Stalin became fascinated with the song.

On 31 May 1934, while watching a newsreel about the May Day parade in Leningrad, Stalin "praised in particular the melodic and rhythmic nature of the music and the quality of the sound, in contrast with a number of our films where the sound is a source of cacophony and 'unintelligible' music." A month later, Stalin watched a documentary about the epic passage of the icebreaker *Cheliuskin* through Arctic ice. Shumiatsky records: "First the documentary was shown without the music accompaniment, but when the piano came in, Iosif Vissarionovich said: 'The cinema really does presuppose music and this latter aids the viewing a great deal.'" On 30 October, upon returning from a long vacation in the resort of Sochi on the Black Sea coast (where he also watched movies), Stalin praised—and not for the first time—the first Soviet musical comedy, *Merry Fellows* (1934; directed by Grigorii Aleksandrov, music by Isaak Dunaevsky), because it was "technically and musically well done," notwithstanding the talk that some writers had criticized it sharply for its "hooligan traits."

On 15 December 1934, two weeks after the murder of Sergei Kirov, Stalin watched *Maxim's Youth*, directed by Grigorii Kozintsev and Leonid Trauberg, with a score by Shostakovich. This was the first sound film to exemplify the biography of a Bolshevik leader who was simple, not university educated, not an émigré talking endlessly in Paris cafés or scribbling in London's British Museum, that is, a film about Stalin's breed of Bolshevik leader. Immensely rich musically—with original songs, accordion solos, urban songs, revolutionary anthems, and the "Internationale" (until 1943, the Soviet national anthem)—the soundtrack was a true revelation. It provided a bright, optimistic, and prophetic dimension in the somber days after Kirov's funeral.

According to Shumiatsky, it was at this time that Stalin's partiality for the triumphant civil war epic *Chapaev* (1934; directed by Sergei and Georgii Vasiliev, music by Gavriil Popov) was redirected to *Maxim's Youth*. On 18 December, with Politburo members and candidate (i.e., nonvoting) members Anastas Mikoian, Lazar Kaganovich, Andrei Andreev, Andrei Zhdanov, and their families, Stalin watched *Maxim's Youth* again. During the scene where prisoners sing the revolutionary song "Varshavianka," a song that Shostakovich would later quote in other works, including his Eleventh Symphony, Stalin's audience started singing along. Art turned into reality. Stalin told Zhdanov, "It's very strong. That will touch the masses of spectators." Stalin praised the work of the cameraman and Shostakovich's music as "good, cultured." He singled out in particular Shostakovich's prologue and the "strong numbers played on accordion."

Not long after, Shostakovich was brought to the attention of the Politburo to be considered for an honorary title—Merited Activist of the Arts of the Russian Federation—for his service in the cause of building the Soviet cinema industry, the only composer nominated in a long list. When the Central Committee reduced the number of candidates, however, and reorganized and changed the form of the awards, Shostakovich's name was left off the final list. He went unrewarded.

On 25 December 1935, together with his children Svetlana and Vasilii, Viacheslav Molotov, and others, Stalin viewed the film *Girlfriends*—a civil war epic directed by Leo Arnshtam with music by Shostakovich—for the third time. Praising the film highly in consideration of its enormous "mobilization significance," Stalin ranked it in line with the best achievements of Soviet cinema. Surprisingly, the only thing that he disliked was Shostakovich's score: "Its lyricism does not harmonize with the main tone of the movie . . . also, there is an awful lot of music [*cherez chur mnogo*]. . . . The music disturbs the viewing," Stalin pronounced.

With this experience of Shostakovich's recent film music fresh in his mind, Stalin went to see his opera, *Lady Macbeth of the Mtsensk District*, a few weeks later. And on 29 January 1936, the day after the infamous editorial "Muddle Instead of Music" appeared in *Pravda*, Stalin evaluated the *Lady Macbeth* affair and the editorial not so much from the standpoint of opera, but from that of music for the cinema. Stalin's strategy for the operational organization of the Soviet music world was disclosed to an inner circle of comrades-in-arms—not including anyone actually responsible for the musical front—prior to a regular late-night Kremlin screening session.

The *Pravda* editorial stated that Shostakovich's opera "titillates the perverted tastes of bourgeois audiences . . . with its twitching, clamorous, neurotic music." Shumiatsky's notes on that late-night gathering on 29

January permit us to draw the inference that what the leader was up in arms against was not so much Shostakovich's opera, but the "unhealthy" tendencies in Soviet film music, about which there was not one word in the editorial. It pointed to a clear-cut evaluation: Shostakovich should continue working and writing important film music instead of useless operas.

The conversation between Soviet leaders about the *Pravda* editorial that was taken down by Shumiatsky is a unique, almost stenographic record. Besides Shumiatsky and Stalin, the others who took part were the People's Commissar of Defense, Kliment Voroshilov, and the Chairman of the Council of People's Commissars, Viacheslav Molotov:

> **Voroshilov** (addressing Shumiatsky): And what do you think about how the issue of Shostakovich's music was raised in *Pravda*?
>
> **Shumiatsky**: It was raised correctly. I have been fighting for clear, life-affirming, i.e., realistic music for a number of years. I have even written about this more than once in the past, last year in *Pravda*, for example. On the other hand, I have been arguing vehemently with composers about that character of music that is based on folklore, on the sources of folk music and the best classical music.
>
> **Stalin**: Yes, I remember the article in *Pravda*. It set the course correctly.
>
> (At this point Molotov arrived. He also participated in the conversation.)
>
> **Molotov**: What did it do for music in the cinema?
>
> **Shumiatsky**: It produced a couple of quite good symphonic and vocal melodies, for example *Golden Mountains* [Shostakovich], *The Tempest* [Shcherbachev], *Aerograd* [Kabalevsky], *Merry Fellows*, and a number of interesting—or rather—the best Soviet mass songs: "The morning greets us with a chill" [i.e., "Song of the Counterplan"], the "March from *Merry Fellows*," "Kakhovka" [Dunaevsky], and others.
>
> **Stalin**: "The morning greets us" is from *Merry Fellows*. All the songs from this movie are good, simple, melodic. They have even been accused of being Mexican in origin. I do not know how many measures they have in common with Mexican folk songs but, in the first place, the essence of the song is simple. And second, even if something might have been taken from Mexican folklore, that's not bad.
>
> **Voroshilov**: No, it was "The song helps us to build and to live" [from Dunaevsky's score to *Merry Fellows*] that was accused of being in Mexican spirit, and "The morning greets us" is, in fact, from *Counterplan*. You mean its music is by Shostakovich?
>
> **Shumiatsky**: Yes, that is his song. Personally, I think that like the

majority of composers, Shostakovich can write good, realistic music, but on the condition that he is directed.

Stalin: That's the crux. They aren't being directed. And thus people are throwing themselves into thickets of all kinds of eccentricities. And they are even praised for this, praised to excess. But now when an explanation has been given in *Pravda*, all our composers should start creating music that is transparent and understandable, and not rebuses and riddles in which the meaning of the work dies. On top of this, it is necessary for people to use melodies skillfully. In some movies, for example, you are brought to deafness. The orchestra cracks, squeals, something screeches, something whistles, something jingles, hindering you from following the visual images. Why does leftism thrive so in music? There is one answer: no one is paying attention, no one places on composers and conductors the demands for a clear mass art. The Arts Committee should take the *Pravda* article as a program for musical art. If it doesn't, it will do badly. In this respect the example of cinema should also be taken into account.

Voroshilov: Shumiatsky is right. Not all of the composers are leftists. There's Knipper, Dunaevsky.

Shumiatsky: Kabalevsky and others.[5] Of course, there are individuals among them with eccentricities. Not many inveterates. If they are taken in hand firmly, the deviations, the cacophony can be averted.

Molotov: That's the point. The article plays right into your hands.[6]

After the appearance on 6 February 1936 of the second *Pravda* editorial, "Balletic Falsehood," attacking Shostakovich's ballet *The Limpid Stream* recently staged at the Bolshoi Theatre, the composer requested a meeting with Platon Kerzhentsev, the newly appointed chairman of the Committee for Artistic Affairs. In reporting the substance of their meeting on 7 February to Stalin and Molotov, Kerzhentsev made no mention of film music. Instead, he informed his superiors that he had counseled the composer to "change his aims, reject his formalistic mistakes, and ensure that his music is understandable to the broad masses." He also advised him that before embarking on any opera or ballet, he should submit the libretto for their approval.[7] Shostakovich would complete no more operas or ballets. But his work in the cinema would continue under Stalin's watchful eye.

In 1940, Shostakovich was nominated for the Order of Lenin, the highest Soviet order, once again for his film music, specifically the "Maxim trilogy"—*Maxim's Youth*, and its successors, *Maxim's Return* (1936–37) and

The Vyborg District (1938)—as well as *The Great Citizen* (directed by Fridrikh Ermler; first series, 1937; second series, 1938–39).[8] In May 1940, the thirty-three-year-old composer was awarded instead the second most prestigious order, the Red Banner of Labor. In other words, Shostakovich's first Soviet decoration honored his services to film. From that point on, awards, titles, and prizes came on a regular basis.[9]

Without striving for nomenklatura status and honors, Shostakovich managed to acquire them with enviable regularity.[10] At the age of twenty-seven, for instance, he was appointed to a committee on gramophone recordings of the Central Committee's Politburo. As a civil servant, Shostakovich began his service at the local level, when he was elected to the Leningrad city council in 1934, at the age of twenty-eight. In 1947, he was elected a deputy to the Supreme Soviet of the Russian Soviet Federated Socialist Republic (RSFSR), representing Leningrad's Dzerzhinsky district, a post to which he was continually reelected until his election to the Supreme Soviet of the USSR in 1962, at first representing Leningrad, and from 1966 representing Gorky (now Nizhnii Novgorod). In 1974, he was elected a deputy to the Supreme Soviet for the last time, representing the Iadrinsky district of the Chuvash Soviet Socialist Autonomous Republic of the Russian Federation. All along, he served on innumerable official boards, committees, commissions, juries, and so forth. From 1934 until his death, Shostakovich's service as a civil servant was constant and uninterrupted.

Shostakovich came under the attentive eyes of the Kremlin's ideological watchdogs very early. His first foreign trip, to the International Chopin Competition in Warsaw in 1927, received tacit approval from the Kremlin. His second trip, as a member of a cultural delegation to Turkey in 1935, received top clearance by the secret police, written acquiescence from Stalin's secretary ("Comrade Stalin does not mind") and formal authorization by the Politburo.[11]

In 1936, during his audience with Kerzhentsev, Shostakovich first expressed the desire to write to Stalin and even to meet with him. But he was dissuaded from pursuing the matter; it was considered unnecessary. The comrades didn't take issue with his film music. In the end, his dressing-down in 1936 played no substantive role in Shostakovich's fate as a nomenklatura beneficiary (titles, awards, responsibilities, rations, housing).

In the Stalinist iconostasis, Shostakovich was de facto the main composer of the Soviet nation. Until 1960, however, when he was elected chairman of the Union of Composers of the RSFSR (not to be confused with the Union of Composers of the USSR), he did not join the ranks of top civil servants.[12] Paradoxically, under Stalin's regime Shostakovich was not required to hold official positions, to join the Communist Party, to "sign" his name to articles in the Party's theoretical journal. He was treasured and protected as a "non-Party-member Bolshevik" (*bezpartiinyi Bol'shevik*). It was the anti-Stalinist Khrushchev who reversed this policy and forced Shostakovich to embrace official responsibilities visibly.

On 16 August 1951, Shostakovich wrote to Politburo member Georgii Malenkov, Stalin's second in command:

> Greatly respected Georgii Maksimilianovich!
>
> On 15 August, General Secretary of the Union of Soviet Composers T. N. Khrennikov spoke with me. He invited me to join the Secretariat of the Union of Soviet Composers [SSK].
>
> I am turning to you with the earnest request to take the following into account: I am prepared to perform any public service within the Union of Soviet Composers of which I am capable. However, to undertake the responsibilities of a Secretary of the SSK is beyond my capacity, since I have no aptitude whatsoever for any leadership duties. Moreover, performing the responsibilities of a Secretary of the SSK will require a great deal of my time and energy and thus will tear me away from creative work which—at least for the time being—I consider my main calling.
>
> With respect to you,
> D. D. Shostakovich
> 16 August 1951[13]

In November 2002, Tikhon Khrennikov confirmed that, at Malenkov's request, he had spoken to Shostakovich about this proposal.[14] Khrennikov traveled to Leningrad and the two composers had dinner at the Evropeiskaia Hotel. Shostakovich agreed to accept the position. But when Khrennikov returned to Moscow the next day, Shostakovich changed his mind. It is unwise to speculate about his reasons. His letter looks not unlike the repudiation of a previous decision. In 1951, Malenkov respected the wishes of the top Soviet composer, issuing an order to Agitprop: "To comrade Kruzhkov. Comrade Shostakovich's request should be honored. Talk again to him and to comrade Khrennikov. G. Malenkov. 18 August."[15]

Six years later, Shostakovich's priorities had evidently changed. In 1957, he accepted election to the Secretariat of the Union of Composers of the USSR, a position he would retain until his death. In 1960, he assumed the chairmanship of the newly created Union of Composers of the RSFSR. The same year he became a candidate member of the Communist Party, becoming a full member in 1961.

The awards distributed at the conclusion of the competition for the Soviet national anthem in 1943 demonstrate the bizarre nature of Soviet cultural policies in dealing with the top artistic nomenklatura. The composer of the winning entry, Aleksandr Aleksandrov, received a much lesser sum, 12,000 rubles, than the losing Shostakovich, who received the highest amount awarded, 32,000 rubles. (Among other losing competitors, Prokofiev was awarded 12,000 and Khachaturian 28,000 rubles). Similarly, the winning poet laureates Sergei Mikhalkov and Gabriel El-Registan were left financially far behind the losing Vasilii Lebedev-Kumach, whose lyrics were discarded.[16] Who then were the winners of 1943 national anthem competition? Judging by the amount of the prize awarded, they were Shostakovich and Lebedev-Kumach. Did their anthems win in the contest? No, they did not.

Attaching numerical equivalents to someone's abstract value was a standard practice of mature Stalinism. Artistic merits, aesthetic considerations, talent, and international fame aside, each particular individual had a financial position in the table of ranks of the Soviet nomenklatura corresponding to his or her value as a fighter on the ideological and cultural front. This position was measured in terms of salaries, awards, honorary titles, Stalin prizes, and benefactions like those enumerated by Shostakovich in his 1946 letter to Stalin quoted above. As the anthem competition proved, by mid-1943 Shostakovich had reached the top of the list of Soviet composers on this elite register.

In the post–World War Two period, Soviet financial and credit policy was overhauled. A new exchange rate was established, billions of rubles of savings were confiscated, food rationing was abolished, and a new, gold-based Soviet ruble was introduced. Stalin also cut privileges accorded to the top nomenklatura.

Judging by surviving documents, one of the main impulses behind the musical scandal in 1948 may well have been economic. Until 1948, when its First Congress was held, the Union of Soviet Composers did not function as an organization juridically equivalent to the Union of Soviet Writers. It had an All-Union Organizing Committee (Orgkomitet) in Moscow and affiliates at the local level, but no Party bureaucracy. The budgetary structure of the Orgkomitet was headed by Khachaturian, Shostakovich, Prokofiev, Kabalevsky, and Popov. This was an exceptional phenomenon in Soviet culture: unlike other disciplines, where Party functionaries held in their hands decision-making power over creative questions, here those powers were held by the most prominent, acknowledged representatives in their field.

Muzfond, the financial wing of the Orgkomitet, was headed by Vano Muradeli, rather less talented in music, but successful in matters of accounting. His deputy, Levon Atovmian, was a certified genius in the distribution of budgetary resources. Khachaturian, Atovmian, and Muradeli were people who were true to their friends. According to a confidential unsigned report submitted to Andrei Zhdanov at the beginning of 1948, on the heels of the scandal over Muradeli's opera, it transpired that Atovmian—identified as a "retainer" of Khachaturian, Shostakovich, and Prokofiev—was in "unchecked disposition of large sums," which he used "mainly to lend support to that group of composers."[17] "Over the last seven years, he [Atovmian] has paid out by way of creative assistance to composers and musicologists 13,190,000 rubles." Moreover, Prokofiev's uncanceled debt to Muzfond amounted to 182,000 rubles; Khachaturian's to 24,000 rubles; Shebalin's to 23,000 rubles. The average monthly salary at this time in the lean and hungry postwar nation was 400 to 500 rubles; Stalin's official salary was 10,000 rubles.

The report noted further: "The same Atovmian, who concurrently holds the job of director of Muzfond's publishing operation, paid out to composers and musicologists over the course of 1947—principally to those very same representatives of anti-realistic music and criticism—2,000,000 rubles. For 1946–47, composer Shostakovich was paid honoraria of 230,200 rubles, Prokofiev 309,900 rubles for the same period, and so forth."[18]

Naturally, Atovmian was fired, by decision of the Politburo, as was the entire leadership of the Orgkomitet. But Stalin had barely passed away before his friends arranged for Atovmian to be appointed director and artistic supervisor of the orchestra of the Committee for Cinematography.[19]

Back then, in 1947, composer Muradeli, the head of Muzfond, submitted his opera *The Great Friendship*—about the civil war in the northern Caucasus—to public scrutiny. To commemorate the thirtieth anniversary of the Great October Revolution, productions of the opera were prepared in twenty theaters. Millions were spent on its staging, on stunning sets, on tremendous crowd scenes with choruses. The Moscow Party activists who auditioned the opera at the Bolshoi Theatre during the 1947 anniversary celebrations didn't fall asleep; they signaled their approval with sustained applause. For the time being, all went smoothly. Bolshoi Theatre soloist and former precentor of a church choir, Maxim Dormidontovich Mikhailov, spoke about the opera's production: "For us it was an enormous event, like Easter is for believers. Yesterday we went to the theater as if to matins, with holy reverence."[20]

The "Easter matins" lasted just until the leader returned from the South. On 5 January 1948, Stalin attended a performance of the opera.

Notwithstanding his evident objections on ethnic grounds, the lavish, tasteless production of Muradeli's opera, ready to be staged in opera houses all across the country, must have appeared the worst example of financial mismanagement in the middle of the massive revamping of the country's finance system.

Suddenly the political economy and financial efficiency of Soviet music became a top priority. In addition to the operational report on Muzfond's activities cited above, in January 1948 a joint investigative team from Agitprop, the Finance Ministry, and the economic counterintelligence department of the secret police prepared evaluations for Zhdanov on the revision of bookkeeping practices, the system of payment, and a scrutiny of the awards of Stalin prizes for music in the years 1941–47.[21] (Although he was not singled out in this scrutiny, Shostakovich had received three Stalin prizes during this period totaling 250,000 rubles.) Minister of Finance Arsenii Zverev reported to Stalin on the revision of budgetary funds allocated for the staging of *The Great Friendship*.[22]

At the meeting with Bolshoi Theatre personnel on 6 January 1948, Zhdanov ranted, "We in the Central Committee watch every film before it is released, but here the opera was concealed from us! . . . In Moscow alone, 600,000 rubles were spent on its production. Its preparation went on in secret, which is completely improper."[23] Who was its author? Muradeli—the chairman of Muzfond. Who was his deputy? Atovmian. This pair distributed millions of the people's money to their friends. And who were their friends? Were they the songwriters, the composers of music for the masses? No. They were the composers of serious music— Shostakovich, Khachaturian, Prokofiev, and those who, for their part, were in charge of the creative union, the Moscow Conservatory, those who served as consultants for musical programming on radio, in music publishing, in other words, those in control of the means of mass information. They served on the Committee for Stalin Prizes. They paid each other fantastic sums of money.

In this matter, Shostakovich was a collateral casualty. He was guilty of being in good relations with those around him, of sitting on innumerable committees and commissions. Yes, he received money and other material blessings in the form of honoraria, loans, and advances. But they were bestowed by representatives of Soviet authority. Were the officials responsible going to scream out to the whole world about the money that had been squandered? In Agitprop they came up with a different strategy: let's tell the nation we are fighting against incomprehensible music that is alien to us, and fighting for understandable music, "our" music.

The apotheosis of Stalin's flirtation with Shostakovich came with the composer's trip to the United States in March–April 1949 as a member of the official Soviet delegation to the Cultural and Scientific Congress for World Peace held in New York.[24] On 16 February 1949, the list of six Soviet delegates, including the composer, was approved.[25] In principle, the non-Party Bolshevik Shostakovich was not consumed with the desire to cross the ocean. On 7 March, he admitted this openly in a letter to Leonid Ilichev, one of the leaders of Agitprop (later to achieve notoriety in connection with Khrushchev's explosion over the abstract artists exhibited at the Manezh gallery in 1962):

> Any public appearance places great nervous strain on me. After all, I perform infrequently and don't have extensive stage experience. Furthermore, the current condition of my health is indifferent. I feel sick the whole time. . . . Therefore, a trip to America, the stay there, the participation in concerts—all of this would place great demands on me. I implore you to take this into consideration and help me. It would be considerably easier for me if my wife, Nina Vasilevna Shostakovich, could make this involved and difficult journey with me. She always accompanies me on my travels and eases considerably all the burdens of the trip, preparation for concerts, daily life, etc. Besides which, if I have to concertize in America, it will be necessary to have tails made.[26]

On 10 March 1949, Ilichev informed his boss, Mikhail Suslov, about a whole range of problems complicating Shostakovich's trip to America. The security organs seemed to signal possible accommodation with the composer's wishes: "Com[rade] Shostakovich also requests that his wife—Shostakovich Nina Vasilevna—be allowed to leave with him. Shostakovich N.V. has traveled before with her husband on foreign trips. Shostakovich's son and his mother will remain in Moscow."[27] They might also have added that his underage daughter, Galina, would be left among the hostages.

The question about his wife aside, the choice of repertory and performers remained, as well as the ordering of an expensive suit from the workshop of the administration of the Central Committee. The super-cautious Suslov couldn't bring himself to resolve such delicate matters. He sent all the documents upstairs, to the curator of external political affairs, Viacheslav Molotov. This was not a good time for Molotov. His wife, Polina Zhemchuzhina, had been arrested in January 1949 in connection with the Jewish Anti-Fascist Committee affair, and he himself was demoted from the post of Minister of Foreign Affairs on 4 March, remaining a deputy prime minister.[28] One can imagine his state of confusion and anguish when he saw Shostakovich's travel dossier on his desk. He may have thought the composer's trip was a trap, the next provocation. Without reflecting for long, he kicked the whole collection of documents up to the Best Friend of Soviet musicians, Stalin.

On the very same day, Stalin phoned Shostakovich at home. Over the years, as he slowly consolidated his power, Stalin's personal involvement in artistic affairs increased proportionately. His unmistakable touch on the literary front was well-known, even to contemporaries. His private letters were leaked in order to shape public opinion. Thanks to a secret police network that initiated, fueled, and controlled gossip, news of Stalin's solicitous personal phone calls to selected members of the elite was circulated immediately. Stalin retained the practice of person-to-person calls until the end of his life. His call to Shostakovich on 16 March 1949 is one of the mythic episodes in the history of the contact between the Zeus on the Soviet Olympus and the leading figures of literature and art. With the difference that in Shostakovich's case, a note with expressions of gratitude for the very fact of that personal contact has been found:

> 17 March 1949
> To Comrade I. V. Stalin
>
> Dear Iosif Vissarionovich!
>
> First of all please accept my most heartfelt gratitude for the conversation that took place yesterday. You supported me very much, since the forthcoming trip to America has been worrying me greatly. I cannot but be proud of the confidence that has been placed in me. I will fulfill my duty. To speak on behalf of our Soviet people in defense of peace is a great honor for me.
>
> My indisposition cannot serve as an impediment to the fulfillment of such a responsible mission.
>
> Once again, I thank you for the trust and attention.
>
> Yours, D. Shostakovich[29]

Comrade Shostakovich's behavior in this matter was beyond reproach. Eight months after his official mission to New York, Shostakovich was named one of the seventy-five members of the committee to organize the celebration of Stalin's seventieth birthday, the only composer on a list that had been carefully selected and approved by the Politburo.[30] His name also figured among the invited guests to the birthday celebrations themselves, to the festivities at the Bolshoi Theatre on 21 December 1949, Stalin's birthday, and to an even more exclusive Kremlin reception the day after.[31] Whether he attended either cannot be verified at this time.[32]

The fourth and last of the letters sent by Shostakovich to Stalin preserved in the leader's personal archive dates from two months later:

> To the Chairman of the Council of Ministers of the USSR
> Iosif Vissarionovich Stalin
>
> Dear Iosif Vissarionovich!
> Some burning issues in our musical life that also touch me personally compel me to disturb you. I beg you to receive me and hear me out. I am in pressing need of your help and advice.
>
> Yours. D. Shostakovich
> 16 February 1950

> Moscow, 151. Mozhaiskoe shosse 37/45, apt. 87. Tel. G 1-22-56. [33]

The register of visitors to Stalin's office does not record such a meeting having taken place in the Kremlin. Whether it took place on neutral territory remains a secret between Shostakovich and Stalin. But on 8 March 1950, three weeks after the composer sent this letter, a front-page announcement in *Pravda* broke the news that Shostakovich had been awarded another Stalin prize, his fourth, for his oratorio, *The Song of the Forests,* and his music to the film, *The Fall of Berlin.* The "burning issues in our musical life" had been settled by the Party.

NOTES

This article, which is chiefly based on archival documents in the collection of the Russian State Archive of Social-Political History (hereafter RGASPI), is a revised and expanded version of "Pod muzyku vozhdei. Stalin i Shostakovich: pis'ma k drugu," *Rodina* (February 2002): 95–98. My sincere thanks to Laurel Fay for her help in shaping the final text.

1. *Pis'ma k drugu: Dmitrii Shostakovich—Isaaku Glikmanu* (Moscow/St. Petersburg: DSCH/ Kompozitor, 1993), p. 5; translation taken from English edition, *Story of a Friendship: The Letters of Dmitry Shostakovich to Isaak Glikman 1941–1975,* trans. Anthony Phillips (Ithaca, N.Y.: Cornell University Press, 2001), p. xiii.

2. RGASPI, f. 558, op. 11, ed. khr. 831, l. 68. Beriia had relinquished his post as head of the People's Commissariat of Internal Affairs (NKVD) in January 1946 to become head of the Soviet A-bomb project; at this moment he was a deputy chairman of the Council of People's Commissars and a member of the Politburo.

3. RGASPI, f. 558, op. 11, d. 831, l. 70. Shostakovich was actually provided two adjoining apartments, with separate entrances, in the building on Mozhaiskoe shosse. In his

reminiscences, Levon Atovmian recalled that a car had been among the gifts showered on Shostakovich at the same time; see L. Atov'mian, "Iz vospominanii," *Muzykal'naia akademiia* 4 (1997): 77.

4. The reports are held in RGASPI; for transcripts, see http://idf.ru/15/doc.shtml; also to be published in *Kremlevskii kinoteatr,* with introduction and commentary by Leonid Maksimenkov (Moscow: Rosspen, forthcoming).

5. On 29 February 1936, Kabalevsky published a directive article in *Pravda,* "Podenshchina v kinomuzyke i ee plody" (On day labor in film music and its fruits), in which, willingly or unwillingly, he developed Stalin's line on film music.

6. RGASPI, f. 558, op. 11, ed. khr. 829, l. 69–74.

7. Archive of the President of the Russian Federation (AP RF), f. 3, op. 35, d. 32, l. 42; translated from Russian text in *Istoriia sovetskoi politicheskoi tsenzury: dokumenty i kommentarii* (Moscow: Rosspen, 1997), pp. 480–81.

8. The nomination was made by the deputy chairman of the Council of People's Commissars, Andrei Vyshinsky, the former Procurator-General in charge of the Moscow show trials; RGASPI, f. 82, op. 2, ed. khr. 957, l. 69.

9. It is one of history's ironies that on the morning of 10 February 1948, the date of the infamous Central Committee Resolution "On V. Muradeli's opera *The Great Friendship,*" the latest of Shostakovich's honors, People's Artist of the RSFSR, was conferred on him. His elevation to the title had been announced in November 1947.

10. In the Soviet period, nomenklatura was a list of executive and honorary positions in all spheres of life that required Politburo approval for appointment and dismissal. (Nomenklatura also refers to the appointees to these positions.) In music, these included membership in the Secretariat of the Composers' Union, directorships of the Moscow Conservatory and the Bolshoi Theatre, nominees for Stalin prizes, for the title People's Artist of the USSR, etc. The classic exposé of this system was written by a political scientist and Soviet defector, Michael Voslensky, *Nomenklatura: The Soviet Ruling Class,* trans. Eric Mosbacher (Garden City, N.Y.: Doubleday 1984). For a recent examination of a segment of the artistic nomenklatura, see Leonid Maksimenkov, "Ocherki nomenklaturnoi istorii sovetskoi literatury (1932–1946)," *Voprosy literatury* (July–August 2003): 212–58; (September–October 2003): 241–97.

11. RGASPI, f. 17, op. 163, d. 1057, l. 7; decision taken on 16 March 1935.

12. The RSFSR was the largest of the fifteen constituent republics of the USSR. From 1948 until the demise of the Soviet Union, Tikhon Khrennikov was chairman of the Union of Composers of the USSR.

13. RGASPI, f. 17, op. 133, ed. khr. 329, l. 55. Malenkov's appended decision to honor Shostakovich's request is dated 18 August 1951. An undated draft of this letter, without the annotation, was published in *Dmitrii Shostakovich v pis'makh i dokumentakh,* ed. I. A. Bobykina (Moscow: GTsMMK, 2000), p. 441.

14. Author's conversation with the Tikhon Khrennikov, Moscow, November 2002.

15. Agitprop (abbreviation for *agitatsiia i propaganda*) is the generic name for the Ideological Department of the Central Committee of the Communist Party, the body that controlled all spheres of culture and ideology in the Soviet Union.

16. RGASPI, f. 82, op. 2, ed. khr. 960, l. 32–36. Lebedev-Kumach was the author of the lyrics for Aleksandrov's "Hymn of the Bolshevik Party," which—with the substitute lyrics by Mikhalkov and El-Registan—became the winning entry in the anthem contest.

17. RGASPI, f. 77, op. 4, ed. khr. 36, ll. 107–8.

18. Ibid.

19. Although this is how Soviet reference sources routinely identify Atovmian's affiliation from 1953 to 1963, the proper name of the institution in question was Main Directorate of Cinematography of the USSR Ministry of Culture.

20. These words were uttered at a hastily convened meeting, attended by Andrei Zhdanov, at the Bolshoi Theatre on 6 January 1948, the day after Stalin had seen the opera; RGASPI, f. 77, op. 1, ed. khr. 786, ll. 1–24. For a more detailed investigation of the events leading up to the Central Committee Resolution of 10 February 1948, see L. Maksimenkov, "Partiia—nash rulevoi," *Muzykal'naia zhizn'* 13 (1993): 6–8; 14 (1993): 8–10.

21. See memorandum of Pokikarp Lebedev, deputy head of Agitprop, dated 9 January 1948; RGASPI, f. 77, op. 4, ed. khr. 36, ll. 121–23.

22. See memorandum of Arsenii Zverev to Stalin, dated 19 January 1948; RGASPI, f. 82, op. 2, ed. khr. 951, l. 85.

23. RGASPI, f. 77, op. 1, ed. khr. 786, ll. 1–24.

24. For a summary of the circumstances of this trip, see Laurel E. Fay, *Shostakovich: A Life* (New York: Oxford University Press, 2000), pp. 171–73.

25. RGASPI, f. 17, op. 163, ed. khr. 1520, l. 128. Molotov's notation reads: "Approved by the CC [*TsK*]." CC is the abbreviation for Central Committee, which on this occasion indicated Stalin.

26. Shostakovich informed Ilichev that he had received a telegram from Arturo Toscanini, Serge Koussevitzky, and others, offering to organize the composer's concerts in the United States during his stay at the peace conference, RGASPI, f. 56, op. 1, ed. khr. 1019, l. 4. Molotov wrote on a copy of this letter: "To Comrade Stalin. I ask you to get acquainted with the enclosed letter from composer Shostakovich. V. Molotov. 16 March 1949" (ibid., l. 3). Copies of the letter were also sent to Politburo members Beriia, Malenkov, Mikoian, Kaganovich, Bulganin, and Kosygin. By doing so Molotov signaled that a formal vote by the Politburo on the Shostakovich trip might have been expected. However, Stalin's personal phone call to the composer resolved the issue.

27. RGASPI, f. 17, op. 132, ed. khr. 242, l. 27; facsimile can be viewed on *DSCH CD-ROM, The Life and Works of Dmitri Shostakovich*, Chandos Multimedia Cultural Heritage Series 1, CHAN 50001, 2001, image K02. In the end, Shostakovich's wife did not travel with him to America in 1949, nor did any other of the delegates' spouses.

28. For the circumstances surrounding Zhemchuzhina's arrest, see Gennadi Kostyrchenko, *Out of the Red Shadows: Anti-Semitism in Stalin's Russia* (Amherst, N.Y.: Prometheus Books, 1995), pp. 119–23.

29. RGASPI, f. 667, op. 1, ed. khr. 17, l. 115. Plans for Shostakovich's concert appearances after the conclusion of the Peace Congress in New York were scuttled when the U.S. State Department peremptorily ordered the Soviet and other Iron Curtain delegates out of the country.

30. "V prezidiume Verkhovnogo soveta SSSR," *Sovetskoe iskusstvo*, 3 December 1949, p. 1.

31. RGASPI, f. 82. op. 2, ed. khr. 516, l. 159.

32. On 21 December 1949, Shostakovich wrote a letter to Isaak Glikman in which he complained about the poor state of health of his immediate family, and his own slow recovery from bouts of flu and angina. He made no mention of Stalin's birthday celebrations. Only critical illness could have justified his failure to attend these important events. The possibility must be considered that he didn't care to mention his attendance to Glikman. See *Story of a Friendship*, p. 38.

33. RGASPI, f. 558. op. 11, d. 831, l. 73.

"The Phenomenon of the Seventh":

A Documentary Essay on Shostakovich's

"War" Symphony

Christopher H. Gibbs

Dmitri Shostakovich has reached the age of thirty-six, and, from the middle of the road, can now look back on a career full of dramatic episodes. Not since the time of Berlioz has a symphonic composer created such a stir. In far-away America, great conductors vie with each other for the jus primae noctis *of his music. The score of the Seventh Symphony, the symphony of struggle and victory, has been reduced to a roll of microfilm and flown half-way across the world, from Russia to Persia, from Persia to Egypt, from Egypt to Brazil, and from Brazil to New York, to speed the day of the American premiere. How the old romantics would have loved to be the center of such a fantastic adventure! But Shostakovich is the product of another age, realistic and collectivist, rather than romantic and egocentric, an age that takes airplanes and microfilms for granted. He is proud of his status as a Soviet composer, and he understands the responsibility that all artistic expression entails in a collectivist society.*

—Nicolas Slonimsky, "Dmitri Dmitrievitch
Shostakovitch," *Musical Quarterly* 28
(October 1942): 415

Composers have been so intent on disposing of him [Shostakovich] as second-rate, that they have missed completely one of his most remarkable attributes—he has made the music of a living composer come fully alive for a world audience. It is not the war fever alone that explains the phenomenon of the Seventh. *Its success was in large measure due to a consciously adopted musical style which is accessible to listeners everywhere. I am not suggesting that Shostakovich has found the solution for our problem—far from it. But all his work, despite the obvious weaknesses, sets that problem before us in an inescapable way. It is the* tendency *he represents, rather than the music he writes, that makes Shostakovich a key figure of the present time.*

—Aaron Copland, "From the '20s to the
'40s and Beyond," *Modern Music* 20
(January/February 1943): 82

Presumably the ballyhoo has never been surpassed in history for the scope of the publicity and the distribution, by means of modern science, of the music. Not only has the symphony come. Ostensibly it conquered. Cruel to relate, in view of all that the work stands for, the tragic circumstances which forged it and the unquestioned sincerity and intensity of feeling with which it was written—it will go soon. It will be remembered much less than the events that gave rise to it. And this is contrary to the destiny of a work of art, which always outlasts not only the emotion but the men and the historical processes that went into its making.

—Olin Downes, "Second View of a Symphony,"
New York Times (26 July 1942)

These three passages touch on the principal issues in the early American reception of what Copland called the "phenomenon of the Seventh": the unusual conditions under which Shostakovich composed his symphony, the stories told about it, as well as those represented musically within, its accessibility to listeners, and, ultimately, its artistic value. In this documentary essay I will examine the initial performances of the Seventh in North America, beginning with Arturo Toscanini's historic broadcast on 19 July 1942. My goal is to consider how perceptions of the work's meaning, significance, and worth mirrored the times and places in which it was heard. The Seventh may seem a very different symphony today than it did in wartime America.

Well before Shostakovich appeared on the cover of *Time* magazine the week of Toscanini's broadcast, reports circulated about the brave young Russian and his "War" Symphony. The effect of the unprecedented attention accorded the work quickly established a "double story," one concerned with its external genesis, performances, and distribution, the other with its internal musical program. The first story is *about* the symphony, involving the fraught circumstances of its creation in a besieged Leningrad, the heroic composer's activities as a fire warden, the emotional first performances in the Soviet Union, the travails of getting a microfilm of the score to New York, and finally the squabbles among star conductors over who would have the privilege of leading the American premiere. The other story is contained *within* the symphony, its "program" as presented to the public at the time, initially coming from the composer himself. Throughout his career Shostakovich shied away from discussing his works in specific detail, and he generally did not write overtly programmatic symphonies (although four have texts and four carry titles bestowed by him). But he talked repeatedly about the Seventh, even before its completion.[1] His wife, colleagues, and Soviet critics also provided abundant information concerning both its context and content.

The Seventh Symphony has no official title and "Leningrad" is derived from Shostakovich's dedication; it quickly found other labels in America, including "War," "Blitz," "Stalingrad," and "The Symphony of Our Times."[2] Although Shostakovich did not name the individual movements in the score, he early on disclosed ones he said he had discarded ("War," "Memories," "The Expanses of our Native Country," and "Victory"), and these became integral to the work's reception as well. Shostakovich's portrayal of the Seventh was as a symphony of and about its time, but not a mere programmatic depiction of it. He was quoted as saying that the work was meant to present not "a naturalistic imitation of war, but nevertheless it is an interpretation of war."[3]

Most American critics in 1942 were keenly alert to the complexity of the interrelated issues of politics, personality, propaganda, and programs with respect to the Seventh Symphony, and yet the word they used most frequently to describe it was "sincere." Olin Downes, the chief critic of the *New York Times*, repeatedly said so (as we can see in the opening quotation), and the other leading American critic of the time, Virgil Thomson, agreed: "I do not find the work objectionable in spirit, and it is certainly sincere and competent music-making. I merely find it thin in substance."[4] The perception of sincerity suggests that the composer's motivations and the work's meaning were crystal clear. In another article Thomson stated just that: "If the music has no mystery and consequently no real freedom of thought, neither does it contain any obscurity or any evidence of personal frustration. It is as objective as an editorial, as self-assured as the news report of a public ceremony."[5] But though Shostakovich's intentions were deemed unproblematic, the programmatic elements of the Seventh, its relation to its own time, and questions of musical style and substance, especially repeated charges that the music was "derivative," aroused considerable debate. Few critics denied that the Seventh was effective—witness its enthusiastic reception from contemporaneous audiences—but some took a longer view and wondered if topicality and weighty political baggage would doom the symphony after all the initial attention.

Much of the American commentary discussed the "story" and "biography" of the work, with many writers using the occasion to explore larger issues of program music, especially in a time of war. Inevitably, the stories about and within the Seventh Symphony became conflated: tales of how Shostakovich struggled to compose it merged with those of the struggles depicted musically within. Such a conflation, of course, was nothing new, as we can see in three older works to which critics compared the Seventh. Berlioz's semiautobiographical *Symphonie fantastique* is a particularly famous example in which what is known about the circumstances of the work's composition overlaps with, and complements, the composer's stated program. If such an intersection in Berlioz's case is at his own invitation, in other instances listeners make connections unintended by the creator. Tchaikovsky's "Pathétique" Symphony, premiered just nine days before his death, soon found life (and death) circumstances projected onto it that cast the work as a farewell symphony. Beethoven's Fifth has been viewed since the composer's own time as a heroic statement of struggles against fate, even though the relevant anecdotes come from dubious sources, rather than from Beethoven himself. (It is also a composition that has successfully been appropriated for a wide variety of political ends.)

Not surprisingly, Beethoven was the composer most often invoked in discussions of the Seventh, raising the stakes (or lowering them, depending on one's perspective) from the geopolitical to the musico-political and biographical. Beethoven's symphonic legacy had dominated the musical politics of the nineteenth century, with the sharply divergent aesthetics of the "New German School" pitted against those of Schumann, Mendelssohn, Brahms, and their followers, and both camps claiming Beethovenian legitimacy. This was the intimidating tradition in which Shostakovich would have to succeed as a great symphonist and the Seventh as a great symphony. But the comparisons between Beethoven and Shostakovich were not just musical, and extended to their respective biographical hardships, both individual and more broadly political. Beethoven's struggles against deafness and the French invasions of Vienna in 1805 and 1809 seemed to foreshadow Shostakovich's against the official censure of his music in 1936 and the German invasion of 1941. "Double stories" have often been told about the symphonies of both composers. If the conflations and converging of the stories about and within musical works often have a long history, Shostakovich's symphonies, like those of Beethoven and of his revered Mahler, are particularly tricky cases and have invited an unusual quantity (if not always quality) of fantasy, speculation, and projection. The stories and programs in all cases—the intended, imputed, and interconnected—are well worth taking seriously because they strongly affect how the composers are viewed and how their music is heard.

I make no naive attempt in this essay to give a complete account of what happened with the Seventh Symphony's initial American adventures, or to claim the "real" meaning of the work. Rather, the generous sampling of representative sources put forth offers a good idea of the chronological unfolding of the symphony's reception and what struck American musicians, audiences, and critics at the time. I trace how the work was packaged and presented to the public, how information about the composer and the symphony, facts and opinions, accumulated during the summer of 1942 and the 1942–43 season. Inevitably this becomes something of a case study of orchestral life in the country at that time— the way concerts were programmed, promoted, and reviewed, the importance of radio, and the type of criticism offered in newspapers and program notes (quite often written by the same person, a possible conflict of interest that is rarely tolerated today).

After summer performances of the Seventh in New York, Tanglewood, and Ravinia, all of the "Big Five" orchestras played the symphony during the first part of the season, as did the NBC Symphony Orchestra and many other ensembles of varying levels of distinction. (Table 1 lists selected American performances during the 1942–43 season; I have concentrated on performances during the first half of the season.) It would be an impossible task to chronicle every performance, and probably unnecessary, as rather clear patterns of presentation and reception quickly become apparent. The process began with the promotion and preparation for the concerts, such as advance newspaper articles meant to generate interest in the symphony and program notes intended to help listeners, and it extended to reviews, reflective "Sunday pieces," synoptic essays, and larger critical studies. The *New York Times, Time,* and other prominent sources provided background information about the composer and his music, much of it derived from Soviet writings translated into English. (The most important Soviet writing appeared in a special August issue of the *Information Bulletin, Embassy of the Union of Soviet Socialist Republics* and the *VOKS Bulletin,* all of which trickled down and out to the public.)[6] The commentary on the symphony was largely repetitive and, as is unfortunately all too often the case with popular journalism and program notes, sometimes bordered on plagiarism. At the risk of trying the reader's patience, I will quote liberally from a broad range of critics so as to convey the information, judgments, and issues that arose at the time.

Table 1

Selected American Performances of
Shostakovich's Seventh Symphony, July 1942 to January 1943

Date		Performance	Conductor
JULY	19	NBC Symphony Orchestra (Broadcast)	Toscanini
AUGUST	14, 16	Berkshire Music Center Orchestra (Tanglewood)	Koussevitzky
	22	Chicago Symphony Orchestra (Ravinia)	Stock
SEPTEMBER	11, 13	Symphony Orchestra of Mexico	Chavez
OCTOBER	7	Symphony Orchestra of Mexico	Chavez
	9, 10	Boston Symphony Orchestra	Koussevitzky
		BSO Tour	
		15 Cambridge, MA	
		20 Providence	
		26, 27 Boston	
	14, 16, 18	New York Philharmonic	Toscanini
	15, 17	Cleveland Orchestra	Rodzinski
	18	Cleveland Orchestra (Broadcast)	Rodzinski
	27, 29, 30	Chicago Symphony Orchestra	Lange
NOVEMBER	3	Cleveland Orchestra (in Detroit)	Rodzinski
	8	National Symphony Orchestra	Kindler
	13	Symphony Orchestra of Mexico	Chavez
	15	Chicago Symphony Orchestra (in Milwaukee)	Lange
		BSO Tour	
		17 Hartford	
		19 New York	
		20 Brooklyn	
	27	Minneapolis Symphony Orchestra	Mitropoulos
	27, 28	Philadelphia Orchestra	Ormandy
	30	Philadelphia Orchestra (Broadcast)	Ormandy
DECEMBER	3, 4, 5	New York Philharmonic	Rodzinski
		BSO Tour	
		8 Buffalo	
		9 Ann Arbor	
		12 Pittsburgh	
		14 Rochester	
	13	NBC Symphony Orchestra (Broadcast)	Stokowski
	15	National Symphony Orchestra (in Baltimore)	Kindler
JANUARY	1, 2	Cincinnati Symphony Orchestra	Goossens
	8	San Francisco Symphony Orchestra	Stokowski
	26	Toronto Symphony Orchestra	MacMillan

Preparing the Public for the Seventh

It requires a fair amount of historical imagination to assess both Shostakovich and his work within their own context—to discard what we know (or think we know) about the Seventh Symphony today, and try to recapture what audiences in 1942 knew (or thought they knew). We now register not only how the Second World War ended, but also how the aftermath (the Cold War) and the aftermath of the aftermath (the demise of the Soviet Union) turned out, at least until the present day. Examining the wartime reception of the Seventh Symphony gives us the chance to consider the loyal Russian, America's crucial ally against the threatening Hitler. Yet the bracketing of our current knowledge is easier said than done; it requires reminding ourselves at all times of the specific historical context in which these events unfolded.

Besides the geopolitical context there is the musico-political one, including the turbulent midcentury aesthetic debates about what contemporary music should be and do—the point to which Aaron Copland alludes in the quotation at the beginning of this article. More specifically, today we know much more about the fate of the thirty-six-year-old Dmitrii Shostakovich, who would go on to write eight more symphonies, fourteen more string quartets, would be denounced again in 1948 (American wartime audiences were already well informed about his 1936 fall from grace), be rehabilitated later, die in 1975, and ultimately emerge as one of the most significant and frequently performed composers of the twentieth century. In this essay, however, I will try to reconstruct a different horizon of expectations, a time when none of this was yet actual and some of it barely imaginable.

In 1942 American concert music audiences were already familiar with some of Shostakovich's music, but the Seventh Symphony offered the opportunity for the composer to exit the arts sections of newspapers and magazines and enter the realm of international news coverage.[7] The *New York Times* correspondent Ralph Parker interviewed the composer not long after the symphony's completion in late 1941, and as the first rehearsals with the orchestra of Moscow's Bolshoi Theatre were taking place in Kuibyshev, the transplanted capital. Parker reports that "Shostakovich wrote the symphony to illustrate the way in which war affects human beings," and quotes him as saying that the opening of the first movement is meant to describe the happy existence of "ordinary, simple people." A major emphasis in this interview, complementing what the composer said elsewhere, is his desire to communicate with a broad public, the point that concerned Copland. We will see the issue arise time and again: Shostakovich is represented, by himself and by others, as someone who writes for the present, not posterity, for the common man, not an elite. Most of the *Times* article is attributed to the composer:

> By ordinary I mean not distinguished by any special features or talents—just ordinary, good, quiet people, going about their daily life. . . .
>
> When Richard Strauss wrote his "Domestic Symphony" he satirized people, taking negative, commonplace types and poking bitter fun at them. I don't want to laugh at people, and I'm not describing silly, commonplace people. I'm simply writing about the man in the street.
>
> After this preliminary theme I introduce the main theme, which was inspired by the transformation of these ordinary people into heroes by the outbreak of war. This builds up into a requiem for those of them who are perishing in the performance of their duty. In the first movement's final passages I introduce something very intimate, like a mother's tears over her lost children. It is tragic, but it finally becomes transparently clear.
>
> The scherzo and adagio movements are of an intermediate character, in which I am moved by the idea that war doesn't necessarily mean destruction of cultural values. The fourth movement can be described by one word—victory. But my idea of victory isn't something brutal: it's better explained as the victory of light over darkness, of humanity over barbarism, of reason over reaction.
>
> I consider that every artist who isolates himself from the world is doomed. I find it incredible that an artist should want to shut himself away from the people, who, in the end, form his audience. I think an artist should serve the greatest possible number of people. I always try to make myself as widely understood as possible, and if I don't succeed I consider it's my own fault. (9 February 1942)[8]

The American public read about the Seventh Symphony in *Time* before Shostakovich appeared on the 20 July cover. A brief report, well in advance of the Kuibyshev premiere on 5 March 1942, underscored the composer's desire to be understood; indeed, his comment to the *New York Times* was repeated verbatim:

> For many war-weary months the people of Leningrad have known solemn, youthful Dmitri Shostakovich was a fire fighter, a trench digger, an embattled citizen like themselves. But the rest of the world

has continued to think of him as the only living composer, aside from Finland's Jean Sibelius, who can make musical history writing a new symphony. Last week musical history was again on the make. In Kuibyshev, secondary Soviet capital, the orchestra of Moscow's Bolshoi Theater began rehearsals on Shostakovich's long-heralded *Symphony No. 7*. Composer Shostakovich has dedicated his symphony, a musical expression of the war's effect on "ordinary, simple people," to the citizens of Leningrad. Says he: "I always try to make myself as widely understood as possible, and if I don't succeed I consider it's my own fault." (16 February 1942)

In April, Parker reported on the Russian premiere, which appears to have had little to do with the common man: Shostakovich "received a thunderous tribute from an excited audience of diplomats, Soviet officials and intelligentsia" for the symphony. "[A]t long last he had answered critics whose threatening challenge seven years previously he had boldly taken up. . . . His Seventh symphony opens a new phase in the young Soviet composer's development." (5 April 1942) The rest of the long article gives a detailed account of his career and ends by reprinting part of Parker's earlier interview with the composer.[9]

The *Time* cover story, however, is what decisively thrust Shostakovich into the public eye on a scale unprecedented for a twentieth-century composer. The illustration is a painting by Boris Artzybasheff with a caption that reads "Fireman Shostakovich—Amid bombs bursting in Leningrad he heard the chords of victory" (see Figure 1). The sensationalized painting, which sets the bespectacled and helmeted composer against a dramatic backdrop of burning buildings, is based on a far more mundane photograph in which the composer stands on the roof of the Leningrad Conservatory wearing his fire warden's uniform. (That image appeared widely in the Soviet and Western press, including *Time*'s earlier report on the symphony, 16 February 1942, and a report in *Life*, 3 August 1942.)

The unsigned article (bylines did not yet appear in *Time*; the principal music writer at the time was Winthrop Sargeant) opens with the old Russian proverb "When guns speak, the muses keep silent," to which "Fire Warden Shostakovich snapped, 'Here the muses speak together with the guns.'"[10] On Sunday afternoon, 19 July, American audiences would have the chance to hear for themselves when Toscanini conducted the NBC Symphony Orchestra in the American premiere of the Seventh Symphony, the composer's "biggest, most ambitious orchestral work to date—the work he wrote last year between tours of duty digging trenches in the outskirts of Leningrad and fire-watching on the roof of the Conservatory.

Figure 1. "Fireman Shostakovich," on the cover of *Time* magazine, vol. 40, no. 3 (20 July 1942). © 1942 Time Inc., reprinted by permission.

. . . Not since the first Manhattan performance of *Parsifal* (in 1903) had there been such a buzz of American anticipation over a piece of music."

Readers are told that Shostakovich witnessed the 1917 Russian Revolution firsthand, at the tender age of eleven, and immediately responded by composing a "Hymn to Liberty" and "Funeral March in Memory of the Victims of the Revolution": "a prodigy and a prodigious event had met."[11] Now, twenty-five years later, audiences could witness how his "Marxist muse" had responded to new prodigious events. *Time* offered some basic background concerning the stories about and within the Seventh Symphony, as well as broad assessments of the composer and his career. The story of the symphony begins with the trying circumstances of its composition, long trek to America, and the "battle royal" among "sleek, platinum-haired Leopold Stokowski, the Cleveland Orchestra's Artur Rodzinski, [and] Boston's Serge Koussevitzky" over who would have "the glory of conducting the premiere." While it first seemed that Koussevitzky had won with a 14 August performance at Tanglewood, *Time* reported that Toscanini, the "old fire-&-ice Maestro," would beat him, conducting the forthcoming special broadcast from Studio 8-H in New York's Radio City.

According to *Time*, the National Broadcasting Company had begun nego-tiations in January, even before the March premiere, and had secured the rights by April. Both Toscanini and Stokowski were then under con-tract with NBC, and the former had first choice—though, as *Time* noted, Toscanini had declined to give the American premiere of Shostakovich's Fifth Symphony four years earlier.[12] Now things were different: "The pho-tostat pages of the score were rushed to Toscanini and NBC held its breath. He looked, said: 'Very interesting and most effective.' He looked again, said: 'Magnificent!'"[13] NBC hired the extra musicians needed to perform the large piece and "night after night, nearsighted Maestro Toscanini, who conducts from memory, never from notes, sat up with eyes buried in the score." (In this regard it is revealing of his working method for a piece he had so little time to learn that the Rose Bampton Collection, housed at the Performing Arts division of the New York Public Library, has Toscanini's handwritten reduction of parts of the symphony.)[14]

The *Time* article also includes a discussion of the symphony. As would most often be the case in critical writings on the work, the opening move-ment received most of the attention, especially the "theme of war":

Written for a mammoth orchestra, Shostakovich's *Seventh,* though it is no blatant battle piece, is a musical interpretation of Russia at war. In the strict sense, it is less a symphony than a symphonic suite. Like a great wounded snake, dragging its slow length, it uncoils for

80 minutes from the orchestra. There is little development of its bold, bald, foursquare themes. There is no effort to reduce the symphony's loose, sometimes skeletal structures to the epic compression and economy of the classic symphony.

Yet this very musical amorphousness is expressive of the amorphous mass of Russia at war. Its themes are exultations, agonies. Death and suffering haunt it. But amid the bombs bursting in Leningrad Shostakovich had also heard the chords of victory. In the symphony's last movement the triumphant brasses prophesy what Shostakovich describes as the "victory of light over darkness, of humanity over barbarism."

The *Seventh Symphony*'s proportions are heroic, most obviously in the 27-minute first movement. The deceptively simple opening melody, suggestive of peace, work, hope, is interrupted by the theme of war, "senseless, implacable and brutal." For this martial theme Shostakovich resorts to a musical trick: the violins, tapping the backs of their bows, introduce a tune that might have come from a puppet show. This tiny drumming, at first almost inaudible, mounts and swells, is repeated twelve times in a continuous twelve-minute crescendo. The theme is not developed but simply grows in volume like Ravel's *Boléro*; it is succeeded by a slow melodic passage that suggests a chant for the war's dead.

As in most of Shostakovich's later music, there are traces of Beethoven, Berlioz, Rimsky-Korsakov, Mahler, moderns like Poulenc and Busoni. The *Seventh Symphony* has been described by those who have already heard it as a modern Russian version of Berlioz's *Symphonie Fantastique*. It has also been called a sound-track for a psychological documentary film on Russia today.

The rest of the article examines the composer's compositional career and personal life. Portraying Shostakovich's professional life, the author tells of his family background, early prodigious talents, and tries briefly to place him within Russian musical history. The great success of the First Symphony, premiered when he was nineteen, is related, along with information about other early symphonies. Shostakovich's trouble in 1936 with the opera *Lady Macbeth of the Mtsensk District* is dealt with candidly: "At the height of the Purge, when Russian nerves were badly frayed and people were plopping into prison like turtles in a pond, Stalin decided to hear *Lady Macbeth*. He did not like it, walked out before it was over." The author quotes from the famous ensuing article in *Pravda* that denounced the piece, and mentions as well the one shortly thereafter that attacked the ballet *The Limpid Stream*. To save himself, Shostakovich "publicly agreed that *Pravda* knew more about music than he did. He withdrew his *Fourth Symphony* (it has never been performed) after one rehearsal. He announced that he would stake his musical future on a *Fifth Symphony*." That work, together with the Sixth Symphony, pleased both officials and the general public.

The last section of the *Time* article offers a glimpse of the private side of the composer in a section entitled "Beer and Soccer." Here readers are assured that the "shy, serious, scholarly" composer is also a real person, and one who likes American sorts of things: "automobiles, fast driving, U.S. magazines," and reads "the U.S. authors who most appeal to Russia— Mark Twain, Jack London, Theodore Dreiser, Upton Sinclair." The intimate portrait concludes by presenting a domestic scene, the composer at home with his wife, two children, mother, sister, and nephew, where he likes to drink beer and write about soccer for the paper *Red Sport*. The article seeks a loftier conclusion by questioning what place the Seventh Symphony might ultimately hold in the history of music:

> Despite the fact that it does not satisfy him as much as a soccer victory, despite its structural looseness and occasional melodic banalities, the *Seventh* is probably the most emotionally mature of Shostakovich's symphonies, is almost certain to be one of his most popular. But it still leaves an important question unanswered: Is Composer Shostakovich the last peak in the European musical range whose summit was Beethoven, or is he the beginning of a new sierra?

The leading critical voice to weigh in before the broadcast and the one who would write most often about the Seventh over the next several months was Olin Downes at the *New York Times*. He also wondered about the symphony's timeliness and its worth within the Beethovenian tradition. An initial Sunday piece begins: "The fortunes of Dmitri Shostakovich are extraordinary. Indeed, they could only be what they are in wartime, and according to the tempo of this confused and desperate era." Downes relates the success of the First Symphony ("a new voice, not very original in its accent"), of the "palpably propaganda music" in the Second and Third symphonies, and the initial triumph of *Lady Macbeth*, which made Shostakovich the "unofficial composer laureate of Russia." (Downes had admired the work when Artur Rodzinski presented it at the Metropolitan Opera House in 1936.) Duly recounted are Stalin's attack on that opera, as well as on *The Limpid Stream*, which led to the withdrawal of the Fourth Symphony, and the rehabilitation that came in the wake of the success of the Fifth and Sixth symphonies. After describing the genesis of the Seventh, its journey West, and the battle of the conductors over "the most sought-after score in the world," Downes offers the following estimate of the composer:

> But to claim, as some already do, that Shostakovich is the young Russian Beethoven, is as premature as it is disproportionate and lacking in perspective. There is gold and there is also much dross in the Shostakovich symphonies. There are pages which are banal and which have not the stamp of a creative individuality. Shostakovich's sense of structure and of dramatic effect are very strong: his contrapuntal equipment by no means of a negligible texture. He can write polyphonically, as well as orchestrally, for dramatic purposes. He uses the orchestra with confidence, personality and with real skill. His greatest strength is in his lyrical slow movements, as in that of the Fifth Symphony.

Downes argues that excepting Jean Sibelius, a composer he ardently supported but who "has not been newly articulate for some time," only Shostakovich can write a "sustained, serene, grandly proportioned slow movement."[15] Sounding themes on which he would elaborate in the months to come, Downes is disturbed that Shostakovich writes too much and too quickly, must behave to please the Soviet authorities, is prone to bombast and banalities, and can be derivative of composers like Mahler and Prokofiev. These faults may prevent him at this time from being the "Russian Beethoven," Downes concludes, "but we have a composer whose art touches urgent experience, who lives in his times and wishes, first as a citizen, then as a composer with a mission, to serve the world and his people. A young man, of striking achievements, he is already a leading figure in modern music" (12 July 1942).[16]

Battle Symphonies

Before a note of the Seventh Symphony was heard in America, the political and musical stakes were well established. This was the war symphony to end all others, and one that had to contend artistically with the legacy of Beethoven. Yet Beethoven's relationship to his public was different from Shostakovich's in ways that go beyond the contingencies of time and place. The contemporaneous reception of Beethoven's works, especially the late ones, showed that a composer might ultimately triumph despite listeners' initial incomprehension. He was accused of "writing only for posterity," not for the public.[17] Nearly a hundred years later, Mahler noted that his "time would come" after death. With the rise of modernism, an increasingly detached and uncompromising attitude among composers further separated new music from the general public. Schoenberg's Verein für musikalische Privataufführungen (Society for Private Musical Performances) was closed to critics; only members and specially invited guests could attend its concerts. Copland identifies the "tendency" in Shostakovich's music of writing for the general public, for the common man, what Shostakovich repeatedly declared and what Copland would himself soon demonstrate in his "Fanfare for the Common Man."

Shostakovich was measured by the standards of the higher Beethoven, the composer of the immortal *Eroica*, not the Beethoven of his own "battle" symphony, the popular potboiler *Wellington's Victory*. Some critics praised the "Russian Beethoven" for writing a symphony that would endure long after the compelling circumstances of its creation, for writing an *Eroica*, not a *Wellington's Victory*. At the same time it was repeatedly emphasized that he composed for the masses, for a "collectivist society." Many American critics, including the most distinguished ones, thought the Seventh programmatic, realistic, and derivative, all too bound to its time, a *Wellington's Victory*, not an *Eroica*, and, as a composition aimed exactly at the common man, one that verged on the simple-minded. They often mentioned the *Eroica* in discussions of the Seventh, and at least one invoked *Wellington's Victory*.[18] (Tchaikovsky's *1812 Overture*, another realistic battle piece, was cited more frequently.)

There are certainly parallels between the battle symphonies of Beethoven and Shostakovich, both works being specifically bound to historical events and musically programmatic. The motivating circumstances were similar, although Beethoven's Viennese audiences were no longer in the heat of battle when the work was premiered, as were Shostakovich's. Napoleon's occupations of Vienna had been traumatic, but the tide had turned with the Battle of Leipzig in 1813. Within the year the Congress of Vienna was convened to reapportion Europe in the aftermath of France's defeat. The triumphant premiere of *Wellington's Victory* there on 8 December 1813 (repeated on 12 December) benefited soldiers wounded in the Battle of Hanau a few months earlier. Among the participants were a particularly impressive list of musicians, including Salieri, Spohr, and Meyerbeer, and some of Vienna's finest performers. The "celebrities" associated with *Wellington's Victory* were comparable to the star conductors allied with the Seventh. The work quickly became one of Beethoven's most popular, despite prevalent complaints about its artistic quality, especially a negative review by Gottfried Weber in the prominent journal *Cäcilia*, which irked Beethoven. Shostakovich was apparently aware of the dangers of a "naturalistic" portrayal of battle. A work like *Wellington's Victory* showed that a great composer could write an occasional piece that succeeds wildly with the public but is an aesthetic embarrassment.[19]

With Shostakovich, the particular critical focus was on the "War" movement of his "War" Symphony. The symphony would have worked better as a single movement work, thought some critics, such as Oscar Thompson, who stated, "That movement is, indeed, the symphony."[20] (Shostakovich is said to have planned the Seventh as a one-movement composition, although this information apparently came many years after its completion.)[21] The movement, especially the famous crescendo in the middle (what Elliott Carter called "the fascist march"), was considered the most beholden to external musical sources, as well as the most programmatic.[22] Indeed, that section is the crux of the debate about the intention, meaning, and artistic worth of the symphony. Shostakovich talked about the movement on many occasions, but for our purposes what matters most is how his views were represented in wartime America, not what he said later, nor what he said he intended, nor what he is said to have said he intended. In program notes and commentary he was quoted as explaining that it was inspired by the outbreak of war in Leningrad in the summer of 1941, when "the war burst into our peaceful life. Its pestilent merciless breath enveloped us."[23] We have already seen his disclaimer about the realistic imitation of war, that rather what he sought was an "interpretation." The various Soviet commentators—David Rabinovich, Aleksei Tolstoy, Eugene Petrov—supplemented Shostakovich. These writings were taken up by Nicolas Slonimsky, the émigré Russian conductor, musicologist, and critic, in the first detailed scholarly American essay, which appeared in the *Musical Quarterly* in October 1942. His analysis of the movement, which included musical examples, reads in part:

> The first movement opens with a vigorous C-major theme, in powerful unisons, punctuated by the rhythmic spurts of the trumpets and kettle-drums. This is the theme of the Leningrad citizen, who has become the hero of the siege. The tonality darkens when an E-flat is introduced in the melodic ascent. The music softens; there is a moment of lyrical lassitude. Suddenly, out of nowhere, a little puppet-like tune is heard in the strings *pizzicato* and *col legno*, against the steady beat of the drum. Relentlessly, it grows, takes on body, spreads over the orchestra, magnified, yet unchanged in its melodic pattern. A Soviet writer [Rabinovich] has described it as a "psychological portrait of the enemy." Alexei Tolstoy saw in it "a sudden outbreak of war, the patter of iron rats dancing to the tune of a rat

catcher." The theme of the citizen-hero struggles through, integrated, from melodic allusions, into a powerful statement. But the "iron rats" leave a path of destruction in their march. The victims are mourned in a threnody intoned by a bassoon solo.[24]

Such is a sample of the issues, information, and intentions presented to the American public in 1942. We can now turn to a detailed record of the performances of the Seventh and the initial responses to them.

The Summer of '42:
New York, Tanglewood, and Ravinia

There was more talk than usual both before and after Toscanini's special broadcast on that Sunday afternoon of 19 July as millions of people around the world tuned in at home and by shortwave.[25] In addition to Ben Grauer, the regular announcer, Edward C. Carter, the president of the Russian War Relief, Inc., addressed the audience and read a telegram from the composer. Grauer recounted how Shostakovich wrote three movements while fighting fire and under fire in Leningrad and finished the symphony in Kuibyshev, where it was premiered on "1 March [*sic*]."[26] He spoke of the circumstances of getting the microfilm of three thousand pages of score and parts to America. An unidentified voice read a "radiogram" from Shostakovich to Toscanini, praising his skill and expressing regret that he could not attend the performance. Toscanini opened the concert with a far from perfunctory rendition of "The Star-Spangled Banner." Following the symphony there were appeals for money from Grauer and Carter, including a request that listeners devote 10 percent of their earnings to buy war bonds, as all the members of the orchestra had already pledged to do. Such "material and moral" aid would help make the "prophecy of music" heard at the concert "become a fact."[27]

Critical reaction from the outset was decidedly mixed, as it would be throughout the season. *Time* reported: "After 73 minutes of non-stop conducting, Arturo Toscanini looked as if he had just come through the siege of Leningrad. The audience jumped up and cheered, as if it had heard news of a Nazi defeat. Thousands of radio listeners, which in many sections had fought a losing battle with static, sighed and turned their dials." Instead of giving its own commentary, the short article summarized critical opinion, stating that some found the work "impressive, sincere, vivid, vast. They also admitted that it was sometimes dull, sometimes theatrical, often derivative." After a sampling of reviews, it concluded by quoting Oscar Thompson from the *New York Sun*: "If it is not a masterpiece to go thundering down the ages, it does thunder—and for a particular time of war and the emotions of war it thunders very well" (27 July 1942). *Newsweek* offered this assessment:

> The result was well worth everybody's time, trouble, and trumpeting. Toscanini, who has never cared particularly for Russian music and who once turned down the premiere of the Shostakovich Fifth, was in magnificent form and seemed to lose years as he and his men encompassed the enormous demands of the work. It was propaganda, yes. But it was great music, too, music that spanned the sprawling might of Russia in terms no words could ever equal. (27 July 1942)

Robert A. Simon, in *The New Yorker*, called the Seventh "a work of unusual impact, and the impact would have moved even one who had not read of the heroic circumstances under which the composer wrote it." Praising Toscanini's "brilliant performance," he noted that "the first movement overshadows the relatively quiet and charming second movement, and the uneven third movement isn't easy to recall after the rousing closer that follows" (1 August 1942). Carl Sandburg published an open letter to Shostakovich in the *Washington Post*, commending him for writing music that tells the story of what is happening in Russia. He noted that no new symphonies were being written in Berlin, Paris, Amsterdam, Copenhagen, Oslo, Prague, Warsaw, and all the other places under Nazi rule, and that Shostakovich gave hope of what the Russian people were able to accomplish.[28]

Nicolas Nabokov, the Russian-American composer and critic (cousin of the writer Vladimir), wrote in *The New Republic*, seconding *Time*'s comment, that the broadcast occurred during the "worst climatic conditions of the year so far as radio interference was concerned." Based on "one imperfect hearing," he stated:

> One point, however, is clear. Despite its grand style, despite its dimensions, despite its somewhat naïve yet profoundly moving sincerity, and even despite its general excellence in technical craftsmanship, it is definitely not the great symphonic work we were prepared to expect. . . .
>
> Shostakovich is writing for the masses, and he makes no bones about it. But is his the way in which the problem of writing music for the masses should be solved? Is it necessary to employ an eclectic

style combining all kinds of clichés like those found in such "popular" pieces as Tchaikovsky's Overture of 1812, the Heldenleben of Richard Strauss, and the Bolero of Ravel? Is this the only way in which one can achieve a new, truly proletarian art? I, for one, do not believe so. The banality, even the tediousness, of this method tends to reveal only too clearly Shostakovich's weak point: his lack of genuine melodic invention. (3 August 1942)

Nabokov elaborated his position at much greater length a few months later in an essay in *Harper's*.[29] Even if he came with his own Stravinskian aesthetic and émigré political agenda, he cogently expressed what many critics felt by emphasizing the disturbing lack of a personal voice he perceived in Shostakovich's music. Looking back at the First Symphony, Nabokov observed: "[T]here was something old about the music, something essentially conservative and unexperimental. I could not feel any definite personality in it, nor did I see very much authentic invention, musical or technical. Every theme, every rhythmic pattern, every technical device, every harmony, however charming and well written, reminded me of another piece of music."

Other critics had similar problems with the Seventh. B. H. Haggin, of *The Nation*, thought it "an excessively long piece of bad music." He remarks in his scathing review from August 1942:

The music . . . is derivative, eclectic: one hears the conventional pastoral style of the past two centuries; one hears this style melodically and harmonically distorted in the manner of Shostakovich—which is derived from Prokofiev; one hears a long crescendo of repetitions of one theme in the manner of Ravel's *Bolero*, including the unceasing snare-drum; among the other things one hears even—surprisingly— a passage for strings in the manner of Sibelius. The music also is diffuse, saying everything at enormously expanded length; it is as pretentious in style as in length; and what it says so pretentiously is feeble, inane, banal. Pretentiousness leaps out at one from that long crescendo of repetitions of one theme—the pretentiousness of the conception, the intention, of the inane theme itself, of the unresourceful, crude, blatant variations in accompanying figuration and orchestration that are devised for the repetitions, of the noise that is resorted to at the end. And these qualities of the music represent the personal resources that are involved with Shostakovich's articulateness in his medium.[30]

While Nabokov and Haggin were most disturbed by the style of Shostakovich's music and his debts to other composers, Olin Downes, in the *New York Times,* focused on the programmatic question and the time-liness of the symphony. Now that he had actually heard it, he weighed in with more concrete opinions. Under the multiple headlines "Shostakovich 7th Has U.S. Premiere—Russian's War Symphony, as Offered by Toscanini, Wins Storm of Applause—By Radio to All Nations—Battles Pictured in Themes—Composer Sends Greeting to Russian Relief Concert," his review begins:

> Following tremendous publicity and in a spirit reflective of the enthusiasm and gratitude that the people of this nation feel today toward Russia, defending in oceans of blood humanity's cause, the American premiere of the much-heralded Seventh Symphony of Dmitri Shostakovich, musical banner-bearer of his people, was given yesterday afternoon in Radio City by the NBC Symphony Orchestra, under the leadership of Arturo Toscanini, to shattering applause.

After praising Toscanini's "passionately devoted reading of the sym-phony," Downes comments on what he called the "double story" at work in the Seventh. He was not thinking of the external genesis and internal musical program I mentioned earlier, but rather the stories about the work and its composer:

> The story of its composition has been told. It is a double story, of the composition of a symphony and of the sudden and spectacular ascent of a composer who, through wartime circumstances and the fact of his exceptional creative gifts, ascended quickly and dizzily, in a few months to new fame.
>
> And this being the case, what of the symphony? Per se? We have been informed of its programmatic meaning: how the first move-ment is Russia, in strife, resisting the invaders, with a passage of epilogue in deathless memory of those who fell, and how the last movement is a paean to victory, humanity's liberation from dark-ness, the triumph of reason and right over barbarism and crime—this in four movements, the last two of which are joined together, and with a number of thematic relations between the principal parts.
>
> Now, if the statement that this was the greatest symphony the mod-ern age has produced would send the last Hun reeling from the last foot of Russian soil, if the further statement that it was the greatest symphony ever written would result in the offensive so long over-

due and so imperatively needed on the western front, we would probably perjure ourselves and declare both these claims to be incontestably true. But we cannot so testify, or even conditionally state that such or anything like it is the case.

For this symphony is far from a work of sustained greatness, either of ideas, workmanship, or taste. That it has its great movements is unarguable. It would only be surprising, with Shostakovich's endowments, such as his long, if not always distinguished melodic line, his orchestral mastery, his flair for dramatic utterance, if it were not so. But much of the score is windy, inflated, put together, in places, with a crudeness which is no help at all to material that is often thin, commonplace in its nature, and too long drawn out. Nor do the presence of certain tricks, perfectly obvious tricks, which are derivations and imitations, put a better face on the matter.

Not that one questions the composer's personal sincerity, or the genuineness of his expressive purpose. But to fuse, to identify the emotion completely with the artistic form is another problem, which must be solved by inspiration and original creative development, seldom present here.

Downes then gives a more detailed description of the symphony's musical features:

The symphony starts with a strong, firm theme, not a very original one, but rythmic and workable, one that is effectively apotheosized later on. A second theme, or sub-theme, in the recapitulation, also finds metamorphosis. The third idea, used for what it is reasonable to assume, is a kind of battle scene, is a page out of Ravel's "Bolero," with some of Richard Strauss's battle scene in "Heldenleben" and a pinch of the extremely noisy instrumentation of Respighi's "Pines of Rome" put together for the show. The short phrase, in the manner of a march, used passacaglio fashion, is first given the strings over a drum tap, repeated, quite precisely, with constantly strengthened orchestration, and with more freedom and complexity in the later variations, a total of eighteen or nineteen times.

It is theatre of a kind, which would do well for a moving picture of a scene of battle and carnage, and no doubt the composer wished to bring such a reality home to our minds. He might say that war is a reality to him, that it is not to us, and that his symphony endeavors to bring the fact home to the world.

But Downes questions whether this is the proper function of art or of the artist. The details are too realistic, "imitation and not interpretation, and at that, bad photography." He finds the scherzo the "most finished and balanced movement," and admires the slow movement as well, but the finale is too long and, although effective, ultimately fails to "add up." In conclusion, Downes remarks:

> We could wish otherwise. We can certainly expect much more of Shostakovich. He believes that social ideology must be back of all music. He writes, he says, to be understood by everybody, and feels that it is his fault if it is not so. We wish, when it comes to composing, that he were free from any conscious ideologies, and also that his countrymen, especially those with not a tithe of his knowledge of music, would cease instructing him as to whether he is or is not properly expressing in his scores the Soviet ideals. If he were let alone to consult purely his inner feeling, in the same way that Beethoven, in the Fifth symphony and his others, consulted his, and without label or propaganda uttered as no composer before or since the cry for liberty—then we would have better and greater music from Shostakovich. (20 July 1942)

I have quoted this review at such length not only because it comes from one of the most powerful critics, but also because Downes addresses many of the central themes of the Seventh's reception: its program, political status, sincerity, derivativeness, and artistic worth within Beethoven's symphonic legacy. Despite his initial and ultimate rejection of the symphony, Downes kept returning to the work in the weeks and months to come, using it as a catalyst for the discussion of a variety of issues. In fact, he returned to it a week later (26 July) in a Sunday piece entitled "Second View of a Symphony," quoted at the beginning of this essay, in which he questions the staying power of a piece so intimately connected with the tragic circumstances of its genesis. He revisits at greater length some of the points made in his review, and enlists the prominent British critic Ernest Newman's review of the BBC premiere on 22 June 1942: "The fact that Mr. Newman's estimate of the musical value of the work coincides with that of the great majority who heard the New York performances— namely that in spite of some great moments it falls far short of being a great symphony, or Shostakovich's best—is of less moment here than his emphasis of the creative principle involved in the matter." (Newman had taken an even harder line than Downes, arguing that a work written under such conditions as Shostakovich's "is certain to be a work of the second or third order.") He continued the discussion the next weekend, reprinting large portions of a letter from the composer Elie Siegmeister, who, although he had not yet heard the Seventh, objected in principle: "What I must, however, disagree with most emphatically is the implication expressed in your article today that such a work could not possibly have been a good one because of the very nature of its inspiration."[31] Siegmeister cites many precedents, going back to the Middle Ages, but predictably concentrating on Beethoven.[32]

Attacks on the Seventh Symphony elicited a strong response from Serge Koussevitzky some two weeks before he was to conduct the work in Tanglewood. The Associated Press disseminated it widely across the country. Koussevitzky was disturbed that so many critics found the work "'banal,' 'uneven,' and 'program music.'" Calling Shostakovich a "genius who possesses the most tremendous appeal to the masses of any composer since Beethoven," the conductor predicted that

> musicians and critics who make such strong criticism today will strongly regret in the nearest future what they have said, for to criticize the work of a man who is without doubt a genius one must listen not once but many times. No one since Beethoven has had the aesthetic sense, the approach to musical material that Shostakovich has. He is the greatest master of musical wealth; he is the master of what he desires to do; he has melody without end; his language is as rich as the world; his emotion is absolutely universal. (2 August 1942)[33]

After much deliberation, the Berkshire Symphonic Festival had been forced to restructure for the summer of 1942. Financial exigencies, the rationing of gas, and conservation of tire rubber made remote Lenox, Massachusetts, a difficult place to reach; sustaining a regular season with the Boston Symphony Orchestra was deemed unfeasible. Koussevitzky, however, was loathe to abandon the festival and its constituent Berkshire Music School. He decided to assemble a student orchestra which would study with principals from the BSO during a six-week season sponsored by the Koussevitzky Music Foundation.[34] Koussevitzky thus gave the first concert performance of the Seventh, in what was again a benefit for Russian War Relief, with a student ensemble, the Berkshire Music Center Orchestra, and not the Boston Symphony Orchestra, as often stated. The event attracted various dignitaries, including the Russian ambassador, Maxim Litvinov, and Princess Juliana of the Netherlands. Despite bad weather and the difficulties of getting to the venue, some five thousand people attended the concert on 14 August.

The event opened with the singing of the "Internationale" and "The Star-Spangled Banner." Evidently the order in which to play them had not been specified and the students began to play the anthems simultaneously.[35] In fact, most concerts featuring the Seventh in the coming season also opened or closed with the American national anthem, and some with the Soviet one as well. This latter practice occasionally elicited comment in the press, as when a Philadelphia critic noted "the incongruity of yesterday's fur-clad, swank audience of Main Line matrons standing for the hymn whose words begin 'Arise, ye prisoners of starvation.'"[36] At Tanglewood there were also various speeches to raise awareness and funds, including one from Dorothy Thompson, who said of the Seventh: "It is a cry of indignation, a prayer of hope, a shout of triumph aimed straight at the heart of all mankind. And as we listen to it we know it is the voice of a great people, full of energy, power and hope, who have refused to be trampled to the ground. It is the voice of heroism."[37] A statement by Koussevitzky on the symphony was also read.

This second American performance, following Toscanini's broadcast, prompted comparisons and reappraisals. Over the coming months many critics attended multiple performances, sometimes with different orchestras. Downes reported in the *New York Times* that Koussevitzky's performance met with "an ovation, which lasted for a good ten minutes, of a shouting, cheering audience which rose to its feet as it extended this homage to the distant composer, to the land and the cause which this symphony symbolized, and to the conductor and the student orchestra, which carried out his wishes with a spirit and technical proficiency that elicited the highest praise." But the chance to hear this "highly dramatic" and "superb" reading did not change his view that it was "essentially far from a first-class symphony." After again recounting various strengths and weaknesses in the work, Downes concluded:

There are great stretches of comparative emptiness, with patent banalities that no amount of patriotism or puffery will cause to endure.

We are too close to Shostakovich, and he is too near his creative beginnings as a composer in his middle thirties for us to be able to designate the precise place that this symphony will take in the perspective of his art. But it is clearly a formative work, not nearly as well and carefully knit together as his First symphony of his nineteenth year, not rising, at any time, to such heights as parts of the first movement and the slow movement of his Fifth symphony. It could be called a battle piece, nobly intended, excitingly scored, with parts and patches of the truly creative spirit of the Shostakovich presumably to mature showing through at times in a very striking but by no means consistently convincing manner. (15 August 1942)[38]

Other critics were more favorably impressed. Henry Simon, of New York's *PM* (a forum to which, as *Time* put it, "nothing Russian is alien"),[39] wrote:

The audience listening tonight must have had the picture of the brave siege of Leningrad in mind. The composer himself has associated the work closely with it. But after a third hearing (two regular performances and a rehearsal), I believe that it is music which transcends even the emotions aroused by contemporary news—that its direct appeal to humanity will live beyond the time those emotions are so immediate as they are now—just as the appeal of Beethoven's *Eroica* has survived the feelings aroused by the world-shaking events which inspired it.

. . . I think there can be little doubt that the Seventh is a great work. Its emotions speak directly, eloquently, unmistakably, and the composer took whatever means came to hand and used his great skill to send home his deeply moving message. The reaction of the audience is only one evidence of his success. (16 August 1942)

There was a further performance during that summer, another benefit for the Russian War Relief. Frederick Stock conducted the Chicago Symphony Orchestra at its summer home in Ravinia Park on 22 August before an audience of some five thousand. (This would turn out to be one of the conductor's last concerts before his death in mid-October, just days away from scheduled performances of the Seventh Symphony in Orchestra Hall.) The concert was billed as the "midwestern premiere" and the press duly noted that it would be the first "regular concert performance by a major orchestra in the western hemisphere," thereby trying to surpass Toscanini's broadcast supremacy and Koussevitzky's student effort.[40] An intermission was placed between the second and third movements at this concert, something that would occasionally happen elsewhere during the coming season.[41]

In advance of the performance, Stock was interviewed by the notoriously acerbic music critic of the *Chicago Sun*, Claudia Cassidy. "It is about 40-60," she reports him saying, meaning 40 percent good music and the rest "emotional grasp of a highly dramatic situation" (21 August 1942).[42] Cassidy offered a rather tepid preview, although audiences were assured that Stock "believes there is much fine work in the Seventh Symphony."

Cassidy's review two days later was cautious. After hearing the broadcast of Toscanini's concert the previous month, she had been eager to encounter the work live, but found the Chicago performance lacking, perhaps due to insufficient rehearsals. (Stock had just two for the long and unfamiliar work, while Toscanini had more.)[43] About the music Cassidy gives a few tentative, but enthusiastic impressions:

> So it still stands in my book of knowledge that the first movement is barbaric and brilliant, with its defiant, almost scornful theme flaunting above the reiterated drive of the drums, and that the finale builds into a brazen excitement that lifts the roof off the stages and the hair off the audience's collective scalp.
>
> The second movement, which Shostakovich calls "Memories," was oddly disappointing, never quite living up to expectations. The much maligned third, on the contrary, developed a good deal of local force, sharing the indomitable courage of which the Shostakovich Seventh is the living symbol.
>
> I still cling to my belief that this is a splendid piece of work with intimations of greatness. But I could not share the Ravinia clamor that mounted to an ovation. What we heard from the Chicago Symphony Orchestra last night is only a hint of what it will do when it has the Seventh Symphony at its sensitive fingertips. (23 August 1942)

C. J. Bulliet, writing in the *Chicago News,* praised the symphony more heartily and found the opening movement the "richest and most varied," although he duly noted "the fine old trick of a drum background, used so effectively by Ravel in 'Bolero,' and by natives of the Congo." In closing, he observed that the work, "composed amidst the clashing of Nazi shells over and against Leningrad, certainly is in the spirit of its time—and that, I think, guarantees its immortality" (24 August 1942). Edward Barry of the *Chicago Tribune* was equally impressed: "All that we had heard in advance about the new work, even the broadcast of July 19, failed to prepare us adequately for the full impact of it." The first movement again comes in for special commendation, particularly its "musical delineation of the coming of war" (23 August 1942). William Leonard offered a dissenting opinion in the *Journal of Commerce,* saying that the Ravinia concert "probably was a greater success financially and socially than it was artistically." He found the symphony uneven, making "a listener grip his chair in rapt attention through the half-hour of its opening movement, and it can bore him the ten minutes of its second movement" (24 August 1942).[44]

The Fall Season Begins: Boston and New York

In October the Seventh Symphony began to make the rounds of the regular season, with a number of orchestras featuring it on opening programs.[45] Given the war, American concert life was not quite business as usual. A few orchestras (for example, Detroit, Toledo, and Portland) had to disband, at least temporarily, and the production of new musical instruments stopped, except for ones used by the armed forces, so as to conserve materials.[46] Edwin Hughes, president of the National Music Council, addressed the Music Library Association in midseason, offering an assessment that was subsequently published in *Musical America*:

> A war, even a world war, does not necessarily mean the disastrous curtailment of all musical activities. Beethoven produced important works while the French were at the gates, and afterward in the streets of Vienna. In our own time, and under heartrending circumstances, Shostakovich has been able to write a "Leningrad" Symphony which has attracted the attention and a decidedly large measure of approbation from the music lovers in the United Nations of two continents.[47]

Koussevitzky gave the first performances of the regular season with the Boston Symphony Orchestra. He intended to perform all of Shostakovich's symphonies with the orchestra (except, of course, the Fourth, which had not yet been performed anywhere), as well as other works, but the plan was not realized.[48] The Seventh took pride of place, opening the season on 9 October and being the featured work on tour to Cambridge, Providence, Hartford, New York, Brooklyn, Buffalo, Ann Arbor, Pittsburgh, and Rochester. The Boston program book was particularly influential, since other orchestras reprinted parts of it. A lengthy note on the symphony by John N. Burk drew liberally from David Rabinovich's and Eugene Petrov's essays in the *Information Bulletin, Embassy of USSR*, included Koussevitzky's statement on the importance of the work, and contained extended quotations from the composer. Shostakovich's essay, "How the Seventh Symphony Was Written," was reprinted from the *Boston Herald*. The program book also featured a long interview with the composer's wife, Nina, which sets the scene of domestic life and relates the challenges Dmitrii Dmitrievich faced writing the work.[49] An anecdote about their son Maxim, then not quite four years old, carries added interest today in light of his later career as a distinguished conductor:

[Galina and Maxim's] most popular tune just now is the theme from the first movement of the Seventh Symphony. They beg their father to play for them and they clamber onto the lid of the grand piano and sit as quiet as mice, all ears. We even took them with us to the general rehearsal of the Seventh Symphony. There they sat in the director's box, and when Professor Samosud, the conductor, asked them "What have you come to listen to?" they replied, "Our symphony." But in the middle of the first movement Maxim started "conducting" with such desperate energy that he had to be taken home.[50]

As would be the case in most venues over the next few months, critical opinion about the Seventh was mixed, although certainly not indifferent. The *Boston Herald* review began:

There will doubtless be better music in Symphony Hall this season than this afternoon, but there will certainly be none louder nor more keenly anticipated. . . . To say the candelabra (and the audience) were shaken to the foundations is to state it mildly.

As is often the case in an over-advertised product, the much discussed Seventh Symphony is something of a disappointment, but this is not to deny its smashing emotional intensity, not to diminish its enormous stature, as the most prodigious example of musical propaganda. That it speaks a message of incalculable inspiration and consolation to the heroic Russian people is simply not to be questioned. Nor can anyone challenge the fact that the symphony's effect is almost as emotionally profound upon many in the American audience. . . . Yes, if we are to judge it by its momentary effect as a message of hope and ultimate victory, it is impossible to deny it a place as a monument to the incredible spirit of our brothers in arms.

Yet it is not so simple as that for, divorced of its shattering implications, the symphony will not do as the work of art its champions claim it to be. Its bones stick out. (10 October 1942)

The *Boston Globe* critic (C. W. D.), who had admired Koussevitzky's Tanglewood performance, was now even more impressed: "The critical argument that the Seventh is flashy and theatrical seems rather specious. No composer was ever more sincere. None ever wrote with more conviction. It is by turn nostalgic and harsh, elegiac and filled with the righteous fire and the tragedy of the embattled Soviet people. This is music of the people, from the commonest upward, and such is what the composer intended." The first movement is praised as "perhaps the finest of all, [it] could be a complete and perfect tone poem, with its vast panoramic mood and its gigantic formal structure" (10 October 1942). L. A. Sloper, of the *Christian Science Monitor,* got a second hearing after the NBC concert in July: "It has the usual virtues and the usual shortcomings of the composer's work. It is brilliant and dull, individual and imitative, terse and repetitious—not all at the same time, but in protracted succession" (10 October 1942). Warren Storey Smith, writing in the *Boston Post,* concentrated his remarks on the first movement with its "celebrated passage, descriptive of the onset of war, that every commentator has likened to Ravel's Bolero." He found other possible models in the fourth movement of Respighi's *Pines of Rome* and in the "August, 1914" section of Ernst Schelling's *Impressions from an Artist's Life.* Smith also admired the solo bassoon threnody that follows the climax, and said the "final reminiscence of the battle-picture is a master stroke." He reported the explosive audience reaction to the movement and the fact that Koussevitzky acknowledged the applause by having the orchestra members stand, and in the end he wryly remarked that there is one thing about which everyone can be sure: "They are not playing it in Berlin" (10 October 1942). The symphony attracted a great deal more critical attention when the orchestra went on tour later that fall.[51]

Toscanini returned to the Seventh in October when he led the New York Philharmonic in three performances at Carnegie Hall.[52] As the NBC summer broadcast had been before an invited audience in Studio 8-H, the Philharmonic concerts gave the general public a chance to hear the work in New York for the first time and elicited substantial reviews from prominent critics.[53] Leading up to the event the great hope was that Shostakovich would himself come to New York to conduct the Philharmonic during the first two weeks of November and, before that, attend Toscanini's performances of the Seventh on 14, 16, and 18 October.[54] The press reported that Toscanini issued the invitation at the request of the president of the orchestra's board of directors, Marshall Field: "Your visit would have great political as well as musical value and would help dramatize the close tie between the United States and the Soviet Union." The composer quickly declined in a cable: "Regretfully admit that I do not master the art of conducting." When Toscanini replied that perhaps he could appear as a piano soloist, the composer again demurred, this time explaining that he was "ever busy with my new symphonic work dedicated [to the] twenty-fifth anniversary [of the] USSR."[55] A commentary in *Musical America* lamented the lost opportunity: "[Shostakovich] is this year's fair-haired boy and his coming might have excited such commotion as not even Tchaikovsky or Dvorak did in the gay nineties. There was no war then to help boost their popularity. And New York had no such special element as now applauds with undisguised fervor whenever the picture houses give them any glimpse of Red Russia or its wartime leaders."[56] After Shostakovich declined, Samuil Samosud, who had conducted the world premiere in Kuibyshev, was invited to lead the weeks set aside for Shostakovich and Soviet music, but he too was unable to travel, citing duties in Russia.[57]

Before the performance, a cable from the musicians to Shostakovich was read:

> Greetings from the men of the Philharmonic-Symphony who this week, while playing your epic symphony, feel so closely the great communion of interest that binds us together. It is eminently fitting that this musical bond shall stand as a symbol of unity of all the forces of culture and progress linked together against degeneracy and barbarism of Fascism. May the symphony of United Nations sound the triumphant liberation of the peoples of Europe and Asia and the victory of civilization so that we may all play a part in the overture to a new era of freedom and happiness for all humanity. With warm friendship and esteem to you and your great people.

The three concerts attracted considerable critical attention. While most reviews were ecstatic about the quality of Toscanini's conducting, and many equally enthusiastic about the work itself, the Associated Press reported that the concert was not completely sold out, partly because of the high ticket prices ($11 for orchestra seats), and because "word had got about that the symphony was too long for its somewhat meager musical talent."[58] Edward O'Gorman in the *New York Post* called the work one of the century's "unbearable pleasures." An admirer of the composer, he found it inferior to the Sixth Symphony, itself less successful than the Fifth, and continued: "In its remarkable power and drive, and in the huge, fundamental story-upon-story way in which its climaxes are built—and it was conducted by Toscanini with fanatical energy—it is an epochal work. It will probably be a hugely successful (as well as notorious) symphony, largely because where it was possible to say no to the artful seductions of the youthful first symphony it is not possible to resist the powerful bullying of its big brother" (15 October 1942). After having heard the work for the fifth time, Henry Simon revisited it in *PM*: "With each performance its vast architectonics become more coherent. As the initial impact of the terrifying march in the first movement wears off, other magnificent passages stand out more clearly and the whole thing hangs together better.

. . . There no longer is any doubt in my mind that here is a great utterance" (15 October 1942). Miles Kastendieck in the *Brooklyn Eagle* stated that "it was one of those thrilling moments in a life of concert going, in this case the more compelling because of the amazing feat accomplished by the 75-year-old wizard of the baton" (19 October 1942).

Louis Biancolli, who wrote program notes for the Philharmonic, contributed a review for the *New York World-Telegram* in which he remarks:

> The symphony's mass appeal was again manifest in last night's stormy reaction. The hard-hitting fury of a people balked of peace by gangster technique pulsed through the vast symphonic fabric. Mr. Toscanini made his audience sense the steady drive of hurtling themes to sure victory. The finale hymn of triumph struck a chord in every hoping heart. . . . The timeliness is only one side of the Leningrad symphony. Its immediate message probes deep. As timeless music, as a symphony, as a sincere welling up of true art it bows into the fellowship of Beethoven and Brahms. (15 October 1942)

Biancolli followed up with a Sunday piece that discussed the Seventh in relation to Mahler's First Symphony, which the Philharmonic was to perform the next week under Bruno Walter, and "the old question of whether narrative guides help the listener or slow up his emotional and imaginative grasp of new music." Biancolli argued that the situation with the Seventh was more complicated because of the circumstances of its creation: "Actually, there was no need for Shostakovich to give the world a table of contents for his symphony. The grim plight of his native city, his participation in its defense and the headlined valor of his country's fighters wrote out the 'program' for him." But Shostakovich wanted more than that—the symphony should not be viewed simply as a "battle-picture with sound effects" because "the theme was larger, more universal." And for this reason, Biancolli observes, Shostakovich gave indications of the work's content:

> Anybody can grasp the picture of the brutal and fiendishly skilled foe hammering at the gates of Leningrad. Also, the will to victory and the requiem strains are easily sensed.
>
> But whether any detailed indexing of poetic and moral issues clarifies the symphony as a whole is another matter. Apart from the manifest realism, its drama is implicit in the musical scheme. In a sense Shostakovich's hymn of hate and love is both program music and absolute music. Adolf Weissmann noted that Mahler's symphonies

were "program music without a program." Reversing the dictum, Shostakovich's Seventh might be termed absolute music with a program. When the last terrifying chords of war have died away the symphony will still be a symphony per se, worthy of high repertory rank. (17 October 1942)

The most substantive comments came from the most substantial New York critics: Downes at the *New York Times* and Thomson at the *New York Herald Tribune*. The former revised his opinion somewhat after hearing what Toscanini brought to his Philharmonic performance in which he "projected a score of highly debatable value with such eloquence and dramatic power that the audience burst into applause between movements and was cheering at the end." The effect was such that "at least one musical observer was obliged to modify his estimate of a work that he had on several previous hearings underestimated." Downes felt that Toscanini became a co-composer: "Thus understood and revealed the Seventh Symphony gave evidence more than ever before that despite the musical unworthiness of much of its material, it was felt and put together with something of that urgency and sincerity that have animated the defenders of the composer's native land."

Downes continued to perceive a visual aspect to the score, as a "tone-picture, genuinely felt in spirit and often of true dramatic power," and to feel more disposed toward the inner movements than the overly praised first movement and finale (15 October 1942).[59] Sunday's *Times* gave yet another opportunity for reflection and praise of Toscanini's interpretation. Despite seeing more virtues in the work, particularly the third movement, Downes concludes:

We are just as sure as ever we were that posterity will consign the piece to the wastepaper basket, and that much quicker than posterity has done with better music. If you are talking of real heroism in music, talk of certain finales of great heroic symphonies of Sibelius that have a grander, nobler stride and a truer simplicity and power of patriotism and nature back of them in ten pages than Shostakovich has in his whole jumbled score. That is music. And the Beethoven Fifth symphony remains the incomparable cry for liberty and chant for freedom, in terms of imperishable architecture and beauty.

Nevertheless, back of this symphony of Shostakovich is the reality and stress of these times, and the unsophisticated, dirty supplications and dreams and furies of a people who have neither time nor more need of art for art's sake. And what is art? In a changing world of endless confusions and transubstantiations of values, Mr. Toscanini made manifest these questions even if he did not profess an answer. (18 October 1942)

Although this was Downes's last substantive comment on the Seventh that season, he continued to cast aspersions on the work when reviewing later Shostakovich symphonies. As late as 1954, the year before his death, he wrote a glowing review of the Tenth Symphony—the composer's "strongest and greatest"—and reflected back on the Seventh: "[T]he war symphony, which then symbolized the conflict and struggle in which Russia and America were jointly engaged. It was excellent musical propaganda, but a second-class symphony."[60]

While Downes was so impressed by what Toscanini brought to his performance of the Seventh, Virgil Thomson saw the situation quite differently. (Downes was an enthusiastic Toscanini supporter and Thomson more often a detractor.) His views on the symphony are well-known from a Sunday piece later that week, reprinted in his collection *The Musical Scene*.[61] The Thursday review in the *Herald Tribune* captured a more immediate response: "There is no getting around it. The Philharmonic is not in good shape. Certainly if anyone can get first-class playing out of any orchestra, Mr. Toscanini can. But he failed to do so with the orchestra last spring, and he has failed to do so this season." It was not just in the new Shostakovich score that Thomson found fault with the execution, but also in the Haydn Symphony no. 99 in E-flat. After lamenting the state of the orchestra, he turned to the state of the symphony:

The Shostakovich Seventh Symphony is easy to listen to but hard to keep the mind on. It is easy to follow, because the tunes are simple, the counterpoint thin and the orchestration very broad and plain. It is experienced work by a man of thoroughly musical mentality; and it is apparently designed for easy listening, perhaps even with a thought to making it possible for the radio listener to miss some of the repetitions without losing anything essential. It is hard to keep one's attention on it in a concert hall because it repeats itself so much. One gets to thinking about something else while waiting for the next section.

As usual with Shostakovich, the quiet passages are less effective than the noisy ones. Even these, with doubled brass and seven men at the battery, are not especially rousing. Like everything else in the work they are a little too simple to be interesting. The symphony seems to need film accompaniment, something to occupy the mind while it goes on and to explain the undue stretching out of all its sections. (15 October 1942)

Thomson elaborated in his Sunday piece, complaining of the symphony's length, which, unlike the long symphonies of Beethoven, Bruckner, and Mahler, he considered unjustified: "merely a stretching out of material that is in no way deep or difficult to understand. . . . It is for the most part straight repetition. . . . It is as interminably straightforward and withal as limited in spiritual scope as a film like *The Great Ziegfeld* or *Gone with the Wind*. It could have said what it says in fifteen minutes, or it could have gone on for two hours more." Thomson felt that Shostakovich, as was his wont, called upon "easy theatrical values." The Seventh Symphony was

a series of production numbers, interspersed with neutral matter written chiefly in the same two-part counterpoint. There is a mechanized military march and the usual patriotic ending, neither of them quite as interesting or imaginative as it might be. And the rest of the episodes are even tamer. The pastorale and the Protestant chorale are competent routine stuff, no more; and the continuity counterpoint, though less static than usual, just sort of runs on as if some cinematic narrative were in progress that needed neutral accompaniment. The opening passage, which is said to represent the good Soviet citizen, is bold and buoyant. But nowhere is there any real comedy, which is what Shostakovich does best.

It was hardly surprising, given the circumstances of its genesis, that this work marked a new maturity, "a wish to put boyish things behind him and an ability to do so without losing confidence in himself." The article offered a damning conclusion:

That it is, in spite of its serious air and pretentious proportions, thin of substance, unoriginal, and shallow indicates that the mature production of this gifted master is likely to be on the stuffy side. That he has so deliberately diluted his matter, adapted it, by both excessive simplification and excessive repetition, to the comprehension of a child of eight, indicates that he is willing to write down to a real or fictitious psychology of mass consumption in a way that may eventually disqualify him for consideration as a serious composer. (18 October 1942)

The Season Continues West:
Cleveland, Chicago, and Beyond

Artur Rodzinski conducted the Seventh with the Cleveland Orchestra on 15, 17, and 18 October. Like Stokowski (but unlike Toscanini), he was an acknowledged Shostakovich champion, having recorded the First and Fifth symphonies with the Cleveland Orchestra, and having led widely acclaimed performances of *Lady Macbeth*. Rodzinski was eager to present an even larger sampling of the Russian's music during the new season, his tenth as music director and the orchestra's twenty-fifth anniversary. [62] (He was just about to be appointed music director of the New York Philharmonic.) According to the memoirs of Halina Rodzinski, her husband had six rehearsals for the concert and conducted from memory.[63] Audience and critical reaction was enormously favorable, according to the *Cleveland Plain Dealer,* and the "ovation which followed the conductor's powerfully dramatic reading of this colossal war epic was almost as tumultuous as the blasts in the finale which herald victory in our present struggle" (16 October 1942).[64] Another report stated that "as a final touch to one of the most unusual emotional reactions ever displayed by a Severance Hall audience, Dr. Rodzinski read the names of six young men in the orchestra who have just signed up to fight for Uncle Sam, and then led the orchestra and the audience in a genuinely heartfelt rendition of the 'Star-Spangled Banner.'"[65] CBS broadcast the final performance, which began with actor Raymond Massey, in Hollywood, reading a text by Carl Sandburg entitled "To Shostakovich," a poetic gloss on the symphony:

> It begins calm with the good earth and with plains and valleys naked for the toil of a man seeking crops and bread. . . .
>
> It goes on with touches like people in peace time having a chance to hunt for themselves, their personal birds of happiness to listen to. . . .
>
> Then come drums and guns and evermore drums and guns and the war is on and the rest of a nation and people—and an ordeal for the whole family of man. . . .
>
> The music marches and fights, it struggles and kills, it stands up and says there are a thousand terrible deaths, it is better to die than to let the Nazis take over your homeland and tell you how you must live. . .
>
> What you say sometimes, Dmitri Shostakovich, is the same as the message MacArthur send by radio to Stalin: "Magnificent! Matchless!"[66]

Two weeks later the Chicago Symphony Orchestra performed the Seventh in Orchestra Hall.[67] In the wake of the symphony's success in Ravinia, Stock had programmed it for the regular concert season, but his unexpected death on 20 October meant that the task fell to associate conductor Hans Lange.[68] Critics praised Lange for learning the new score so quickly, although generally the responses were rather tame in comparison with other cities, "polite instead of exuberant," in the words of one critic.[69] Some commented that the second evening performance was far more effective than the initial matinee.

William Leonard, in *Journal of Commerce,* opined: "Gigantic and uneven, it is electrifying and boring by turns—music of great entertainment value, but of construction that shows the haste with which it was assembled." He found it had more melody than usual in the composer's music, and less "brittle little rhythms" and "witticisms." He concludes, "Perhaps the inspiration for the 'Leningrad Symphony' is all packed into that overwhelming first movement, with the rest of the work in the nature of addenda, but the wonder is that it was written at all, under the circumstances" (28 October 1942).[70] Felix Borowski, one of the orchestra's program annotators who also wrote criticism for the *Chicago Sun,* attended both performances and gave a "close and critical study of the orchestral score." He wrote two scathing reviews of the work, protesting its banality and derivative elements (28 October and 30 October 1942).[71] C. J. Bulliet, in the *Chicago News,* remarked that the staid Tuesday afternoon audience, "composed largely of women," heartily greeted the work (especially the first movement) and that without all the extraneous fanfare that had accompanied the Ravinia performance in August, the symphony was now received on its own terms, along the lines of Shostakovich's "classic" Fifth Symphony: "That is to say, it is likely to endure when the immediate excitement of its composition has become accepted as 'history'—as in the case of Beethoven's 'Eroica'" (28 October 1942). This hopeful prediction of the Seventh's ultimate worth was challenged by Cecil Smith (another of the orchestra's annotators) in the *Chicago Tribune*:

> If you want to be completely swept away by this symphony you will do well to concentrate at least half your thoughts upon Russia, the siege of Leningrad, and the brave stand of the Russian armies. Strip the music of its timely connotations, and there is remarkably little left to substantiate the claim that this is one of the great symphonic works of our time, or of any time at all. It is most conspicuously a piece of program music which leans much too heavily on its program, in the hope of concealing appalling shortcomings of technical

workmanship. Tchaikovsky's "1812" overture is both a more effective piece of program music and an infinitely better work of art. . . .

I wonder what it will sound like after the war? (30 October 1942)

By November the symphony had been heard live and in broadcasts across the country. *Life* ran a photo spread on a Stokowski performance for some fourteen thousand soldiers at an army desert camp in Southern California. As *Time* reported, "Discreetly Conductor Stokowski had cut the symphony's torturous length by nearly half, but as he boomed and rattled into the home stretch of the first movement the audience shuffled and groaned impatiently, electricians began jabbering over their microphones, newsreel men noisily ground their cameras. Suddenly Stokowski stopped the orchestra. Said he: 'Men, there is a little more of this symphony to play. I do not know whether you want to hear it and it does not matter to us'" (26 October 1942).[72] The performance resumed and, as composer Robert Ward wryly observed, "a bad time was had by all."[73] The *Life* feature noted:

By now it is almost unpatriotic not to like Dmitri Shostakovich's Seventh Symphony. Written last winter during the siege of Leningrad and widely played now in the U. S. during the stubborn defense of Stalingrad, this work has become a symbol of the Russians' heroic resistance. People who temper their praise of the Seventh or express dislike of it are looked upon as musical fifth columnists who are running down our brave Russian allies. No other symphony has ever achieved this special character of the Seventh which is, in fact, quite able to stand up and be judged upon its own musical merits. (9 November 1942)

The Philadelphia Orchestra was the last of the major orchestras to perform the symphony, which is somewhat curious given that under Stokowski the ensemble had presented the American premieres of the First, Third, and Sixth symphonies (and would later present numbers Four, Thirteen, Fourteen, and Fifteen under Ormandy), and had recorded the First, Fifth, and Sixth with Stokowski.[74] The orchestra played a lot of Russian music in 1942–43, opening the season on 2 October with a program consisting of Tikhon Khrennikov's Symphony no. 1, op. 4, Stravinsky's *Firebird* Suite, and Shostakovich's Fifth Symphony. Ormandy's Seventh on 27 and 28 November was presented on an all-Shostakovich program that opened with Two Pieces for Strings, op. 11 (originally for string octet). The performance on Friday, 27 November was broadcast nationally—the third after Toscanini in July and Rodzinski in October.

Critical opinion was divided, as usual. Arthur Bronson, writing in the *Philadelphia Record,* applauded the symphony: "As Shostakovich's picture of the Soviet people today, struggling in battle, confident of victory, it is a remarkable work, titanic and stirring. It has a fine opening movement of imposing stature and a magnificent close. What appears today as a tribute to a gallant fighting race tomorrow will be a monument" (28 November 1942). Linton Martin in the *Philadelphia Inquirer* was less impressed by a piece "heralded by more blare and fanfare of publicity than any other musical work has had in all time." He wrote:

> Certainly if ballyhoo and hullabaloo could make for musical greatness, this Shostakovich would be the symphonic masterpiece of all time. Instead, it is at best a work uneven in interest, originality, ideas and inspiration, derivative to a degree, haphazard and scattered in construction, far too long for what it has to say. In short, an overblown bore. . . .
>
> This Seventh Symphony is in every way inferior to the same composer's Fifth. . . . It has lots of imitation-Tchaikovsky, amounting almost to "quotes" from the "1812" Overture and the Fourth and Fifth Symphonies.
>
> There are suggestions of the "Ein Heldenleben" of Richard Strauss, and also of Sibelius, especially the second movement of the Fifth Symphony. The analogy to the Ravel "Bolero" already has been mentioned. (28 November 1942)

Betty Stine was equally unmoved, arguing in her *Evening Bulletin* review: "If one listened to the Leningrad Symphony without benefit of the program notes and dramatic incidents of its composition, it can be conjectured that the reaction to the music itself would be one of interest and not much more" (28 November 1942).

"The Decrescendo of the Great Crescendo": The Decline of the Seventh

In November Hans Kindler conducted the Seventh with the National Symphony Orchestra, and Dimitri Mitropoulos led the work in Minneapolis.[75] John K. Sherman in the *Star Journal* called the latter's performance "one of the most impressive and thrilling events of music in the annals of the Minneapolis Symphony orchestra," and again commented on its programmatic aspect in relation to its time:

But one of the important points about this "Leningrad' symphony—
probably THE important point—is its cargo of message, its inspiration
and its purpose. You know that the war motivated the work, and
feel it keenly throughout—in fact you never forget it anywhere.
This is "program" music closely linked with the headlines of today,
giving flaming expression to the ideals of free men and their valor
in fighting for them against brute aggression. (28 November 1942)

The extraordinary status of the Seventh is evident not only in the fact
that New York saw performances by the NBC Symphony Orchestra, New
York Philharmonic, and Boston Symphony Orchestra all within the space
of less than four months, but also that the NBC and Philharmonic both
presented the work with different conductors within the same period.
Stokowski finally got his chance to lead the work in New York with the
NBC in a broadcast, the fourth nationally, from Studio 8-H on 13 December
and Artur Rodzinski conducted the symphony with the New York Philharmonic at Carnegie.[76] Oscar Thompson remarked in the *New York Sun*
that Rodzinski's

> was a generally lyrical presentation which was to the advantage of
> the lesser movements standing in the shadow of the colossal first alle-
> gro, which might be presented alone as a symphony in one movement.
>   For one who had heard the earlier performances there was a
> further loss in the impact of the protracted middle section of that alle-
> gro, where the Ravel of the "Bolero," the Sibelius of the pizzicato of
> the Fifth Symphony and the Mossoloff of the "Iron Foundry" were
> leagued together in a huge upbuilding of the clangorous sonorities
> the defense of Leningrad is assumed to have inspired. The perfor-
> mance was a spirited one and it seems fairer to attribute the blunting
> of the impact of the work's most sensational pages to the deleterious
> effect of too many and too immediate repetitions—the nature of the
> music being what it is—rather than to the conductor or the admirable
> ensemble at his command. But it does not speak well for the future
> of the symphony. Much of it sounded thin last night and there were
> places where only its momentum seemed to hold its structure together.
> (4 December 1942)[77]

By December, more than a dozen orchestras had tackled the Seventh
and, in Thompson's words, "The decrescendo of the great crescendo
continues, as conductors seem determined to play the Shostakovich Seventh
Symphony to death." A few further performances in early January can round

out this survey of the first six months of the Seventh in North America. On New Year's Day 1943 Eugene Goossens opened his Cincinnati Symphony Orchestra concert featuring the Seventh with "The Star-Spangled Banner" and the United Nations National Anthem no. 9 (The Netherlands), before playing, in one of the more innovative examples of programming, Haydn's "Military" Symphony no. 100 in G Major. Stokowski conducted the Seventh with the San Francisco Symphony Orchestra on 8 January before an audience of 9,300—hundreds are reported to have been turned away. The event again benefited Russian War Relief.

In January 1943, Shostakovich, together with Prokofiev, was made an honorary member of the American Academy of Arts and Letters. (The Seventh had already won the Stalin Prize in the Soviet Union.) Just as the symphony's fortunes began to diminish, there were some larger retrospective looks at the composer, including a book rushed into print by Victor Seroff, in collaboration with Shostakovich's aunt, Nadejda Galli-Shohat, who lived in Philadelphia. In a review in *Modern Music* Donald Fuller remarked on the "undue haste," and stated that it was an "extended version of the typical newspaper blurb."[78]

In February, Ralph Parker wrote an article for *The New York Times Magazine* entitled "The Symphonist of Russia's Travail: The Story of Dmitri Shostakovich and of His Great Composition Honoring Leningrad"(7 February 1943).[79] Much of it was devoted to a profile of the composer and his career; the information about the Seventh was largely familiar, except for some details that went against all other accounts and evidence.[80] The article included comments Shostakovich allegedly made to Parker (the fictions earlier in the piece do not inspire much confidence in the reporting), who visited the composer's hotel in Kuibyshev: "I am deeply happy that the American people have enjoyed my Seventh Symphony. . . . What is really important is that the music be widely understood." Shostakovich stated that he was not surprised at the reaction, "You see, I have had so many evidences to prove that ordinary people in the Soviet Union have understood the symphony, so many letters have come to me from ordinary people, that it is not a surprise that Americans should have understood its meaning as well." Parker asked if it was not necessary to have suffered directly from the war, as Russians had, and reminded the composer that when last they had talked he had stated that the first movement "evoked the lost joys of peace and the growing and finally overwhelming sorrow of war." Shostakovich responded: "I think that the American understanding of the 'Leningrad Symphony' shows that the American people understand what the war is, that Russian and American people have feelings in common about war and peace, all of which opens their hearts in the same way to the music."

Yet the Seventh soon faded from American concert life, especially from the repertory of the leading orchestras. (Less prestigious ensembles that had not performed the work took their turns offering local premieres, especially as performance materials became more easily available and, perhaps, less expensive.) Given the heated initial competition among conductors over the work, one might have predicted a comparable race to record it, but a ban on all recording by the musicians union delayed any such undertaking.[81] The first recording came only in 1946, with William Steinberg leading the Buffalo Philharmonic Orchestra.[82] After that, the Seventh virtually disappeared for many decades, which is perhaps not surprising given the Cold War. If other Shostakovich symphonies, particularly the First and Fifth, continued to be performed, and his new ones premiered, the original circumstances around the Seventh may have been too painful a reminder of a very different time in American-Soviet relations. Table 2 lists the subsequent seasons in which the Seventh Symphony was performed by the leading five orchestras. After so many performances in 1942, the work was not again performed at Carnegie Hall until 1977 (Temirkanov conducting).

The "phenomenon of the Seventh" should be considered not only within the context of the war, but also of American musical culture of the time, especially the programming offered by orchestras and the musical politics of new music in general. This can be found in an overview of the

---

Table 2
Postwar Performances of the Seventh Symphony by the Leading Five American Orchestras

New York Philharmonic:	1962 (Bernstein), 1990 (Temirkanov) 1994, 1998, 2000 (Masur)
Philadelphia:	1977 (Temirkanov), 2000 (Temirkanov)
Boston:	1948–49 (Bernstein), 1984 (Slatkin), 1995 (Gergiev)
Chicago:	1984 (Slatkin), 1986 (Herbig), 1988 (Bernstein), 1995 (Wigglesworth)*
Cleveland:	1995 (Ashkenazy), 1999 (Wigglesworth)

*The Chicago Symphony Orchestra also performed the symphony at the Ravinia Festival, in 1947 with Richard Steinberg, and in 1984 with James Levine.

---

repertory that American orchestras played during the 1942–43 season, a "'state of the nation' symphonically," as *Musical America* deemed it. Beethoven was the most performed composer, followed by Wagner and Brahms. (The country may have been at war with Germany, but that did not mean people stopped listening to German music.) Tchaikovsky's Fifth Symphony and Wagner's *Meistersinger* Overture were the two works programmed most frequently.[83] Among living composers, Richard Strauss, hardly a politically attractive choice, took the lead, followed by Shostakovich. The two modern works dominating the charts were Shostakovich's Seventh and Rachmaninoff's Second Piano Concerto.[84]

Although more American music was played than during the previous season, up 2.4 percent from 6.5 to 8.9 percent of the concert fare, no works captured the collective imagination in any way comparable to Shostakovich's music.[85] But as the United States became more involved in the war, composers increasingly addressed the times, with Shostakovich's Seventh standing as an imposing model.[86] Edwin Hughes, president of the National Music Council, declared in midseason: "Our serious composers have begun to feel the urge to write music connected with the war, but so far we have not had anything brought to popular attention which looks like an American counterpart of the 'Leningrad' Symphony."[87]

Most new American pieces in 1942 and 1943 had little or no overt political baggage (for example, Schuman's Fourth Symphony, Barber's Second Essay for Orchestra, Diamond's Cello Concerto, Carpenter's Second Symphony), but some did, such as Copland's *Lincoln Portrait* (premiered 14 May 1942) and Morton Gould's *A Lincoln Legend* (1 November 1942).[88] On 26 February 1943, Koussevitzky led the Boston Symphony Orchestra in the premiere of Roy Harris's Fifth Symphony, a work dedicated "to the heroic and freedom-loving people of our great ally, the Union of Soviet Socialist Republics, as a tribute to their strength in war, their staunch idealism for world peace, their ability to cope with stark materialist problems of world order without losing a passionate belief in the fundamental importance of the arts."[89] Copland's "Fanfare for the Common Man," was first performed by the Cincinnati Symphony Orchestra on 12 March 1943.[90] Originally one of eighteen fanfares by various composers that Goossens commissioned for the orchestra, Copland's brief brass and percussion piece, with its Shostakovichian title and melodic content, eventually won wide recognition when it was incorporated into his own "war" symphony, the Third.[91] A particularly fascinating case is Samuel Barber's Second Symphony, op. 19. Commissioned early in 1943 by the U.S. Air Force, Koussevitzky premiered the work with the Boston Symphony Orchestra on 3 March 1944 in an Office of War Information broadcast to Allied troops and other nations. The model of the Seventh is clear, but Barber soon became dissatisfied with the symphony, revising it in early 1947, withdrawing it in 1964, and destroying all scores, copies, and parts a few years after that. He stated: "Such times of cataclysm are rarely conducive to the creation of good music, especially when the composer tries to say too much." He seems to have particularly regretted the work's programmatic elements and realistic effects.[92]

While the fading "phenomenon of the Seventh" is most evident in its quick disappearance from the repertoire, interest in Shostakovich nonetheless remained strong and the symphony's extraordinary success left its mark as well, and not just on Harris, Copland, and Barber. The most pointed musical commentary was Bartók's snide one in the fourth movement of his *Concerto for Orchestra,* in which he parodied the central march theme of the first movement.[93] As Richard Taruskin has noted, Stravinsky, Schoenberg, and Bartók all took considerable interest in the Seventh and one can only guess at the extent of their jealousy and resentment over all the attention given the work and its composer.[94] In 1943, Marc Blitzstein succinctly called the Seventh "the symphony which composers run away from, and conductors can't get enough of."[95]

As John H. Mueller has noted in his social history of American orchestras, there was a certain paradox to the fact that the communist's symphony was subjected to "the normal capitalistic competition between two national radio chains and the Eastern orchestras."[96] Shostakovich's American fortunes by no means faded completely after the phenomenal Seventh, an event that could hardly be duplicated. While NBC had secured the performing rights for the Seventh, two years later the rival network CBS paid $10,000 for the Eighth Symphony.[97]

The Changing Seventh

In 1942 an American critic in Minneapolis's *Morning Tribune* suggested that people listen to the Seventh not "with any fine, critical detachment":

> Leave it to the scholars of 1975 to determine whether it's another "Ninth" or an overlong and uneven tour-de-force chiefly memorable for its topical significance. So far as you're concerned, it's an experience of a sort you've never had before. You'll be listening to Russia's greatest composer endeavoring to translate into music his first-hand impression of his own Russia's magnificent stand against a modern Genghis Khan. Accept it primarily as a message from a gallant, fighting ally, a cry, if you will, from an agonized country rising

by sheer force of will to one of the supreme feats of resistance of all time. Taken in that spirit, it's impossible that it could leave you cold. (27 November 1942)[98]

As we have seen, the Seventh Symphony rarely left critics cold. Even among those who disliked it, the work aroused a good amount of passionate discussion. The unprecedented wartime hype, duly noted at the time, may have engendered some of the attacks, just as it probably did the unusually enthusiastic audience responses. Those critics who unreservedly praised it tended to be lesser, now long-forgotten ones; they rarely offered much to support their claims. The voices critical of the piece usually proved more concrete in stating what they perceived as its compositional weaknesses. Although critics argued about the artistic value and long-term prospects of the Seventh, we have seen broad agreement about two things: that the composer and the work were "sincere" and that the symphony was "derivative," both of other composers' styles and of many specific works.

Shostakovich is said to have anticipated that people would hear *Boléro* in the first movement, telling Khachaturian and others who heard him play it through on the piano, "Forgive me, will you, if this reminds you of Ravel's *Bolero*."[99] Isaak Glikman reports the composer made a similar comment to him: "I suppose that critics with nothing better to do will damn me for copying Ravel's *Bolero*. Well, let them. That is how I hear war."[100] But this obvious similarity, acknowledged by Shostakovich, commented upon by countless critics, and repeatedly invoked in the secondary literature on the symphony, may divert attention from the fact that so many commentators at the time found so much else in the symphony also derivative. The list of pieces we have seen mentioned as connected to the first movement alone includes Sibelius's Fifth Symphony, Strauss's *Ein Heldenleben,* Respighi's *The Pines of Rome,* Tchaikovsky's *1812 Overture,* Berlioz's "March to the Scaffold" from the *Symphonie fantastique,* Grieg's *Gnomenreigen,* as well as such curiosities as Mosolov's *Iron Foundry* and Shelling's *Impressions from an Artist's Life*.[101] Less specifically, critics invoked Beethoven, Rimsky-Korsakov, Mahler, Busoni, Prokofiev, Poulenc, and others.[102] The long list of alleged allusions and quotations (and self-quotations) has continued to grow ever since, with the principal change being that now the sources adduced are increasingly viewed as keys that can unlock hidden meanings within the work.

The use of the word *derivative* in the wartime criticism is in itself significant because responsibility is placed on Shostakovich, not on the listener, with the implication that he is unoriginal. Yet when critic Douglas Watt reviewed Toscanini's NBC broadcast premiere, he was reminded of

Fats Waller's "Ain't Misbehavin'." There was obviously no charge of this being a source for Shostakovich, rather it was simply one critic's associations. The observation was not about the intentions of the composer, but rather the reception of the listener. Indeed, Watt's fanciful hearing of the first movement tells its own story, the idiosyncratic way he heard the music. After a blissful pastoral opening,

> a tiny little figure appears, a ridiculous-looking fellow. He is small, but he is out of place. As he comes nearer, you notice he wears the oddest smile. The perspective is wrong, too, because he keeps getting bigger, much bigger than he should. Before you know it you can't see the landscape anymore. There is only one he, gigantic now and malevolent. The whimsical patter of his boots has risen to a thunder. He is all murder. He is the surprise attack. (20 July 1942)[103]

No American critic of whom I am aware questioned that this murderous figure was Adolf Hitler or that Shostakovich was not less than completely sincere in writing a work that stood up to the German attack on the Soviet Union in the summer of 1941. More recent writings have suggested otherwise. The "scholars of 1975," the year of Shostakovich's death, uncannily invoked in the review at the beginning of this section, have broadened the range of interpretation from its original wartime associations. In a future article I hope to compare the initial American reception of the Seventh Symphony with current appraisals of the work. Most striking are suggestions nowadays that the symphony is as much, or more, about Stalin than Hitler, a notion that did not occur to any American critic during the war.[104] In our era the "phenomenon of the Seventh" has been revived, revisiting old debates with new twists. The resurrection of the Seventh, of course, is far less a mass event, since classical music plays an ever decreasing role in the general culture. Nonetheless, after decades of near oblivion in America, performances and recordings of the symphony surged in the 1990s, just as those subscribing to the view of a "New Shostakovich" expounded what they argued was the work's "real" meaning, questioning in the process the supposedly all too clear meaning apparent to everyone in wartime America, if not explicitly questioning the composer's "sincerity."[105]

The "derivative" issue remains, although that pejorative word is no longer used. As the symphony's overdetermined meaning expands, so too does the list of pieces to which it is said to owe a debt. Critics today, writing from a postmodern perspective, may have more sympathy for Shostakovich's eclectic montages of styles and allusions. (The same shift has happened with Mahler's reception.) We may also make finer distinctions between a composer's intention and a listener's reception: what the former consciously puts into a work and what the latter hears. For the Seventh has invited listeners to hear what they want—be it Ravel or Fats Waller, Hitler or Stalin. The central first movement march section in particular may still be considered derivative, but what exactly it is derived from keeps expanding, from Russian, German, or other sources, or, more recently, self-quotation (a possibility the American wartime reception never considered).[106] Furthermore, the sources now adduced tend to be used to promote specific readings of the work.[107] It would, of course, be quite a feat for Shostakovich to have been simultaneously inspired by, copied, alluded to, stolen from—whatever term one wants to use—a dozen or more pieces, but that is what the reception tells us.

While Shostakovich was often criticized in 1942 for relying too much on the compositions of others, some commentators now praise him for subtle allusions that convey meaning. But no interpretation reveals the music's real meaning or the composer's true intentions. Rather they mirror how listeners respond to the work in particular times and places, be it in 1942 or 2004, in Leningrad/St. Petersburg or New York City. Richard Taruskin has eloquently urged that we consider the Seventh Symphony's fortunes in this larger historical, musical, and political context:

> The history of Shostakovich's "Leningrad" Symphony is an exceptionally rich and eventful one, touching both inspiringly and dispiritingly on many of the most terrible circumstances of the twentieth century. It subsumes the history of its own reception in varying geographical and political climates and illuminates (or at least illustrates) many of the most pressing aesthetic-cum-social controversies of our time. It gives the lie to the dear old dichotomy between the "purely musical" and the "extramusical," which cannot even be disentangled within the work, let alone in any symbolic explication of it. The importance of this symphony to the history of twentieth-century music, then, is immense.[108]

This documentary essay has attempted to pursue just one chronological and geographical aspect of that remarkable history. The Seventh Symphony has not died in large part because Shostakovich has emerged as a more potent force than many imagined in 1942. And even if some critics' predictions that the Seventh would be remembered as the twentieth-century *Eroica* have yet to be vindicated, the fact that musicians and audiences continue to find pain and pleasure in the work, discover and invent new associations and meanings, suggests that it will endure. One might say that the "Leningrad" has become the "St. Petersburg" Symphony, a different work for a different time. This validates, at least in part, the view that the symphony was not fatally bound to the circumstances of its genesis. But musical works are always heard within history, a testimony not only to their time of creation, but also to their subsequent realizations and rehearings. The Seventh is always changing.

NOTES

My thanks to Laurel Fay for her helpful guidance and suggestions. I am grateful to Christopher Hatch for his insightful comments. I greatly appreciate the help I received from the archives and publicity departments of Carnegie Hall and of the orchestras discussed in this essay, and from the staff of the music division of the New York Public Library for the Performing Arts.

1. The most important sources are listed in the "Editor's Note" of *D. Shostakovich: Collected Works in Forty-Two Volumes* (Moscow: Muzyka, 1979–1987), vol. 4 (hereafter cited as *Collected Works*) and in the Preface by Manashir Yakubov, *Dmitri Shostakovich Symphony no. 7 "Leningrad," op. 60 (1941); Facsimile Edition of the Manuscript* (Tokyo: Zen-On, 1992), pp. 7–10 (hereafter *Facsimile*). My concern here is with what the American audiences knew at the time; some of Shostakovich's 1941 and 1942 articles and statements were reprinted in the United States and will be discussed below.

2. Nicolas Slonimsky pointed out that "Leningrad" was not an official title very early; see "Soviet Music at Quarter-Century Mark," *Musical America* (10 February 1943): 21. The last two names cited were far less common, but see, for example, *The Etude* 66 (February 1943): 142; and Charles Mills, "Over the Air," *Modern Music* 20 (1942): 62.

3. *VOKS Bulletin* no. 1–2 (1942): 55–56; Cleveland Orchestra program notes (15, 17 October 1942).

4. *New York Herald Tribune,* 15 October 1942.

5. Virgil Thomson, *The Musical Scene* (New York: Alfred A. Knopf, 1945), p. 102.

6. The 10 August 1942 issue of the *Information Bulletin* contained an announcement of the upcoming Tanglewood performance, articles by Aleksei Tolstoy ("Shostakovich's Seventh Symphony"), Koussevitzky ("The Simplicity and Wisdom of Shostakovich"), Vera Vassina ("Growth of an Artist"), Eugene (Evgenii) Petrov ("A Triumph of Russian Music"), Constantin Finn ("Shostakovich Speaks for Our People"), and an interview with the composer himself. The July issue already had offered David Rabinovich's "Portrait of a Soviet Citizen" (18 July 1942); I have been unable to obtain a copy, but the article appears to · be the same, or quite similar, to what appeared in *VOKS Bulletin* at the same time; see David Rabinovich, "Symphony of Struggle and Victory," and Shostakovich, "My Seventh Symphony," *VOKS Bulletin* no. 1–2 (1942): 55–60.

7. On the question of familiarity, see Kate Hevner Mueller, *Twenty-Seven Major American Symphony Orchestras: A History and Analysis of Their Repertoires, Seasons 1842–43 Through 1969–70* (Bloomington, Ind.: Indiana University Press, 1973), pp. 315–16. Shostakovich's opera *Lady Macbeth of the Mtsensk District* had also been performed in various cities and there were multiple recordings of selected symphonies.

8. Ralph Parker, "Shostakovich, Composer, Explains His Symphony of Plain Man in War," *New York Times*, 9 February 1942, p. 17. Reprinted with permission.

9. Ralph Parker, "Shostakovich—A Major Voice of the Soviets, His Seventh Symphony Hymns the Heroic Potentialities of the People," *New York Times*, 5 April 1942.

10. *Time* may have gotten the motto from Shostakovich's statement in *Izvestiia* (12 April 1942), see *Dmitry Shostakovich: About Himself and His Times,* trans. Angus and Neilian Roxburgh (Moscow: Progress Publishers, 1981), p. 96. Excerpt from *Time* reprinted with permission.

11. The former supposedly dates from 1915–16, before the revolution; see Derek Hulme, *Dmitri Shostakovich: A Catalogue, Bibliography, and Discography,* 3d ed. (Lanham, Md.: Scarecrow Press, 2002), p. 11

12. Artur Rodzinski conducted the premiere with the NBC Symphony Orchestra on 9 April 1938.

13. Although the press often alluded to the contest among various conductors to give the premiere, the extent and details were unknown at the time. Grigorii Shneerson later published letters requesting permission from the Soviet authorities written by Koussevitzky (15 January 1941), Ormandy (16 September 1941), Stokowski (12 February 1942), and Rodzinski (17 February 1942); see "Aus der Aufführungsgeschichte der 7. Sinfonie von Dmitri Schostakowitsch," *Musik in der Schule* 27 (1976): 62–63; see also Krzysztof Meyer, *Dmitri Schostakowitsch: Sein Leben, sein Werk, seine Zeit* (Munich: Gustav Lübbe Verlag, 1985), pp. 285–86. The now-famous exchange of letters between Toscanini and Stokowski only became known after the former's death, in liner notes by Irving Kolodin that accompanied the first commercial release of Toscanini's broadcast of the Seventh in a centennial collection honoring the conductor (*A Toscanini Treasury of Historical Broadcasts* [1967; RCA LM-6711]). Stokowski's letters are given in Oliver Daniel, *Stokowski: A Counterpoint of View* (New York: Dodd, Mead, 1982), pp. 454–59; and Toscanini's in Harvey Sachs, *The Letters of Arturo Toscanini* (New York: Alfred A. Knopf, 2002), pp. 385–86; see also Sachs's *Toscanini* (Philadelphia: J. B. Lippincortt, 1978), pp. 279–80.

14. There are 35 pages of music, NYPL/PA; JOB 89–2, folder no. 23; my thanks to John Shepard for bringing this to my attention.

15. Concerning the critic's support of Sibelius, see Glenda Dawn Goss, *Jean Sibelius and Olin Downes: Music, Friendship, Criticism* (Boston: Northeastern University Press, 1995).

16. Other forums also prepared the public for Toscanini's broadcast, if more on the level of gossip. Irving Kolodin, in the *New York Sun,* went into more detail about the conductors' battle over who would lead the premiere. He reported that Koussevitzky had arranged to give the first performance at the Berkshire Music Center and that Toscanini would present it with the New York Philharmonic in October. But NBC's Moscow correspondent acquired the rights and Toscanini agreed to "break his inviolable period of summer rest to conduct the first worldwide broadcast of the much-publicized score" (6 July). On 18 July, "The Talk of the Town" in *The New Yorker* gave further details about the challenges in preparing a performable score. The route of the microfilm is expanded from those given elsewhere: "from Moscow to Kuibyshev, by plane from Kuibyshev to Teheran, by automobile from Teheran to Cairo, and by plane from Cairo to the United States, via South America"; it arrived on 25 June and was printed within a week. But problems arose from the fact that the film was underexposed and that there was a shortage of matte printing paper, which required the use of glossy paper difficult to read under the performance lights. According to the brief program note for the NBC broadcast, there were also difficulties because the "Russian film differed in the size of its frames from any used in America and could not be reproduced with standard equipment." Toscanini's score and a copy of the program are in the Toscanini Legacy Collection at the New York Public Library for the Performing Arts (hereafter NYPL/PA) (JPB 90–1 A224 and JPB 90–1 L235).

17. Beethoven addressed charges that he composed "only for posterity" in 1814, see *Thayer's Life of Beethoven*, ed. Elliot Forbes, rev. ed. (Princeton, N.J.: Princeton University Press, 1967), p. 586.

18. B. H. Haggin, *Music in the Nation* (New York: W. Sloane Associates, 1949), p. 111.

19. For the reception of *Wellington's Victory*, see Stefan Kunze, *Beethoven im Spiegel seiner Zeit* (Laaber: Laaber-Verlag, 1987), pp. 267–88; and *The Critical Reception of Beethoven's Compositions by His German Contemporaries*, ed. Wayne M. Senner (Lincoln and London: University of Nebraska Press, 2001), vol. 2, pp. 5, 180–81, 224; for a more recent appreciation, see William Kinderman, *Beethoven* (Berkeley, Calif.: University of California Press, 1995), pp. 170–75.

20. Oscar Thompson, "Shostakovich Seventh Has Premiere," *Musical America* (August 1942): 4.

21. See the "Editor's Note," *Collected Works*, vol. 4, and *Facsimile*, p. 8. As there has been considerable discussion in recent years about the chronology of the Seventh it is worth emphasizing that plans for *a* Seventh Symphony may be quite different than the reality of *the* complete Seventh Symphony. Some of Shostakovich's early plans were even known in America at the time; for example, his statement in December 1940 that "In 1941, I hope to complete my Seventh Symphony, which I shall dedicate to the great genius of mankind—Vladimir Ilich Lenin" (program notes for the Cleveland Orchestra [15, 17 October 1942]).

22. The Carter quote is in *Modern Music* 21 (1943): 52.

23. *VOKS Bulletin* no. 1–2 (1942): 55–56; Cleveland Orchestra program notes (15, 17 October 1942).

24. Nicolas Slonimsky, "Dmitri Dmitrievitch Shostakovitch," *Musical Quarterly* 28 (October 1942): 435–37; the quotation from Tolstoy is not exactly the same as in the *Information Bulletin*, but perhaps Slonimsky had the original Russian or was paraphrasing.

25. Irving Kolodin later recalled that there were plans by the Office of War Information to film a documentary on the symphony, its travels to America, reconstruction from the microfilm, and so forth leading up to the NBC performance. The project fell through and Verdi's *Hymn of the Nations* was done instead; see Kolodin's liner notes to *A Toscanini Treasury of Historical Broadcasts* (RCA LM-6711). A copy of the proposed script for the film, dated 16 April 1943, is in the Toscanini Legacy collection, NYPL/PA (JPB 90–1, L 105D).

26. Much of the American press at the time reported the date of the Russian premiere as 1 March, not 5 March. (The error continues to be found in various sources to this day. The confusion may have come in part from a private performance on 1 March, the official premiere coming four days later.) The modest two-page program book, which gave the correct date, contained the program announcement and a brief essay "The Odyssey of a Symphony" that discussed the circumstances of the symphony's composition and travels to America, NYPL/PA (JPB 90–1 L235).

27. Although pirated copies of the famous broadcast circulated for decades, it was not until 1967, to mark the centennial of Toscanini's birth, that a recording of the broadcast was released commercially in *A Toscanini Treasury of Historical Broadcasts* (RCA LM-6711). It is possible to hear the opening and closing announcements (some 8 and 5 minutes, respectively) in an archive tape at the NYPL/PA (LT 10 6238/39).

28. Excerpted in Dmitri and Ludmilla Sollertinsky, *Pages from the Life of Dmitri Shostakovich* (New York: Harcourt Brace Jovanovich, 1980), p. 107.

29. Nicolas Nabokov, "The Case of Dmitri Shostakovich," *Harper's* 186 (March 1943): 422–31, especially p. 423; reprinted in a revised and updated form in *Old Friends and New Music* (London: Hamish Hamilton, 1951), pp. 190–209.

30. Haggin, *Music in the Nation*, p. 109 (article reprinted from vol. 115 [15 August 1942], p. 138).

31. Downes had worked with Siegmeister on *A Treasury of American Song* (New York: Howell, Soskin & Co., 1940). The extended quotations from Downes are reprinted with permission.

32. Elie Siegmeister, "Sources of the Art of Composers," *New York Times*, 2 August 1942.

33. *Syracuse Herald-American*, 2 August 1942; abridged in *New York Times*, 2 August 1942; other comments by the conductor are in the *Information Bulletin, Embassy USSR* (10 August 1942), pp. 1, 3, 6. For reactions, see Hugo Leichtentritt, *Serge Koussevitzky: The Boston Symphony Orchestra and the New American Music* (Cambridge, Mass.: Harvard University Press, 1946), pp. 179–81.

34. *Time* (24 August 1942); *Musical America* (June 1942): 6; after 1942 all activities ceased until 1946 (Leichtentritt, *Serge Koussevitzky*, p. 181).

35. Louis Biancolli, "Leningrad Symphony," *New York World-Telegram*, 15 August 1942.

36. Arthur Bronson, "Shostakovich's 7th Played by Ormandy," *Philadelphia Record*, 28 November 1942.

37. Henry Simon, "New England Receives a Message for Russia and Understands It," *PM*, 16 August 1942.

38. Downes offered some further comments after the repeat performance two days later, see "Season Concluded by Koussevitzky," *New York Times*, 17 August 1942.

39. *Time*, 27 July 1942.

40. *Chicago Tribune*, 22 August 1942.

41. The Kuibyshev premiere had an intermission after the first movement, see Laurel E. Fay, *Shostakovich: A Life* (New York: Oxford University Press, 2000), p. 131.

42. *Chicago Sun*, 21 August 1942. This lack of enthusiasm is supported by another account in the *Chicago Times*, 23 August 1942, in which Stock comments, "As you know, it's not all that it should be, but we have to do our best."

43. *Newsweek* reported four 2½-hour rehearsals (27 July 1942), but others place their number at five or six.

44. In addition to this sample of reviews, another voice of some historical interest was heard in the press. Conductor Nicolai Malko, who gave the world premieres of Shostakovich's First and Second symphonies in Russia and who was at the time music director of the Chicago Women's Symphony, was interviewed in the *Chicago Times* (23 August 1942) about his relationship with Shostakovich. After relating a few anecdotes, he commented that the Seventh was too long and not as good as the Fifth or Sixth, or the First, which he considered best: "But one of the really interesting aspects of the 'War' symphony is its dynamic development, especially in the first movement and in the finale. Another is the combination of lyricism and humor in the second. The whole has a strong pictorial character. But without touching upon its symphonic qualities, we must admit that today this work has become a political factor and must be treated as such. Hence I appreciate everything that it can accomplish towards spiritual uplift in difficult times such as these." For more about his relationship to Shostakovich, see Malko's memoirs, *A Certain Art* (New York: William Morrow, 1966).

45. Carlos Chavez, another conductor who had expressed great interest in the symphony, performed the work in Mexico in September with the Symphony Orchestra of Mexico; see *Musical America* (September 1942): 25; (25 November 1942): 34; and (10 December 1942): 34.

46. Edwin Hughes, "Music Alert to Wartime Task," *Musical America* (10 February 1943): 110.

47. Ibid.

48. Only symphonies 5, 6, and 7 were performed that season. Koussevitzky, in fact, had not conducted much Soviet music before 1941, see Moses Smith, *Koussevitzky* (New York: Allen, Towne & Heath, 1947), p. 258. The opening concert also featured Beethoven's Second Symphony.

49. Both Shostakovich's explanation of the symphony and the interview with his wife were reprinted elsewhere in advance of the concerts on the BSO tour.

50. Boston Symphony Orchestra program book, 9–10 October 1942.

51. When Koussevitzky brought the Boston Symphony Orchestra to Carnegie Hall in November, he paired the Seventh, as he had for a second Tanglewood performance in August, with Haydn's Symphony no. 88 in G Major.

52. This was the last time Toscanini conducted the work; indeed, he rarely performed Shostakovich's music. He had conducted the First Symphony with the New York Philharmonic in 1931, with the BBC Orchestra in 1937, and with the NBC in 1939; see Mortimer H. Frank, *Arturo Toscanini: The NBC Years* (Portland, Ore.: Amadeus Press, 2002), pp. 65–66, 201.

53. Audiences had ample opportunities to hear a large amount of Shostakovich's music. Toscanini presented his first Philharmonic performance on 14 October. The night before, Eugene Ormandy conducted the Philadelphia Orchestra in the Fifth Symphony at Carnegie. The First Symphony served as the music for Léonide Massine's ballet *Rouge et Noir* at the Metropolitan Opera House, and there was the chance to listen to Artur Rodzinski's national broadcast of the Seventh Symphony with the Cleveland Orchestra on Sunday 18 October. Because Toscanini had an exclusive contract with NBC, the New York Philharmonic concert could not be broadcast as usual on Sunday afternoon.

54. "Russian Declines Philharmonic Bid," *Musical America* (September 1942): 9; see also Oscar Thompson, "Shostakovich on the Horizon," *New York Sun*, 12 September 1942.

55. *New York Times*, 30 September 1942; see also *Musical America* (September 1942): 4.

56. "Mephisto's Musings," *Musical America* (September 1942): 9.

57. *New York Herald Tribune*, 16 October 1942.

58. The article reports a performance time of 66 minutes, which is some 7 minutes shorter than Toscanini's NBC concert in July; I consulted the AP item, which presumably was picked up across the country, in the *San Francisco Chronicle*, 15 October 1942. Walter Toscanini's meticulous timings are probably more accurate; for the 14 October concert he gives: 27:00, 10:02, 16:45, 14:05 (67:53 total), see the draft of his letter to Spike Hughes in NYPL/PA (JPB 90–1, folder L235).

59. Olin Downes, "Shostakovich 7th Wins Ovation Here," *New York Times*, 15 October 1942.

60. *Olin Downes on Music: A Selection from His Writings During the Half-Century 1906–1955,* ed. Irene Downes (New York: Simon and Schuster, 1957), p. 426.

61. Thomson, *The Musical Scene*, pp. 101–4.

62. The archives of the orchestra contain selected correspondence between general manager Carl J. Vosburgh and Am-Rus Music Corporation, "the exclusive distributors of Russian and Soviet music for North America." In preparation for the fall season, Vosburgh wrote to Am-Rus in mid-August that he was "amazed" at the $500 fee demanded for three performances, adding that with the "additional cost of quite a number of extra players for rehearsals and performances, the cost is practically prohibitive." He further explained that a planned third performance would be a Sunday afternoon broadcast on CBS, for which the network would pay, and that the concert would be given without an audience (it was later agreed that selected patrons could attend). Vosburgh informed Rodzinski that the total costs of mounting the Seventh, including rental fees and the additional musicians, "would very greatly limit us in the performance of other works which you might wish to perform," and he urged dropping the symphony. Eventually the matter was resolved, with a fee of $400 for the two public concerts and broadcast, to which $100 was added when it was decided to do a run-out concert in Detroit on 3 November.

63. Halina Rodzinski, *Our Two Lives* (New York: Charles Scribner's Sons, 1976), p. 218. The concerts opened with Mozart's Symphony no. 40 in G Minor, conducted by Rudolph Ringwall.

64. Herbert Elwell, "'Leningrad Siege' Is Given Ovation," *Cleveland Plain Dealer,* 16 October 1942.

65. Elmore Bacon, "Thrilled Patrons Give Standing Ovation to Symphony Dedicated to Leningrad," *Cleveland News,* 16 October 1942.

66. Minneapolis Symphony Orchestra program book, 27 November 1942, p. 135.

67. As in Ravinia, an intermission was placed between the second and third movements (the concert opened with Brahms's *Tragic* Overture). The review in the *Musical Leader* questioned the wisdom of splitting the symphony; see Paul Hugo Little, "Shostakovich Seventh Featured" (November 1942): 3–4.

68. The *Chicago Times* reported that at lunch the day before his death, Stock discussed the desirability and possibility of making cuts in the long work with Hans Kindler, conductor of the National Symphony in Washington, who performed the Seventh in November. Stock decided that the public should be given the chance to hear the work unabridged several times before any cuts were made (Remi Gassman, "Shostakovich's New Work Needs Pruning," *Chicago Times,* 28 October 1942).

69. Herman Devries, "Music in Review," *Chicago Herald-American,* 28 October 1942.

70. William Leonard, *Journal of Commerce,* 28 October 1942. He returned to the next performance two days later and found it more convincing: "The symphony's faults—its loquacity, its repetitions, its lack of originality—don't disappear with repeated performances. Its merits become more manifest" (30 October 1942).

71. Felix Borowski, "Shostakovich's 7th Called Banal Rather than Heroic," *Chicago Sun,* 28 October 1942; he also preferred the second performance, but concluded "the symphony is too long, and that much of it is repetitious and not always original" ("Shostakovich Seventh Repeated by Hans Lange," 30 October 1942).

72. "Tank Corps," *Time* (26 October 142): 50–51. The Los Angeles Philharmonic does not have a record of Stokowski's performances, which were certainly not regular subscription concerts, but *Time* (26 October 1942), *New York Times* (11 October 1942), and *Musical Leader* (December 1942) reported the performances. *Life* states that it was the "Los Angeles Symphony" that gave the performance (9 November 1942, pp. 99–100).

73. Robert Ward, "Letter from the Army," *Modern Music* 20 (1943), 171–72.

74. *The Philadelphia Orchestra: A Century of Music,* ed. John Ardoin (Philadelphia: Temple University Press, 1999), pp. 231, 243.

75. The Kindler program featured Weber's *Oberon* Overture and Bach's Brandenburg Concerto no. 3 on the first half; when they played the Seventh in Baltimore the following month the concert opened with Kindler's arrangement of the Sinfonia from Bach's Cantata no. 29 and Strauss's *Don Juan.* In the Mitropoulos, "The Star-Spangled Banner" was followed by Gluck's *Alceste* Overture and the first two movements of the symphony, before intermission.

76. The concert opened with Sir Thomas Beecham's arrangement of a suite from Handel's *Il Pastor Fido.*

77. Thompson had made a similar comment earlier, reviewing Toscanini's October performances with the Philharmonic: "Rehearings serve to underline, rather than eradicate, the impression that about this gargantuan opus there is considerably more than a trace of Mossoloff's 'Iron Foundry' of the not completely forgotten recent past. Though the work has no such detailed program, so far as has been made known, the clanging of actual machines and factories may have been in the composer's consciousness when he unleashed the furies of his counterpoint at the climax of the ten-minute crescendo of the first movement. But that crescendo is less stunning on the second and third experience

than when heard for the first time. This commentator must confess that the basic melodic ideas sounded more trite, and either empty or bombastic,"; *New York Sun,* 15 October 1942. See also his article in *Musical America* on the premiere (August 1942): 4.

78. Victor Seroff, *Dmitri Shostakovich: The Life and Background of a Soviet Composer* (New York: Alfred A. Knopf, 1943); for Fuller's review see "Biography, Premature or Overdone," *Modern Music* 21 (1944): 126; the book was also reviewed in *Time* (23 August 1943): 38–40.

79. *The New York Times Magazine,* (7 February 1943): 10, 33.

80. According to Parker, Shostakovich had finished the symphony in Leningrad and planned to take it with him to Kuibyshev "to work out the full orchestration." He was "depressed" at the thought of leaving and "was dissatisfied with the finale." With his wife and "child" (*sic*), he carried the score, which had "never left him" since he started. But as he entered the Douglas plane, some pages flew out of his hand—they were never found and Shostakovich stayed in Leningrad to rewrite the finale. He was "ill" and "anxious." One day he heard sounds from the street, and looked out the window to Nevsky Prospect where he saw a large crowd from which came "a loud, grumbling, menacing, but triumphant sound." The group had captured some German pilots and from the "cry of triumphant anger" Shostakovich took his inspiration for the finale. Parker reports him saying, "It means the triumph of light over dark, of good over evil." (This was a sound bite that the composer stated elsewhere on radio, in interviews, and in writing.) For an account of the chronology of the composition of the symphony and of Shostakovich's leaving Leningrad, see Fay, *Shostakovich: A Life,* pp. 125–26.

81. *Life* (9 November 1942): 99.

82. The recording was made in December 1946 in Kleinhan's Music Hall and lasts 69:29. Hulme gives the date as c. 1950, but the first Buffalo performance was 1946, the date given on the Dante CD reissue (LYS186); see *Shostakovich: A Catalogue,* p. 211.

83. Ronald F. Eyer, "Nation's Symphonic Diet Subject to Survey," *Musical America* (May 1943): 22–23.

84. Ronald F. Eyer, "Our Orchestras vs. the Modern Composer," *Musical America* (June 1943): 7–8.

85. "Native Musicians Gain in Favor," *Musical America* (10 December 1942): 17.

86. See Henry Cowell, "In Time of Bitter War," *Modern Music* 19 (1941): 83–86.

87. *Musical America* (10 February 1943): 200.

88. However, Barber said about his Second Essay that "Although it has no program, one perhaps hears that it is written in war-time"; see Barbara B. Heyman, *Samuel Barber: The Composer and His Music* (Oxford: Oxford University Press, 1992), p. 206.

89. Nicolas Slonimsky and Laura Diane Kuhn, *Music Since 1900,* 6th ed. (New York: Schirmer Reference, 2001), p. 376; see also *Modern Music* 21 (1943): 209f. which compares the Shostakovich Seventh with the Harris Fifth. Harris later encountered problems when the work was performed in 1952 at a festival in Pittsburgh. He conducted his symphony in the Soviet Union in 1958, at which time he met Shostakovich; see Dan Stehman, *Roy Harris: An American Musical Pioneer* (Boston: Twayne Publishers, 1984), pp. 102–3.

90. Slonimsky, *Music Since 1900,* pp. 366–76.

91. Howard Pollack, *Aaron Copland: The Life and Work of an Uncommon Man* (New York: Henry Holt, 1999), p. 360. Goossens commended Copland for the Fanfare, stating that its "title is as original as its music." Compare the descending scale of the infamous "war" theme in the Seventh with the Fanfare; I am grateful to Richard Taruskin for pointing this out to me.

92. Heyman, *Samuel Barber,* pp. 215–31; see also Nathan Broder, *Samuel Barber* (New York: G. Schirmer, 1954), pp. 36–37, 81–87. Barber's 1951 recording and a set of parts discovered in England in 1984, after his death, have allowed the work to live on despite the composer's wishes.

93. Benjamin Suchoff, *Bartók: Concerto for Orchestra: Understanding Bartók's World* (New York: Schirmer Books, 1995), pp. 157–59.

94. Richard Taruskin, *Defining Russia Musically: Historical and Hermeneutical Essays* (Princeton, N.J.: Princeton University Press, 1997), p. 485. Hindemith was also interested in the symphony; see Reinhold Brinkmann, "Reading a Letter," in *Driven into Paradise: The Musical Migration from Nazi German to the United States* (Berkeley, Calif.: University of California Press, 1999), pp. 11–12.

95. "London: Fourth Winter of the Blackout," *Modern Music* 20 (1943): 118.

96. John H. Mueller, *The American Symphony Orchestra: A Social History of Musical Taste* (Bloomington, Ind.: Indiana University Press, 1951), p. 227.

97. *Time* reported: "A large radio public agreed with the Carnegie Hall audience that CBS had not been gypped" (10 April 1944): 70.

98. William J. McNally, "The Shostakovich 'Seventh,'" *Morning Tribune*, 27 November 1942.

99. Elizabeth Wilson, *Shostakovich: A Life Remembered* (Princeton, N.J.: Princeton University Press, 1994), p. 148.

100. *Story of a Friendship: The Letters of Dmitry Shostakovich to Isaak Glikman, 1941–1975,* with a commentary by Isaak Glikman, trans. Anthony Phillips (Ithaca, N.Y.: Cornell University Press, 2001), p. xxxiv. Shostakovich also called attention to the similar technique used in Glinka's *Kamarinskaia* and Grieg's "March of the Dwarfs" from *Peer Gynt* (perhaps he meant *Lyric Suite*, op. 54); see *Dmitri Shostakowitsch: Erfahrungen* (Leipzig: Verlag Phillip Reclam jun., 1983), p. 97. See also Artur Lur'e, "O Shostakoviche (vokrug 7-oi simfonii)" *Novyi zhurnal* 1 (New York) (1943): 367–72; in the German translation by Ernst Kuhn, Arthur Lourié, "Über Schostakowitsch und seine Siebente Symphonie," in *Dmitri Shostakowitsch: Komponist und Zeitzeuge* (Berlin: Verlag Ernst Kuhn, 2000), p. 241.

101. The "March to the Scaffold" and *Gnomenreigen* come from Lur'e's 1943 essay, "O Shostakoviche (vokrug 7-oi simfonii)."

102. The similarity to the aria "Da geh' ich zu Maxim," from Franz Lehár's *Merry Widow,* went unmentioned in all the commentary from the time that I have read, and may have entered the American critical discourse with respect to Bartók's *Concerto for Orchestra*; see Suchoff, *Bartók*, pp. 157–59, and Antal Doráti, "Bartókiana (Some Recollections)," *Tempo* 136 (March 1981): 12–13.

103. *Sun*, 20 July 1942; Watt suggests the following titles for the movements: "Surprise Attack," "Adjustment," "Uncertainty and Tragedy," "Victory."

104. This view is stated most influentially in *Testimony: The Memoirs of Dmitri Shostakovich as Related to and Edited by Solomon Volkov*, trans. Antonina W. Bouis (New York: Harper & Row, 1979). The impact of Volkov's discussion is apparent in most program and liner notes today; for some recent examples see Michael Steinberg, *The Symphony: A Listener's Guide* (New York: Oxford University Press, 1995), pp. 550–58; Jonathan D. Kramer, *Listen to the Music* (New York: Schirmer Books, 1988), pp. 667–72; Douglas A. Lee, *Masterworks of 20th-Century Music: The Modern Repertory of the Symphony Orchestras* (New York: Routledge, 2002), pp. 352–56.

105. Ian MacDonald, *The New Shostakovich* (Boston: Northeastern University Press, 1990).

106. For a discussion of the self-quotation of the "power" motive from *Lady Macbeth*, see Bernd Feuchtner, *Dmitri Shostakowitsch: "Und Kunst geknebelt von der groben Macht"* (Kassel: Bärenreiter, 2002), pp. 144–46; Michael Koball, *Pathos und Groteske: Die deutsche Tradition im symphonischen Schaffen von Dmitri Shostakowitsch* (Berlin: Verlag Ernst Kuhn, 1997), pp. 180–81. For connections to the Eighth Symphony, see David Gow, "Shostakovich's 'War' Symphonies," *Musical Times* 105 (1964): 191–93. Among the more recent additions are Beethoven's Piano Sonata in C Minor, op. 10, no. 1 (Leo Mazel, in *Shostakovich Reconsidered*, ed. Allan B. Ho and Dmitry Feofanov [London: Toccata Press,

1998], p. 483f; and Taruskin, *Defining Russia Musically,* pp. 488–89); Tchaikovsky Symphony no. 6, third movement (Feuchtner, *Shostakowitsch,* p. 144); Nielsen's Fifth Symphony (Roy Blokker, *The Music of Dmitri Shostakovich: The Symphonies* [London: Tantivy Press, 1979], p. 82); the end of the funeral march of Beethoven's *Eroica* (Koball, *Pathos und Groteske,* p. 186); the last movement of Sibelius's Symphony no. 2 and the "invasion" march from Prokofiev's *Alexander Nevsky* (Steinberg, *The Symphony,* pp. 550–58); and the works adduced by Ian MacDonald (see the next note).

107. Ian MacDonald, for example, argues that "the 'war symphony' legend [of the Seventh], along with the composer's programme and movement titles, was, like the Fifth's similar accoutrements, a bodyguard of lies for his deeper intentions" and goes on to give his own reading in which the German qualities of the theme, drawn from *The Merry Widow* and "Deutschland über Alles," combine with the distinctly Russian first theme of Tchaikovsky's Fifth Symphony (*The New Shostakovich,* pp. 159–61). Timothy Jackson hears a "klezmer" dance melody at rehearsal number 45 ("The Composer as Jew," in Ho and Feofanov, *Shostakovich Reconsidered,* pp. 617–19); and see also Koball, *Pathos und Groteske,* p. 179.

108. Review of *Facsimile* in *Notes* 50 (December 1993): 761.

PART II
ESSAYS

Shostakovich as Industrial Saboteur:

Observations on *The Bolt*

SIMON MORRISON

Long concealed by the industrial haze of the Soviet cultural revolution, Shostakovich's second ballet, *The Bolt*, merits study for its paradoxical combination of popular and serious music and dance—its mapping, in other words, of Komsomol medleys, Red Army marches, circus acrobatics, and vaudeville antics onto traditional balletic structures. Over the course of the three long acts, the twenty-five-year-old composer combined what the eminent historian Katerina Clark calls the "periphery" and "center" of Soviet musical culture.[1] In *The Bolt*, as in his foxtrot-laden first ballet, *The Golden Age* (1930), Shostakovich brought together the content of low art and forms of high art. From our post-Soviet vantage point, his industrial ballet seems to have been an ingenious experiment, a work that fused the "iconoclastic" and "icon-creating" facets of proletarian drama.[2]

Shostakovich's contemporaries, however, held their applause. In fact, *The Bolt* raised the ire of the press, even though the ballet appears to have been scaled down during the rehearsal period to avoid controversy.[3] Its first performance on 8 April 1931, at the Leningrad State Academic Theatre of Opera and Ballet, was also its last. Critics argued that while the subject matter was topical—industrial sabotage and the first Five-Year Plan—its realization was superficial and irreverent, a slap in the face of the Soviet cause. Melodrama became burlesque, with the "positive" (proletarian) and "negative" (bourgeois) characters cast in the same grotesque light. They less resembled flesh-and-blood participants in a class struggle than poster boards. The ballet critic for *The Worker and the Theatre* complained:

The intrigue is confined to five minutes of havoc in the third act, while the first two acts live independent lives, repeating the long-familiar devices of ballet divertissements. There is a gym class, a choreographic interlude about the opening of a workshop, and an episode, bearing absolutely no relationship to the story line, based on grotesque pantomimic movement, specifically the dances of negative characters. There is also an interlude spurred by a get-together in a club. Thus, from the perspective of effective drama, all the devices of the old ballet remain. When this kind of material falls into the hands of the stage director [Fyodor Lopukhov (1886–1973)], he not only evinces his complete lack of understanding of the material, specifically the atmosphere of a factory, but also quite clearly demonstrates his political non-preparedness for the creation of a Soviet spectacle.[4]

This tendentious assessment was recapitulated by a critic for the newspaper *Shift Change* and, with less fervor, critics for the morning edition of *Red Newspaper* and *Leningrad Pravda*. The first writer scorned the "notorious 'dancification' (*otantsovyvanie*) of industrial processes,"[5] the second the "provincial decorative design of the last act,"[6] and the third the "blatant vulgarity and banality" of the music-dance interaction.[7] Technical details in the reviews are few and far between, focusing on the links between Shostakovich's score and the hurdy-gurdy-like sounds of music hall spectacles. The quoted writers ignored, rather than overlooked, the bald fact that *The Bolt* was conceived as a satire, a caricature of proletarian dramaturgy, notably the factory parables staged by the Theatre of Worker Youth in the late 1920s.[8]

The press likewise suppressed comment on the self-consciousness of the ballet, a self-consciousness embodied in a plot that was "ripped from the headlines." Manashir Iakubov, the editor of the piano score of *The Bolt,* comments, "In 1930 [Russia] was shaken by a much-publicized trial of industrial saboteurs, a trial which became known as the 'Industrial Party Trial.'"[9] The plot of *The Bolt,* fittingly, concerns a drunken lout, Lazy Idler (*Len'ka Gul'ba*), who upon being sacked from his factory post seeks revenge on his employers by convincing a hapless sidekick, Goshka, to hoist an impossibly large bolt into one of the workshop lathes.[10] The scheme succeeds: the lathe short-circuits. Lazy points the finger of blame at an upstanding member of a team of shock workers, Boris, but the guilt-ridden Goshka confesses to his role in the crime. Lazy is captured by the factory guards, this prompting a celebration among the foremen and laborers, who cheerfully return to their mind-numbingly repetitive posts on the production line. In discussing the story line, Iakubov asserts that the ballet's scenarist, the civil war veteran and second Moscow Art Theatre (MKhAT-2) director, Viktor Smirnov, was a literary hack. Iakubov clarifies that, despite many rewrites, the "simplicity of the plot and the professional incompetence of its author" remained "striking."[11] The prolific dance historian Vera Krasovskaia seconds this view, pointing out that Smirnov, after penning his "vacuous anecdote" about industrial sabotage, "immediately dropped out of contemporary critics'—and then ballet historians'—field of view."[12] It should be noted, however, that the triteness of the plot complemented rather than contradicted the music and dance. Neither Shostakovich nor his choreographer, Lopukhov, sought to repair the short-circuited dramatic apparatus. Each feature of the ballet's interdisciplinary totality, in effect, undermined the precepts of theatrical verisimilitude.

In what follows, I will explore the infrastructure of *The Bolt* with the dual aims of understanding how the work came into being and understanding the target of its satire. Did Shostakovich sabotage his own ballet by representing the utopianism of Soviet industrial policy in an anti-utopian guise? Did he aspire to highlight flaws in other Communist Party–line, proletarian stage works? Or was the ballet unwittingly misconceived, an ill-timed and ill-fated reading of the volatile cultural climate of early 1930s Russia?

Shostakovich wrote the music of *The Bolt* at *udarnik*—"shock worker"—pace. Involved at the time in multiple projects for stage and screen, he freely recycled and retooled his scores to meet simultaneous deadlines and to satisfy his own irrationally exuberant production quotas. His comparative inexperience with ballet obliged him to seek the advice of his collaborators on *The Bolt*. Thus, irrespective of his frenetic compositional method, its music cannot be properly "heard" without consideration of its interaction with the décor and dance. The décor, a multilevel, multipurpose assemblage by the Constructivist wife-and-husband team Tatiana Bruni (1902–2001) and Georgii Korshikov (1899–1944), did not survive the 1931 staging; Nancy Van Norman Baer claims that *The Bolt* "was reconstructed in Leningrad in 1979 with costumes and sets remade after the original under Bruni's supervision."[13] Yet although many of the visuals were remade, the ballet was not actually restaged, as Baer seems to imply.[14] Unlike Bruni's designs, Lopukhov's choreography is unrecoverable; it does not survive in notated form, was not photographed in performance, and was not taught to subsequent generations of dancers. To paraphrase the British dance and theater historian Lesley-Anne Sayers, to study Lopukhov's contribution to *The Bolt* is to face the "presence" of this contribution's "absence."[15] My evaluation of the décor-dance-music relationship, and the satiric thrust of this relationship, is thus provisional.

1. Décor and Dance

To begin with, some historical context. *The Bolt* was not the first dance-based work of the period to be based on industrial themes, nor was it the first to interrogate the relationship between man and machine. In 1921, the Futurist artist El Lissitzsky (1890–1941) sketched an electronic mechanism for a hypothetical choreographed version of the opera *Victory Over the Sun* (1913). Joachim Noller comments that the sketch anticipated the invention of "a mechanical ballet," one that would replace the singers of the fantastic twice-performed opera with tin and wire robots, whose physical gestures would be powered by electric currents of various voltages.[16] In 1922, the Moscow choreographer Nikolai Foregger (1892–1939) created his oft-discussed *Dance of the Machines,* whose performers mimicked "the movements of a flywheel gyrating around an immovable axis."[17] Elizabeth Souritz adds that a subsequent variation required male and female dancers "to imitate a train—by swaying, stamping their feet against the floor, and banging sheets of metal together, even by swinging burning cigarettes in the air so that sparks flew all over as if from a locomotive's smokestack." Yet another variation entailed imitating the turning over of "a transmission" and the revolving of "a conveyer belt." The dancers also "created an image of hammers of various sizes—the smallest, by using their fists, and the largest, by lifting and lowering a dancer held upside down."[18]

The 1927 ballet *Le Pas d'acier* (*The Steel Step*), performed in Paris by the Ballets Russes and inspired by Foregger's machine dances, represents the most provocative artistic treatment of industrial themes in the modern canon.[19] The music was composed by Sergei Prokofiev (1891–1953), the set designed by the Constructivist artist Georgii Iakulov (1884-1928), and the choreography developed (with limited participation by the composer and set designer) by Leonid Massine (1895–1979). *Le Pas d'acier* was a *succès de scandale* with the critics and the public, and gained the attention of political commentators, who viewed the ballet as a parable about the pitfalls of factory life, notably Soviet factory life. Humans neither benefited from their machines nor even controlled them; they were instead imprisoned by them.

Though most of Prokofiev's score was performed by the Ballets Russes, most of Iakulov's interactive set—operated by the dancers in the finale—was not built. This aspect of the ballet is perhaps best described as hypothetical, an example of paper architecture whose most daring aspects did not make the transfer from study to stage. In her exceptionally thorough research on this ballet, Sayers reveals that the original drawings of the set and the lone black-and-white photograph of the model indicate that Iakulov did not intend to critique the cause of industrialization but to ennoble it.[20] His conception of *Le Pas d'acier,* in short, differed from its realization. The original drawings, Sayers observes, depict man and machine lifting and pulling in harmony, and call for dazzling smoke and lighting effects, a puffing steam engine, and flashing advertisements. The set, she adds, would also have included self-conscious references to its own status as part of a ballet: the light poles would have "stood" in third and fifth position and mobile discs would have assumed the guise of human faces.

Le Pas d'acier was not staged in the Soviet Union. Noting the positive reception of the ballet in "decadent" Paris, proletarian organizations ridiculed the work for its anti-proletarian sentiments. Iakulov, a citizen of Soviet Armenia, died too young to suffer the abuse, and his reputation, burnished by his involvement in the 1924 design contest for the Lenin Mausoleum, remained unsullied. Since he was regarded as a leading force in the Constructivist movement, it stands to reason that Bruni knew of his work on *Le Pas d'acier*—although, admittedly, I have not found concrete evidence to this effect. Bruni's décor for *The Bolt,* featuring a factory workshop, a village chapel, and a factory lounge, is a playful, funhouse-mirror reflection of Iakulov's décor for *Le Pas d'acier,* which offsets images of down-at-the-heels peasants in the countryside with images of multitasking in the factory. The original scenarios of both ballets, moreover, envisioned movement in silhouette behind gauze. The Soviet art historian Grigorii Levitin describes Bruni's décor for *The Bolt* as follows:

> The factory was conceived as a generalization, almost an abstraction: three rows of windows, one atop the next. A lifting crane was plainly sketched in black against the white backdrop. Closer to the wings were three small squares, where the "machine dances" would have been performed. [. . .]
>
> If the "factory" scene was conceived, in effect, graphically, the "village" was conceived with features from landscape portraits placed "*sur la pointe.*" Huts and plainly sketched birch trees could be seen on three "branches" in the depths of the stage. On the stage stood a chapel with a round plank onion dome. The chapel's walls were fortified by taut ropes which slackened in the drinking scene in a way that made the chapel move like an accordion. The sides of the stage moved in tandem. The entire décor danced.

The last act—the "Scene in the Club"—was conceived by the artists [Bruni and her husband] as a gigantic panorama of the achievements of the Soviet Union. Flats painted in bright primary colors framed a large model of Volkhovstroi with a "natural" dam. Against this backdrop—or exhibition—agit-brigades performed a concert divertissement.[21]

In a glasnost-era interview about the 1931 production, Bruni embellished this description somewhat, remarking that the Act 1 factory workshop housed a furnace, and that one of the workers repeatedly pushed a trolley back and forth across the stage. This trolley concealed a spotlight whose beam was reflected by mirrors across the white backdrop. In Act 2, the chapel "danced," but so too did the dilapidated huts and sheds that decorated the three curved tiers of the backdrop. The mural of Act 3, moreover, featured actual running water. For the interview, Bruni supplied a sketch of the dancing chapel, with its cross swinging to the left side and the dome beneath it swinging to the right. The ballet's villain, a vodka bottle balanced on an outstretched hand, enjoys the show. In the distance, the trees and huts lean helter-skelter.[22]

These details, while colorful, pale compared to Bruni's remarks on the political context of the staging. Though her memory may have faded or, in the heyday of glasnost, become malleable, her comments both enrich the historical record of *The Bolt* and raise complex questions about the ontological status of its décor, dance, and music. The title of her interview translates as "On Ballet, with Undying Love"; the section of the interview under discussion bears the subheading "This Is How the Lie Began":

The pity is, we were too late with *The Bolt*. Boundlessly passionate about Lopukhov and his poster-board spectacle, we did not notice that at this time art had veered sharply to the side of realism. The "terrible" words "Soc[ialist] Realism" appeared. [. . .]

And herein begins the lie. The lie that the spectacle, according to the official record, failed. At the time, the dress rehearsals were open to the public at large. The theater seemed overcrowded. As soon as the curtain opened, applause rang out; when the factory started to move, it transformed into an ovation that did not let up until the end of the spectacle. The dancing chapel and individual costumes delighted the public. I swear by all that is sacred this took place. The catcalling of those in opposition (manifest philistinism!) was drowned out by the applause.

The spectacle was withdrawn. . . . Not one drawing was left to me. Some of them [the collection of drawings] were destroyed in the theater by particularly zealous "Soc[ialist] Realists." The majority of the costumes are in the [St. Petersburg] Theatre Museum. I made the drawing of the Act 1 décor (by this time after Korshikov's death) for the A. A. Bakhrushin Museum. Some costumes might also be there. We did not make drawings of the décor, only a model.[23]

Socialist Realism was not codified as the official artistic doctrine of the Soviet Union until 1932, thus Bruni's emphasis on the term is somewhat anachronistic. Nonetheless, Bruni's gloss on the hair-raising atmosphere surrounding the staging of the ballet demonstrates that political trouble was brewing for iconoclastic artists. In the interview, she twice mentions that some of her designs for *The Bolt* were destroyed when the work was withdrawn; the editor of the journal in question embellishes the point, claiming that "almost all" of them were destroyed.[24] These claims explain why two of the images I have seen are double-dated 1931 and 1979; the rest are undated but bear, with the exceptions of the satiric poster-board images, similar color schemes and poses. Bruni re-created them—albeit with a much advanced artistic technique—for posterity's sake. The images, then, are idealized reimaginings, and in this respect have features in common with the ballet's scenario and music, themselves beneficiaries of revision and renewal.

Bruni's artwork for *The Bolt* is housed in the Russian Museum and the Museum of Theatre and Music in St. Petersburg, the Bakhrushin Theatre Museum in Moscow, and several private collections, most notably that belonging to Nina and Nikita Lobanov-Rostovsky. Her reimagined décor for Act 1 (Figure 1), which was in fact her husband's conception, is much richer in detail than the 1931 original described by Levitin in his 1986 monograph. Beyond simple black-on-white graphics, the re-creation offers an ingenious glasnost-era paraphrase of Constructivist aesthetics, which center on the "de-aestheticization" of stage design through the transplantation and transformation of artistic "images" into actual "objects."[25]

The backdrop contains the base of a pyramid, with two characters outfitted in red and black sitting atop the entrance in the guise of sphinxes, a visual hint that the sketch harbors a Constructivist riddle. On the left-hand side, six characters form the upper and lower halves of pistons. The lower three figures push and pull against crimson cords (or giant rubber bands), these seeming to symbolize kinetic forces. On the right-hand side, five additional characters form a ladder or, as Levitin claims, the base of a crane. Further study of the sketch indicates, however, that the figures

Figure 1. Tatiana Bruni, Act 1 décor for *The Bolt,* 1979, based on Georgii Korshikov's 1931 original. Courtesy of Bakhrushin Museum, Moscow.

are not full-size humans, but miniature ones. They denote electronic devices: transistors, spark plugs, maybe even vacuum tubes. From this vantage point, the backdrop becomes an angled, upright circuit board, and the crimson cords electrical cables. The miniature humans are involved in the production of electricity—the machine-age, nonhuman equivalent of kilocalories. This observation in turn intimates that the various squares, triangles, and octagons in the drawing may be symbols for full-size physical gestures, the circuit board an abstraction of geometric graphemes, the shapes that the visionary Soviet choreographer Aleksandr Larionov, a colleague of Bruni's, used to notate modern dances.[26] In this reading, the sketch becomes a fantastic depiction of a movement notation (choreological) laboratory, one in which, perhaps, *bras* and *pas* patterns are mixed and matched in the test tubes of the human body. Machine dances are denoted by geometric shapes, with each line and angle designating a sequence of gestures. The pyramid-like center of the sketch, moreover, makes clever reference to Larionov's fascination with "Egyptian pictograms."[27]

Here one solves the riddle of the sketch: for a choreographic "image" to become an "object," dancers should not produce movement patterns;

rather, movement patterns should produce dancers. The factory work-shop literally embodies the graphic signs, the choreographic notation for the performance it hosts. The "five-minute" intrigue that takes place within its walls is literally etched into those walls. Bruni wrote the word "Caution!" (*Ostorozhno!*) in jagged, electric-bolt-sized letters in the top left-hand corner of her sketch. She informs us, perhaps, that the factory workshop in *The Bolt* denotes an unstable reality, a malleable space in which image and object, signifier and signified pass into each other. The ballet depicts a factory that depicts ballets.

As *The Bolt* was assembled and reassembled (by Lopukhov and Shostakovich in 1931, and by Bruni in the interregnum between 1931 and 1979), the "positive" and "negative" characters took on the guises of Red and White Russians, Komsomol members and kulaks, Bolsheviks and Mensheviks. Their costumes, moreover, were mixed and matched, like those of the paper dolls and department store mannequins that they—in the opinion of some—resembled. The critic for *Shift Change*, one of the "Socialist Realists" derided by Bruni, asserted that the costumes were incorrect, with the Komsomol members outfitted in drab gray suits and dresses, and the Red Army Cavalry in hussar outfits.[28] The same writer also carped about a disconnect between the physical appearance of the principals and their description in the program—that Olga, a sentimental, benevolent lady is the director of a Komsomol brigade could only be gleaned from the cast list, as could the identity of the team of shock workers. The Soviet airmen of Act 3 looked like vaudeville extras.

Bruni's reimagined 1979 costume drawings include images of a textile worker, a participant in the factory phys-ed activities, slim and trim Olga (Figure 2), and the plump, excessively muscular girlfriend of the impudent, foxtrot-whistling factory clerk Kozelkov (Figure 3). (Either she gained weight between 1931 and 1979 or else Kozelkov had two girlfriends, since another, earlier image puts her in high heels, beret, and a skintight dress.)[29] Lazy's female companion, whom Bruni calls a "prostitute," is also ample, but distinguished from Kozelkov's by galoshes, headband, a dirty handprint on her midriff, and scraped knees. Her splayed, hands-on-hips posture contrasts markedly with that of the Act 3 image of a female Komsomol worker hanging from latticework (or rope ladder), hypothetically gesturing to those on the ground below. Two other images, tagged "American fleet" and "Japanese fleet" (Figures 4 and 5), are re-creations of figures from the amateur concert from Act 1 (as Bruni indicates in her reminiscences) or Act 3 (as Iakubov indicates in his edition of the piano score). The first features a morbidly obese, missile- (rather than cigar-) puffing American capitalist, the second a Japanese officer with fanglike teeth, skeletal fingers, and shoulder flashes of outsized bayonets. These figures were created for the episode that lampooned an actual historical event: the naval disarmament talks between the United States, Japan, and two other nations—all "enemies" of the Soviet cause—in 1922. They are not actual characters in the ballet, but sandwich boards, akin to the wooden placards of strongmen and glamour girls that one finds at Coney Island or Brighton Beach. They were worn in the performance by two dancers whose faces were visible through holes in the top and whose torsos swayed to and fro behind white tulle skirts depicting bobbing South Pacific waves. A tenth drawing of a whip-cracking drayman, a cantankerous relic of pre-revolutionary Russia, was conceived for the amateur concert of Act 3; an eleventh, featuring a spectacled bureaucrat with legs made out of bundled stacks of paper, was intended for the amateur concert of Act 1. The bureaucrat was joined onstage by another buffo figure, the tuxedo-clad Bungler (*Golovotiap*).[30]

Of the available 1931 photographs of the primary and secondary characters, four match descriptions in the scenario, while a fifth does not.[31] Photograph one shows Leonid Leontev (1885–1945) in the role of the drunken Lazy. Arms clasped around his chest, a vacant expression on his sullen, wasted face, he hunches slightly forward, prevented from falling over by his outsized galoshes, which rise up over his knees, fastening him in place. Photograph two shows either Z. Vasileva or N. Bazarova (both dancers are named in the sources) in the trouser role of Lazy's juvenile sidekick Goshka, whose name recalls that of Grishka, the gullible and ultimately repentant villain in Nikolai Rimsky-Korsakov's opera *The Legend of the Invisible City of Kitezh and the Maiden Fevroniia* (1904), but whose demeanor suggests—at least for those of English descent—Charles Dickens's Artful Dodger. The implication here is that Goshka, a caricature, brings to mind other caricatures, just like the opening music of *The Bolt*, a mock (polonaise-derived) fanfare, brings to mind another mock (polonaise-derived) fanfare, that at the beginning of Pyotr Tchaikovsky's Fourth Symphony (1878). Likewise, the beginning of the Act 3 "Dance of the Drayman," a representation of a beaten-down horse-cart driver, brings to mind "Bydlo" from Modest Musorgsky's *Pictures at an Exhibition* (1874), a representation of a beaten-down oxcart driver. The distractingly *outré* quality of these references is one of the ways in which *The Bolt* defines the grotesque.[32]

Photograph three shows the shock worker Boris wooing coquettish, curvaceous Olga, and photograph four shows the Komsomol members in their neutral garb, a lone Soviet airman standing behind them. Photograph five defies both description and logic. It features a short male (or female in trouser role) with sculpted, slicked-down coiffure, posed like a toreador with a bemused expression on his face. His costume includes a white bow tie and black (vinyl-textured) waistcoat, the lapels emblazoned with sunbeams. His right arm curls around a lance bearing, at the top, a swastika and what seems to be a boxing glove. The role occupied by this figure in the ballet is ambiguous: he may have been featured in the Act 3 amateur concert, with its spoofs of fascists, NEP-men, capitalists, and counterrevolutionaries.[33] He may also be the aforementioned Bungler, though Bruni's drawing of this Chaplinesque character has him holding a cane and crowbar rather than a swastika and boxing glove. Given that Lopukhov sometimes included quick-change artists in his ballets, the character may have occupied two or more roles, his costume multilayered. The swastika, the most striking feature of the photograph, is also the most beguiling, since it is right-handed (assuming that the photograph has not been printed in reverse) rather than left-handed, the opposite of the emblem aligned with the Nazi Party after 1920. Right-handed, the swastika suggests associations with the Finnish Air Force, whose planes displayed it in this way during the First World War, or with "*völkisch*" nationalism in the nineteenth century.[34] Mounted at the end of a lance, it resembles an oversized key. Finally, both the form and content of the photograph establish a link between *The Bolt* and Shostakovich's first ballet, *The Golden Age,* whose Western capitalist villain, the rival of a visiting Soviet soccer team's captain for the hand of a showgirl, goes by a name that no self-respecting Soviet lass would place on her dance card: "Fascist." The swastika would have been more at home in this ballet than in *The Bolt,* since it has historically been used by sports teams, including, oddly enough, a girls' hockey club in Edmonton, Alberta, Canada in 1916.[35] The role of "Fascist" was performed by Leonid Lavrovsky (1905–67), who bears no likeness to the figure in the photograph from *The Bolt*.

2. Scenario and Music

The swastika-bearing figure, like most of the other incidental figures in the ballet, is not listed in the piano and orchestral scores.[36] This fact is less odd than it might appear, since the "five-minute" intrigue of the ballet was merely a hub around which various comic vignettes were arranged and rearranged. The mutability seems to have been as much a part of the ballet's genesis as it was its performance. The assembling and reassembling of *The Bolt,* in other words, was the true drama, insofar as it reflected

Figure 2. Tatiana Bruni, 1931/1979 drawing of Olga for *The Bolt*.

Figure 3. Tatiana Bruni, 1931/1979 drawing of Kozelkov's girlfriend for *The Bolt*.

Figure 4. Tatiana Bruni, 1931/1979 drawing of an American Capitalist for *The Bolt,* featured in the Act 1 (?) skit about naval disarmament talks.

Figure 5. Tatiana Bruni, 1931/1979 drawing of a Japanese officer for *The Bolt,* featured in the Act 1 (?) skit about naval disarmament talks.

the instability of Soviet culture, the continuous revolution taking place within the domains of music, dance, and theater. Just as lower-level bureaucrats supplanted upper-level ones in the government ministries, so too did fringe cultural groups supplant the artistic establishment. The perverse logic of this process was its guaranteed self-replication.[37] Each institutional upheaval begat another; the "Red Wheel" (to refer to the subtitle of Aleksandr Solzhenitsyn's first book on the revolution) kept turning.

Fittingly, the process of creating *The Bolt* bore its own circular logic; the musical and visual material routinely changed while basically staying the same. Shostakovich's two summaries of the scenario, one predating the premiere, the other postdating it, add a generous dose of slapstick to the historical record. His first summary comes from a 10 February 1931 letter to the musicologist Ivan Sollertinsky (1902–44), a close friend. It refers to an early draft of the scenario, which Shostakovich received at the time he accepted the commission from the State Academic Theatre to write the music:

> Comrade Smirnov read to me his story for the ballet *At the New Machine*. The content is very topical. There was a machine, then it broke down (the problem of wear and tear). Then it was mended (the problem of depreciation), and they also bought a new one. Everyone then dances round the new machine. Apotheosis. The whole thing takes three acts.[38]

Shostakovich's second, longer summary comes from a 24 August 1934 letter to another friend, Levon Atovmian (1901–73):

> *1st scene*. The workers come to the factory. They do their morning exercises. Among them is Lazy Idler, drunk from yesterday's hang-over.
>
> *2nd scene*. A celebration of amateur talent on the occasion of the opening of a new workshop. Lazy Idler and his cronies (Ivan Corkscrew and Fyodor Beer) behave like hooligans. They are evicted.
>
> *3rd scene*. The workshop operates.
>
> *4th scene*. Day off. Suburban village. The priest dances. The Komsomol members dance. The old women dance. Drunk, Lazy Idler cavorts with the girls. He wants to continue into tomorrow. To this end he incites an irresponsible lad to lodge a bolt into a

machine. Then the factory will stop, and he can continue cavorting. This is overheard by Gusev, a Komsomol member, who wishes to expose the conspiracy. Lazy kills Gusev.

5th scene. The lad lodges the bolt. Gusev (revived) exposes him and Lazy Idler. They are arrested. General rejoicing. Dances.

Apotheosis.

End.[39]

Beyond sarcastically condemning Smirnov's dramatic skills, these summaries present two subtle ironies. *The Bolt* was performed once in 1931, yet even after it was consigned to the scrap heap of agitprop, the scenario continued to evolve. Shostakovich's letter to Atovmian reduces a ballet of seven scenes (three acts) into one of five scenes. The Komsomol worker Boris is referred to as Gusev, after Pyotr Gusev (1904–87), the dancer cast in the role of the hero before the ballet was staged, but not in the staging itself. (This point is clarified below.) His name may have stuck in the composer's mind because he, like his onstage partner Tatiana Vecheslava (1910–91), "found it difficult to assimilate the music of the ballet; it was full of complex harmony which acquired grotesque overtones."[40] These "grotesque overtones" may have been enhanced because the dancers consciously bungled their steps.

The St. Petersburg division of the Russian State Archive of Literature and Art contains two of Smirnov's draft scenarios.[41] These are undated, but indicate, based on the level of visual and choreographic detail within them, a late stage in the creative process. For this reason, perhaps, they are nowhere near as trite as Shostakovich asserts in his letters. In fact, the level of musical and choreographic information within them evinces both Shostakovich's and Lopukhov's influence on Smirnov.

The principal difference between drafts 1 and 2 concerns the addition of a preface, in Smirnov's words, describing the inspiration he received for the ballet from a visit to the club of the Red Hercules factory, which included a peculiar display of the objects that had been mangled in the machines, and a banner proclaiming the factory administration's intolerance for acts of sabotage. The plotting and carrying out of one of these incidents became the source of Smirnov's scenario, which he initially sought to flesh out with scenes from peasant life (in the style, perhaps, of *Le Pas d'acier*), but avoided doing so in favor of a dramatization of the interaction of factory and village life. Smirnov's preface includes a polemic about the necessity of developing new choreographic set pieces based on the dynamics of labor, and for the transfer of these set pieces from the theater into public spaces. This second proposal accords with the aesthetic platform of the Theatre of Worker Youth.

The two drafts contain three acts, the last partitioned into two scenes, with a five-minute pause allowing for a change of décor. Act 1 of both drafts shows the workshop being inspected, retooled, and then triumphantly restarted. Komsomol members decorate the walls with murals attesting to the achievements of socialist labor throughout Russia. The hooligans arrive late, their heads throbbing from a few too many the night before. Unable to work, they leave their posts to share a bottle, thus causing lathes to jam and (in draft 2) the chief engineer to report them for dereliction of duty. The Komsomol leader, Petka, spars with the ringleader, but despite the threat of physical harm, the encounter comes to naught. The hooligans are replaced at their posts, and the tempo of the workshop hastens as the curtain falls. The names of the ensemble and solo pieces are almost identical in the two drafts, though in the latter the words *mime* and *pantomime* are replaced with the word *dance*. More significant, perhaps, is the renaming of the two episodes that represent the activity of the workshop: the two "dances of man and machine" in draft 1 become "machine dances" in draft 2. Since the décor did not feature actual machines, the change in the description suggests that, during the creative process, the dancers went from being workers *at* machines to workers *as* machines. The dancers, in other words, came to imitate the mechanics of pistons and pulleys. In both drafts, Smirnov mentions that "compared with all of the devices" in the factory, the workers would appear "miniscule." Based on the reviews, this visual effect does not appear to have been part of the actual staging of the ballet.

Act 2 takes place in a rustic village, with a wooden church, tavern, and scattered log huts. Bored to tears, the priest procrastinates by hopping about to the sound of accordions played in the distance by Komsomol members. The music attracts the parishioners, who also begin to dance, though they are soon led into church by the priest (who uses his incense burner like a ball and chain) and his hapless bell ringer. During the episode, the movements of the parishioners modulate from leaden shuffling to a "shuffle-shuffle-hop-kick-kick" pattern and back again. Lopukhov may well have supplied this pattern to Smirnov. Kozelkov, the pretentious factory clerk, tries to impress the Komsomol members with a dance he learned in the city, but becomes, with his female friends, an object of their mockery. During the service, the hooligans stumble out of the tavern into the church square, where they hatch their plan to sabotage the factory, the aim being to secure a day off on Holy Trinity. Petka chances upon the group while making his way to work. In draft 1 of the scenario, he guesses the substance of the hooligans' conversation; in draft 2, he does not. The outcome is the same in both instances: the hooligans, suspecting Petka of eavesdropping, pounce on him and beat him senseless. As the church service concludes, the hooligans leave him lying unconscious behind a log. Emerging from the church, the priest sees one of the hooligans holding a bolt and deduces that he and his cohorts intend to sabotage the factory. He offers them his blessing. Petka staggers up and gestures for help to a passing guard. The guard dismisses him as a vagrant.

Act 3, scene 1 is almost identical in both drafts. The action takes place in shadow behind a factory window. Through the glass, we see a young lad steal into the workshop and lodge the bolt into a lathe; Petka dashes in to retrieve the object, but upon doing so finds that he has been locked inside by the hooligans, who, stifling their laughter, summon the factory guards. Petka is handcuffed and led away. Dismayed, Tania curses the hooligans for their treachery. The scene changes to show the factory club and the arrival of members of the Red Army on leave. Musicians from the club orchestra also appear, this providing the pretext for the performance of a set of satiric dances. In draft 1 of the scenario, Smirnov indicates that the dances mock naval peace talks as well as such ne'er-do-well pre-revolutionary characters as a Conformist, Intelligentsia Lady, Textile Workers, Drayman, Capitalist, Bureaucrat, and Blacksmith. In draft 2, however, these dances are replaced by five Red Army dances: an "Aviators' dance," "Artillerymen's dance," "Cavalrymen's dance," "Seamen's dance," and a general number that "draws in all of the youth." The remainder of the scene is the same in both drafts: the hooligans, drunk again, pick a fight with physical trainers. The latter soon depart, leaving the hooligans to squabble among themselves. The ringleader mistakenly strikes a sharp blow on the head of his accomplice in crime. Upon coming to his senses, the young lad confesses to his role in the sabotage, leading to the detention of the ringleader, Petka's liberation, his joyful reunion with Tania, and the apotheosis. This is the section in draft 1 where the Red Army divisions perform their concert; in draft 2, which introduces the Red Army earlier, the apotheosis features a mass round dance and the unfurling of banners reading "Protect the Machines" and "Saboteurs Go Home." More concise than draft 1, draft 2 omits the Conformist, Intelligentsia Lady, and the other comic figures while also abridging the finale. These comic figures, Bruni claims, eventually became part of Act 1.

The differences between the first and second drafts of the scenario pale in comparison to those between the second draft and the scenario included in Iakubov's 1996 edition of the piano score. The latter was not Smirnov's final version, that is to say, the version printed in the program for the 8 April 1931 premiere. Iakubov instead chose to compile his scenario from a wide variety of documents. In the "Commentary" to his edition, he notes that "the autographs and authorized manuscripts of the ballet score" housed in the Russian State Archive of Literature and Art in Moscow and the Glinka State Museum of Musical Culture neither accord with "the synopsis of the ballet set out in the booklet issued for the premiere" nor with "the list of numbers in the ballet" supplied in a 1965 "notational and bibliographic guide" to Shostakovich's music.[42] Iakubov also identifies differences between the program, the manuscript of the eight-part suite of the ballet housed in the Composers' Union library in Moscow, and the orchestral and piano scores edited by Sergei Sapozhnikov, who based them on materials housed in two St. Petersburg collections.[43] From this account, it emerges that Iakubov did not himself consult all of the source materials on the ballet: in one instance, he relied on a 1965 handbook, and in another on a later edition of the score. He acknowledges, in fact, that he transferred the climactic episode, "The Revelation of the Conspiracy (the Young Lad's Narrative)" from the sixth to the seventh scene of Act 3 in accord with Sapozhnikov, who "relied on the original version of the libretto preserved in the V[iktor] F[yodorovich] Smirnov family archive."[44] To the best of my knowledge, there is no such archive in St. Petersburg. The archive in question appears to be the *fond* in the Russian State Archive of Literature and Art that contains the two draft libretti described above. Neither of these documents, however, contains an episode titled "The Revelation of the Conspiracy (the Young Lad's Narrative)." The title is a slight variation of that provided in the actual program of the 1931 premiere.

Comparison of the 1931 program with the cast list and scenario compiled by Iakubov for his edition of the piano score reveal four discrepancies and one striking correspondence.[45] The edition includes a Chief Engineer, Red Army Soldier, and Red Army Sailor that the cast list does not include. Iakubov renames "The Georgian" of Act 2 "The Caucasian," a geographic and demographic shift to the north. The correspondence between the 1931 cast list and the edition concerns the renaming of the hero and heroine from Petka and Tania to Olga and Boris. According to Bruni, Lopukhov named the characters in his ballet after the dancers who performed their roles.[46] The available evidence indicates that the roles of the original hero and heroine, Petka and Tania, were assigned to Pyotr Gusev (whom Shostakovich mentions in his 1934 letter to Atovmian) and Tatiana Vecheslava. Before *The Bolt* received its premiere, however, these two dancers were replaced by Boris Shavrov and Olga Mungalova (1905–42);

the hero and heroine, accordingly, became Boris and Olga. Vecheslava ended up dancing a minor role in the ballet; Gusev, who remained the hero until late in the rehearsal process, dropped out of the ballet altogether.[47]

The 1931 scenario is cast in three acts of seven scenes, not the three acts of four scenes found in the two drafts. Iakubov's version of the scenario is likewise cast in three acts of seven scenes, but deviates in large and small ways from the 1931 scenario. The most important alteration concerns the conclusion of scene 2 and scene 4. In the 1931 scenario, the passages in question are tagged "Start-up of the workshop" and "The workshop operating: rhythmic scenes." In the edition, they are tagged "Starting-up of the workshop (dance of the machines—I)" and "Operation of the workshop (dance of the machines—II)." Though the music for the "dances of the machines" survives in the archives, the dances do not appear to have been staged. Supporting evidence for this assertion comes from Bruni, who recalled that the dances "were withdrawn from the first dress rehearsal" to accommodate ideological requirements.[48]

Two other discrepancies between the 1931 scenario and Iakubov's edition merit commentary. First, the scenario for Act 2 includes choreographic information that is absent from the edition: the Komsomol members, playing hooky from church, amuse themselves by dancing a quadrille, the aristocratic forerunner of the rural square dance. (In his music for this number, Shostakovich furnishes entrance cues for four couples and a concluding gallop.) Second, in the 1931 scenario for Act 3, the happy ending is celebrated by a raucous concert featuring Red Army soldiers and then the full complement of factory workers. In Iakubov's edition, however, this concert frames, rather than caps, the resolution of the plot. Red Army officers meet with Komsomol members in the factory club, spurring the Komsomol members to mount an agitprop concert. Several dances later, Lazy is arrested, and Boris (Petka) is happily reunited with Olga (Tania), who asks to be forgiven for initially doubting his innocence in the intrigue. The concert then resumes, with the Red Army taking over from the Komsomol members. Iakubov's reordering of Act 3 decreases, rather than increases, the dramatic effect of the ballet. This is an unpleasant irony, given that *The Bolt* was criticized in 1931 for a purported lack of drama.

These editorial concerns reveal, at the very least, that the scenario of the ballet was subject to wholesale manipulation both in the months leading up to the premiere and in the years afterward. The essential framework of the plot, inspired as it was by a banner in the Red Hercules factory, nonetheless remained intact, despite Shostakovich's disdain for it. This disdain, along with time constraints and the need to move on to other musical commissions, compelled the composer to cut corners in the creative process. The composer recycled music into the ballet from earlier works and out of the ballet for later works. He also changed the titles of some numbers to accord with changes in the scenario, though, significantly, he did not change the actual musical content of the numbers. Harried, Shostakovich resorted to sleight of hand to fashion the score.

On these points, it should be noted that the musicologist Alla Bogdanova has identified correlations between the E-flat major march of the workers into the workshop in Act 1 of *The Bolt* and the opening march of Shostakovich's incidental music to Vladimir Mayakovsky's play *The Bedbug* (1929).[49] Citing Bogdanova's finding, Iakubov points out a similar kinship between the B-flat major dance of the cleaning ladies in Act 1 and the concluding march from *The Bedbug*.[50] Both he and Bogdanova overstate the degree of similarity between the play and the ballet: the marches in question are not reproductions but variants of their prototypes—a relationship akin, say, to that between the surface and background whites in Kazimir Malevich's Suprematist painting *White on White* (1918). Other passages from *The Bedbug*'s score derive from Shostakovich's music for the anticapitalist film *New Babylon* (1929). The source of the recycled music in *The Bolt* is recycled music.

To complicate matters further, Iakubov claims that at least two of the dances in the ballet were written for another, inchoate work:

Some of the numbers in the autograph piano score have names without any connection whatsoever with the content of the libretto of the ballet *The Bolt* familiar to us. Thus the number receiving the name "The Dance of the Machines" (No. 14, Start-up of the Workshop and No. 17, Operation of the Workshop) in the final edition of the orchestral score is called "The Dance of the Silhouettes" in the piano score (RGALI, f. 2048, op. 2, ed. khr. 41, l. 29). The number designated "The Mime of the Installation of the Machines" in the orchestral score is called "The Destruction of the City" in the piano score. This provides a basis for supposing that the composer was at first guided by some other libretto for the ballet that has not come down to us, or else that he included in the ballet numbers composed earlier for other purposes.[51]

From the two drafts of the ballet's scenario, we know that "The Man and Machine Dance of the Silhouettes" (as it is called in the first draft) and "Dance of the Silhouettes" (as it is called in the second draft) are not the original names of the items labeled, in Iakubov's edition, "Dance of the Machines I" and "Dance of the Machines II." Rather, they are the original names for the item that Iakubov calls "The Scene with the Bolt." It would appear that "The Dance of the Silhouettes" was not conceived for another ballet, as Iakubov posits, but for an earlier version, and a different section, of the same ballet.[52]

Gerard McBurney, the British composer with a keen interest in Shostakovich's theater music of the period, suggests that Iakubov might also be mistaken on another assumption: "The Destruction of the City" was not the original title for "The Mime of the Installation of the Machines," but the title given to the number when it was reused by the composer in the 1931 revue *Uslovno ubityi*, a comedy of errors centering around the activities of *Osoaviakhim* (the Soviet civil defense, aviation, and chemical construction league). The nettlesome title of this work has been translated as *Declared Dead* by Laurel Fay in accord with the details of the plot. McBurney speculates that Shostakovich may have taken the piano score of "The Mime of the Installation of the Machines" from his ballet folder, renamed it "The Destruction of the City" for the theater revue, orchestrated it for the theater revue, and then returned the piano score to his ballet folder without erasing the new name. Thus, in the Russian State Archive of Literature and Art, which houses the documents in question, what now appears to be a section of one work (*The Bolt*) with two titles might actually have been a section of two works (*The Bolt* and *Declared Dead*) with two titles.[53]

McBurney's comments come on the heels of his celebrated reorchestration of twenty-one numbers from *Declared Dead*. It was issued on compact disc by Cala Records in 1993 as *Hypothetically Murdered*, McBurney's imaginative translation of the title. Fay, who has also researched the theater revue, documents that the music—intended to accompany a street chase, singing and dancing waiters, and a paradoxical episode in Communist heaven—both derived from and was destined for several other Shostakovich scores. Her concordance of works with equivalent or near-equivalent music to *Declared Dead* ranges from *The Bolt* to the opera *Lady Macbeth of Mtsensk District* (1932), to the incidental music for the play *Hamlet* (1932), to his third ballet *The Limpid Stream* and beyond.[54] Shostakovich's light music traveled so much that, even within the Soviet Union, it merited a multi-entry visa.

The Bolt thus emerges as one of a family of compositions whose contents less comprise autonomous ballet, theater, and cinema numbers than recyclable templates. The "positive" characters could, as noted, be revolutionaries or workers or revolutionary workers; the "negative" characters could be internal or external to Soviet society, antagonistic toward Marxist-Leninist ideology or simply in need of political reeducation. The alterations began before *The Bolt* was premiered and continued after it was withdrawn; the ballet occupied just one spot on a long production line. "Socialist Realism" precipitated tinkering between the dress rehearsals and the premiere. Once the ballet was yanked off the stage, discussion immediately began about remounting it with an improved scenario. As Sergei Radlov (1892–1958), the director of the State Academic Theatre, put it, the thin plots of the Romantic ballets "*Raimonda* and *Coppelia* seem like Shakespeare's works compared to the dramaturgy of *The Bolt*."[55] Yet judging both from Bruni's unhappy 1991 memoirs of the 1931 premiere and the reaction by the Artistic-Political Council of the State Academic Theatre, *The Bolt* was dead: nothing came of Radlov's planned revival, enabling Shostakovich to recycle some of the music in (perhaps fittingly) *Declared Dead,* whose satiric content roiled the Soviet cultural police anew.[56] Three decades later, the composer sanctioned the insertion of the aforementioned "Dance of the Drayman" into Valerii Panov and Konstantin Boiarsky's film-ballet *Baryshnia i khuligan* (1962), whose title can be roughly translated as *Lady and the Tramp*.

The process of creating *The Bolt,* a factory ballet, thus became a fitting imitation of an age-old factory process (though the goods it yielded did not always appeal to Party-minded consumers). Just like molten metal is poured into carved wooden blocks in traditional cast-iron making, Shostakovich, teamed with an amateur scenarist, filtered his music through multiple dramatic contexts. His industrial method resulted in a group of stage works whose music seemed estranged from—or unconcerned with—events taking place on stage.

3. Dance and Music

Support for this last point comes from Sollertinsky, who noted a disconnect between the music and dance of the ballet in his essay "*The Bolt* and the Problem of Soviet Ballet," which was included in the "Viewer's Guide" distributed to the audience at the Leningrad premiere. The essay is beguiling insofar as it pays more attention to the ballet's negative qualities than its positive ones. *The Bolt* was panned before it even reached the stage, an obvious—if odd—indication that it was self-reflexive in nature, with its negative reception in the Soviet press anticipated and perhaps even encoded into the music and dance. Though obligated to talk up the ballet for the Soviet public, Sollertinsky talks it down, and in this respect comes close to replicating the self-critiques that typify commedia dell'arte (revived in Russia during the Symbolist era).[57] Sollertinsky remarks, for example:

> The divertissement character of the spectacle is still not liquidated. True, the places of "Bluebird," "Prince Whooping-Cough," and "Cinderella," are in turn taken by the stage "entrées" of *osoaviakhi-movtsy,* motorcyclists, cavalrymen, and so forth. But all the same the old devices of ballet "plot development" make themselves known.[58]

The contradiction here is hard to miss: Sollertinsky describes the ballet as a "divertissement," the implication being that it lacks plot development, yet he also contends that it exhibits the "old devices" of plot development. In his brief discussion of the music, Sollertinsky contradicts himself once again. He reports that, in *The Bolt,* "Shostakovich travels the path of ballet symphonization, that is, along Tchaikovsky's and Stravinsky's path," but he also reports that "Shostakovich's music is concretely theatrical," the implication being that it adheres to the traditional ballet number format.[59]

The writer also anticipates a negative critical reaction to *The Bolt* by describing Lopukhov's choreography as transitional in nature, the first phase in the politically motivated reconception of physical expression. In his early ballets, Lopukhov imported "phys-ed" or, more accurately, "physical culture" (*fizkul'turnyi*) gestures into classical ballet set pieces. These "acrobatic drills," Sollertinsky writes,

> inarguably bore within themselves more vital elements than the affected classicism of the eighteenth century. But they also harbored an essential error: revolutionary ballet was initially understood to mean revolutionary dance form. Dance at first remained inexpressive, characterless. Thematic, conceptual considerations were also absent. The human body was transformed into an ideal working mechanism, devoid of classical characteristics. If classicism reflected a courtly and feudal way of life, then acrobatic dance corresponded sociologically to the mechanized culture of a grand capitalist city. On the Soviet stage unintelligent acrobatic thematics led to formalism.[60]

In *The Bolt,* Sollertinsky continues, Lopukhov turned a new page in ballet history. He supplanted "physical culture" choreography—that which had led to abstract "formalism"—with a "dance spectacle" based on "Soviet thematics."

Lopukhov, in essence, inaugurated two choreographic revolutions in his career: he first disbanded classical dance, and then he disbanded the acrobatic dance that had replaced it. *The Bolt* rejected ballet norms, but also rejected the rejection of these norms. Lopukhov's masterstroke, Sollertinsky suggests, resides in his balletic expression of dialectical materialism. To quote a recent (and appropriately self-ironizing) commentator on Leninist philosophy, Lopukhov's choreography articulated a "Hegelian 'negation of negation': first the old order is negated within its own ideologico-political form; then this form itself has to be negated."[61]

Lopukhov's treatment of *The Bolt*'s scenario accorded with Shostakovich's treatment insofar as he situated his dancing somewhere between abstract and mimetic gesture, or what he labeled "classical" (and "semi-classical") and "character" (and "semi-character") dancing, the former typified by "soft" *plié* landings, the latter by "hard" ones.[62] To Lopukhov, this middle ground was the realm of the "Grotesque," the third and, for the Soviet avant-garde, most relevant category of dance. In part 1 of his 1925 treatise *Paths of a Ballet Master,* Lopukhov writes:

> We know that movements having the hard *plié* as their basis came first while movements having a soft *plié* as their basis came second. Yet we also know that there exist many movements, conceived after the advent of classical dance and continuing to be conceived even now, that are neither suitable for the performers of character dance nor the performers of classical dance. Those individuals who execute them likewise possess certain striking physical features that are not observed in performers of character and classical dance. What, then, are these movements? Precisely those that contain within themselves the twin foundations of choreographic art, that is, the hard and the soft *plié*. In order to execute these movements, in order to direct oneself away from the ground and toward the ground at one and the same time—or, in other words, to switch immediately from a hard to a soft *plié,* one must of course have a physical form that allows for this execution. Such a form must be strictly proportional, that is, no one part of the body should dominate another.[63]

Lopukhov here hypothesizes that the choreography of the future would at once consolidate the past while also providing new movements for new physiques. Immediately before the lines given above, he inserts a graph into his text showing the physiological in-between-ness of "Grotesque" dance versus "character" and "classical" dance; immediately after, he makes the bold declaration that "new concepts require new gestures and movements."[64]

The "new gestures" in *The Bolt*, to recap, blended "movement" and "mimed" episodes, or what might otherwise be called "dance" and "non-dance" episodes.[65] Yet they also, of course, united opposites in the same way that Bruni's Constructivist drawing of the factory workshop did. Her fusion of "images" and "objects" became Lopukhov's fusion of abstract and representational choreographic forms. From the reviews, one senses that the combination of these two modalities had a disorientating effect on the 1931 audience, with part of the "semiosis" being "purely introversive (as in pure dance)," and the remainder adhering to the narrative format of "story ballet."[66] These two parameters of expression served in eighteenth- and nineteenth-century ballet to depict fantastic and realistic events, "negative" and "positive" characters. In *The Bolt,* these binaries are dissolved; the two parameters of expression are conjoined. Lopukhov's choreography occupies the grotesque middle ground between introversive ("pure," "abstract") and extroversive ("narrative," "storytelling") gestures.

The great irony of Lopukhov's method was its guaranteed malfunction. In the late 1920s and early 1930s, critical debate about dance reform—one which, in the opinion of Soviet soothsayers, would spirit in a future-perfect "TRAM [Theatre of Worker Youth] ballet"—centered on the wholesale abandonment of the introversive, formalist elements of ballet syntax in favor of greater nationalist content and more affective acting.[67] Classical technique was seen to occupy a domain external to the concerns of the actual world. The turning-out of the leg, like the five positions of the feet and arms, obliged the dancer to adopt sculptural, figurative poses. Moreover, the emphasis on salutary gestures and low bows in classical technique attested to its baroque (rococo) origins. Though seemingly abstract, ballet harbored within itself traces of discredited aristocratic rituals. Proper reform of ballet necessitated rescuing pantomime from its subservient place in the dramatic framework and enhancing its emotional content. Improvisation, method acting, and training in gymnastics were all viewed as crucial to the renewal of the art. Hybridizations of ballet and sport, ballet and acrobatics, and ballet and circus, however, were regarded as dubious enterprises, more likely to estrange than engage the viewer, and thus further distance the art from the pressing concerns of Soviet life.[68] For this reason, perhaps, the hybridization of these genres in "high" and "low" art venues met with skepticism in the press. In the 1930 production of *The Football Player* at the Bolshoi Theatre, L. Lashchilin and I. Moiseev sought to invigorate classical variations and ensembles by infusing them with goal-scoring headers and penalty kicks. The reviewer for *The Worker and the Theatre* argued that the fusion of "pure classicism, built on the adagio and the simplest classical variations," with phys-ed routines "did not work at all."[69] A month earlier in the same journal, another writer called into question the insertion of ballet ensembles into

Moscow and Leningrad music hall spectacles. Upon listing such items as "The Pioneer Dance," "The Red Navy Dance," the "Hammerers'" display and other ditties of "proletarian provenance," the author concluded that the battle between "high" and "low" art had ended in a "draw." Regarding the "effort" that was made in the music hall spectacles "to abandon uncoordinated 'divertissement' for circus-theater-style *represen-tation*," the author simply stated that the struggle needed to continue.[70]

In *The Bolt*, the conflation of "dance" and "non-dance" routines, introversive and extroversive semiosis, served as the underpinning for a much larger conflation between dramatic layers. Like the ballet mentioned above, Shostakovich and Lopukhov's ballet merges standard dance narrative with vaudevillian insertions. These insertions take the form of the amateur concerts in Acts 1 and 3. They are extraneous to the main action insofar as they neither propel nor enhance the plot line, but simply provide ambiance. To borrow language used in writings about film musicals, the amateur concerts illustrate the "myth of entertainment," in which "multiple levels of performances and consequent multiple levels of audience combine to create a myth about musical entertainment permeating ordinary life."[71] *The Bolt*, as a dance-based work, does not portray "ordinary life" in the manner that the spoken-dialogue sections of a film musical do; the ballet does, however, allot the "positive" characters in the drama the kind of impossible talent characteristic of the film musical. The amateur concerts, the "entertainments" in question, are mounted by the factory workers with shock-worker initiative at breakneck speed. These workers perform a "professional" rather than an "amateur" tribute to the "Blue Blouse Troupe," an agitprop ensemble that, during the 1920s, "performed" the headlines in the guise of "Living Newspapers." The amateur concerts likewise featured a mimicry of "ROSTA windows," political posters issued by the Russian telegraph agency for display in storefronts.[72]

From the preceding points, it stands to reason that the choreography of the amateur concerts would differ in method and approach from the choreography of the surrounding drama. One imagines this inner narrative layer being distinguished from the outer narrative layer by the self-consciousness of the choreography. In the amateur concerts, time would not progress in continuous, unbroken phrases but would be segmented, partitioned into discrete units. The performers would not be one with their performance, but would be seen to grapple with their movements. These traits clearly apply to *The Bolt*. However, instead of assigning this self-conscious mode of performance only to the amateur concerts, Lopukhov, according to the reviews, made it the basis of the entire ballet. Rather than distinguishing the inner and outer narrative layers, Lopukhov conflated them, transforming all of the dancers into poster-board look-alikes, and all of the dances into rough-edged, blocklike assemblages. Far from a "dynamic" time-space continuum, the choreographer privileged a "static" one.[73] In accord with Constructivist aesthetics, "images" fused with "objects": the two-dimensional figures featured in the amateur concerts could not be distinguished from their three-dimensional prototypes.

Opponents of *The Bolt* heaped scorn on the grotesque conflation of type and persona, the abnormal and normal, but did not entertain the possibility that it was intentional, that, artistically, it meant something. They noted that Lazy Idler, Ivan Corkscrew (*Ivan Shtopor*), Fyodor Beer (*Fedor Piva*), and Manka Luck (*Man'ka Fart*) and the other figures in the main plot were just as stereotyped as the "absentee," "drunkard," "malingerer," and "job-changer" portrayed in the inserted numbers. Thus the ostensibly "fictional" figure of the blacksmith (who, lurching to and fro, uses two oversized hammers to disgorge flames from molten iron) garnered as much abuse as the "actual" Red Army cavalrymen (who perform a gallop while sitting on bentwood "Viennese" chairs). The Act 2 vignette between Heavenly (*Podnebesnenskii*), the hapless priest, and his parishioners seemed better suited for a variety show than a ballet, as did the Act 3 dances by a gypsy and an unidentified "easterner."[74] Though the Komsomol ensemble of the finale was praised for its expression of "the optimism, energy, and 'feeling of camaraderie' common to the Soviet people," critics noted that the happy-go-lucky gestures came from an earlier Lopukhov ballet, *The Red Poppy* (1927).[75] In the Act 1 rehearsals, "the actors represented a crane, a tractor, and a mechanical loom (twenty-four female dancers in two rows, moving up and down)," and thus mimicked Foregger's machine dances.[76] The latter, however, were not used by Foregger in a serious dramatic context, and were thus out of place in a ballet about industrial sabotage. Reviewers of the premiere did not comment on the machine dances because, according to Bruni, they were removed beforehand, a point that, at the very least, needs to be factored into editions of the score. The premiere of the ballet offered something less than the complete ballet.

The critical denunciations and the attendant allegations of professional incompetence focused almost as much on the dance as the scenario. Dance, a medium that embodies physical and mental creative processes, proved suspicious in the Soviet context because the thoughts and emotions it engendered tended to be mixed, its message uncertain. In the early 1930s, ambiguity became as much the enemy of the cultural thought police as subversion. Later—albeit a very short time later—Soviet cultural critique became deadly business, and the intellectual liberalism, if not free play, of the 1920s flipped over on its head to become its negative antipode: intellectual imprisonment. Dance, especially improvisatory dance, proved problematic because it offered more interpretive license to performers than music. It depended as much for expression on individual dancers and the particulars of their bodies as it did on prescribed *bras* and *pas* patterns. With little time to mount the work, Lopukhov less authored than guided the choreography of *The Bolt*. He established the loose parameters within which his Blue Blouse Troupe imitators moved. Opponents of his approach, evincing an ideological bias toward controlled, nonaleatoric artistic expression, voiced distrust, or what might be called a Leninist "hermeneutics of suspicion," for the ontological frailty of dance forms.[77] Predisposed to favor Shostakovich—who led the musical division of the Theatre of Worker Youth—over Lopukhov, the critics for *Daily Life Newspaper*, *Proletarian Musician*, and *The Worker and the Theatre* ascribed the ideological failings of the ballet less to the unfree mechanics of the human consciousness than to the spontaneity of the body.[78] Even the most hostile opponents of *The Bolt* entertained the possibility that it was not conceived as proletarian kitsch, but inadvertently transformed itself into proletarian kitsch once performed.

This ontological consideration should not be construed as an attempt to counter the academic consensus that the ballet was planned as a satire. It was—as the political fallout from the rehearsals and premiere attest. Lopukhov assessed this fallout in a self-effacing, Khrushchev-era summary of the ballet's perceived failings. As the sole testament to his (and Shostakovich's) intentions, it merits quotation at length:

> Creating the ballet, we saw before us the innovations of the Blue Blouse and TRAM, and dreamed of doing something of equal value.
>
> But all the same the ballet did not make the grade. It is not the business of ballet to ironize the news of the day, but to reproduce true life as one sees it. It is not possible to place in the center of a spectacle negative characters, except in a satiric review. Having excluded favorable heroes with a grand plan from *The Bolt*, having avoided making the best qualities of Soviet man the main feature of the spectacle, we actually excluded the most powerful and attractive element of the art of dance. A large ballet cannot consist of grotesque numbers alone. Of course, this only came to me many years later, when I repeatedly mulled over what I had done, and searched for the root causes of my failures. The failure of *The Bolt*

began with the dramatic outline, with the choice of subject, and with the treatment of that which is contrary to ballet, but not, one could say, contrary to drama, which possesses immeasurably grand possibilities for unmasking, satire, and so on.

However if I failed overall, in places I managed to achieve some results. We were drawn to the possibility of infusing dance with motives of political satire inspired by "ROSTA Windows." It seemed and still seems to me that the attempt to choreograph political satire in *The Bolt* bore an influence on variety shows and will certainly become part of the mature ballet spectacles of our day. For the scene in the workshop I composed a "Dance of the Textile Workers," and I am certain that it looked realistic, though the "dancification" of industrial processes was perhaps somewhat archaic. For all of its faults, *The Bolt* showed and proved that in ballet new heroes such as factory workers are possible, and that if one extracts from labor the poetry of dance one can represent a factory workshop onstage. This bears great potential. Unfortunately, our attempt remains singular: up to now ballet theater has not been attracted to industrial motives, and has not made factory and mill workers dramatic protagonists.[79]

This gesture of repentance does not mark Lopukhov as an outsider to Soviet culture, but as a quintessential insider. In tone, it brings to mind the self-critiques written by Shostakovich at regular intervals during the roller-coaster ride of his career, self-critiques that straddled the line between lip service and genuine contrition.

For this reason, we can apply to Lopukhov's choreography a point that has recently been made about Shostakovich's Fifth, Seventh, and Eleventh symphonies and their ambivalent, was-he-or-was-he-not-a-dissident narrative content: "The inner distance towards the 'official' Socialist reading of his [art] makes [Lopukhov] a prototypical Soviet [artist]."[80] However paradoxical the notion may seem, "this distance is constitutive of ideology," because those artists "who fully (over)identified with the official ideology," who tried too hard to toe the Party line, ran "into trouble."[81] The cultural climate of 1931 was such that, no matter how sincere a choreographer's or composer's attempt to celebrate the proletarian cause, to depict it in the most glowing light, the endeavor always fell short of the creative and technical mark because this mark was constantly being moved out of reach. Nothing was ever satisfactory; the work always needed to improve. The vehemence of journalistic attacks on artists only increased as the 1930s, the worst decade in the history of Russia, progressed. To represent the situation using black humor, as Lopukhov and Shostakovich did, was not to undermine the proletarian cause but to support it through earnest cultural critique. This is the reason why their dancers moved, both literally and figuratively, one step forward and two steps back.

4. Music and Dance

Not surprisingly, this type of motion typifies Lazy, the wayward antihero of the ballet, whom we meet near the start of Act 1, as he leaves for work after an all-night binge. Shostakovich's music for the scene is an intoxicated waltz, whose upper and lower lines move in and out of sync with each other, and then alternately disappear, as though they had fallen out of the score into a gutter somewhere. The musical syntax is blurry, moving from a B-flat minor nexus at rehearsal number 35 to an E-flat minor nexus at rehearsal number 36.[82] In the second half of the waltz, this same tonal relationship is reversed a half-step lower: D minor flows down to a resigned, wayward A minor. Overall, however, the texture is chromatic, with the melodic gestures saturated with semitones, and the upper and lower lines grinding dissonantly against each other. Three measures before rehearsal 37, for example, offers us a D♮ in the bass register against a D♭ in the treble. Hearing the music, one "sees" Lazy's halting, lumbering steps, his unkempt physical state, his fruitless efforts to tidy himself up, and his unconvincing attempt to appear sober as he enters the workplace (this last event is represented by a buffo-like melody in the bassoon). The frequent alterations in meter and rhythm relate to Lazy's changes of pace as he loses and regains his sense of direction; the frequent silences relate to his confused pauses. The emptiness of many of the staves, moreover, suggests close interaction between Shostakovich's music and Lopukhov's choreography. The latter perhaps swapped places with the former in the ballet. Physical gestures may have bridged the gap between musical gestures; visual lines of movement may have substituted for aural lines of movement. One could argue, in fact, that the absent choreography of the ballet accounts for the absent melodic and accompanimental lines in the waltz.

The thinness of the texture, however, could also be symbolic, highlighting Lazy's shallowness. In Soviet dramaturgy, the personalities of villains tend to be vacuous, their sinister motivations transparent. Lazy's lack of ethical and moral substance is expressed through a lack of musical substance. His mood and disposition is marked not by melodic and harmonic detail, but by substandard, sub-canonic orchestration: the solo English horn denotes abjection, the solo bassoon absurd pride (Example 1).

Example 1. Lazy Idler, *The Bolt,* Act 1, rehearsal number 35, mm. 1–17.

Instrumentation likewise plays a role in the depiction of the Conformist, or Yes-Man (*Soglasitel'*), one of the figures from the former tsarist society lampooned in the Act 3 amateur concert given by the Komsomol brigade. Despite being a caricature, a poster-board look-alike, the depiction of this character is more finely wrought than that of Lazy. To represent the Conformist's willingness to please, the xylophone and solo bassoon—and then the xylophone and full orchestra—come to cadential agreement at the ends of phrases in the four measures preceding rehearsal numbers 616 and 620. From rehearsal number 621, the brass endorses the agreement with a pompous repetition of the bassoon's and xylophone's melodies. Lengthy, if simple variations of the eight-measure melody introduced by the clarinet one measure after rehearsal number 612, and an uproarious contrast between the xylophone and muted trumpets one measure before rehearsal 622, enhance the sense of burlesque. Shostakovich incorporates body portraiture into the number, infusing the melodic line with obsequious nods and bows, and sustaining a tempo that allows for prancing about and gesticulating.

The number is saturated with acoustic gestures taken from Big Top marches, these adding to the cheerful banality. The Conformist is clearly distinguished from the other characters from the past (the Lady Aesthete, Colonial Slave Girl, and Drayman) that are lampooned in the amateur concert. As in Lazy's waltz, Shostakovich leaves room in the number for choreographic responses to the music. Much as the bassoon and xylophone mime each other's gestures before rehearsal numbers 616 and 620, so too, one imagines, do the Conformist and the xylophone mime each other's gestures in the span between rehearsal numbers 620 and 621. There, the musical texture is reduced to single pitches, leaving room for the dancing to be, as it were, "heard" (Example 2).

This kind of hypothetical music-dance interaction cannot be gleaned from the ensemble dances in the ballet, whose music forges its own logic, with the consciousnesses of the individual performers subservient to the *über*-consciousness of the collective. The ensemble dances are, on the whole, the domain of the "positive" characters, not the "negative" ones, and they take place in the factory, where the only work that seems to take place is the work of looking busy. The machines clink and clank, but the Komsomol brigade charged with their upkeep devotes most of its time to leisure activity. In accord with the old Soviet saying, the state pretends to pay the workers, and the workers pretend to work.

To justify these points, we can turn to two of the ensemble numbers, the (rehearsed) Act 1 "Dance of the Machines" and the (staged) Act 3 "Apotheosis." The title of the first number is doubtless a joke: people, not machines, dance, unless the machines in question have been made into people, or, in accord with the modernist nightmare, people have been made into machines, with aluminum flesh and mercury blood. Shostakovich's music is explicitly mechanical, offering standard musical imitations of automated processes. Rehearsal number 146, the very opening of the number, presents a simulacrum of well-oiled pistons moving up and down with a larger, slower hydraulic system supplying power underneath. At rehearsal number 147, we "see" this operation from another angle: the upper-line rhythm changes from even eighth notes to alternating quarter and eighth notes. Following rehearsal 150, the level of activity turns up a notch, with the upper line introducing scalar runs and the lower line covering fully twice the intervallic range it did at the opening. The harmonic pattern in the two measures preceding rehearsal number 151 compresses a chain of perfect fifth relationships into one of major seconds. The D major triad progresses to C and B-flat triads, rather than to G, C, F, and B-flat ones. Every other gear in the tonal wheel is left out: V–I relationships become V/V–I relationships.

Example 2. The Conformist, *The Bolt,* Act 3, rehearsal number 619, m. 4 to rehearsal number 621, m. 9.

The music perpetuates the illusion that events in the workshop are moving too fast for the employees standing around to absorb.

Toward the middle of the number, the music ceases to unfold in real time. It instead begins to move in parallel, or simultaneous times, offering us the aural equivalent of a cinematic montage (a technique with which the composer became acquainted while working on *New Babylon,* but also during his student years, when he earned money working as a silent film accompanist). As the dancers move from platform to platform, position to position in Bruni and Korshikov's décor, the musical focus shifts from eight-measure phrases in B-flat and E-flat major to eight-measure phrases in B and E major. What first sounds like a modulation of a semitone from B-flat to B major at rehearsal number 152, a modulation of a diminished fourth from B to E-flat major at rehearsal number 155, a modulation of a semitone from E-flat to E major at rehearsal number 157, and a modulation down an augmented fifth from E to B-flat major at rehearsal number 159—is actually a montage of simultaneous tonalities. Shostakovich "cuts" from key to key, musical scene to musical scene. The blocklike structure of the music—the abrasive tonal shifts and the conflation of six- and eight-measure phrases—is alleviated somewhat by other features, notably a gradual increase in dynamic level and gradual enrichment of the orchestration. The majestic fanfare of sustained B-flat major chords in the sixteen measures following rehearsal number 167 suggests self-congratulation, even triumph. The music lauds itself for smoothing over the seams in its own blocklike structure.

In this regard, the "Dance of the Machines" is self-assembling and self-regulating, capable of generating eight-measure phrases and rhythmic patterns from two-measure ones, and a full orchestral sound from smaller string and brass ensembles. The music seems to compose itself, the implication being that it is representing the sounds of a factory that, in whole or in part, makes factories. (Here we might recall Bruni's fanciful 1979 drawing of the Act 1 and 3 workshop, which includes graphic notation of the dances performed within.) The brass and string pistons and pulleys double, triple, and quadruple in size in a manner redolent of the demonic brooms in Johann Wolfgang von Goethe's tale *The Sorcerer's Apprentice* (1779). The operations of the factory (evidently curtailed before the ballet's premiere) are redundant. Shostakovich represents an over-bureaucratized complex whose output is its input or, to put it another way, whose process is its result. In *The Bolt,* the Five-Year Plan more than exceeds its quota.

The last number of the ballet, an apotheosis featuring Komsomol cadets, Red Army conscripts, and the men and women of the factory, fastens together the tonalities of B-flat and C-flat major in a simulacrum of a grand ballet finale. In Shostakovich's hands, the ever-accelerating cadential whirl endemic to the genre is tempered, its mettle cooled. The apotheosis becomes a "climax to nothing" in the sense that the music simply repeats, the melodies and harmonies recurring in square eight-measure units. The time and space of the frenetic final ensembles of ballet lore—that scored, for example, by Borodin for his Far Eastern Polovtsians and by Ravel for his Mediterranean Bacchantes—cedes to something modern but mundane: a celebration of the end of the workday by blue-collar types.[83]

The three sections of the apotheosis—covering rehearsal numbers 812 to 818, 818 to 821, and 821 to 825—are denoted less by melodic and harmonic contrasts than rhythmic ones. Section 1 is prefaced by a bi-tonal sonority, a C-flat triad above an F pedal tone, the latter the dominant of the home key. The dissonant relationship between the upper and lower pitches becomes the mechanism that drives the three-part form forward. (This relationship may also tell us something about the choreography. Lopukhov may have intended the movements of the Red Army soldiers and factory workers to conflict with one another, if not on a lower-torso metric level, then on an upper-torso gestural one.) The Cb–F conflict resolves in a series of V–I cadences in B-flat. These decrease in volume at rehearsal number 812, the beginning of section 1. The section contains six eight-measure phrase units, whose melodic content consists of repeated eighth notes, stepwise motion in quarters, and leaps of fourths and fifths in mixed values. The voice-leading is unconventional, with the string basses obliged to slide in and out of B-flat major in order to remain consonant with the solo trombone. (One is reminded here of Charlie Chaplin trying to keep pace with the conniving conveyor belt in *Modern Times*.) In section 2, Shostakovich reorchestrates the melody for trumpets. He also harmonizes it, thus transforming its awkward intervallic structure into an awkward chordal one. The two measures preceding rehearsal number 819 feature two sonorities—F-Bb-C-G to F-Bb-E-C—containing the pitches of V and V/V of B-flat. (The kinks in the syntax are worked out a measure later.) Section 3 involves a detour into B major, the enharmonic equivalent of the aforementioned C-flat major. Here the sound becomes less diatonic and more chromatic, with the extended coda—rehearsal numbers 826 to 833—threatening a semitonal fade-to-black. Rehearsal number 829 constitutes the nexus of the disorder; it compresses, piston-like, pitches from B and C major in a clatter of eighth notes and triplets. The initial Bb–Cb configuration of the apotheosis shifts a half-step higher. Rehearsal 830 witnesses a reversal of the shift and a corrosion of the texture. The apotheosis, and the entire ballet, concludes with unison Bbs.

The semantic sameness of the musical language, its leadenness and obtuseness, here neutralizes the drama, and thus contradicts the Soviet vision of the factory as utopian domain, with man and machine happily toiling together, their energies organically combined. Critics and colleagues liked his music far more than they liked Smirnov's scenario and Lopukhov's choreography; however, the similarity and simplicity of many numbers taxed their patience. The composer Maksimilian Shteinberg (1883–1946) made the following diary entry about the 7 May 1931 dress rehearsal:

> The Act 1 overture, blacksmith's dance, concluding ensemble and a few incidental things went over well. In Act 3—the textile workers' ensemble and some other passages. The rest was either dull or deplorable, both musically and scenically, in particular Act 2. By no means a success.[84]

Given Shteinberg's conservative musical tastes, it is unlikely that his comments reflect the general critical or public opinion about the quality of the score. His comments do, however, allow us to assess the score within a general ideological context.

Shostakovich's insistent repetition of chords and motifs can be regarded as intentionally "bad" composition, unintentionally "bad" composition, or the product of haste. In all three instances, the blandness of the score allows for a colorful interpretation as a none-too-subtle comment on the hectoring ideological doctrine of his time. If, according to Marxist-Leninist philosophy, "thought bears a certain determinate relation to matter, serving as its "'image' or 'reflection,'" one could, I think, argue that *The Bolt* provides a moribund "image or reflection" of reality, Soviet or otherwise.[85] Shostakovich's intentional or unintentional satire depends upon a deadening of the cognitive processes that, according to dialectical materialism, not only mirror the real but also govern it. To refer to Marxist-Leninist philosophy once again, "The world of consciousness is the material world 'translated into forms of thought.'"[86] Shostakovich drains his score of subjectivity; the music probes neither feeling nor cognition. It represents socialist (proletarian) reality as a construct, a "reflection" of an "ex-" or "non-" consciousness, the mind of an automaton, not a person.

5. *The Bolt*

Though it would be crude to insist that Shostakovich, as a compositional shock worker, threw a wrench into his own ballet, or that his critics wore industrial fasteners in their necks, it bears emphasizing that neither he nor Lopukhov sought to improve upon Smirnov's sparse scenario. Unwittingly (of course), they ensured that *The Bolt* would be panned in *The Worker and the Theatre* and elsewhere. The composer and choreographer hammered together a mock ballet made up of mock music and dance, a work whose "in-between" syntax adhered neither to "classical" nor "character-based" modes of denotation. Paradoxically, perhaps, the target of their satire was the cultural organizations that they themselves participated in. Like other pro-labor artistic bodies, the Theatre of Worker Youth reduced socialist discourse into Communist Party–minded catch-phrases and "living newspaper" sound bites. The organization's actors claimed to be former blue-collar workers, but their stage works represented these workers superficially, in a near comic-book guise. True romance was replaced by clandestine encounters by the wrecking ball or in the railway yard. On this issue, Clark observes that the Theatre of Worker Youth "tried to overthrow the most fundamental conventions of theater, and with them, the way in which its audiences perceived reality."[87] However, in the end, it only managed to stage "primitive and pedestrian melodramas and comedies of the factory floor."[88]

The Bolt, in essence, relied on satire to highlight the inside-out, upside-down relationship between the proletarian experience and its representation by the Soviet avant-garde. In creating the ballet, Shostakovich (like Lopukhov) seems to have adopted the creative outlook of the writer Mikhail Zoshchenko (1895–1958), a practitioner of the everyday speech–derived literary genre known as *skaz,* who called into question the function and purpose of the "agitprop of the Komsomol."[89] "In my stuff," Zoshchenko wrote in an autobiographical essay, "I'm parodying the imaginary but genuine proletarian writer who would exist in the present-day environment. Of course, such a writer cannot exist, at least not yet."[90] Jeremy Hicks explains that Zoshchenko set out to parody the "mentality" and "naive philosophy" of proletarian artists.[91] His writings express ambivalence about proletarian culture, but not, it must be emphasized, the proletarian cause.

Satire is not the same thing as parody, but Shostakovich emulates Zoshchenko by casting aspersion on the paths being taken by Soviet culture in the late 1920s and early 1930s. He engages in "formalism" as a means to countermand the "blathering anti-formalists," the cultural dilettantes who purported to be the standard bearers of the brave new proletarian art.[92] The composer's detractors could not grasp, much less appreciate, his satire because they, like the Theatre of Worker Youth, were in its sights. Shostakovich's detractors, in other words, clung to the "naive philosophy" that *The Bolt* ridiculed. Subtle proof for this claim comes from the title of a strident political critique of Shostakovich's music for stage and screen: "Who's Against? It's *Unanimous*: An Open Letter to D. Shostakovich" (italics added). Signed by members of Leningrad ballet, theater, and musical organizations, this article takes the young composer to task for spreading himself too thin, simultaneously writing music for opera, ballet, music hall, and film studios, and for daring to charge that Soviet musical culture lacked refinement and sophistication.

"Who's Against? It's Unanimous" was written in response to Shostakovich's "Declaration of Responsibilities," published in the fall of 1931 in *The Worker and the Theatre*. In this article, the composer decries the simplistic and reductive handling of music in proletarian cinema, operetta, and vaudeville. The creators of such "light" genres assign music a trivial role in their works, reducing it to the level of aural wallpaper, where it merely serves to "accent" feelings of "'despair' and 'ecstasy.'" [93] Soviet musicals, Shostakovich notes, tend to recycle the same "'standard' numbers in the music: a drum strike for a new hero's entry, 'cheerful' and 'spirited' dance for the positive personages, a foxtrot for the 'denouement,' and 'cheerful' music for the happy ending." Though the composer omits the Theatre of Worker Youth from his critique (doubtless owing to his involvement in its musical division), he nonetheless repudiates "the total one-hundred-percent impotence of our musical theaters to create Soviet musical spectacle," a phrase whose overemphasis on adjectives mimes agit-prop to a T. There ensues a critique of those dramatists who believe that music should "aid the digestion" of the visual action by assigning high notes to tenors and *fouetté* rhythms to female dancers. Shostakovich contends that composers have become industrial laborers, stamping out score after score without passion or inspiration. To reduce his production quota and enhance the quality of his goods, he assigns himself a *piatiletka*, a "five-year plan." In the final two sentences of his article, he vows to decline all "commissions" to write music for "dramatic theater and sound cinema," and to commit himself to serious genres, notably a "large symphony dedicated to the fifteenth anniversary of the October Revolution."

Shostakovich's ballet emerges, then, as a send-up of the industrialization of Soviet culture in the service of industrialization. Music, like choreography, cannot be reduced to slogans, a point he and his choreographer make obvious by emphasizing surface over depth, semantic sameness over variance. Their ballet is consciously "bad" insofar as it replaces substance with rhetoric, nouns with adjectives, things-in-themselves with clichés. To refer to the title of an infamous 1936 *Pravda* article, the music and choreography represent a "balletic falsehood" that nonetheless tells the truth.[94]

It is thus oddly fitting that, in his "Declaration," Shostakovich called *The Bolt,* and his earlier ballet *The Golden Age,*

> a severe failure. I hasten here to exclude all of the ballet master Lopukhov's work on *The Bolt*. His work was wonderful, but Lopukhov found himself in the thrall of the theater and took on a libretto of poor quality, the result being a pasquinade.[95]

This remark, like some of Sollertinsky's remarks in his pre-premiere article on the ballet, is a marvel of contradiction. Shostakovich lauds the feature of *The Bolt*—the choreography—that the critics denounced, and denounces the feature of the ballet—the music—that the critics favored. It is also curious that he neglects to mention the attitudinal similarities between *The Bolt* and his opera *The Nose,* which, just before the quoted passage, he singles out for praise for its meta-theatrical innovations. The ballet and the opera exist in a kind of comic symbiosis, each furnishing buffo variations of "high" and "low" musical genres. And whereas Shostakovich intimates that his ballet flopped because it clung to shopworn theatrical formulae, he also intimates that it flopped because it did not uphold these standards: the music and dance suffered from Smirnov's "libretto of poor quality."

Shostakovich claims that his balletic intentions went unrealized, that *The Bolt* actually expresses the opposite of what he wanted to express. Here again, the composer emulates "the poetics of *skaz,*" in which the "author" undermines his own text by having the narrator, or individual characters, speak in a contradictory and paradoxical manner.[96] Because Shostakovich himself speaks in this manner, we are left in the dark as to whether or not he actually considered his ballet to be a miscalculation. *The Bolt* is a satire; so too, perhaps, is the composer's self-critique. The only certainty of the "Declaration" is uncertainty; "images" and "objects" have again become confused. In Shostakovich's compositions and in his writings about his compositions, "in-between-ness" becomes the remedy for a political and social milieu of absolutes, black humor the remedy for this milieu's dark side. Satire, a hardware store clerk might write, is both *The Bolt*'s dramatic fastener, locking the three disparate acts together, but also its dramatic tensioner, helping them to cohere.

NOTES

I would like to express my sincere gratitude to Laurel Fay for her invaluable comments on the draft of this essay, for directing me to crucial sources on *The Bolt*, and for allowing me to use her notes on an archival source. I am also extremely indebted to Mariia Ratanova for gathering and sending me visual and journalistic materials on the ballet from St. Petersburg, to Elena Strona for background information about the décor, and to the late Viktor Varunts for details about metamorphoses of the ballet in the 1970s.

1. Katerina Clark, *Petersburg: Crucible of Cultural Revolution* (Cambridge, Mass.: Harvard University Press, 1995), p. 240.

2. Ibid.

3. Reference is made here to the testimony of the artist Tatiana Bruni. See n. 48.

4. M. Iankovskii, "Bolt," *Rabochii i teatr* 11 (21 April 1931): 11. For an overview of the genesis and critical reception of the ballet, see Manashir Iakubov, "*The Bolt*: An Unknown Ballet by Dmitri Shostakovich," in Dmitrii Shostakovich, *The Bolt, op. 27: Piano Score,* ed. Manashir Iakubov (Moscow: DSCH, 1996), pp. 269–76.

5. B. Rod., "'Bolt,'" *Smena,* 12 April 1931, p. 4.

6. Iur. Brodersen, "Neudavsheesia perevooruzhenie baleta ('Bolt' v gosteatre opery i baleta)," *Krasnaia gazeta [utrennii vypusk],* 11 April 1931, p. 4.

7. V. G., "Prisposoblencheskii spektakl': 'Bolt' v gosbalete," *Leningradskaia pravda,* 10 April 1931, p. 4.

8. For the history of the theater, see Clark, *Petersburg,* pp. 266–73.

9. Iakubov, "*The Bolt*: An Unknown Ballet," p. 271.

10. In the published piano score, the name is translated by Cindy Carlyle as "Lyonka Tippler" (Shostakovich, *The Bolt,* p. 10). I will be relying on Carlyle's translations of the other characters' names in this essay.

11. Iakubov, "*The Bolt*: An Unknown Ballet," p. 270.

12. Vera Krasovskaia, *Pavlova. Nizhinskii. Vaganova. Tri baletnye povesti* (Moscow: Agraf, 1999), p. 478.

13. *Theatre in Revolution: Russian Avant-Garde Stage Design 1913–1935,* ed. Nancy Van Norman Baer (London: Thames and Hudson, 1991), p. 191.

14. Several excerpts from *The Bolt* and Shostakovich's third ballet *The Limpid Stream* (1935) were used in a stage piece premiered 9 January 1976 at the Stanislavsky and Nemirovich-Danchenko Musical Theatre in Moscow. Called *Dreamers,* it featured a time-traveling libretto by Natale Ryzhenko, Viktor Smirnov-Golovanov, Sergei Sapozhnikov, and G. Iungvald-Khilkevich. According to a positive review in *Culture and Life,* the production had "two parts, the first narrating the 1930s, the second brings the viewer forward to our time for the construction of BAM [the Baikal-Amur-Mainline]. The protagonist [Pavel] unifies the two halves. First he builds the Metro; then, after many years, he journeys to Siberia to help young workers tame the wilderness." In an aside, the author of the review assures us that "Shostakovich responded excitedly to the idea of creating a spectacle about contemporary events. He opened his personal archives to the directors, provided the scores of his ballets from the 1930s, offered advice, and requested that the spectacle be given a beautiful and romantic name" (Unsigned, "Mechtateli," *Kul'tura i zhizn'* 6 [1976]: 29–30). This second remark represents Soviet spin at its grimmest. Shostakovich died on 9 August 1975 after protracted illness, making it unlikely, to say the least, that he had a hand in the production.

Also in 1976, Iurii Grigorovich (b. 1927), the director of the Bolshoi Theatre Ballet in Moscow, commenced rehearsals for another *Bolt* metamorphosis. Like the collective responsible for *Dreamers,* he created a new scenario and new choreography for the ballet, transforming it from a factory parable into a "living portrait" of the period between the

Russian revolutions of February and October 1917. The hero, a Bolshevik activist, and the villain, an officer of the tsarist guard, play out their antipathy against the backdrop of the tsar's abdication, the establishment of the Provisional government, and the Bolshevik dismantling of the government. Grigorovich assembled his dancers into wedgelike formations and instructed them to lunge toward and through invisible obstacles in a simulacrum of sacrificial dance. The choreography recoded—or retooled—the ostinato-based music that Shostakovich intended to represent the actions of pistons and pulleys. To resuscitate a failed ballet, Grigorovich relied on fail-safe dancing, those gestures that accorded with the tenets of the official artistic doctrine of Socialist Realism. This new *Bolt* was not, however, staged; Grigorovich went on to revive Shostakovich's *The Golden Age*. (Information in this paragraph comes from *Yuri Grigorovich: Master of the Bolshoi,* directed by Yuri Aldokhin, narrated by John Benson [Moscow: Sovinfilm, 1986].)

15. Lesley-Anne Sayers, "Diaghilev's 'Soviet Ballet': Reconstructing Jakulov's Set Design for *Le Pas d'acier* (1927)," in *Preservation Politics: Dance Revived, Reconstructed, Remade. Proceedings of the Conference at the University of Surrey Roehampton, November 8–9, 1997,* ed. Stephanie Jordan (London: Dance Books, 2000), p. 31.

16. Joachim Noller, "Maschine und Metaphysik: Zur Symbolik der modernen Kunstfigur," *tanzdrama magazin* 43:4 (1998): 17.

17. Neil Edmunds, *The Soviet Proletarian Music Movement* (Oxford, Eng.: Peter Lang, 2000), p. 74.

18. Elizabeth Souritz, "Constructivism and Dance," in *Theatre in Revolution: Russian Avant-Garde Stage Design,* p. 137.

19. The following information on the ballet comes from Lesley-Anne Sayers, "Re-Discovering Diaghilev's *Pas d'acier,*" *Dance Research* 18:2 (Winter 2000): 163–85.

20. Ibid.

21. G[rigoii] M[ikhailovich] Levitin, *Tat'iana Georgievna Bruni* (Leningrad: Khudozhnik RSFSR, 1986), pp. 34–35. Volkhovstroi is the site on Lake Ladoga where an enormous hydroelectric plant was built in accordance with the first Five-Year Plan.

22. Tat'iana Bruni, "O balete s neprekhodiashchei liubov'iu," *Sovetskii balet* 5 (September–October 1991): 36. In a preface to the article on page 33, the editor notes that Bruni drew this image "with her left hand, since her right was paralyzed from a stroke," hence its style differs from that of the other extant images.

23. Ibid.

24. Ibid., p. 33. In a related article from the Soviet period, Tatiana Drozd downplayed the matter, stating that "all of the drawings of the décor" were "lost" rather than "destroyed." Drozd confirms, however, that some of them were "restored" by Bruni in the 1970s for the Bakhrushin Museum ("Roman ee zhizni," *Sovetskii balet* 4 [July–August 1984]: 31).

25. Souritz, "Constructivism and Dance," p. 129. The sketch in question is reproduced on p. 140.

26. Nicoletta Misler, "Designing Gestures in the Laboratory of Dance," in *Theatre in Revolution: Russian Avant-Garde Stage Design,* p. 165.

27. Ibid., p. 159.

28. Rod., "'Bolt,'" p. 4.

29. This latter hypothesis seems more likely, since one of Smirnov's draft scenarios for Act 2 of the ballet, discussed below, describes Kozelkov performing a dance "with two girlfriends from the factory offices" (see n. 41 for the reference).

30. These images are reproduced in various sources. The textile worker can be found in *Paris-Moscou 1900–1930,* 2nd ed. (Paris: Centre Georges Pompidou, 1979), p. 389; the phys-ed participant in *The Great Utopia: The Russian and Soviet Avant-Garde 1915–1932* (New York: Guggenheim Museum, 1992), plate 649; Olga, Kozelkov's girlfriend, the

American and the Japanese fleets in *Tat'iana Georgievna Bruni: Vystavka k 100-letiiu so dnia rozhdeniia,* ed. Valentina Korshikova (St. Petersburg: Gosudarstvennyi muzei teatral'nogo i muzykal'nogo iskusstva, 2002), p. 4; the second, earlier image of Kozelkov's girlfriend, Lazy's girlfriend, and the female Komsomol worker from Act 3 in *Khudozhniki russkogo teatra 1880–1930,* ed. John E. Bowlt (Moscow: Iskusstvo, 1994), plates 360–62; the Drayman in Levitin, *Tat'iana Georgievna Bruni,* p. 28; the Bureaucrat in Souritz, "Constructivism and Dance," p. 141; and the Bungler in Drozd, "Roman ee zhizni," p. 31. Variants of the female Komsomol worker, Bureaucrat, and another figure, the bow-legged, pencil-thin Lady Aesthete (alternately named the Intelligentsia Lady), are included in Bruni, "O balete s neprekhodiashchei liubov'iu," pp. 32 and 33. These latter images date from 1991 and were drawn by the artist with her left hand (see n. 22).

31. The first three are reproduced between pp. 128 and 129 of A[lla] Bogdanova, *Opery i balety Shostakovicha* (Moscow: Sovetskii kompozitor, 1979); the fourth and fifth can be found on *DSCH CD-ROM: The Life and Works of Dmitri Shostakovich,* Chandos Multimedia Cultural Heritage Series 1, CHAN 50001, 2001, images N28F and N27E.

32. For a list of popular song allusions in the score, see Sergei Sapozhnikov, "Dmitry Shostakovich's Ballet *The Bolt* at the Bolshoi," *Music in the USSR* 2 (April–June 1986): 78.

33. The supporters of the New Economic Policy, a free-market system introduced by Lenin in 1921 to assuage Russia's fiscal crisis, but abandoned by Stalin in favor of further State economic control. Elizabeth Wilson clarifies that, in the late 1920s, "the term 'Nepmen' was coined as a pejorative not only for the entrepreneurs who were able to exploit the free market, but for all those who indulged in such 'bourgeois' pastimes as dancing, American jazz, living it up in restaurants, and so on" (*Shostakovich: A Life Remembered* [Princeton, N.J.: Princeton University Press, 1994], p. 68).

34. The secondary literature on the swastika is immense. For a detailed history, see Malcolm Quinn, *The Swastika: Constructing the Symbol* (London and New York: Routledge, 1994), esp. pp. 1–21.

35. Ibid., plate 3.

36. On this point, see Iakubov, "Kommentarii," in Shostakovich, *The Bolt,* p. 277.

37. Slavoj Žižek, *Did Somebody Say Totalitarianism? Five Interventions in the (Mis)Use of a Notion* (London and New York: Verso, 2001), pp. 121–22.

38. L. Mikheeva, *I. I. Sollertinskii: Zhizn' i nasledie* (Leningrad: Sovetskii kompozitor, 1988); quoted in Iakubov, "*The Bolt*: An Unknown Ballet," p. 270.

39. *Dmitrii Shostakovich v pis'makh i dokumentakh,* ed. I. A. Bobykina (Moscow: Glinka State Central Museum of Musical Culture, 2000), pp. 221–22.

40. Tat'iana Vecheslava, *O tom, shto dorogo* (Leningrad: Sovetskii kompozitor, 1989); quoted in Wilson, *Shostakovich: A Life Remembered,* p. 93.

41. Russkii gosudarstvennyi arkhiv literatury i iskusstva Sankt-Peterburg (RGALI SPb), f. 337, op. 1, ed. khr. 73, ff. 7–10 (draft 1) and 23–36 (draft 2). A detailed summary of the contents of the two drafts was generously supplied to me by Laurel Fay. My overview of the drafts, and my brief quotations from them, come from her notes.

42. Iakubov, "Kommentarii," p. 277. Carlyle's translation of this text, from which mine derives, appears on p. 278. Iakubov refers in the quote to E[fim] Sadovnikov, *D. D. Shostakovich: Notograficheskii i bibliograficheskii spravochnik* (Moscow: Muzyka, 1965), pp. 30–34.

43. Sapozhnikov arranged the music of *The Bolt* for the 1976 ballet *Dreamers* (see n. 14). It begs comprehension why Iakubov would consult *Dreamers,* a ballet that deviates in form and content from *The Bolt,* to produce his edition of *The Bolt.*

44. Iakubov, "Kommentarii," p. 277.

45. Reference is made in this and the next two paragraphs to "Cast" and "The Ballet's Plot," in '*Bolt' (V pomoshch' zriteliu). Balet v 3-x deistviiakh. Libretto V. V. [sic] Smirnova.*

Muzyka D. Shostakovicha (Leningrad: Gosudarstvennoe izdatel'stvo khudozhestvennoi literatury, 1931), pp. 11 and 12–16; and Iakubov, "Synopsis," "Cast," and "Contents," in Shostakovich, *The Bolt*, pp. 5–6, 9, and 279–80. I am extremely grateful to Mariia Ratanova for finding and sending the first of these two sources to me.

46. Bruni, "O balete s neprekhodiashchei liubov'iu," p. 36.

47. Ibid. Bruni recalls a stage in the creative process where the hero and heroine were named Pyotr (Gusev) and Olga (Mungalova).

48. Ibid. "The blow brought upon us by the Council for the Arts [*khudsovet*] was terrible: the machine dances were withdrawn from the first dress rehearsal. But the supports for the machines—the cubes and cylinders that signified nothing—remained; we were unable to remove them."

49. Bogdanova, *Opery i balety Shostakovicha*, p. 138.

50. Iakubov, "*The Bolt*: An Unknown Ballet," p. 272 n. 26.

51. Iakubov, "Kommentarii," p. 277. RGALI is the acronym of the Russian State Archive of Literature and Art.

52. Of course, in order for "The Dance of the Silhouettes" to be the original title of "The Dance of the Machines," as Iakubov claims, the music would have to be the same. However, the music of "The Scene with the Bolt," which took the place of "The Dance of the Silhouettes" in the scenario, is unrelated to the music of "The Dance of the Machines." It may be that Shostakovich retitled "The Dance of the Silhouettes" "The Dance of the Machines," transplanted the number from Act 3 to Act 1, and then composed new music under the title "The Scene with the Bolt."

53. Gerard McBurney, personal communication, 22 June 2003. My thanks to the author for his counsel on this matter.

54. Laurel E. Fay, "Mitya in the Music Hall," unpublished colloquium typescript, 1995. An abbreviated version of this essay was published in Russian as "Mitia v miuzik-kholle," *Muzykal'naia akademiia* 4 (1997): 59–62. I am grateful to the author for sharing the English-language text with me.

55. Unsigned, "Pererabotka 'Bolta' (Beseda s khud. rukovoditelem Teatra opery i baleta S. E. Radlovym)," *Rabochii i teatr* 12 (30 April 1931): 22. Radlov proposes a "radical revision or removal of such episodes as 'the blacksmith,' 'the colonial slaves,' a significant reconfiguration of the look and dancing of the philistines, and a complete reworking of the Red Army's final dances." Radlov adds that his biggest challenge concerned enhancing the dramatic meaning of the pantomimed episodes.

The revision was to be performed once on 28 June 1931. For the bulletin announcing the remounting, see "Za 10 dnei," *Rabochii i teatr* 16 (11 June 1931): 15; for the bulletin announcing the cancellation of the remounting, see "Za 10 dnei," *Rabochii i teatr* 17 (21 June 1931): 15. The latter reads: "Owing to entire series of organizational miscommunications, no work has been conducted on the withdrawn ballet *The Bolt*, and this spectacle has been permanently removed from the repertoire without any redevelopment. *The Red Poppy* will take the place of the scheduled performance of *The Bolt* on 28 June."

56. RGALI SPb, f. 337, op. 1, ed. khr. 73, includes, according to Fay's notes, the minutes of the artistic and political council of the State Academic Theatre from 22 September 1930 (folio 1 recto and verso) and 7 September 1931 (folios 2–3). Folios 4–5 contain information about the planned reconstruction of the ballet as well as a 28 June 1931 letter from V. Loginov of the Factory named after Karl Marx.

57. On this subject, see J. Douglas Clayton, *Commedia dell'Arte/Balagan in Twentieth-Century Russian Theatre and Drama* (Montreal and Kingston: McGill-Queen's University Press, 1993).

58. I[van] Sollertinskii, "'Bolt' i problema sovetskogo baleta," in *'Bolt' (V pomoshch' zriteliu)*, p. 8. Iakubov comments on this same quotation in "*The Bolt*: An Unknown Ballet," p. 273.

59. Sollertinskii, "'Bolt' i problema sovetskogo baleta," p. 9.

60. Ibid., pp. 6–7.

61. Slavoj Žižek, "Between the Two Revolutions," in *Revolution at the Gates: Selected Writings of Lenin from 1917,* ed. Slavoj Žižek (London and New York: Verso, 2002), p. 8.

62. Fedor Lopukhov, *Puti baletmeistera* (Berlin: Petropolis, 1925), p. 44. Other portions of this treatise can be read in translation in *Fedor Lopukhov, Writings on Ballet and Music,* ed. and intro. Stephanie Jordan; trans. Dorinda Offord (Madison: University of Wisconsin Press, 2002).

63. Ibid., p. 45.

64. Ibid.

65. Marianne Shapiro, "Preliminaries to a Semiotics of Ballet," in *The Sign in Music and Literature,* ed. Wendy Steiner (Austin: University of Texas Press, 1981), p. 226.

66. Ibid.

67. In a 1930 interview about the future of LENTRAM (Leningrad Theatre of Worker Youth), M. Sokolovsky, the director, declared that the "methods" of the organization should be applied "to the various branches of art. In tandem with IZORAM [Worker Youth in the Fine Arts], it is time to consider MUZORAM [Music] and ballet RAM, which will be unified within the council of RAM organizations" (S. R., "TRAM na zavtra," *Rabochii i teatr* 11 [26 February 1930]: 4). For context on this interview, see Clark, *Petersburg,* p. 267.

68. Information in this paragraph comes from A. Gvozdev, "O reforme baleta: Kharakternyi tanets," *Zhizn' iskusstva* 4 (24 January 1928): 4–5; I[van] Sollertinskii, "Poiski sovetskogo tantsa: Iz zametok o balete," *Rabochii i teatr* 45 (14 August 1930): 2–3; L. Iakobson, "Na povestne—baletnyi teatr," *Rabochii i teatr* 26 (8 October 1931): 6–8.

69. Ravich., "Bol'shoi teatr na perelome ('Futbolist' na stsene mosk. Bol'shogo teatra)," *Rabochii i teatr* 22 (21 April 1930): 13.

70. Sim. Dreiden, "Seans zariadovoi gimnastiki ('Attraktsiony v deistvii')," *Rabochii i teatr* 16 (21 March 1930): 9.

71. Jane Feuer, "The Self-Reflective Musical and the Myth of Entertainment," *Quarterly Review of Film Studies* 2:3 (1977): 161.

72. Elizabeth Souritz, *Soviet Choreographers in the 1920s,* trans. Lynn Visson (London: Dance Books, 1990), pp. 284 and 318. ROSTA is the acronym for Russian Telegraph Agency (Rossiiskoe Telegrafnoe Agenstvo).

73. These terms, and the preceding information in this paragraph on time-space relationships in choreography, come from Maxine Sheets, *The Phenomenology of Dance* (Madison and Milwaukee: University of Wisconsin Press, 1966), pp. 10–31, esp. 18–19.

74. Empa., "'Bolt' i BOLTlivye formalisty," *Bytovaia gazeta,* 15 April 1931, p. 2.

75. G[alina] Dobrovol'skaia, *Fedor Lopukhov* (Leningrad: Iskusstvo, 1976), p. 200.

76. Souritz, "Constructivism and Dance," p. 140.

77. Žižek, "Between the Two Revolutions," p. 8. For an entertaining gloss on the double-voicedness of Shostakovich's music, one to which I refer below, see the same author's *Did Somebody Say Totalitarianism?,* pp. 123–27.

78. Clark, *Petersburg,* p. 270.

79. Lopukhov, *Shest'desiat let v balete: Vospominaniia i zapiski baletmeistera,* ed. Iu. Slonimskii (Moscow: Iskusstvo, 1966), pp. 257–58.

80. Žižek, *Did Somebody Say Totalitarianism?,* p. 125.

81. Ibid.

82. I refer here and in what follows to Iakubov's published piano edition of the score; my further comments on instrumentation derive from the complete recording of the ballet by Gennady Rozhdestvensky and the Royal Stockholm Philharmonic Orchestra issued on two compact discs by Chandos Records, CHAN 9343/4, in 1995.

83. Reference is made here to the rhythmic accelerandi of Aleksandr Borodin's Polovtsian Dances from *Prince Igor,* staged by the Ballets Russes in 1909, and to the 5/4 ending of Maurice Ravel's *Daphnis et Chloé* (1912). Michel Fokine created the choreography for both works.

84. Ol'ga Dansker, "Shostakovich v dnevnikakh M. O. Shteinberga," in *Shostakovich: Mezhdu mgnoveniem i vechnost'iu. Dokumenty. Materialy. Stat'i,* ed. L. G. Kovnatskaia (St. Petersburg: Kompozitor, 2000), p. 108. The conductor of *The Bolt,* Aleksandr Gauk (1893–1963), unsurprisingly took the opposite stance, claiming that reviewers "all remarked on the success of the musical side; but the music, unfortunately, was not enough to guarantee the ballet's success" (*Aleksandr Vasil'evich Gauk: Memuary, izbrannye stat'i, vospominaniia sovremennikov* [Moscow: Sovetskii kompozitor, 1975]; quoted in Wilson, *Shostakovich: A Life Remembered,* p. 92).

85. Allen Wood, "Dialectical Materialism," in *The Oxford Companion to Philosophy,* ed. Ted Honderich (Oxford, Eng.: Oxford University Press, 1995), p. 198.

86. Ibid.

87. Clark, *Petersburg,* p. 272.

88. Ibid.

89. V. G-v, "V bor'be za tramovskogo dvizheniia" (*Zhizn' iskusstva* 19 (12 May 1929); quoted in Clark, *Petersburg,* p. 268.

90. Mikhail Zoshchenko, "About Myself, About Critics, and About My Work" (1927); quoted in Jeremy Hicks, *Mikhail Zoshchenko and the Poetics of Skaz* (Nottingham, Eng.: Astra Press, 2000), p. 161. For context on the relationship between Shostakovich and Zoshchenko, see Clark, *Petersburg,* pp. 235–36.

91. Hicks, *Mikhail Zoshchenko and the Poetics of Skaz,* p. 161.

92. This phrase derives from the punning title of the review of the ballet printed in *Bytovaia gazeta,* "'Bolt' i BOLTlivye formalisty," which translates as "*The Bolt* and Blathering Formalists," or in Carlyle's rendering, "*The Bolt* and Formalist Chatterboxes" (Iakubov, "*The Bolt*: An Unknown Ballet," p. 274 n. 35).

93. This and the other quotations in the paragraph come from D[mitrii] Shostakovich, "Deklaratsiia obiazannostei kompozitora," *Rabochii i teatr* 31 (20 November 1931): 6. M. Iankovskii, the author of "Who's Against? It's Unanimous," opined, "You [Shostakovich] are trying to reassign blame for your own mistakes, for your own loss of direction and confusion concerning Soviet theater and Soviet cinematography. Now who's responsible for this crisis? [. . .] Isn't it you who has recently taken the path of least resistance? Isn't it you who—in flailing about between the ballet and music hall, the music hall and TRAM [Theatre of Worker Youth], TRAM and the cinema studio, the cinema studio and the operetta—has begun to lose your creative personality?" ("Kto protiv—edinoglasno: Otkrytoe pis'mo D. Shostakovichu," *Rabochii i teatr* 32–33 [7 December 1931]: 10).

94. Unsigned, "Baletnaia fal'sh'," *Pravda,* 6 February 1936, p. 3.

95. Shostakovich, "Deklaratsiia obiazannostei kompozitora," p. 6.

96. Hicks, *Mikhail Zoshchenko and the Poetics of Skaz,* p. 3.

The Nose and the Fourteenth Symphony:

An Affinity of Opposites

LEVON HAKOBIAN

TRANSLATED BY DIMITRI SHAPOVALOV

Within Shostakovich's legacy, his witty youthful opera, *The Nose* (1928), and his gloomy penultimate symphony, the Fourteenth (1969), occupy opposite poles. And yet they have something in common. Unlike most other large-scale works by the composer, they were created by a free man, one burdened neither by political pressures nor by the voluntarily assumed mission of the "artist-citizen," the chronicler of his own time, the humanist who pleads for "mercy for the fallen." Both works communicate as expressive in the highest degree because they are "pure"; that is, they are politically, ideologically, and sociologically untainted illustrations of a worldview deeply rooted in the literary tradition of St. Petersburg that bloomed opulently under Soviet rule. This worldview may be characterized succinctly as a nondialectical split vision of the world, together with a precariously intimate stance toward the sphere of the otherworldly.

Many commentators have pointed to the organic dependency of Gogolian humor on the well-known genius loci of St. Petersburg—this "city of the half-mad," where the human soul is "subjected to the gloomiest, most aggressive, and strangest influences," and where doctors, attorneys, and philosophers were able to carry out their "most treasured inquiries" (Dostoevsky). Shostakovich was destined to be born and live just shy of forty years in this wholly artificial city—in Dostoevsky's words, "the most intentional in the world"—the burial ground for the thousands of slaves who built it, and which thereafter acquired the infamy of being a cursed spot in Russian history. Moreover, the beginning of the composer's conscious existence was fated to coincide with a moment in history that in a most emphatic fashion confirmed the deeper truth of St. Petersburg's genius loci empirically. At that turning point, a band of malicious homunculi, fuming with vengeful violence as if they were Peter's slaves risen from their graves, massacred the sugar-pampered offspring of the dreadful demiurge. It is not surprising that Shostakovich's older contemporaries often perceived the events of the first years following the 1917 Revolution as unfolding in some otherworldly space, on the other side of reality: "The dead are firing at the dead. So it does not matter who will win. By the way . . . are you afraid? Me neither. Not at all. And that's how things should be. It's the living that will be afraid . . . later."[1]

A similar perception of reality (qualitatively different from any kind of humanism) was also characteristic of Shostakovich's contemporaries, the writers of the group Oberiu, whose work has been rightfully regarded as inspired by Gogol's literary legacy.[2] The double influence of an original Petersburgian tradition inherited from Gogol and of the new reality these writers—who referred to themselves as "Oberiuty"—experienced while living in the "cradle of the revolution" resulted in a remarkable hybrid far removed from the official Soviet model of the world but upon which it was simultaneously dependent and of which it was a distinctive form of critique. The critique, in this instance, is not a refutation of specific details of this model (otherwise we would be dealing with social satire or with protest literature) but rather the rejection of some of its most basic gnoseological and ontological principles. Thus, in one of Daniil Kharms's miniatures, we can observe how the idea featured in Gogol's "The Nose" receives new treatment. If in the Gogol "the crack dissecting the world" separates a man from his own nose, Kharms has many such "cracks" that dismember the human body, dividing it into mutually estranged parts, thus irreversibly erasing the line between being and nonexistence. The ontological problem broached in this miniature touches upon many pressing questions of Soviet actuality; in his presentation, however, Kharms carefully avoids any concrete associations:

There was a red-haired man who had no eyes or ears. He had no hair either, so he was called "red-haired" only by convention.

He could not speak, because he did not have a mouth. He had no nose, either.

He did not even have arms or legs. Nor did he have a belly, nor did he have a back, nor did he have a spine, nor any intestines. He had nothing! So nobody knows who we are talking about.

Maybe we had better not talk about him then.[3]

Shostakovich belonged to the same generation and social milieu as the Oberiuty. Although none of them participated in the creation of the libretto for *The Nose,* the opera's musical-dramatic design turned out to be surprisingly close in spirit to the ideas promoted within their literary circle. (This is not to deny the significance of other sources of influence on the opera, among which Meyerhold's staging of Gogol's *The Inspector General* and Berg's *Wozzeck* are the best known and commonly recognized ones.) Shostakovich's opera views Gogol's text through the lens of experiences common to both the composer and the Oberiuty.

At first glance, the opera appears to be the product of an unimpeded youthful imagination. It is filled with extravagances such as singing and playing in extreme registers; naturalistic sound imitation; sudden switches from simple triadic harmony to radical atonality and vice versa without any external justification; passages of intentionally muddled, quasi-aleatoric texture; parodic quotations and stylistically foreign interpolations that abound with "wrong" notes and appear, it would seem, in the most inappropriate contexts; and so forth. It is as if Shostakovich wants to convince us that at any given moment in *The Nose* anything is possible. However, this seeming anarchy reveals its affinity with a particular principle of Oberiu theater, as delineated in the movement's "Manifesto":

> We take a plot—a dramatic one. It develops at first in a simple manner, and then it is suddenly interrupted by apparently unrelated events that seem clearly ridiculous. . . . That is why a *dramatic* plot would not appear to the audience as an unambiguous plot-building device; rather, it flickers, as it were, in the background of the action. It is supplanted by a *scenic* plot that spontaneously arises out of all elements of our play.[4]

The principle of combining two different "plots" is realized in practice in "Elizaveta Bam," a play by Kharms staged for the first time in 1928. The arrest of the heroine, accused of an unknown crime, comprises the play's "dramatic" plot. This plot is interrupted by elements of a "scenic" plot: a series of scenes that are diverse in character, logically unconnected or mutually contradictory, and for the most part acutely grotesque and funny. An analysis of Shostakovich's opera reveals at least three interlocking "plots," two of which are fully analogous to the "scenic" and "dramatic" plots of the Oberiuty. Episodes that parody various musical genres conform to the "scenic plot" of the opera. (In the present instance it would be better to call this the "music genre" plot.) These include the church chorus in scene 4; the eight-part canon of the yard-keepers in scene 5;

the folk songs in scene 6 (the solo number of the servant Ivan) and in scene 7 (the chorus of the policemen); several grotesque gallops in the first and third acts; and the numerous short fragments with easily recognized genre traits that are dispersed throughout the opera. All of these episodes arise spontaneously in the musical stream of consciousness and align themselves according to a single principle of construction: melodic and rhythmic elements typical of one or another popular genre are inserted into a context that proves to be decidedly "disharmonious." The beginning of Miss Podtochina's "romance" from Act 3, scene 8, may serve as an example. While preserving its original rhythm and character of motion, the initial accompaniment figure gradually degenerates into a pattern of seemingly random sounds that contrasts sharply with the melodic content of the vocal part.

Example 1. Shostakovich, *The Nose,* Act 3, scene 8, rehearsal number 436–437.

Gogol's tale of the loss, search for, and reacquisition of the Nose functions as the "dramatic" plot of the opera. Its components, which include the original text (with some insertions borrowed primarily from Gogol's other works), are set to music according to principles that bear a close relationship to Musorgsky's musicalization of Russian speech in his unfinished opera *The Marriage*. Despite the thoroughly dissonant, atonal context into which Gogol's text is placed, this plot line—if taken by itself, dissociated from the multilayered structure of the opera—hinges in its entirety on reasonably traditional means. The greater part of Shostakovich's effort is focused on a precise (or, if necessary, purposefully imprecise, hyperbolized) translation of the intonations and intricacies of spoken speech, while issues of specifically musical form-building interest him comparatively little. More or less extensive aria-like episodes are rare. Structures with solid genre traits extending over long portions of music do not play a vital role. When they do appear, such structures manifest themselves as spontaneous "spillovers" of musical speech-streams rising from the depths of the "dramatic" plot level to reach the more superficial plot level of "musical genre"—that is, they appear as elements whose purpose is to create the effect of the absurd. A characteristic case is shown in Example 2, a segment from the Doctor's "arioso" advising Kovalev how to treat his "illness." The arrival of what in terms of genre amounts to a polka (mm. 5–9 in our example) in the midst of a lengthy semi-recitative set in prose is a typical Oberiu device. It recalls possibilities for interaction between the dramatic and scenic plots described in the Oberiu manifesto: an actor portraying a Russian peasant suddenly switches to Latin, while an actor portraying a minister begins to howl like a wolf and crawls across the stage on all fours.[5]

If Shostakovich, when he was organizing the opera's musical material, had limited it to two "plots" according to the model offered by the Oberiu theater, it would already have been sufficient for a good-quality comic opera with a distinct accent on the absurd. But the composer goes further and constructs a new, third "plot," substantially enriching the structure of the work as a whole and intensifying its dramatic "Kafkaesque" aspect. Essentially, the structure of the opera results from the interaction of not two but three stylistically heterogeneous layers. The "dramatic" plot, the *fabula* of Gogol's short story, is superimposed in this structure over the deepest layer of the opera, a kind of a second dramatic plot in its own right that truly "flickers in the background of the action" and serves as the backbone for the entire musical-dramatic construction. In Gogol's tale, this deepest level is practically nonexistent. Just as with the "musical genre" plot, it is entirely Shostakovich's invention and reveals the composer's spiritual affinity with the Oberiuty. Its theme consists of the persecution, torture, and massacre of a victim. This theme is only superficially explored in Gogol's short story (less so than in some of his other works), whereas in the oeuvre of Kharms, Oleinikov, and other poets of the Oberiu circle, it plays a paramount role.

Example 2. Shostakovich, *The Nose,* Act 3, scene 8, from rehearsal number 416 + 5mm.

The creators of the early literature of the absurd keenly perceived the primacy of an atavistic, crude force as an integral part of their lives which they assimilated into their art as well. Shostakovich shared the Kharmsian notion of human interrelationships in a world where regular tributes in the form of "the bones of slaves" were necessary to attain desired order. Such a view withholds completely any kind of sympathy for the weak side, that is to say, the victim. Of course, this contradicts the hallowed tradition of Russian humanist literature but, on the other hand, accurately captures the spirit of the newly triumphant absurd.[6] The unfinished dramatic miniature by Kharms reproduced below, which is in some respect a modernized version of Gogol's "The Tale of How Ivan Ivanovich Quarreled with Ivan Nikiforovich," fashions human relationships in the new society more accurately and eloquently than entire volumes of satiric or denunciatory politically charged literature:

GRIGORIEV (*hitting SEMENOV in the mug*): So here you go, it's winter! Time to light up the fireplace. What do you say?

SEMENOV: Yes, taking your point into consideration, I would say that it is indeed time to kindle up the fireplace.

GRIGORIEV (*hitting SEMENOV in the mug*): So what do you say, is this winter going to be cold or warm?

SEMENOV: Well, judging by the fact that we had much rain in the summer, the winter is going to be cold. If it rains much in the summer, the next winter is always cold.

GRIGORIEV (*hitting SEMENOV in the mug*): But I'm never cold!

SEMENOV: This is absolutely correct that you say you are never cold. You are that way.

GRIGORIEV (*hitting SEMENOV in the mug*): I never get cold!

SEMENOV: Ow!

GRIGORIEV (*hitting SEMENOV in the mug*): "Ow" what?

SEMENOV: Ow, my face hurts!

GRIGORIEV: Why does it hurt? (*Punching SEMENOV in the mug right then.*)

SEMENOV (*falling off the chair*): Ow! I have no idea why.

GRIGORIEV (*kicking SEMENOV in the mug*): And I'm not hurting anywhere!

SEMENOV: You son of a bitch, I'll teach you how to fight! (*Trying to get up.*)

GRIGORIEV (*hitting SEMENOV in the mug*): Yeah, right, you're gonna teach me now!

SEMENOV (*falling flat on his back*): You rotten scum!

GRIGORIEV: Hey, watch your language there!

SEMENOV (*straining to get up*): I've been tolerating this for a long time, brother. But enough already! You don't understand normal language, it seems. It's your own fault, brother . . .

GRIGORIEV (*hitting SEMENOV with the heel of his boot*): You keep talking, keep talking! We're listening!

SEMENOV (*falling flat on his back*): Ow . . .[7]

The plot of the persecution/torture/massacre of a victim materializes in the opera *The Nose* as a series of scenes that become more and more populated and intense as the action progresses. The scenes comprising this "secondary" dramatic plot display extreme structural primitivism and adhere to the same pattern: they all end with the repetitive hammering out of some basic ostinato figure, just like the periodic "hits in the mug" from the miniature about Grigoriev and Semenov quoted above. Thus, every episode from this plot line comes to a dead end with no other recourse than to switch immediately into either of the other two remaining "plots." By itself, this mechanism serves as a powerful means for creating effects quite in the spirit of the Oberiu theater of the absurd. A comparatively simple and telling illustration is an excerpt from scene 2, the chasing down of the barber Ivan Iakovlevich by curious pedestrians, before the entrance of the policeman at rehearsal number 61. Example 3 shows the final part of this episode, the moment when it degenerates into metaphorical "hits in the mug." A switch to the "musical genre" plot takes place immediately afterward as the policeman, accompanied by domras, delivers his phrase in pellucid C major.[8]

The chase scene in question is still comparatively innocuous—as is the episode that precedes it, when Praskovia Osipovna, Ivan Iakovlevich's wife, throws her husband out into the street. Her hysterical shrieks, "Out! Out! Out!," onto which the meek, apologetic babble of Ivan Iakovlevich is superimposed, function here as the prevalent ostinato element. The atmosphere becomes more menacing later, in the pantomimic chase after that same long-suffering barber by a detachment of policemen (the famous entr'acte for percussion between the second and third scenes). Act 2 does not contain analogous episodes. From the dramatic standpoint, they are replaced in part by the instrumental fragment (the "interlude") that will be examined below. But in Act 3, we encounter three chase episodes; moreover, each new one surpasses its predecessor both in terms of scope and in the number of characters involved. The first episode is the attack by policemen on the pretzel vendor in scene 7, after rehearsal number 346. The lewd shouts of the policemen ("Ah! Ah! Ah!") respond to the equally monotonous wails of the street vendor ("Oi! Oi! Oi!"). The second episode, from the same scene, depicts a crowd attacking and beating the Nose while shouting, "Get him! Get him!" Finally, the third episode features yet another bloodthirsty crowd running around aimlessly looking for the Nose and its eventual dispersal by the police. (This happens at the end of scene 8, after rehearsal number 501, when the policemen answer the crowd's repeated question, "Where? Where? Where? Where is he?" with their own cry, "Break it up! Break it up!"). None of the episodes described

Example 3. Shostakovich, *The Nose*, Act 1, scene 2, from rehearsal number 59 + 3mm.

above appear in Gogol's text: they are either wholly conjured up or they stem from casual phrases like the mention of the Nose being "captured almost on his way there," as he attempts to dash off to Riga. In each case, the music mimics the atavistic, primitive automatism that drives the crowd. Examples 4a, 4b, and 4c illustrate the underlying pattern.

Thus, the structure of Shostakovich's first opera consists of three inter-penetrating "plots," each of which employs its own specific means of organizing musical material. This "counterpoint of plots" allows us to discern the latent theme of the entire work—the theme of unreasoning cruelty, ruthlessness, bloodthirstiness—as presented from a displaced "absurdist" angle, thereby revealing the kinship between Shostakovich's conception of music theater and the ideas that were taking shape within the Oberiu literary circle at the same time. The only place in the opera that operates outside this absurdist realm is the orchestral interlude between the fifth and sixth scenes. Its centrality is underscored by its

Example 4a. Shostakovich, *The Nose,* Act 3, scene 7, from rehearsal number 346 + 4mm.

Example 4b. Shostakovich, *The Nose,* Act 3, scene 7, rehearsal number 356.

Example 4c. Shostakovich, *The Nose,* Act 3, scene 8, ending.

topography. The interlude is situated in the middle of the second act, in between two vividly grotesque episodes that belong to the "musical genre" plot: the octet of the yard-keepers and the little ditty of the servant Ivan. A fugato takes up the larger part of the interlude in question. However, here it is not a caricature of a serious genre but a quite genuine specimen of genre, defiled neither by nonsensical, unconnected thematic writing (such as the canon of the eight yard-keepers) nor by the idiotic dialogue of a noseless Major and his own Nose General (such as the church chorus from scene 4, which otherwise is quite elegantly stylized). The fugato makes a pedantic point about discharging the requirements of its genre. Here we find such well-recognized hallmarks of traditional contrapuntal writing as tonal answers, countersubjects, the theme in inversion, stretti, and so forth. The theme, presented first in a fairly clear G minor with alternating seventh degree (see Example 5) appears in almost all minor keys as the fugato proceeds.

Example 5. Shostakovich, *The Nose,* Act 2, orchestral interlude between scenes 5 and 6, rehearsal number 238.

The interlude from the second act is the only more or less extensive integral episode in the opera that allows us to consider the presence of a musical *logic* as such. As far as the rest of the material of the opera is concerned, it is built on three principles. The first is the complete rejection of any immanent musical logic. This is true for most places in the music that belong to the "dramatic" plot on the primary level. The same can be said with respect to the composition of the opera as a whole, with its characteristically unpredictable, capricious relationships between the "plots." The second principle is the grotesque violation of "proper," long-established, and logically verified correlations between the thematic writing and its context (as in the episodes of the "musical genre" plot). Finally, the music may reduce its logic to the level of the most primitive tautology (as in the episodes of the "dramatic" plot of the secondary level). Metaphorically speaking, the interlude from Act 2 is the only island of relative stability and order that survives the all-crushing typhoon of the absurd.

Continuing the comparison of the poetics of Shostakovich's opera with the poetics of "Petersburg" literature of the absurd in the 1920s, we might recall the peculiar semantic function of the lyrical undertones that occasionally punctuate the opera. A ballad by Nikolai Oleinikov, "Gluttony," is telling in this respect, as it contains the following lines concerning the death of the "lyric hero":

Buried, forgotten,
I lay in the ground,
Covered with a horse-cloth,
I tremble with fear.
I tremble because
I have started to rot
But I want to eat and drink
Twice as much.
I crave food,
I crave meatballs,
And pretty tea,
And pretty sweets.
Love I do not need,
I do not need passions,
I want some lemonade
And vegetables!
But my pleas go unanswered—
Only the boards creak,
And melancholy crawls
Into the poet's heart.[9]

In regard to the last lines, a respected scholar has written:

This is real melancholy, and it belongs to a real poet. But these are
not the melancholy and the poet bequeathed to us by poetic tradition. . . . Any real poet . . . needs elevated words that reflect his longing
for true values. How does he come by a new elevated word? He does
not invent them; he takes eternal words—*poet, death, melancholy* . . .
—and lets them into the thick mix of a verbal haberdashery. And
there, they mean something they have never meant before. . . .
Milled through many words with the opposite value sign, the all-
poetic word has retained its emotional halo but given away its
inherited meanings.[10]

The longing for "true values" contained in the elevated poetic Word,
even if this Word is distorted and defiled by a nonsensical context, raises
the poetics of the absurd above the level of a simple play with "opposite
value signs." The interlude from Act 2 of *The Nose* functions as the musical equivalent of such a Word. This is the place where, having acquired
a specific quality surrounded by "opposite value signs," the longing of a
real artist for true values crawls into the music of this absurdist opera.

Thus, behind the anarchic surface of the work a rather clear-cut picture of the world emerges, one governed by the desire to demarcate the sphere of the "internal" (a storage space for comparatively reliable and long-established values) from the sphere of the "external" (populated by some kind of grotesque and terrifying creatures). This worldview continues the traditional Petersburgian "mythology," in which the most important topic—at least since the time of Pushkin's "The Bronze Horseman"—has been the incompatibility of a private individual's internal life with the amorphous, inhuman environment. The eminent thinker Vasilii Rozanov (1856–1919), one of the comparatively late exponents of this outlook, formulated his credo in one of his notebooks, *Solitary Thoughts*:

> My God is special. It is only *my* God; and nobody else's. If "somebody else's"—then I do not know and am not interested in that.
>
> "My God" is my infinite intimacy, my infinite individuality. Intimacy resembles a cone, or even two cones. From my "social I" stems one cone, shrinking down to a point. . . . Beyond this point, another cone is located: this is not a shrinking infinity but, on the contrary, an expanding one. This is God. "There-God."[11]

In Shostakovich's opera, the realm of inner life and subjective expressivity (the realm of "Here-God," so to speak) is symbolically represented in musical episodes written in complex, fully developed polyphonic forms, while the surrounding world is portrayed predominantly by such means as exaggeratedly mechanistic ostinato and grotesque distortion of traditional genre paradigms. In his later works, Shostakovich occasionally turned to an analogous method of style juxtaposition, endowing it with transparent, extramusical meaning. He also used elements of twelve-tone composition—a technique that makes its way into his stylistic arsenal beginning with the penultimate movement of the Thirteenth Symphony ("Fears")—as part of this method. There is no need to remind the reader that Shostakovich never handled twelve-tone structures according to the rules of serial composition. For him, "twelve-toneness" functions rather like a means for constructing abstract, at times deliberately lifeless, melodic lines that often contrast with an altogether different kind of music, one that points (as does the orchestral interlude from *The Nose*) to the sphere of noble, lofty traditional values.

The case of the Fourteenth Symphony—for soprano, bass, strings, and percussion to words by Garcia Lorca, Brentano, Apollinaire, Küchelbecker, and Rilke—is especially telling in this respect.[12] Dodecaphonic melodic lines predominate in nine of its eleven movements. Many of the twelve-tone rows scattered throughout the score cannot be reduced to a common denominator. A relatively crude differentiation results in the following classification: in movements 2, 5 (especially in the instrumental parts), and 8, rows based on fourths and/or fifths are most prevalent, particularly those in which these intervals are overlapping or adjacent. Movements 1, 3, 4,

Example 6. Shostakovich, Fourteenth Symphony, twelve-tone rows of the first and second types. Rows of the first type: a through f. Rows of the second type: g through o.

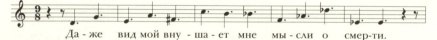

Example 6a. Movement 2, after rehearsal number 10.

Example 6b. Movement 2, after rehearsal number 11.

Example 6c. Movement 3, after rehearsal number 32.

Example 6d. Movement 5, the refrain.

Example 6e. Movement 5, after rehearsal number 71.

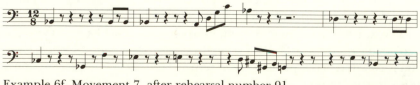

Example 6f. Movement 7, after rehearsal number 91.

(1)　(2)　(3)　　　　(4)　(5)　(6)　(7)　(8)　(9)　(10)　(11)　(12)

Example 6g. Movement 1, beginning, see also movement 10.

За - мол - чй - те,　е - пис-коп!　По-мо-ли - тесь　и　верь - те:

Example 6h. Movement 3, after rehearsal number 26.

Example 6i. Movement 3, after rehearsal number 50.

Example 6j. Movement 4, after rehearsal number 60.

Example 6k. Movement 4, after rehearsal number 62.

И　вот　　　по - э - то-му хо - чу　я стать кра-си　－　вой.

Пусть яр － ким　фа-ке-лом　грудь у ме-ня　го － рит,

Example 6l. Movement 5, after rehearsal number 70.

Example 6m. Movement 7, beginning.

Example 6n. Movement 7, after rehearsal number 96.

Example 6o. Movement 7, after rehearsal number 103.

7, and 10, on the other hand, emphasize rows based on seconds and thirds (sixths). Generally speaking, rows of the first type are connected with the topoi of cold indifference, of monstrosity, and of the meaninglessness of death, and rows of the second type with the topoi of living human emotions: grief, sorrow, compassion. Characteristically, when semantically appropriate, rows of the first type can also be found in movements 3 (see five measures after rehearsal number 32, with the text "even my looks arouse thoughts of death in me") and 7 (the instrumental canoninterlude fulfills a clearly illustrative function). Several rows of both types are given in Example 6; they by no means exhaust the profusion of twelve-tone structures employed in the symphony.

Twelve-tone rows form a specific environment—a kind of distorting mirror—for motives scattered across the score that possess a symbolic meaning for Shostakovich's oeuvre as a whole.[13] Setting aside the brief "Conclusion," which is cut short abruptly, the only movement free of any twelve-tone configurations is the ninth (the elegy "O Delvig, Delvig!"). In its dramatic function, this strictly tonal piece—which is essentially an emphatically traditional lyrical romance—is comparable to the orchestral interlude from *The Nose*.

It is commonly accepted that the Fourteenth Symphony explores the idea of death. We should note, however, that the theme of death is completely missing not only from the movement "O Delvig, Delvig!" but also from the movement that directly precedes it ("The Reply of the Zaporozhian Cossacks to the Sultan of Constantinople"). In the movement immediately preceding "The Reply of the Cossacks" (the seventh, "At the Santé Jail"), death is invoked only as a metaphor for the loss of freedom. In one of my publications, I have advanced an interpretation according to which the Fourteenth Symphony follows the canonic structural layout of the requiem.[14] The absence of death in the eighth and ninth movements can be explained by the fact that, in the context of the work as a whole, these movements function respectively as the equivalents of the Sanctus and Benedictus. I will not develop this hypothesis further here. I would simply like to stress that death is by no means the leading "character" of the symphony. The essence of the work, its "gist," lies in another sphere. Although the symphony, in contrast with the opera, does not manifest a direct connection to the Petersburgian mythology mentioned above, it continues the line that was first broached in *The Nose*: an examination of a world in the process of disintegration. The opera and the symphony may be perceived as two meditations on the same theme; only one of these "meditations" assumes a humorous and rather undisciplined identity, while the other is more somber and comparatively ordered. In the earlier case, it is empty repetitiveness and "wrong" harmony that serve as musical symbols for universal and ubiquitous decline and destruction; in the latter, this function is carried out by artificially constructed twelve-tone rows (that is to say, something that in the USSR of the 1960s was perceived as empty and improper). In both cases, a certain space is reserved for subjective utterance (the equivalent of Schumann's "Der Dichter spricht"—the poet is speaking) that is embodied musically by means of traditional forms in which the "optimal" ratio between the fundamental categories of order and freedom is preserved.

Shostakovich's attraction to the theme discussed here could be linked, if so desired, to his direct, lifelong experience of the inhuman and decomposing Soviet system. However, *The Nose* and the Fourteenth Symphony belong to those of Shostakovich's works that do not lend themselves to facile interpretation using terms like "civic mourning," "Aesopian language," and other, by now worn-out clichés of the same kind. The author of *The Nose* and the Fourteenth Symphony engages not so much in a critique of the society in which he was obliged to live, as in an analysis of the fundamental and insuperable dualism of human existence within empirical reality (to use Rozanov's terminology, the dualistic realms of "Here-God" and "There-God"). Thus Shostakovich reveals his connection with the subculture of Russian Gnosticism, which developed especially vigorously under the yoke of the Soviet regime as an unofficial, "shadow" counterweight to the strictly monistic official ideology.[15] Shostakovich emerges in *The Nose* as a precursor, and in the Fourteenth Symphony as a representative, of the post-Stalinist Soviet musical avant-garde, the senior colleague of Gubaidulina, Schnittke, Silvestrov, and Pärt, whose works from that time belong to the same Gnostic subculture. All of these composers readily employed "risky" contemporary Western techniques to depict low, "shadow" spheres of imagery, thus pointedly setting off the transcendent, ideal images that were depicted using completely different means, usually an emphatically conservative musical language. (This kind of a stylistic dualism, reflecting the idea of mutually alienated, ontologically incongruous realms, became something of an idée fixe for the nonconformist Soviet music of the post-Stalinist era.)[16]

Thus, the place occupied by *The Nose* and the Fourteenth Symphony within Shostakovich's legacy, and also their similarities, are defined by the fact that they were written by a truly free artist, one not burdened by the necessity to prove or defend himself, to respond to the events of the day or—as recent studies have claimed—to get things off his chest by deceiving the censors. This is precisely why these two works manifest, in such an outspoken and uncompromising fashion, the most important metaphysical theme of Shostakovich's work—the theme of the decline of the universe, the disruption of the "correct" order of things.

NOTES

1. Georgii Ivanov conveyed these words of Aleksandr Blok in his *Peterburgskie zimy* (Moscow: Kniga, 1989), p. 384. The dialogue took place in March of 1921, during the Kronstadt uprising.

2. The best known members of Oberiu (which is an acronym for *Ob"edinenie real'nogo iskusstva* [Association for Real Art]) were: Nikolai Zabolotsky (1903–1958), Aleksandr Vvedensky (1904–1941), and Daniil Kharms (1905–1942). Nikolai Oleinikov (1898–1937) was also close to Oberiu. All these writers became victims of repression in the 1930s–1940s and all, except Zabolotsky, perished.

3. D. Kharms, "Golubaia tetrad' no. 10" (Blue notebook no. 10), in *Vanna Arkhimeda: sbornik*, comp. A. A. Aleksandrov (Leningrad: Khudozhestvennaia literatura, 1991), p. 229.

4. "Manifest Oberiu," *Vanna Arkhimeda*, pp. 461–62.

5. Ibid., p. 461.

6. We should recall that at approximately the same time, at the opposite end of Russia's spiritual topography, the following significant words were uttered by Maxim Gorky: "Humanism, in the form in which we have absorbed it from the Gospels and from the sacred writings of our artists about the Russian people and about life, is a very bad thing"; quoted in Benedikt Sarnov, *Prishestvie kapitana Lebiadkina: sluchai Zoshchenko* (Moscow: RIK Kul'tura, 1993), p. 376. Not long after, Shostakovich would display his solidarity with Gorky's thesis in his *Lady Macbeth of Mtsensk District*.

7. Untitled miniature, in *D. Kharms: tom 2* (Moscow: A. O. Viktori, 1994), pp. 122–23.

8. Frequently encountered in Russian folk orchestras, the domra is a type of long-necked lute. *Trans.*

9. *Vanna Arkhimeda*, pp. 310–11.

10. L. Ginzburg, *Chelovek za pis'mennym stolom* (Leningrad: Sovetskii pisatel', 1989), pp. 394–95.

11. V. Rozanov, *Sochineniia* (Moscow: Sovetskaia Rossiia, 1990), p. 57.

12. All sources list G. Apollinaire as the author of the text for the third movement ("Lorelei"). However, his "Lorelei" is not an original poem but a translation of the ballad by the German Romantic poet Clemens Brentano (1778–1842), published in 1801. Shostakovich selected a translation of the translation for his symphony, and it is not logical to regard the text as Apollinaire's.

13. For a detailed analysis, see L. Akopian (Hakobian), "'Khudozhestvennye otkrytiia' chertyrnadtsatoi simfonii' ('The artistic discoveries' of the Fourteenth Symphony), *Muzykal'naia akademiia* 4 (1997): 185–92.

14. Ibid.

15. It should be remembered that, narrowly conceived, Gnosticism (from the Greek *gnosis,* knowledge) refers to those early Christian heretic schools of thought according to which the real world was created not by a benevolent deity who kept aloof from its affairs, but by the most base and darkest of forces. More broadly understood, Gnosticism represents a rejection of the fundamental, ontological unity of the corporeal and the spiritual,

and a perception of world creation through the lens of the ontological multiplicity of "partial" worlds—be it the world of good and evil, of light and darkness, of the spirit and the body, or of the "I" and of other human beings, and so forth. Only through acquisition of the mystical, intuitive *gnosis* can man overcome this multiplicity (in this particular case, dualism) of worlds—by shedding everything earthly, including his base nature (corporeal and spiritual)—and attain true spiritual unification with the transcendence of the true God, which, for Gnostics of any sort, has nothing to do with the "official" God of the Church and of theologians.

16. See L. Akopian (Hakobian), "O vozmozhnykh tochkakh soprikosnoveniia mezhdu teoreticheskim muzykoznaniem i glubinnoi psikhologiei" (On possible points of contact between theoretical musicology and in-depth psychology), *Muzykal'naia akademiia* 1 (1999): 206–12.

Shostakovich and the Russian

Literary Tradition

CARYL EMERSON

Shostakovich came of age as a musician in an era that loved the literary word. This reverence was not that of the great Realist novelists of the nineteenth century, however, for whom language was primarily a window to what exists, an accomplice in clarifying the world. Nor was it any longer the extreme language experimentation of the radical Futurists. Early in the revolutionary era, Futurists had stunned Petrograd with their passion for the "word as such," celebrating its phonetic, rhythmic, and semantic aura in addition to (or in preference to) its referential meanings. *Zaum* or "trans-sense" poets tantalized the ear with strings of quasi-nonsense syllables. But by the mid-1920s, many had come to consider such experiments elitist and sterile. Although the sensuous, sonorous aspects of the word were still prized highly, proletarian art adequate to the new Bolshevik culture now had to communicate in more concrete down-to-earth ways: in street language, in the rhythms of factories and dancehalls. As Katerina Clark notes in her study of revolutionary Petersburg, in a chapter suggestively entitled "Straight Talk and the Campaign against Wagner," by the second half of the 1920s the monumental spectacles, patriotic pantomimes, and "exaggerated heroic pathos" of the early revolutionary years had given way to a cult of everyday speech, even substandard speech.[1] In Oberiu, the "Association for Real Art," the literary avant-garde took steps to democratize itself. Stimulated by the 1927–28 Leningrad premieres of operas by Krenek and Berg, debates were launched over new ways to de-automatize and reinvigorate the coupling of music and the speaking Russian word.[2]

Among Romantic predecessors, the greatest practitioner of this pungent "substandard" speaking aesthetic was Nikolai Gogol, whose bizarre comic genius had come back into fashion in the 1890s together with poetry and the short form. The young Shostakovich was personally acquainted with several writers of the "Gogol school" recognized today as Soviet-era classics—Mikhail Zoshchenko, Vladimir Mayakovsky, Evgenii Zamiatin, Iurii Olesha, Mikhail Bulgakov. Prose of their eccentric and often naively comic sort appealed keenly to the composer in his formative years. In these passions he was supported by his close friend Ivan Sollertinsky, a polyglot philosopher and literary critic turned music scholar, whose private wit and professional advice on modern performance art (ballet, opera, libretto art, film scores) became indispensable to Shostakovich, beginning in 1927.[3] In September of that same year, as part of a questionnaire on the creative process (see the translation in this volume, p. 27), the twenty-one-year-old composer was asked to define his attitude toward the other arts. Literature came first in importance, then ballet, sculpture, and architecture, and then (a poor fourth) painting. As regards literature Shostakovich wrote: "Above all a preference for prose literature (I don't understand poetry at all and do not value it . . .): *Demons, The Brothers Karamazov,* and in general Dostoevsky; together with him Saltykov-Shchedrin; and in a different category, Gogol . . . And then Chekhov. Tolstoy as an artist is somewhat alien (although as a theorist of art, much of what he says is convincing)."[4] As the composer grew older, poetry would rise in his estimation, but these prosaic loves would remain. "In spite of being generally considered a symphonist," Esti Sheinberg writes in her remarkable recent study of irony in Shostakovich's music, "Shostakovich seems to be rather a 'literary' composer."[5]

What this appellation "literary" might mean in the context of Shostakovich's settings of Russian texts is the subject of the present essay. His pioneering opera (if it can be called that) premiered at the Maly Opera Theatre in 1930: a musical amplification of Nikolai Gogol's deadpan surreal fantasy "The Nose." His final song cycle (if it can be called that) is a musical dramatization of some very bad, very funny poems by Captain Lebiadkin, drunken buffoon from Dostoevsky's 1872 novel *Demons.* In between those two prosaic grotesques, op. 15 and op. 146, Shostakovich set an astonishing variety of Russian literary texts to a large number of solo and choral musical genres, several of them hybrids of his own devising. Alongside pellucid song cycles on lyrics by Pushkin (1936, 1952), Aleksandr Blok (1967), and Marina Tsvetaeva (1973), he set five "Satires," far less lyrical, of the early twentieth-century poet and children's writer Sasha Chorny (1960), incidental music for Meyerhold's 1929 staging of Mayakovsky's dystopian farce *Klop* (*The Bedbug*), and contributed to the Pushkin Jubilee of 1936 a musical score for Pushkin's "Folktale about the

Priest and His Workman, Blockhead," a "film-opera" realized in the form of a cartoon (1935). A full-length opera based on Nikolai Leskov's 1864 tale *Lady Macbeth of Mtsensk District* was mounted in 1934, with devastating repercussions two years later. A second musicalization of Gogol (his 1842 dramatic sketch *The Gamblers*) was started in 1942 but abandoned by the end of the year, after eight scenes had been set word for word. The composer's first choral setting, in 1921–22, was of two fables by Ivan Krylov. And of the four vocal symphonies (three of them choral), no. 13 is a monumental setting for bass and male chorus of five politically provocative poems by Evgenii Yevtushenko (1962).

These musical treatments of Russian literature range from restrained poetic partnerships between vocal melody and clarified instrumental line to an aggressive (some would say savage) pursuit of the "prose of life" in music, rhythmically as well as intonationally. But unlike the orthodox pioneers in this "prosaic," words-first enterprise, notably Musorgsky, Shostakovich did not disdain the resources of the orchestra.[6] (That he so inventively orchestrated his own song cycles— even, as in the case of op. 62, twice at great interval—suggests an abiding curiosity in the acoustic continuum between instrument, voice, and word. His own creativity could be stimulated by intervention in the work of others; for example, his interest in vocal music intensified after 1962, upon completing his orchestration of Musorgsky's *Songs and Dances of Death*.)[7] Even the fifty-minute stretch of *Gamblers* music, which begs comparison with Musorgsky's (also aborted) musical treatment of Gogol's *The Marriage,* owes its integrity less to the vocal line than to the orchestration, which is more relaxed and euphonious than that of *The Nose*. In such unconventional operas, the line that carries the words is often not closely synchronized with the activity of the orchestra.[8]

In all his marvelous inventiveness, Shostakovich never appeared to feel the tension of words *versus* music, that is, of words crippled, enslaved, or overpowered by music. That ancient feud, which had fueled the most radically "realistic" voice-setting in the nineteenth century, is transcended in his practice by a daring, virtuosic concept of orchestral voice. Shostakovich's orchestra is not limited to mere commentary on events taking place onstage. While it does, of course, make use of reminiscence motifs that prompt conscience or memory in a character (as does, say, Lensky's theme in the orchestra, passing through Tatiana's frantic mind during the final scene of Tchaikovsky's *Eugene Onegin*), in Shostakovich, an instrumental line has its own autonomous tasks as well. It can reinforce the emotional moods and memories of individual singers in their own present, but it can also address—and undermine—the literary plot, genre, or "generation" in which these individuals are embedded. In the self-conscious

Russian tradition, where the literary canon was not just known but known by heart, genres and generations were acutely marked.

As the Act 3s of both *The Nose* and *Lady Macbeth* demonstrate, Shostakovich had no scruples about supplementing the plotline of classic literary narratives with episodes drawn from other texts of the same author, period, or style. But musically he would often realize these interpolated episodes through twentieth-century genres, deployed ironically: the cancan, galop, foxtrot, silent film chase, perversely imbalanced waltz. A strong rhythmic insert of this sort could serve several purposes. It could jolt the audience, defamiliarizing its expectations and encouraging a fresh approach to the psychology of the nineteenth-century heroes depicted on stage. Or it could function as an internal genre parody. In the two Act 3s noted above, the relevant parodied object is the operatic convention dictating some sort of "group" (or mob) activity in the third act—usually a dance or a ballet, but why not a chase, a lineup, a riot? Such an insert could even take off on its own, animating a scene in a direction quite different from the inner life of the heroes and infecting the audience with a sense of the liberating—not only the distorting or pathological—potential of the grotesque.

This revolutionary achievement in concrete word-music-rhythm relations was noted by Boris Asafiev in an appreciative essay on *Lady Macbeth* in 1934, soon after the premiere. "Not losing sight of the word for a single moment, Shostakovich is nevertheless not distracted by externally descriptive naturalistic tendencies: he does not imitate the meaning of the words through music, he does not illustrate the word but rather symphonizes it, as if unfolding in the music the emotion not fully spoken by the words."[9] Although there are, of course, illustrative and "naturalistic" moments in Shostakovich (the infamous pornophony of the seduction scene in *Lady Macbeth* and the gross orchestral yawns, sneezes, and grunts in *The Nose*), Asafiev's insight is a sound one. The uttered word is context-specific and semantically ambiguous. It communicates through inflection and intonation, and it can mean something new in each new environment. Thus its "symphonization" would tend to make interpretation more—not less—difficult, intricate, and provisional. The symphonized word has nothing in common with a caption "explaining" a photograph.

In his musical dealings with Russian literature, Shostakovich had another ally during the 1920s: the cinema. It is often remarked that the young composer's tedious job as pianist for silent films, with its emphasis on the chase, the capture, the cameo love scene, and other slapstick or sentimental routines, perfected his improvisatory and "storytelling" skills, sensitizing him to the relationship between the visual and the aural in movement. But the reverse is surely also true, that Shostakovich's early intimacy with silent film must have impressed upon him the many strategies (in addition to musical ones) available for undermining the tyranny of the verbal sign. During these pioneering years, Russian Formalist critics spoke of film as a sort of "inner speech" that was a more immediate and flexible record of the psyche than was plotted verbal narrative. Exploring this potential, Iurii Tynianov, a Formalist critic and novelist whose work was very likely known to Shostakovich, produced an expressionist filmscript for Gogol's story "The Overcoat" in 1926. (In 1927, Tynianov published an essay, "On the Basics of Cinema," which ended with a stylistic analysis of Gogol's "The Nose.")[10] Meanwhile, the film theorist Sergei Eisenstein was at work defining techniques of montage. His parameters were less spatial than they were temporal, dynamic, even musical. He distinguished between metric, rhythmic, tonal, and "overtonal" montage according to tempo, rhythm, intensity, pitch, shrillness or haze of light, and major or minor harmonies.[11] By the end of the 1920s, film had been established as a new language for the Soviet masses, a language more directly accessible to them than the bound volumes of literary classics. Perhaps film would prove even more accessible than music— although many critics (including Tynianov) assumed that film's special, if not exclusive, strength would be limited to the comic genres. The soundtrack was still at the mercy of the moving image. "In the cinema, music is swallowed up," Tynianov wrote as early as 1924, ". . . and that is a good thing: music, which is in itself interesting, would distract you from the action."[12]

The task for the new opera, then, was to reintegrate the literary word, which had been enriched as well as compromised by these media innovations. Summing up the strategies for "embodying the word" that had gained currency by the end of the first Soviet decade, Shostakovich's biographer Sofia Khentova finds four of special importance: the declamatory-conversation style of vocal parts; musical dramaturgy that imitated the framing techniques of film; a peculiar use of orchestral timbres, especially percussive; and the advent of a special dramatic hybrid, the "theatrical symphony."[13] Khentova's fourth item must be approached cautiously. Shostakovich had in mind something quite different from Meyerhold's musical theater, which had so successfully staged Gogol's *The Inspector General* in 1926 by granting full artistic license to the director to alter the words, pace, and even dramatic concept of the original. A "unified music-theatrical symphony" in Shostakovich's sense of the term presumed a rigorous fidelity to the author and to the received text (which could include its drafts or variants). It also implied a more objective musical structure, one where, in the composer's words, the aria-recitative distinction is replaced with an "*uninterrupted symphonic current,* although without leitmotifs."[14]

How does this "current" deliver its shock? If earlier rebels in vocal dramaturgy, such as Musorgsky, took extreme stands on "which comes first, the music or the words," then Shostakovich devises scandals in another realm. What excites and appalls us in his work are the textures and shameless rhythms of this "symphonic current"—the drums, bells, gongs, hammering stretches of ostinato and unexpected glissando passages into which a snatch of sincere lyrical line always threatens to fall and be profaned. One aspect of the composer's literary credo (the "*Nose*-to-Lebiadkin" line, as it were) remained constant throughout his life: that surprise, incongruity, abrupt juxtaposition, and "gracelessness" in a literary text can always find its equivalent, and perhaps even its most precise fulfillment, through music. In a recent essay, Gerard McBurney remarks on these startling priorities. The world of Shostakovich and Sollertinsky, he writes, abounded in people "interested in language as cliché or as nonsense, language and inarticulate sound as incantation, as a window into a trance . . . [people who] played with the preposterous and simultaneously horrifying effect of long lists . . . or dreary repetitions." If, like Gogol, the new Soviet-era artist appeared to delight in "trance-inducing babble," it was "not so as *not* to think but as *another way* to think."[15] To further this "other way" of thinking, however, a composer had to command a robust slate of devices for musical humor, parody, and ambiguity, as well as a new definition of coherence.

Such issues have been long and ardently debated in Shostakovich's music, where—most listeners agree—it is easy to hear stories. And stories take a stand. They are narrated from a point of view; personalities come alive within their borders and begin to evaluate their world. A skeptic will ask, not unreasonably, how many disconnected points of view can be tolerated inside a story before the whole thing falls apart. And, this skeptic might add, are not the stories that do cohere in Shostakovich's operas, morally speaking, pretty miserable affairs, far worse than their literary sources: the mob's vicious pummeling of the eponymous hero down to its proper size in Act 3 of *The Nose* (an episode not found in Gogol's whimsical tale), the sadomasochistic rapes and whippings in *Lady Macbeth*, orchestrated with such naturalistic relish, during which a murderess is transformed into a lyrical heroine and victim? Russian literature, it could be argued, was not born for this task. Its mission was always the high ethical road. Those famous nineteenth-century transposers of the Russian classics—from the rough and "realistic" Musorgsky to the more elegant genius of Tchaikovsky and the fantastical Rimsky-Korsakov—altered the plots and rewrote the words, but they were not accused of being depraved or gratuitously nasty, as Shostakovich routinely was.

One defense against such subjective evaluations is to apply the formal method, that is, to step back from one's likes and dislikes and classify techniques. The most thorough scholar to attempt this type of rehabilitation recently is Esti Sheinberg, in her *Irony, Satire, Parody and the Grotesque in the Music of Shostakovich*. As the first serious study to ground the composer's use of musical parody in philosophies relevant to both the literary practice and the literary theory of the era, her argument merits attention. It will equip us with useful terms for the four case studies from the Russian literary tradition that follow: first, Shostakovich's two completed operas, and then, at opposite poles near the end of his life, his most poetic and his most prosaic song cycle.

Musical and literary parody: Sheinberg's thesis

Early in her study, Sheinberg suggests why Shostakovich was drawn to "Shakespeare, Gogol, Dostoevsky, and Chekhov" while tending to avoid "literary figures like Tolstoy and Pushkin" or film directors like Sergei Eisenstein. The former, she writes, were masters at semantic ambiguity, the latter committed "to clear-cut artistic communication that sometimes became straightforward propagandistic art."[16] Although the presence of Pushkin in that list is not quite just, overall the generalization holds. Writers who value irony—the principled distance, or alienation, between two or more layers of meaning sensed simultaneously in a single utterance—cannot be reduced to a sermon or a political tract. If their utterances *are* so reduced, they become satirists. If (in the other direction) their statements are cluttered even further by distortions, incongruities, cacophony, and gross misbehaviors of the body, they enter the domain of the grotesque. None of these qualities are static. In a temporal art like music, irony is inevitably "going somewhere" en route to being resolved. And here Sheinberg, drawing on Kierkegaard, identifies three dynamic types of irony, each of which she eventually provides with its own characteristic musical expression.[17]

There is, first, irony employed as a stimulus or device. Like satire, irony as stimulus is normative, finite, stern, and strives toward singular resolution. A given set of norms can be violated by a variety of techniques: the removal of an essential thing, the piling up of nondirectional inessential things (redundancy, banality, Muzak), the insertion of an incongruent element, exaggeration both qualitative and quantitative (82–120). Sheinberg's most telling examples of quantitative exaggeration ("overload") are from *The Nose*. There is the "mechanized canon" of the yard-keepers in the newspaper office that, unlike its source in the medieval hocket, consists of incoherent chopped-off cries and shouts that pointedly fail to come together in a "musically meaningful picture" (114–15). Even more boisterous and bizarre is the policemen's lament in Act 3, where the "whooping" folk song of Russia's northwest frontier is caricatured alongside the new Soviet folk song, culminating hilariously on a dog's howl (134–45). "Overload" is additive: it is felt whenever repetition is absolute, lasts too long, hammers too persistently, or resists harmonic change. When juxtaposed suddenly to maudlin sentimentality, these devices can mechanize, dehumanize, and make ludicrous.

In contrast, irony as terminus—as an end in itself—is infinite and admits of no resolution. A common reaction to infinite irony is also laughter, but of the uneasy absurd variety, what Sheinberg calls puzzlement or "irony's vertigo" (40). Here is the home of "non-satirical parody" (147), where we detect two incompatible and even clashing styles, but under such conditions that we are not swayed to prefer one over the other. Such serious, ubiquitous musical procedures as quotation, allusion, and stylization can turn ironic with only a slight slippage in proportion: if a passage continues unchanged for a few seconds too long, if the context is a little off, if pitch values are slightly distorted, if the tessitura is pushed too high or the tempo tweaked unnaturally in one direction or another. Dance forms, being so strongly marked rhythmically and relatively firm in their sociocultural connotations, are excellent material for such parodies. At the extreme end of irony as terminus is the ambivalent category of the grotesque: "an unresolvable ironic utterance, a hybrid that combines the ludicrous with the horrifying" (207).

The richness of the grotesque comes in our freedom to interpret its monstrous lack of proportion in diametrically opposed ways. It can be seen as infinitely negating or subtractive (when we equate formlessness with chaos and despair) or as infinitely affirmative and additive (when we celebrate, as did Mikhail Bakhtin, the tolerance of the grotesque for impulsive cross-fertilization and improvisation). What is always present in the grotesque is hyperbole registered on the human body. Therefore both abundance and violence are natural to it. Boundaries of all sorts are blurred. Although the default position of a grotesque organism is most certainly death rather than beauty, this death is cyclical and warm to the touch, not tragic. "While irony and satire communicate through concepts," Sheinberg writes, "the grotesque uses visual images and physical empathy" (215).

A third and final type of irony is the existential (316–19). It draws its force from the fact that we are all grotesque and ludicrous simply by virtue of being mortal, dependent upon bodies that are subject to error, aging, illness, and carnal folly. Shostakovich's irony is often of this attractively modest, panhuman sort. Sheinberg provides few musical examples of this category, but Shostakovich frequently spoke and wrote of it. The sentiment surfaces, and somewhat surprisingly, in the final paragraph of the composer's preface to the 1930 libretto of *The Nose*. "The music does not carry any deliberately 'parodying' overtone," Shostakovich wrote. "No! Despite all the comicalness of what is happening on stage, the music does not make things comical [*ne komikuet*]. I consider that appropriate, since Gogol lays out all these comic events in a serious tone. In this lies the strength and dignity of Gogolian humor. It doesn't 'try to be witty [at someone's expense]' [*ne 'ostrit'*]. The music tries also not to be witty."[18]

Sheinberg's three types of irony all exploit ambiguity and invite parody in its technical sense: the imitation of the distinctive style of an author, text, or tradition for purposes of critical reevaluation. But in the spirit of Shostakovich's comment on *The Nose*, parody need not imply ridicule or degradation. It requires only repetition with a difference. In order for parody to register as such, "originals" and earlier statements of the theme must be kept clearly in mind. The one cultural skill indispensable to successful parody is memory. In the compact and auto-referential Russian literary tradition, varieties of affectionate, creative parody were so widespread that the Russian Formalists devoted whole books to them; among Tynianov's most influential works is a study of parody in (and of) Gogol and Dostoevsky, Shostakovich's two favorite writers. Parody is not obliged to laugh predecessors down or discredit them as cultural values. Quite the contrary; parody serves to keep earlier forms alive by constant rejuxtaposition and recontextualization.

Such creative use of earlier material—parody intended as lifeline and tribute—is clearly the case with our first operatic transposition, *The Nose*. The work was intended by its authors to be both a new Soviet musical genre and a model for Soviet composers desiring not to reject but to recuperate and "re-accent" Russian masterpieces of the past. In his preface "Why *The Nose*?" Shostakovich wrote: "About the libretto. The libretto is composed according to the principle of literary montage."[19] The adjective is significant. Shostakovich does not refer to montage in its spatialized, "film frame" sense familiar from visual art, nor even to the various musicalized categories of dynamic montage (rhythmic, overtonal) that Eisenstein was so painstakingly defining for film. Instead, the centrally marked moment is the literary one. Keeping in mind Sheinberg's classification of musical and literary irony, how might this priority be understood?

i. *The Nose:* literary montage

The literary source text for an opera is a block of words, variously appropriate for singing and acting, which must be rearranged and reconstituted into a target text (libretto) to fit a new medium and genre. Gogol's 1836 story would seem an unlikely candidate for such transposition. A civil servant wakes up one morning without his nose; a barber finds a nose in a hot roll; and the nose itself (a singing role) morphs from a facial organ into a state councillor and back again. A "montage" approach to this absurd string of nonsequiturs would call for juxtaposing and musically animating out of this block of words a series of Gogolian "pictures," more or less isolated in their frames. Thick walls between events are already implied in the structure of Gogol's tale, where causality is arbitrary and at crucial moments the narrator abdicates altogether, a given "incident is enshrouded in mist, and what ensued is totally unknown" (end of chapter 2). Shostakovich's operatic equivalent to these "shroudings" between episodes is the entr'acte. They are either conventionally instrumental or, as in the famous entr'acte separating scenes 2 and 3, an extensive interlude for unpitched percussion. The withdrawal of tuned instruments—an abdication of the melodic line and a withdrawal of voice even in instrumental form—is an ingenious strategy, especially in a darkened hall, for expressing the chaos left behind when narrators declare themselves incompetent to continue their story. Arguably, such a percussive solution is even more effective than the original "abdicating" words, which, after all, must remain on the page.

In collaboration with two gifted writers for the stage, Georgii Ionin and Aleksandr Preis, Shostakovich created a libretto calling for ninety characters plus chorus. It is exceptionally faithful to the spirit, authorship, and plotline of its literary source. Large chunks of Gogol's prose are declaimed or sung as arioso almost unchanged. Frequently what appear to be changes in the early-Soviet-era canonical text of "The Nose" are in fact variant lines taken by the librettists from earlier nineteenth-century editions of Gogol (1842, 1855), where some passages are given in a colloquial style more amenable to first-person—and thus to operatic—delivery.[20] Unusually for libretti derived from prose works, where a severe compression of direct discourse is the rule, Gogol's "The Nose" offered insufficient usable (that is, singable, actable, first-person) text. Additional material had to be found, which the librettists researched with great care. Act 3, set in the "suburbs of Petersburg," grew out of a single line near the end of Gogol's chapter 2, in which we learn that the Nose had been sighted walking in the Tavricheskii Gardens. The supplementary phrases that fill out this "ensemble" act, down to the most fragmentary, are all taken from other works of Gogol: "Old-World Landowners," *Taras Bulba,* "Christmas Eve," the tale of the two Ivans, *The Marriage,* and even a five-word utterance from *Dead Souls*.[21]

The only other author incorporated into the libretto is Gogol's most distinguished disciple and successor, Fyodor Dostoevsky. At the beginning of Act 2, scene 6, Kovalev's servant Ivan "lies on the couch, plays on the balalaika, spits at the ceiling and sings."[22] What he sings is Shostakovich's word-for-word setting of a mawkish song found in part 2, book 5, chapter 2 of *The Brothers Karamazov* (1881), two stanzas of couplets trilled out "in a sweetish falsetto" by the lackey Smerdiakov for the benefit of a young neighbor, Mariia Kondratevna. "By an invincible force I am bound to my dearie. Lord have mercy on her and on me, on her and on me, on her and on me."[23] As we shall see in our discussion of the Lebiadkin Songs, Shostakovich knew his Dostoevsky well. No context, it appears, is accidental. Why, of all the filler available for *The Nose,* was Smerdiakov selected? He and Gogol's Ivan are both lackeys, to be sure. But whereas Kovalev's lackey is a sidekick, a ludicrous overtone, Smerdiakov is more serious fare, a lackey of the new revolutionary type: impudent, craven, an embittered bastard and a parricide, the true villain of the novel. Soon after he strums these lines (the chapter title is musically marked: "Smerdiakov with a guitar"), he confides to Mariia Kondratevna: "I hate all of Russia. . . . The Russian people need thrashing, miss." He then sings a final couplet (which Kovalev's Ivan does not sing) about leaving for the capital, where he will not mourn the filth he has left behind. But Smerdiakov does not leave; he shams an epileptic fit, commits murder, implicates two innocent Karamazov brothers, and before the trial, hangs himself. Lord have mercy on them and on me.

Here, then, is one example of literary montage: three prose texts not so much juxtaposed side by side as glinting through one another: 1836–1881–1928. The first and third are parodic grotesque, the second grimly serious. But the final entry in any sequence always comes with the prior contexts (in effect, whole other worlds) attached to it. In this accretion of contexts and worlds lies the essence of Russian literary tradition, where not infrequently—as Tynianov wrote in 1921, apropos of Dostoevsky's parody of Gogol—a parodied tragedy becomes a comedy, and a parodied comedy takes on the potential for tragedy.[24] In his study of Dostoevsky and music, Abram Gozenpud remarks that the young Shostakovich felt a special intimacy with the great novelist, and "not only because Kovalev's servant Ivan sings Smerdiakov's little song."[25] That little song (to speculate on Gozenpud's enigmatic remark and fill it with positive content) is only a marker, a portal to the interpolated world of Act 3, where the Nose is thrashed down to its "real" size. For the crowd-turned-mob is a Dostoevskian signature: idle curiosity that becomes voyeurism which then passes, naively and even gaily, into mass violence and torture. Gozenpud argues that the "ironic phantasmagoria" of Gogol's tale moves us to another plane, where the "humor of the music and the entire ominous setting of the action are close to the atmosphere that reigns in [Dostoevsky's early tale of schizophrenia] *The Double*." That Shostakovich chose to set these couplets to a twanging subcanonical instrument like the balalaika, and to a metrically irregular melody recalling both an ornamented folk song and a cheap urban romance, reinforces the "Russianness" of this little musical interpolation, so rich in sinister associations.

There are, however, other ways to understand "literary montage" in *The Nose*. In addition to juxtaposing episodes and lines from Gogol's "The Nose" to one another, to other Gogol tales, and to Dostoevsky's Smerdiakov (all instances of citation and allusion, a rather straightforward form of intertextual dialogue), the opera also realizes, in amplified form, an essential truth about Gogol's stylistics. Which is to say, it realizes not just the literary word as a carrier of stories, but also the *aesthetic tasks* of that word as Gogol understood it. By the time of the revolution, two major schools of Gogol criticism were well developed in Russia. The first had dominated the nineteenth century and still found favor among Party-minded readers in the early Bolshevik era: Gogol as tendentious civic critic, singer of the downtrodden clerk and lampoonist of big-city bureaucracy, who all the same was a prophet of Russia's future greatness. Readers in this tradition assume that Gogol employs irony in a closed-ended satirical way (in Sheinberg's terms, as a stimulus or device) in order to expose society's shortcomings. Many accomplished Soviet scholars of Shostakovich's *The Nose*—for example, Alla Bretanitskaia—partake of this line in modified form. Alongside subtle study of the accentual shifts in the libretto and a keen appreciation of the ambivalence of reciprocal laughter (Kovalev's "laughing return to himself" that structures the plot as a mirror), she remains committed to the politically correct thesis that social disharmony and satire against "petty-bourgeois, clerkish Petersburg" lie at the core of the work.[26] The second school of Gogol criticism routinely resists this conclusion. Dating from the 1890s, the beginning of the Symbolist era, it has seen Gogol as consummate stylist and religious mystic, an apolitical (if not reactionary) visionary for whom all grotesques were self-projections and self-portraiture.

Several Russian Formalists in the mid-1920s were Gogol scholars of the first rank. They were eager to liberate their author from both these inherited burdens, which in their view were equally one-sided and humorless, by inquiring more objectively into the formal strategies of his art. One essay that made a major stir was Boris Eikhenbaum's "How Gogol's 'Overcoat' Was Made" (1918/1924). It argued that Gogol didn't care about characters or events; what did matter to him was the soundscript (*zvukopis'*) of wordplay, mimicry, puns, weird phonic envelopes for names, and oral intonation (folkish, pathetic, or ludicrous) behind the telling of events— what in Russian literary terminology is called *skaz*. Eikhenbaum claimed that "The Overcoat" was made, as all of Gogol's Petersburg Tales were made, over a void. Absurd anecdotal gossip alternates crazily with melodramatic outbursts, but at no point can one extract the author's unified ethical position or authentic voice because no plane exists for registering it. Thus Gogol's genius is pure juxtaposition—in a sense, pure montage—or, in Sheinberg's terminology, "irony as terminus, as an end in itself," infinite and admitting of no resolution. "The result," Eikhenbaum concluded, "is a grotesque, in which the mimicry of laughter alternates with the mimicry of sorrow—and both create the impression of being a performance, with a pre-established order of gestures and intonations."[27]

Whether Shostakovich knew this essay is uncertain (although there are grounds to believe he did, if only through Sollertinsky, who was well connected in literary circles). In any event, its relevance to the operatic *Nose* is considerable.[28] One student of that opera, Alexander Tumanov, has even suggested that Shostakovich devised an "orchestral, or symphonic, *skaz*" that was competent to register a given character's perception of events (albeit only locally, unstably, and superficially, since *skaz* is always a language mask).[29] Its scope in the opera is considerable, for not all characters and situations are equally grotesque. Much of *The Nose* is colloquial speech set quite "reasonably," in such a way that musical phrase coincides with spoken utterance. Although stretches of such speech might be hyperbolic and overexcited, it is still capable—as the grotesque often is—of evoking sympathy. But a moment of distorted, extremely low or high-register vocal sound announces the onset of that other aspect of grotesque art, the horrifying. It is a sign that the person being addressed is in a state of terror. Among such moments are Ivan Iakovlevich the barber hearing his wife's repeated high-pitched shrieks, the menacingly shrill counter-tenor policeman tracking the barber as the latter tries to rid himself of the rogue nose, and the repeated bullet shots of "*Bubliki! Bubliki!*" from the pretzel vendor. Vocal imagery of this sort, Tumanov argues, reflects Gogol's mystical and metaphysical side, unavailable to a simpleminded *skaz* narrator but expressible through music, where we can hear the message as perceived in exaggerated form by its most unnerved recipient.

In its sophisticated fusion of formal and psychological devices, Shostakovich had hoped that his opera would become the model for a new Soviet genre. In this he was disappointed. Despite active preparation of the audience and enthusiastic early runs, *The Nose* disappeared from repertory in 1931, to be revived only in 1974, one year before its composer's death. But it made a disproportionately large contribution to the Russian literary tradition all the same. Not only was the opera not reviled for infidelity to its source—a worthy fact, given the baleful charge made against so many operatic transpositions of the very great classics, from *Eugene Onegin* to *War and Peace*—but it actually participated, in its own time, in confirming the best literary criticism being written on its baffling source text.

ii. *Lady Macbeth of Mtsensk District:* the triumph of tragedy-satire, or the confessional grotesque

The rise and fall of Shostakovich's second opera between 1934 and 1936 is the most famous scandal to befall the musical world during the Stalinist era. The *Pravda* editorial "Muddle Instead of Music," which denounced the opera and its prodigiously popular twenty-nine-year-old composer at the end of January 1936, sent shock waves throughout the cultural establishment at the time. That scandal is still being investigated, with startling results.[30] Here only one aspect of this well-known story is addressed: the role of Shostakovich's second opera in the Russian literary tradition, taking into account the genre that the composer himself assigned to it in 1932: "tragic-satirical opera."[31] One important fact must be emphasized about this hybrid genre. The tragic component is concentrated almost entirely in the heroine, Katerina Izmailova. Arraigned against her are wimps, buffoons, lechers, dandies, and thugs—in a word, human material far more easily satirized than heroicized. Until the final "Siberian" scene, when intonations of tragic lament and psychological cruelty spread evenly throughout the population on stage, satire dominates the outer context of the opera, tragedy the inner landscape of the title role. Shostakovich was explicit and unembarrassed about his sympathy for this multiple murderess. As he wrote in a 1933 essay, the author of the nineteenth-century source text, Nikolai Leskov, had demonized his heroine and could find no grounds on which to justify her, "but I am treating her as a complex, whole, tragic nature . . . , as a loving woman who feels deeply and is in no way sentimental."[32] He noted with satisfaction the remark of a fellow musician at one of the rehearsals that the operatic Katerina had been cast as a Desdemona or a Juliet of Mtsensk, not as a Lady Macbeth.[33]

This lyrical purification of the title role remains the most puzzling and disputed aspect of Shostakovich's transposition. Leskov's 1864 story was also no stranger to dispute. But the original "Lady Macbeth of Mtsensk District" had startled its readers not so much for its grisly plot—the nineteenth century was raised on gothic horror stories and not easily shocked—as for its mode of narration. Its style is languid, sensuous, studded with the repetitions and rhythmic idiom of Russian folk dialect. This stylized surface is almost impenetrable. Events, no matter how horrific, are related in an objective, matter-of-fact manner, as if the narrator were a museum guide describing a gorgeous tapestry embroidered with brutal scenes. (Leskov framed his story as a "sketch for notes on a criminal court case.") There is no innerness to his Katerina, who moves as if in a trance and whose acts are depicted without emotion, as "evidence," exclusively as they appear on the outside. Why Shostakovich was attracted by this glossy, brittle tale as material for opera—a genre in which the inner life of heroines is the very stuff of arias—is an intriguing question, often and inconclusively discussed.[34]

During the first decade of Soviet power, Leskov's "Lady Macbeth" was in the air. It had enjoyed a popular revival in the 1920s: a silent film version appeared in 1927, and in 1930 a handsome edition of the tale was published with illustrations by the celebrated artist Boris Kustodiev (1878–1927). Kustodiev had close friends among contemporary writers and was passionate about music. His daughter Irina had been Mitia Shostakovich's classmate; through her, Mitia and his older sister Marusia became intimate with the entire family. Marusia even served the artist as an occasional model, and Shostakovich's first public performance of his own music, in May 1920, took place at an exhibition of Kustodiev's paintings.[35] For all his indifference to painting as an art form—in the 1927 questionnaire he calls painting a "meaningless activity," insofar as it reduces a dynamic world to stasis—Shostakovich knew Kustodiev's work well. Kustodiev's illustrations to Leskov, influenced by the *lubok* (woodcut) style of Russian folk art, were surely familiar to him. But seven years earlier, when the artist was still alive, this Kustodiev–visual art connection might have played an important *literary* role in the subsequent lyricization of "Lady Macbeth." The intermediary here is Evgenii Zamiatin, master writer of modernist and ornamental prose, minor collaborator on *The Nose* libretto, and admiring friend of Kustodiev, who illustrated several of his stories.

Zamiatin was a highly distinctive prose stylist and polemicist. In 1918 he delivered his first public lecture on Neorealism, an artistic credo that attempted a dialectical synthesis of mimetic, earth-bound Critical Realism and its triumphant antithesis, the otherworldly abstractions of Symbolism. Neorealists believed in concrete matter and movement: energy as opposed to entropy, the efficiency of a synecdoche, sudden laughter brought about through unexpected contrast. During and after the war years, many of them were turning away from the modernized, mechanized cities "into the backwoods, the provinces, the village, the outskirts" in search of "hut-filled, rye-filled *Rus'*," which they described elliptically, in abrupt, compact phrases ringing with the "music of the word."[36] Much as Eisenstein would explore visual montage in terms of temporal dynamics, so Zamiatin developed for literature a theory of prosaic meter, what he called the "prose foot," measured not by the distance between stressed syllables but by the distance—often devoid of explanatory verbs—between stressed words and images.[37] In his own prose Zamiatin followed these metric directives carefully. Among his exemplary Neorealist tales is the 1923 story "Rus," which appeared as a preface, or prefatory "Word," to a small book of portraits entitled *Rus': Russkie tipy B. M. Kustodieva* (Kustodiev's Russian types).[38] Zamiatin later explained how he had come to provide this verbal "illustration" to an art book. The publishing house Akvilon had commissioned from him an article reviewing Kustodiev's art. He wasn't in the mood to provide a conventional piece of criticism. "So I simply spread out in front of me all those Kustodievan beauties, cabbies, merchants, tavern-keepers, abbesses—and stared at them." After a few hours, an act of "artificial fertilization" took place: the figures came to life, sedimenting out into a story like a "supersaturated solution."[39] The plot of Zamiatin's "Rus" is a pared-down, purified, lush and more passive version of Leskov's "Lady Macbeth of Mtsensk District."

Almost certainly, Shostakovich knew the volume *Russkie tipy*. (That very summer, Mitia and his sister had vacationed with Kustodiev at a sanitorium in Gaspra on the Crimean peninsula.) Did Zamiatin's 1923 variant on Leskov's tale impress the young composer? In an interview from 1940, Shostakovich credited Boris Asafiev for recommending to him, a decade earlier, Leskov's story.[40] However, the critic Mikhail Goldshtein has claimed that Shostakovich, in private conversation with him, named Zamiatin as the source for the idea of an operatic "Lady Macbeth," and that Zamiatin "even jotted down a plan for the opera."[41] Goldshtein's claim has not been confirmed. But the fact that Shostakovich did not repeat his remark—if indeed he made it—could be explained by Zamiatin's emigration in 1931, rendering impossible any positive public reference to him or his works within the Soviet Union. Let us assume that Zamiatin's Neorealist story was indeed one lens through which Leskov's nineteenth-century tale passed on its way to the twentieth-century stage, and that the young Shostakovich was alert to it. How might "Rus" have influenced the opera?

Zamiatin's story opens on a vast coniferous forest, more the backdrop to a fantastic fairy tale than mapped historical space. Its elements are wood, fire, water. Deep in this forest is Kustodievo, a town without vistas or prospects—for "this is not Petersburg Russia, but *Rus'*," its components are "alleys, dead ends, front yard gardens, fences, fences."[42] Marfa Ivanovna, a naive and timid orphan, is being married off by her aunt, now an abbess. In her youth this aunt "was called Katia, Katiushenka"; now she wants her niece settled, for she "knows, remembers" the ways and temptations of the world (11). Marfa draws lots among her suitors and the rich merchant Vakhrameev wins, a man old enough to be her father. In keeping with Zamiatin's synecdochic aesthetics, we never see all of the young heroine—only the rounded bust, white neck, downcast eyes. What we do know is that she is not some "fidgety wasp-waisted girl from *Piter* [*piterskaia vertun'ia-osa*]" but "weighty, slow, broad, full-breasted, and as on the Volga: you turn away from the main current toward the shore, into the shadows—and look, a whirlpool" (10).[43] Vakhrameev shows off his young wife to his shop, visits the bathhouse with her (a direct transposition of Kustodiev's famous portrait of a nude "Russian Venus," no. 14 in *Russkie tipy*), feeds her sweets, and returns to his trade. There is no violence, no cruelty, only apples ripening in the heat, buzzing insects, and the "coal-black gypsy eye" of the shop assistant, trying to catch her gaze. Vakhrameev leaves for the fair. Marfa is alone, thirsty, idle, rustling in her silks, and when the coal-black eye invites her into the garden one warm May night ("Marfa Ivanovna!" . . . "Marfushka!" . . . "Marfushenka!"), she turns away angrily, "the silk rustling tightly across her breast." She says nothing—but goes to the garden. The next morning everything is as if "nothing had been" (21).

Vakhrameev returns from the fair with gifts. Marfa is silent. Several days later he dies; the cook had mixed in poison mushrooms with the morels. Although he departs "in a Christian fashion," still, people begin to talk—but "what won't people talk about" (21). The widowed Marfa remarries, but her new bridegroom, it turns out, was not one of Vakhrameev's jealous rival merchants. The silence of the forest takes over. The entire event is like a stone cast into still water: circles, ripples, spreading out and fading away, "no more than faint wrinkles in the corner of eyes, from a smile—and again, a smooth surface." In the expanse of *Rus'*, words are muffled by broad rivers, by massive trees, by the "copper velvet" of bell ringing on the evening air. Characters, after coming temporarily to life, reenter the space of portraiture, where stasis, not movement, is the rule.

Such concentration on the visual and aural surface of things is very much in the ornamentalist and Gogolian tradition. But the effect of this texture in Zamiatin is fundamentally different from the pace and feeling of Gogol's nervous marionettes, whose nonsequiturs define the Petersburg Tales. Zamiatin's objects do not collide percussively and mechanically, as do objects in "The Nose." They slumber, glide, ripen, circle round. In the capital city, energy lies on the surface and is openly spent; in the forest and the provinces, energy is bottled up, spent in private, stingy with spoken words. Natural cycles control and redeem all; human interference is quickly effaced. This "rural Neorealism" of Zamiatin's Marfa Ivanovna—her mysterious organic and lyrical depth—left a trace, I suggest, on Shostakovich's operatic Katerina Izmailova, created ten years later.

Zamiatin presents his shy, massively Kustodievan variant on Leskov's Lady Macbeth as an innocent creature caught in a trap. She speaks little. Rather than declare herself, she prefers to cast lots, rustle silks, or bow her head. Her mode of expression is ideally suited to the private, heartfelt genre of the aria, where inner truth is communicated to the audience in the hall, not to one's captors on stage. Far more than Leskov's callous, lascivious protagonist, Marfa Ivanovna is part of nature and moves instinctively with it. (We can imagine Zamiatin's heroine singing the aria in scene 3 that precedes Sergei's knock at her bedroom door—"The young colt hurries toward the filly," a lament on her unnatural and unmated life—whereas Leskov's Katerina has no such sentimental resources.) Zamiatin describes Marfa Ivanovna as a "transplanted apple tree" blossoming in vain behind the merchant's high fence; when the "coal-black gypsy eye" is sent in by Vakhrameev to treat the mistress of the house with apples and nuts, how could she be blamed for her fall (16)?[44] In the primeval Eden that is *Rus'*, all emphasis is on the tree and its fruit; the human seduction scenario is fated, forgiven, and all but forgotten in advance. The underwater whirlpool follows its own laws. It is not really a crime.

In his preface to the 1934 libretto, Shostakovich emphasized these new, lyrical, "natural" priorities—and in the process, he condemned his earlier practice in *The Nose*. "I have tried to make the musical language of the opera maximally simple and expressive," he wrote. "I cannot agree with those theories, which at one time were quite widespread in our country, that in the new opera the vocal line should be absent and the vocal line is nothing other than conversation in which intonations should be emphasized. Opera is first and foremost a vocal artwork, and singers must occupy themselves with their primary obligation—which is to sing, not to converse, declaim, or intone."[45] In his *Lady Macbeth,* this pervasive singing, melodious and rhythmically bold, would eventually encompass all emotional registers: lyrical, melancholic, lecherous, raucous. And in all genres—high-, middle-, and lowbrow—singing would be supported by an uninterrupted instrumental line and by richly orchestrated interludes between scenes. The world is thick and harmonious. It evokes our lament and awe, like the coniferous forest on which Zamiatin's "Rus" opens, the deep pool of water on which it closes, and the lake in the forest with the huge black waves of which Katerina sings in Shostakovich's final Siberian scene. Out of this lyrical landscape will come the opera's tragedy.

However, this fated "Kustodiev–Marfa Ivanovna" component works solely in the interests of the heroine. No other aspect of the opera partakes of it. Through Zamiatin's story, Shostakovich had a chance to cleanse his Katerina morally, to justify her (as Leskov did not) in her intoxicating physicality and intensely Russian-style unfreedom. Kustodiev's mysterious, Mona Lisa–like portraits are a shield that irony cannot penetrate. And such a defensive shield is necessary, because the other side of Shostakovich's hybrid "tragic-satirical" genre is a veritable battering ram of devices from his well-tested, avant-garde operatic vocabulary: an antic pace, musical caricature, and pitiless juxtapositions of lyricism with violence. Indeed, the singing fabric of *Lady Macbeth of Mtsensk District* is punctuated throughout by shockingly violent scenes of graphic naturalism. High-pitched female shrieks are no longer peripheral to the plot, like the pretzel vendor was in *The Nose,* but respond to abuse taking place in front of our eyes: whips we both see and hear, percussive strikes that coordinate with a murder instrument being wielded on stage. No such violence is present in Zamiatin's "Rus," nor is it the dominant note in Leskov's tapestry.

In the opera, violence is often prelude to the bluntest satire. The prolonged flogging of Sergei in scene 4, an unbearable episode, segues almost unbroken into serving up the mushrooms and from there to Katerina's faked lament over her poisoned father-in-law and the priest's little jig preceding his travestied requiem. In scene 6, the shabby peasant stumbles drunk onto the corpse of Zinovii Borisovich to the tune of a boisterous fanfare, a mood carried merrily over to the policemen's chorus and its moronic interrogation of the teacher in scene 7. When Boris Timofeevich has a moment of legitimate lyrical sorrow in scene 1 (over the absence of an heir in the Izmailov house), he is allowed only a line or two of relaxed music before collapsing back into his thumping, lecherous profile. His massive aria that begins scene 4 ("That's what old age means: you can't sleep") clearly parallels the heroine's "not being able to sleep" in the opening scene, but it is a parodied parallel: the father-in-law's lament quickly transforms itself into an active prowl, a sexual fantasy to be acted out on the body of his son's wife. The workman Sergei also has moments of lyrical self-pity (most expansively during his initial visit, in scene 3, to Katerina's bedroom "to borrow a book"), but they occur only before consummation of their love, not after. We sense his lyricism as a mask, as a seduction strategy pure and simple, and this suspicion is confirmed by his corrupt courtship of Sonetka in the final scene. Only Katerina's lyrical outpourings, whenever they occur, are spared this sort of framing and parodic distancing. From the start they are introspective, needy, in touch with a deeper truth, and potentially confessional.

This intimate juxtaposition of tragedy, violence, and satire confused some of the opera's first listeners. The composer, however, defended his hybrid of a lyrical heroine in a satirized world. In an article in *Krasnaia gazeta* a year into *Lady Macbeth*'s wildly successful run, he remarked that some musicians who had heard his opera were pleased to note that "here, finally, in Shostakovich we have depth and humanness. When I asked what this humanness consisted of, most answered me that for the first time I had begun to speak in a serious language about serious tragic events. But I cannot consider 'inhuman' my striving toward laughter. I consider laughter in music to be just as human and indispensable as lyric, tragedy, pathos, and other 'high genres.'"[46] For all the general truth of that statement, the ennobling and humanizing aspects of laughter are not much in evidence in this opera. A tragedy can always be laughed down or turned into a travesty or a burlesque, but the reverse procedure is extremely delicate: it takes real work to elevate a debased, satirized tragic-lyrical moment so that we can again put our trust in it. For this reason, one of the remarkable achievements in Shostakovich's *Lady Macbeth* is the moral insulation the composer succeeds in wrapping around his heroine. However she might act, we are never tempted to doubt the necessity of her deeds, her sincerity or pathos. Can a "tragic-satirical opera," so seamlessly combining lyricism with graphic cruelty and outright *bouffe*, be considered a variant of the grotesque? And if so, of what kind?

We recall that Sheinberg distinguishes between two types of grotesque. There is the route of infinite negation, where the horrifying overpowers the ludicrous and drives the body to disfigurement or suicide. And then there is the affirmative celebratory grotesque, more like an infinite acceptance that frees the body from stereotyped judgment and makes reality itself open-ended and "unfinalizable." Each type comes at considerable cost—despair at one end, utopia at the other—and both types, it seems, occur in this opera. The laughter that Shostakovich values is clearly the celebratory grotesque; the lyricism that he wishes us to respect (and pity) is that of infinite despair, and it accrues only to Katerina.

Sheinberg herself approaches the problem differently, through visual art. She devotes ten pages to an analysis of Shostakovich's Katerina Izmailova in the context of Kustodiev's paintings.[47] No mention is made of Zamiatin's "Rus." Had she discussed that story, her thesis would probably have suffered, for she sees in Kustodiev's ample women not a mysterious, lyric affirmation, not a stylized extension of the rotund Russian earth, its natural cycles stripped of responsibility and blame, but a more tainted ambiguity, the "unexplained charm of their devotion to their own sensuality" that "borders on the grotesque." For her, Kustodiev's famous *kupchikhi* (merchants' wives) are on a continuum with his monstrously over-sized cab drivers, his gross Russian Venus in the bathhouse, and his giant "Bolshevik" (1920) striding over the city. Applying Realist rather than Neorealist criteria, Sheinberg finds Katerina's soaring vocal line wholly, tragically inappropriate to the love that the heroine feels for Sergei. "The grotesque stems not just from this incongruity but also from Katerina's total unawareness of the situation," she writes. "When balanced against the murders she commits for the sake of this love, the mixture of compassion, repulsion, mockery and admiration we feel for her is transformed into a chilling macabre grotesquerie." We feel this chill in the ostinato-like rhythms that creep into her most passionate love songs. Sheinberg's intuitions here are plausible, but could easily be subsumed by the category of the pathetic—and in any case are restricted to the insulated heroine. They do not shed light on the larger issues raised in the *Lady Macbeth* wars.

What those wars involve, and their significance for the Russian literary tradition, are questions closely tied to the ambivalence of grotesque genres such as the "tragic-satirical." Shostakovich's fall from grace in 1936 was ostensibly caused by his opera's "deliberately dissonant quacking, hooting, panting, grinding, squealing"—all verbs taken from "Muddle Instead of Music"—and by the unembarrassed licentiousness of its plot. In addition, *Lady Macbeth* was accused of lacking precisely what its composer, in his 1934 preface to the libretto, had insisted was central to his reformed operatic aesthetic: "simple, accessible musical language." Yet this second opera (for all its naturalism) was so much more luxuriantly song-like than its predecessor *The Nose,* and so much more successful with its public, that these censures seemed perverse. Shostakovich came to qualify as a bona fide victim of prudish, vicious Stalinism, an image polished to high sheen by Solomon Volkov in his 1979 book on the composer. This image swept the West off its feet. But a powerful dissenting voice soon made itself heard, in the person of Richard Taruskin. Between 1989 and 1997, while fully respecting Shostakovich and his genius, Taruskin laid out a case for *Lady Macbeth of Mtsensk District* as itself a Stalinist opera— or at least as an opera that tried hard to accommodate Stalinist ideological priorities within a popular (and thus all the more dangerous) dramatic-musical language.[48] Taruskin saw grotesquerie not on the stylistic or musical plane, but on the social and moral.

Taruskin made the following case for the opera's moral depravity. Leskov had designed his Katerina to be seen as a sinner, nymphomaniac, and quadruple murderer. In recruiting this horror story as source text for the first in a planned series of operas on heroic Russian women, Shostakovich cleanses her image at its most filthy points. The suffocation of the young heir and nephew by the (then pregnant) Katerina is eliminated; in fact, that entire pregnancy, toward which Leskov's heroine was callously indifferent, disappears from the libretto. Boris Timofeevich moves from doddering eighty-year-old to vigorous patriarch, eager to exercise a father-in-law's rights over the young wife of his wimpish middle-aged son. Katerina does agree to commit the murder of these obnoxious creatures, but by their deeds and their music these men are presented to us as soundly deserving of being dispatched; moreover, in the case of Zinovii Borisovich, it is Sergei and not his mistress who actually wields the murder weapon. As soon as is dramatically feasible, Shostakovich's Katerina has nightmarish visions of ghosts and guilt reminiscent of her Shakespearean prototype (or, closer to home, of Tsar Boris Godunov, an opera amply cited in the music). When the police come to arrest the couple at their wedding, and when Katerina realizes that it is too late to flee, she begs forgiveness of her bridegroom and holds out her hands to be bound. Sergei, however, tries to escape. The final Siberian act is a full-scale lyricization of Katerina's fate. Even in this new, more awful captivity, she trusts in love and justice—and is betrayed. All that is ludicrous and satirical drops out of the opera. Only the tragic is left.

Taruskin correctly identifies the literary source for this cleansed, lyrical Katerina in Aleksandr Ostrovsky's famous play from 1859, *The Storm*. Katerina Kabanova also marries into a rich and repressive merchant household, falls illicitly in love with another man, suffers a tyrannical in-law, is victimized by her bigoted environment, and drowns herself. Indeed, it was against the cult of Ostrovsky's sentimental, martyred Katerina that Leskov, several years later, had constructed his chilling counterstory. In

1927, in response to that questionnaire on the creative process, Shostakovich had remarked that he "didn't much like Ostrovsky."[49] By the 1930s, however, he had come to see the usefulness of this canonically pure heroine, sacrificed to the viciousness of a mercantile world that, conveniently for Communist ideologues, had been tsarist Russia's emergent capitalist class. In effect—so Taruskin argues—Shostakovich restores Ostrovsky's sentimental plot in the service of a new regime. If that regime had been musically more sophisticated and less capricious in rewarding its servants, Shostakovich's opera might have become the first in his series of Socialist Realist tributes to Russian women: long-suffering, eternally mistreated, but women with nerves of steel, capable of murdering a class enemy yet remaining lyrically vulnerable, even in defeat. In Taruskin's eyes, this project qualifies as a moral grotesque.

The debate is not yet over. In 2000, in the first major post-Communist rethinking of the fidelity issues surrounding this opera, Vadim Shakhov took to task both the anti-Stalinist readings and Taruskin's counterattack—for roughly the same reasons.[50] Shakhov notes ruefully that the West picked up this much-battered topic pretty much where the Soviet Union had left off (245). And this is unfortunate, because the status of Stalinist victim and of Stalinist collaborator or fellow traveler are equally overpoliticized. Great works of art rarely benefit from being analyzed on that plane. Since Shostakovich and his co-librettist Aleksandr Preis did follow the basic shape of Leskov's plot (which, as librettos go, is a reasonably faithful transposition), and since this plot is so gruesome, most critics have been more intuitive than precise in their judgments about it, neglecting to do close, episode-by-episode comparisons of story and libretto. Shakhov provides his reader with just such a comparative chart (249–54). But he refuses to play by the usual rules in "fidelity studies," which always humiliate the derived text. He takes the libretto as his basic artistic text—that literary artifact, after all, is the relevant narrative under consideration—and, working backward, measures the adequacy of the original against it. Which operatic episodes are also present in the original Leskov, he asks, and which are absent? How did the librettists, working under a performance imperative, improve on the images provided by the written text? Which of the two stories is more effective for opera?

His findings are instructive. Even discounting the whole of Act 3 (the antics at the police station and the wedding, both absent in Leskov), the bulk of the episodes set to music can be traced back to a line or two of Leskov's text, a mere hint at a scene, or else they have no "original" at all. The libretto certainly recalls Leskov—the setting and the characters' names are the same—but in fact, Shakhov concludes, "it is an autonomous dramatic reworking, which has not that much in common with the text or the events of [Leskov's] sketch." (254). The heroine, in Shakhov's view, is not a merchant's wife copied from a Kustodiev canvas (261); she is not Ostrovsky's timid and accommodating Katerina; and she is not the objectified murderess of the original, whose criminal life was written up in the style of a police report. The operatic heroine is a new and viable psychological construct: Leskov's story as experienced through the eyes and heart of its title character (270). Although Shakhov does not adduce this parallel, we might note that Tchaikovsky accomplished a similar feat several decades earlier in his equally beloved, and equally controversial, operatic *Eugene Onegin*: the updating and recasting of Pushkin's novel-in-verse to resemble a novel by Turgenev, narrated (in keeping with Turgenev's own sympathies) from the perspective of its heroine, Tatiana.[51]

Shakhov's larger argument is a plea for the right of an opera transposition to coexist peacefully in its own time (and for all time) as an aesthetic whole, not lashed to some ideology and not as a derivative of some jealous "original." (After all, the Katerinas of Shostakovich and Leskov are as different from each other as both are from their Shakespearean namesake.) He has some impatient words for Western critics, whose sex-centric Freudian reflexes render them both too offended and too fascinated by Shostakovich's "naturalistic" treatment (which in any event is more in the staging than in the music or the sung text [288])—and further blinds them to the Russian literary tradition, in which Russian women consider self-sacrifice not pathological but sweetly fulfilling (289). In his view, the "tragedy-satire" label is not a political category but an aesthetic one, part of the twentieth-century's striving to "maximally dissociate polar extremes" in staged art and thereby to enhance dramatic effect (271).

For all of Shakhov's cogent argumentation, however, there is still an element of the grotesque, of unbridgeable incongruity, at the center of this opera. I would suggest that it be sought neither in politics nor in plot per se but in those moments of trust that Katerina, true to her cleansed and deepened image, cannot help but extend to the outside world. The exclusive lyricization of one personality within a naturalistic musical drama is a risk-laden project. This risk is even greater if the drama is transformed, even for the stretch of a single scene, into a circus. For if everyone else is caricatured, debased, made shallow or silly, then the lyrical heroine is without interlocutors. No one is worthy of her confessions. (The end of Act 3 is an excellent example: does it make any sense to offer yourself up honorably to the Keystone Kops?) If the repenting subject is not to sing her arias into a void, then repentance, confession, and spiritual conversion require a worthy confessor. The Old Believer Marfa has Dosifei, Tatiana has a rapt Onegin, Natasha Rostova her loyal Pierre Bezukhov or dying Prince Andrei. But there is literally no one on stage in Shostakovich's *Lady Macbeth* who can register evidence of Katerina's moral growth. In other times and cultures, of course, this recipient would be God. But in a Soviet Socialist Realist opera, such a divine interlocutor is impossible.

There is, of course, the audience in the darkened hall, the conventional recipient of aria speech. But such an addressee, were it to represent the sole locus of seriousness, would tend to lift the heroine out of her surroundings and cease to make character and context answerable to each other. Either way, the radical aloneness of Katerina creates an odd incongruity. She is both a direct product—that is, a victim—of her environment, thus not blamed for her crimes, and at the same time she is irrevocably cut off from that environment, increasingly unable to address it or anything beyond it. This situation gives rise to what we might call the "confessional grotesque," an especially black variant of infinite negation. It is not a familiar presence on the Russian cultural horizon, traditionally rich in spiritual resolutions. But it might help explain the moral and psychological confusions inherent in this operatic masterpiece, where tragedy and satire almost cancel each other out and invite no transcendence.

Summing up this section, we might review the trajectory of this Russian "Lady Macbeth" and suggest a revised genealogy. The starting point, of course, is Shakespeare. Macbeth's wife offers a full range of potential behaviors. Although at first she fears that "the milk of human kindness" might hinder her husband in his ambition "to catch the nearest way," once the murders are committed she comes to experience terror, guilt, and the fatal burden of responsibility. Leskov's Russian version of the plot sustains the cold-bloodedness throughout, replaces politics with sexual jealousy as the primary motivation for murder, and embeds the whole in a curiously stylized police report that suppresses any "realistic" empathy with the sinful heroine. Shostakovich selected this text as the first part of a larger, politically correct plan to portray operatically a series of courageous and energetic Russian women. There is reason to believe that he also saw in it a tale amenable to the genre requirements of more traditional opera, where the unhappy diva longs for love, sins, confesses, and sings her most moving aria on the brink of death. As Shakhov demonstrated, the composer's task in this transposition was complex. He had to reactivate the innerness and moral suffering of the title role while at the same time retaining a Russian sheen to the story, emphasizing the brutality of the enemy (mercantile) class, and imparting to Katerina Izmailova a sense of agency and of moral outrage. The heroine—however her crimes are explained—could not become an agent as long as guilt was pervasive. So the first task was to get rid of the guilt. Here Zamiatin's "Rus" might have provided the link.

For even more than Leskov's "naturalistic" Katerina Lvovna, Zamiatin's Neorealistic Marfa Ivanovna is a folk stylization, the animation of several enigmatic portraits. Unlike Leskov's heroine, however, Marfa is justified by her context, shielded from any personal blame for her life's course, and at the end is reintegrated into the natural world that had confined her and nourished her. It remained for Shostakovich, as a Soviet composer intent upon defining a new operatic ideal, to add a didactic, proactive element to this exonerated image, some intonation that would prove women stronger, smarter, and more progressive than their male captors, even as comedy and violence remain in place to draw the common viewer in. We sense these somewhat prudish, Socialist-Realist "inserts" acutely whenever they occur in the opera, for they compete, and not always persuasively, with Katerina's more conventional operatic roles as kept woman, slave of passion, repentant sinner, and martyr. (One prominent example is Katerina's moral lecture to Sergei before their hand wrestling in scene 2: "You men certainly think a lot of yourselves, don't you. . . . And don't you know about those times when women fed the whole family, gave the enemy a beating in wartime.") Thus does the Soviet-era diva sing in her own defense what the nineteenth-century literary tradition had long canonized, from Pushkin's Tatiana to the legendary Decembrists' wives up through Turgenev's heroines: that men are "superfluous," impulsive, and selfish, women are loyal, tenacious, and indispensable. The capacious image of Lady Macbeth can accommodate itself even to this deeply Russian message.

Our remaining two case studies from the Russian tradition are song cycles dating from the final three years of the composer's life. The first is "maybe the most intimately personal of all Shostakovich's song cycles," a perfect harmony of poetic sentiment with music that works toward transcending our fate in this world.[52] The second is surely the most down-to-earth, prosaic, and parodic of all the verse Shostakovich set to music. Together they illustrate not only the enormous range of the art song as Shostakovich created it but also the inventiveness, craft, and craftiness that the composer brought to sociopolitical topics. This latter issue remains perennially timely, for the image of Shostakovich as a citizen of his nation and age continues to suffer gross simplification.

iii. The Tsvetaeva songs:
pure poeticity and transcendence

"The piano was my first mirror," Marina Tsvetaeva wrote in her 1935 essay "Mother and Music." "My first awareness of my own face was through blackness, through its translation into blackness, as into a language dark and incomprehensible. That is how it has been my whole life: to understand the simplest thing I had to plunge it into verse, to see it from there."[53] Shostakovich experienced the opposite evolution. As a young man he had confessed (again in the 1927 questionnaire) to neither liking nor understanding poetry, with partial exceptions for the eighteenth-century Derzhavin and twentieth-century Mayakovsky. His musical and literary selves were most stimulated to collaborate when he was, as it were, plunged into prose. The composer came late to Tsvetaeva, but intensely. In a letter to his friend Isaak Glikman in August 1973 he laconically announced his completion, after several weeks' concentrated work, of op. 143, a setting for contralto and piano of six poems by Marina Tsvetaeva. (In 1974, he would arrange the cycle for voice and chamber orchestra as op. 143a.) But Shostakovich provided no commentary on this new composition, remarking only that his physical deterioration prevented him from writing out the words and the music for his friend, as he would have liked, and that a good pianist would be necessary to perform the cycle since he himself was no longer even up to playing *Chizhik* (rendered by the translator as "Three Blind Mice").[54]

From these remarks it is easy to see the Tsvetaeva songs as part of a preparation for death: part tragic, part ludicrous, part grotesque. Death and the poet had been a familiar theme for Shostakovich since the Fourteenth Symphony in 1969. In the summer of 1973 he had just returned from his exhausting trip to America, where Washington doctors confirmed what the Moscow specialists had diagnosed: that his condition was incurable. Glikman recalls that two years earlier Shostakovich had set to music a poem by Yevtushenko, "Yelabuga Nail," about Tsvetaeva's homely suicide weapon.[55] (Recently repatriated with her two children, Tsvetaeva hanged herself in that Russian village in 1941.) Also in 1971, Shostakovich became acquainted with the settings of three Tsvetaeva lyrics by his friend and fellow musician, Boris Tishchenko. Requesting the score of those songs, he wrote to his friend: "I've grown to love them and want to have them around, to play occasionally."[56] Throughout July 1975, his final summer, Shostakovich was reading Tsvetaeva's verse as well as the memoirs of her daughter Ariadna.[57] The art and fate of this poet were on his mind. Part of the message of that fate was that bodies were dysfunctional and doomed. But op. 143 is remarkable for its radiant optimism about the survival of art.

Tsvetaeva is a poet's poet. "Fate has given Marina Tsvetaeva an enviable and rare gift, that of singing," wrote Vladislav Khodasevich, one of the very great poets of the emigration, in 1923. "Tsvetaeva's 'music' is foreign to any pursuit of external effect, very complex in its inner structure and orchestrated in the richest possible way."[58] Technically virtuosic and highly inventive semantically, her condensed, highly rhythmic verse hardly seems to invite the competition that any external musical setting would offer it. Yet Shostakovich, a master at double-voiced satire, succeeded in setting these poems with no friction at all, and with none of the ironic undertow that Sheinberg detected in Katerina Izmailova's love songs, contaminating them with the grotesque. Here, the shimmering intent of the word is perfectly realized in the music. Whatever grotesqueries there are (and there are some) come from within the scene described by the words.

The poems Shostakovich chose to set to music, written between 1913 and 1931, seem at first an unusual cluster. The opening poem was composed by Tsvetaeva in 1913, on the theme of her own first verses, "written so early" and now languishing in bookstores unread. The second, a love lyric "Whence this tenderness," dates from 1916 and is dedicated to Osip Mandelstam. The third, "Hamlet's dialogue with his conscience" (1923), belongs to Tsvetaeva's Ophelia poems and to a larger category in her work as a whole: laments over failed lovers. The fourth and fifth are from the 1931 cycle "Verses to Pushkin"—poems as percussive, public, and hortatory as the others are shrouded and intimate. The final song sets another early dedicatory poem, Tsvetaeva's 1916 tribute to Anna Akhmatova. Two features of this sequence stand out. First is the predominance of poems dedicated to other poets. Second is Shostakovich's play with temporal perspective and with the weight—precisely the weight—of future greatness in the two deeply personal framing poems (Tsvetaeva to herself, and Tsvetaeva to Akhmatova), as contrasted with the timeless and weightless confrontations apostrophized in the two poems to Pushkin.

Tsvetaeva wrote "To my verses" when she was twenty-one. She wrote the tribute to Akhmatova—it was the older poet's favorite of several that Tsvetaeva would offer her—at age twenty-four. Yet Shostakovich sets both of these poems largo, in a stately manner, for an older, deeper, more experienced voice with a matured perspective. (The composer had in mind for his new cycle the Leningrad mezzo Irina Bogacheva, for—he said—her strong and beautiful voice resembled what he imagined for Tsvetaeva herself: "thick, powerful, shrouded in the bitterness of homegrown tobacco, a voice that smoked, smoked as it wept."[59])

Tsvetaeva at twenty-one compares her adolescent verse with precious wines "whose time will come" (*nastanet svoi chered*). But only the music, added in 1973, was absolute witness to the arrival of that triumphant time, thereby rendering provisional and transitory the insecurity of the poem's present. The tribute to Akhmatova is subject to a similar temporal layering. It was written by Tsvetaeva decades before the advent of those national tragedies—political terror, purges, the Second World War— that Akhmatova would chronicle in *Requiem* and elsewhere, which would transform her into the conscience of the nation. A half-century later, the musical setting of this 1916 lyric gives voice to the grandeur of the poet as only Shostakovich, not Tsvetaeva, could know her. These poems from the 1910s are early promises—promises remembered, made good, and performed by their aged poets.

Such proof of survival is a driving force behind any cultural tradition. But the interaction of words with music in the Tsvetaeva songs is of a different sort than in the operatic *Nose* or *Lady Macbeth,* where Shostakovich's music revitalizes Gogol, Leskov, and Zamiatin. In this cycle, a good part of the work is "perspectival," accomplished by the mature poets on their own younger selves. It is worth noting that Tsvetaeva had a well-elaborated theory about poets and time. Poets, freed from their own histories, are all contemporaries of each other. Poets who possess special communicative powers were persecuted or martyred.[60]

Thus the two magnificent poems to Russia's founding poet Pushkin at the center of the cycle: "Poet and Tsar" and "No, the drum was beating." In the first, we find ourselves in the "otherworldly hall of tsars," confronting a marble-and-gold statue of Nicholas I, "pitiable gendarme of Pushkin's fame" and butcher, censor, *pevtsoubiitsa* (poeticide, murderer of singers). In the second, a historically accurate scene that develops musically from the first almost without pause, we witness Pushkin's funeral in 1837. The drum and fife are beating and the body is being carried out— but the authorities, making a show of honoring the slain poet, so fear a public demonstration that the coffin is sneaked out at night and the site is packed with police. Their "gendarmes' chests and mugs" are lined up shoulder to shoulder, seam to seam. Tsvetaeva invokes a positively Gogolian landscape of uniformed body parts, gossip, rumor, and cringing conformity before the powerful, which must have assaulted and thrilled Shostakovich's ear. In such a world, the poet of genius will live and die a misfit, a thief, a willful child kept under surveillance—but all the same, this poet will be acknowledged by the tsar himself as "the wisest man in Russia." By the 1970s, when Shostakovich set these poems in the Soviet Union, "Poet and Tsar"—free creative artist versus state authority—was a richly contemporary theme. As a music professional, Party member, and target of the regime's displeasure, Shostakovich had served honorably on both sides of the divide.

Tsvetaeva herself would have failed to understand why such dual service was considered by some to be so scandalous. In her essay "Art in the Light of Conscience" (1933–34), she asserts that the artist should feel guilt in two cases only: in the refusal to create an artwork, and in the creation of an inartistic work.[61] Guilt, although real, comes later, at the receiving end (and creative artists are also on that end, for they must answer for the effects of their work just as they must respond to the work of others). Here the choices are hard and absolute. The greater the artwork, the more keenly we must answer for our personal behavior in response to it. "One person reads *Werther* and shoots himself, another reads *Werther* and, because Werther shoots himself, decides to live. One behaves like Werther, the other like Goethe. A lesson in self-extermination? A lesson in self-defense? Both." For (as Tsvetaeva paraphrases Goethe) "who can calculate the effect of any one word?"

These provocative essays were circulating clandestinely in Russia by the mid-1960s. We know that Shostakovich was an eager reader of Tsvetaeva's prose. How reassuring it would be if this essay had reached him—a great poet's generous, if idiosyncratic, prosaic envelope for the tribute to poetic immortality that his 1973 vocal cycle would become. For who can calculate the effect of any one musical message?

iv. The Lebiadkin songs:
bad poetry, bad prose, bad politics, bad ends

Shostakovich's penultimate opus, no. 146, "Four Verses of Captain Lebiadkin," is a puzzling farewell to Russian literature. It belongs to a well-developed line in the composer's work, that vein of Musorgskian musical satire and parodic citation that begins with the two Krylov fables (1922), moves through *The Nose* (1930) and the slapstick episodes of *Lady Macbeth* (1932), and culminates in the post-Stalinist period with the Sasha Chorny "Satires" (1960), the texts from *Krokodil* (1965), and "Preface to the Complete Collection of My Works" (1966). These compositions are often hilarious, but—it is often asked—are they profound, and do they evoke the humanizing, ennobling laughter that the composer professed to admire? As we learn from the diaries of Shostakovich's composition teacher, Maksimilian Shteinberg, the Lebiadkin poems were on this precocious student's mind as a term of rebuke early on. In 1928, having just finished *The Nose,* "Mitia" irreverently remarked of Shcherbachev's Second Symphony (a setting of poems by Blok) that it was "not Blok at all, but the poetry of Captain Lebiadkin from *Demons*."[62] But in 1974, the proximity of this paradigmatically ugly Dostoevskian buffoon to the radiant Tsvetaeva and Michelangelo cycles, each of which is a testimony to artistic transcendence and survival, seemed incongruous. In Malcolm MacDonald's words, the "doggedly syllabic setting" of the cycle, its textures "spare to the point of dessication," its harmony "almost entirely limited to bare octaves, with the occasional buzzing dissonance," make it "in some ways the oddest and most opaque of Shostakovich's late works."[63]

Ignat Lebiadkin is a petty but pivotal scoundrel in *Demons:* thief, schemer, sponger, blackmailer, permanent drunk, brother to the mad lame girl whom the novel's enigmatic hero, Nikolai Stavrogin, secretly married on a bet. He serves Stavrogin as his jester, and he is a poet. Strewn throughout the novel are a half-dozen examples of his wretched stanzas, which ever since the 1920s have attracted the occasional interest of Dostoevsky scholars and of poets curious about the limits and cadences of the grotesque. Vladislav Khodasevich, the émigré poet who so appreciated the musicality of Tsvetaeva's verse, wrote an essay in 1931 on "The Poetry of Ignat Lebiadkin," in which he remarked that most of Dostoevsky's characters adored poetry (the singular exception is Smerdiakov), even though very few could create successfully in it beyond botched recitation or pastiche imitation; Khodasevich concluded that poetry was important to the great novelist largely as one more form of caricature.[64] More recently, Ksana Blank has shown that Lebiadkin's extravagantly vulgar metaphors, rhyme patterns, and archaic metrics in fact travesty—and rather cleverly—important eighteenth-century neoclassical genres and poets: the fable, the celebratory ode, the convention of occasional verse, and Derzhavin's practice at its wildest and most startling.[65] Shostakovich's knowledge of classic Russian literature was very thorough. He must have delighted in these grotesque resonances and debased parodies. Recall his early fondness for Russia's great revolutionary poets on either side of her Golden and Silver Age, Derzhavin and Mayakovsky.

According to the musicologist Abram Gozenpud (an acquaintance of the composer through Sollertinsky and the author of a monograph on Dostoevsky and music), Shostakovich had reread Dostoevsky's *Demons* in the summer of 1971. When queried by Gozenpud on his attitude toward the novelist, Shostakovich replied that "it was easier to have dealings with Shakespeare than with Dostoevsky," for "he has too powerful an effect on me, so powerful that it is difficult for me to organize my impressions."[66] Lebiadkin must have provided some focus. Here was a voice (comfortably travestied and grotesque) through which to filter a bit of the wisdom imparted by the huge prose mass of this conspiratorial novel. For his first three songs, Shostakovich gathered up Lebiadkin's scattered lines of doggerel verse, together with some prosaic context clinging to them. Then, as his final song, he set a poetic text, also doggerel and a parody, that was not written by Lebiadkin but is centrally important to the novel's catastrophic finale.

Finishing the cycle in August 1974, Shostakovich wrote to Glikman that "the image of Captain Lebiadkin has much of the buffoon about it, but there is considerably more in him that is sinister [*zloveshchee*, literally, 'bearing evil tidings']. It has turned out to be a very sinister composition."[67] On the following day he also wrote to Tishchenko, repeating his phrase about Lebiadkin being a buffoon, and at the same time "it seems to me, a sinister figure [*figura zloveshchaia*]." The letter to Tishchenko continues: "I don't have a copy of *Demons* to hand at this moment, therefore I can't point out to you the pages where the above-mentioned verses are found. But I'd like you to read them through. Ah, here I've just found *Demons*. Look at the verses on pages 126, 140, 261 (I unified those into a single number). And then cf. pp. 188, 493 and 369." That Shostakovich should go to this trouble locating the relevant swatches of verse in Dostoevsky's novel to ensure his friend's sequential rereading suggests that for him, a knowledge of the larger contexts was essential to his musical settings. The page numbers tagged to the verses proceed chronologically, except for the final song. Significantly for my interpretation of the cycle, Shostakovich ends his letter to Tishchenko with the caveat: "In such an order they must be performed."[68]

Lebiadkin is sinister, ominous, a buffoon and bearer of evil tidings. The songs he sings are brazenly self-confident, full of the vanity of performance. Performance vanity—the singer as author, hero, improviser, and commentator on his own song—is key to the resilience and infectiousness of the cycle. Vladimir Ovcharek, leader of the Taneev Quartet, recalls that after hearing its pre-premiere performance of the Fifteenth Quartet in October 1974, Shostakovich was in such "magnificent spirits" that he "told lots of jokes, and even sang the Songs of Captain Lebiadkin for us; at the time they had still not been performed in public."[69] In the whole of the Russian canon arguably only Dostoevsky's *Demons*—a very funny book, and Shostakovich's favorite prose work—succeeds in combining, on a large scale, the irresistibly comic performance with unspeakable and irreversible evil. It would seem that anyone concerned with the composer's politics would have to grasp the dynamics of this novel and the behavior of its inhabitants.

Most scholarship on this song cycle has emphasized either its generic connections with other satirical text settings by Shostakovich, or the personality of its morally repellent protagonist. Dorothea Redepenning, in her survey of the various interpretations of the Lebiadkin cycle, sees a range of influences stretching from the Romantic-folkloric (she notes the link with Musorgsky's beggar-monks and quasi-sacred holy fools) to the caustically political (the composer's disgust with corrupt Party bureaucrats of his own time).[70] She herself prefers a biographical and confessional lens. In her view, the brutal simplicity of these settings looks back to the "methods of socialist realism," their doggerel recalling texts of the Stalinist period that Shostakovich himself undertook, willingly or no, to musicalize for the glory of the regime. Redepenning ends her analysis on this mournful note. But to perform the cycle in a mocking spirit, as the composer did for the Taneev Quartet, might also have offered a chance to seize control of the context and thereby ease the guilt.

Sheinberg also discusses op. 146. But she limits her analysis to the first of the songs (the "love epistles"), noting a similarity between its rhythmic settings and the "unison, heavy, stamped waltzes" in other works (*Lady Macbeth,* the Eighth String Quartet, and the Fourth, Fifth, and Tenth symphonies). She reminds us that in Shostakovich, distorted or compulsive dances are often a prelude to mob violence, which in itself is ample evidence that the first Lebiadkin song qualifies as a grotesque of the most sinister sort.[71] Gozenpud too remarks upon the cycle's use of grotesquely parodic musical reminiscences. Eclectic snatches of tune pair up with the poetic fragments of Afanasii Fet and Nestor Kukolnik that float wantonly into the drunken captain's memory: intonations from Verdi's *Rigoletto,* a Tchaikovsky romance, a triumphal cantata.[72] My discussion below supplements these earlier readings from a less commonly pursued perspective: the Lebiadkin songs in the context of the novel itself. This context Shostakovich knew intimately, and it can fairly be said that he expected his listeners (not only Tishchenko) to know it. For we are dealing here with an audience that did not require libretti to follow the plot of a transposed classic. Among the more thrilling aspects of literary culture in that country is that Russians of Shostakovich's circle could *recite* the classics, not just recall them.

The first song of the cycle, "The Love of Captain Lebiadkin," stitches together three separate poetic missives that the love-struck buffoon sends to Elizaveta Tushina (from Part One, III, ch. 3; Part One, IV, ch. 2; and Part Two, II, ch. 2 of the novel).[73] The opening two quatrains, which immediately recall the hilarious nonsequiturs in the "Tale of Captain Kopeikin" from Gogol's *Dead Souls,* are delivered to the narrator by the drunken

Lebiadkin himself, on the street, in the middle of the night. "A cannon-ball of flaming love/exploded in Ignat's chest/and again with bitter anguish groaned/the armless one from Sevastopol." Before singing a "variant" of the above verse (in fact, a totally different text), Lebiadkin amends the sentiments expressed in a line of prose, which Shostakovich also sets: "Although I wasn't in Sevastopol and wasn't even armless, still, what rhymes!" This comment sets the pattern for Lebiadkin's literary mentality, which is a staple of the Gogol-Dostoevsky school: tasteless hyperbole featuring colorful lies that are instantly revealed as such for the sake of pleasure in the form.

The second installment, several pages later, is not performed by Lebiadkin in the novel but delivered to its love object, who indignantly hands it to the narrator and his friend Ivan Shatov to read. This is a love epistle, "To the Perfection of the Maiden Tushina," rhyming couplets of irregular length and high-blown diction that mimic eighteenth-century amateur versifying. In their defense Lebiadkin appends a love letter in prose (which Shostakovich does not set), with this piece of wisdom: "Look at it as verse and nothing more, for verse, after all, is nonsense, and jus-tifies what in prose is considered an impertinence." Again, hilarious poetry is explicated and deflated by a prosaic addendum: poetry is a means for getting away with something you could not get away with in prose, and it creates the ground for an illusion that prose will sooner or later expose. The subtext for this hypothesis (which Shostakovich also did not set) is found in the conversation that follows the first installment of Lebiadkin's courtship lyrics, spoken to the narrator by his crony Liputin: "He's in love, in love like a tomcat, and you know, it actually started with hatred." Here again we recognize Dostoevsky's trademark psychology, becoming ever more politically relevant and painful, albeit still uttered by one shameless buffoon about another. We love and hate, collaborate and resist, all on the same plane.

The final snatch of amatory verse, inspired by Elizaveta Tushina's horseback riding and clumsily entitled "On the Occasion if She Should Break Her Leg," combines high abstraction with indecently gross innu-endo ("The beauty of beauties broke her member/and became doubly interesting"). The larger context is now turning ominous. Lebiadkin recites these four lines to the novel's hero, Stavrogin, boasting that this bit of nonsense in the style of Gogol is "raving, but a poet's raving," and that "even a louse has the right to be in love." At this point Stavrogin flies into a rage and confronts Lebiadkin with a list of his vices: drinking, lying, extorting money, mistreating his sister, sending insolent letters. Stavrogin promises to announce his marriage publicly in the near future, which will release him from the need to subsidize this blackmailer. Enter a new theme, so familiar as a source of guilt in conspiratorial societies: that of the cynical nihilist (Stavrogin) sacrificing his own freedom to curtail the abuses of his turncoat jester. Shostakovich ends his first song on this third installment of love lyrics, setting as his coda the signature from the second poem: "Composed by an unlearned man during a quarrel."

And quarrel there will be. The second song in the cycle, "The Cockroach," occurs during the novel's first big scandal scene, in the drawing room of Stavrogin's imperious mother, Varvara Petrovna. (Its melodic base is a thumping parody of the children's song *Chizhik,* which "nearly every Russian child can play with one finger on the piano."[74]) During this scene Stavrogin confronts—inconclusively—his mad crippled wife (whose status as legal spouse is still secret), his mother (desperate to know if the rumors of her son's disgraceful marriage are true), and eventually every major conspirator in the town, including for the first time its most sinister villain, Pyotr Verkhovensky. Into this gathering Lebiadkin stumbles, temporarily sober, and recites his senseless Cockroach piece, itself a triple parody on a Krylov fable.[75] Here Shostakovich sets, in a style reminiscent of the most radical of Musorgsky's topical satires and perhaps in affectionate allusion to Musorgsky's final vocal satire "The Flea," the prose text surrounding the inserted fable. Lebiadkin is thus simultaneously in the novel and in the song. He sings his verses, then sings Varvara Petrovna's confused response to them, then insists that no one interrupt him, then starts over, and finally provides a self-satisfied prose explication: that despite falling into a glass full of flies, the cockroach "*ne ropshchet*" (doesn't murmur), even when Nikifor sensibly "dumps the whole comedy into the tub, despite all the shouting." Shostakovich ends his vocal setting on a final clarification from Lebiadkin: "As regards Nikifor, he represents nature." To portray this absurd dramatic situation accurately requires ingenuity from the singer-performer as well as from the audience, which is both listening to the song being performed in the recital hall and (as soon as the prose passages begin) dragged into the world of the novel, as one more witness to scandal unfolding in Varvara Petrovna's drawing room. Sycophancy and craven impudence combined with burlesqued classical allusion: such is the essence of Lebiadkin the jester. But the third and fourth songs will reveal his more sinister (*zloveshchee*) side.

In the second half of the cycle, Shostakovich sets texts that are increasingly distant from Lebiadkin's grotesque self. But as the buffoon withdraws in person, the subtexts and secondary parodies mount—and Lebiadkin's sly, greedy, shameless spirit diffuses rapidly throughout the remainder of the plot. The third song, in honor of the governesses, occurs in

Dostoevsky's text as the first (unscheduled) piece of art performed at the fête. Thus it serves to inaugurate the novel's apocalyptic catastrophes: the death by fire of Lebiadkin and his sister, the death by drowning of the ex-conspirator Shatov, the death of Elizaveta Tushina at the hands of an outraged mob, the suicide of Stavrogin by hanging. Lebiadkin's ditty opens innocently enough ("Greetings, greetings, governess!") but quickly descends into vulgarity and provocation. Be you "retrograde or George-Sander," you teach French to snot-nosed children but in fact you only want to get married; however, even a priest is hard to nab without a dowry; so grab the capital we're raising for you here, make a run for it, "spit on everything and triumph!" Although sung as a parody of a triumphal cantata by its putative author in the cycle, in the novel it is not Lebiadkin who recites this ditty at the fête but his evil sidekick Liputin, the jester's fool, in a calculated move to transform the ball into a mob whose violence will then mask a number of planned political murders. In the final song, "Svetlaia lichnost" (variously translated as a Radiant personality, a Shining light, and a Pure soul), this nihilistic intonation is carried through to its inevitable conclusion. Captain Lebiadkin is no longer connected to it.

"Svetlaia lichnost" is Dostoevsky's parody of a poem, "The Student," by the radical émigré Nikolai Ogarev. In 1867 Ogarev dedicated it enthusiastically to the charismatic nihilist, anarchist, and political fraud Sergei Nechaev, a disciple of Bakunin.[76] Two years later, Nechaev engineered the murder of a recalcitrant ex-radical student in Moscow, with the aim of blackmailing those members of his "revolutionary cell" who had begun to doubt his authority. Dostoevsky was horrified when news of this murder reached him in Dresden, and he placed the event at the center of his novel in progress, *Demons*. The "Svetlaia lichnost" poem-parody (quite a bit worse than Ogarev's original) plays a crucial role in the denouement of the novel's plot. It melodramatically recounts the story of a brave student revolutionary who fled abroad after inciting rebellion; now the Russian people, "from Smolensk to Tashkent," await his return to avenge "marriage, church, family—all the evildoing of the old world!" At the proper moment Pyotr Verkhovensky, the novel's Nechaev double (and double agent), insinuates to the gullible governor of the province that this poem refers to none other than Ivan Shatov (whose grisly murder Verkhovensky is himself planning). But in true double-agent style he makes a show of begging the governor to save the fellow, an old friend, for sentimental reasons, cursing himself all the while for his softheartedness. That Lebiadkin should sing this poem in Shostakovich's cycle is quite appropriate. Its context in the novel is completely Lebiadkin's voice zone—although this zone has now been taken over by a far more skilled and dangerous scoundrel. As Malcolm MacDonald points out, the structure of the final song differs from the earlier three in the cycle. They are "open-ended and continuously developing . . . [whereas] this last one is a simple strophic song, with a pawky little refrain on the piano," a "scrap of tune" that bears some resemblance to the satirical "A Career" in the Thirteenth Symphony.[77]

This entire Nechaev/*Demons*/Shatov story was of course known by heart among the Soviet intelligentsia of Shostakovich's generation. It resonated like a cliché beneath the staged murder of the Party chief Sergei Kirov in Leningrad in December 1934, the event that set off the purges. Although Dostoevsky was a proscribed author during the Stalinist period, having been discredited by Maxim Gorky as a writer incompatible with the task of building socialism, *Demons* was at last reissued in a limited press run in 1956, the year Khrushchev initiated tentative de-Stalinization at the Twentieth Party Congress. The resurrected novel quickly became synonymous with political corruption—and with the right, at last, to expose that corruption.

As it occurs in Dostoevsky's novel, the poem-parody "Svetlaia lichnost" is a portal to revolutionary violence. It is also a perfect example (in Sheinberg's terminology) of irony as device. Its one-way dynamic leads directly from venality through betrayal to violence and death. But Shostakovich's setting of that poem and its kindred verses as his final vocal cycle in 1974—as well as his delighted performance of it when in "magnificent spirits"—becomes infinite irony, irony as terminus. Its laughter is absurd, grotesque, even sinister, but also double-edged and productive. The performance of a multiple parody always celebrates the right of the performer-survivor to re-accent and re-voice the originals. Anguish is both acknowledged and released. In the Russian literary tradition that inspired Shostakovich to so many masterpieces, such double-voicedness was the norm for art, not the exception. It is a lesson that Western observers of the Russian scene have been slow to learn: that this culture, whether tsarist or Stalinist, was not divided into collaborators versus martyrs. The double-voiced collaborators most often *became* the martyrs. And many of these martyrs, reflecting on their duty as creative artists, would seek ways to re-accent their work so as to continue to serve. They did so not only out of fear but because art in Russia was taken so seriously, subsidized so generously, and assumed by its best practitioners to be an end and not a means. Art, which complicates consciousness and thus keeps it alive, is more necessary under closed regimes than open ones.

The Russian literary tradition is conventionally divided into two great currents: Gogol and Dostoevsky on one side, Pushkin and Tolstoy on the other. Shostakovich was attracted to the first pair; Prokofiev, in his maturity, to the second. The second pair of writers, with their crystalline, confident relation to language and their "eighteenth-century" sobriety, appealed less to Shostakovich's musical imagination. (Pushkin, the most beloved and most musicalized of all Russian writers, receives only a handful of songs and one comic fairy tale; Tolstoy, fully co-opted by the Soviet establishment and a certifiably acceptable source text, merits only one wry allusion in "The Kreutzer Sonata," the last of the Sasha Chorny "Satires," where the opening bars of Beethoven careen off into a cheesy urban romance.) It was with Gogol and Dostoevsky that Shostakovich made his home. Their faulty or defaulted narrators, rumor-laden plots, and distrust of the sleek sermonizing word were a perfect complement to music that relished grotesque effects and abrupt changes of direction. But with art of this sort, pitfalls await the critic. A parodying energy is perhaps the most dangerous of all energies to contain and define. For a commitment to infinite irony—such as Shostakovich appeared to honor—is not necessarily nihilist, nor does it preclude a political identity. Gogol and Dostoevsky ended their lives in a frenzy of Russian patriotism, yet both were ironists and parodists of the genius class. Although the twentieth century put ghastly new burdens on artists of this creative temperament, delight in parody continued to coexist with a deep, often defensive patriotism and civic conscience. Bred in an age of patronage, Shostakovich became one of his country's most subtle and least servile interpreters.

NOTES

1. Katerina Clark, *Petersburg: Crucible of Cultural Revolution* (Cambridge, Mass.: Harvard University Press, 1995), pp. 224–41, esp. p. 226.

2. For an account of Shostakovich's outspoken participation in this ultimately unsuccessful campaign, centered around (but not limited to) his own first opera, see Laurel E. Fay, "The Punch in Shostakovich's *Nose*," in *Russian and Soviet Music: Essays for Boris Schwarz*, ed. Malcolm Hamrick Brown (Ann Arbor, Mich.: UMI Press, 1984), pp. 229–43.

3. The polymath and polyglot Ivan Sollertinsky (1902–44) possessed a photographic memory for literary as well as musical texts (he knew twenty-five languages and could reproduce a score after a single glance). In 1927, soon after his friendship with Shostakovich began, he joined the Leningrad Philharmonic, where he served as lecturer, head of publications, and eventually musical director. Biographers of Sollertinsky credit him with shaping many of the young Shostakovich's tastes and techniques; the composer concurred. See L. Mikheeva (L. V. Sollertinskaia), *I. I. Sollertinskii: Zhizn' i nasledie* (Leningrad: Sovetskii kompozitor, 1988), pp. 70–75. For a two-page biography of this remarkable figure in the context of the Bakhtin circle (he was a respected intimate in that company), see Katerina Clark and Michael Holquist, *Mikhail Bakhtin* (Cambridge, Mass.: Harvard University Press, 1984), pp. 104–5.

4. "Anketa po psikhologii tvorcheskogo protsessa," in *Dmitrii Shostakovich v pis'makh i dokumentakh*, ed. I. A. Bobykina (Moscow: Glinka State Central Museum of Musical Culture, 2000), pp. 473–74. Unspaced ellipses [. . .] in the original. The specific question posed (no. 4) was "Your attitude toward the other arts (level of professionalism, degree of interest and so on)."

5. Esti Sheinberg, *Irony, Satire, Parody and the Grotesque in the Music of Shostakovich: A Theory of Musical Incongruities* (Aldershot, U.K.: Ashgate, 2000), p. 153.

6. For a brief survey of the correlation between Shostakovich's operatic style and the style of symphonies being composed at the same time, see Geoffrey Norris, "The Operas," in *Shostakovich: The Man and His Music*, ed. Christopher Norris (Boston: Marion Boyars, 1982), pp. 105–24, esp. pp. 118–20.

7. For a discussion of this watershed, see Malcolm MacDonald, "Words and Music in Late Shostakovich," in Norris, ed., *Shostakovich*, pp. 125–47, esp. pp. 125–26. A case could be made that Shostakovich's efforts at orchestrating Musorgsky's great song cycle on death were not in that earlier composer's best interests. Musorgsky, a profoundly pianistic composer for whom brilliant, consoling orchestral textures in combination with the singing voice were alien, stripped down his cycles to let in the necessary air and loneliness. Orchestration can clog them.

8. For a good discussion of this aspect of the new librettistic word as it gained notoriety in the later 1920s, see Clark, *Petersburg*, pp. 228–30.

9. "O tvorchestve Shostakovicha i ego opere 'Ledi Makbet'" (1934), in B. Asaf'ev, *Ob opere: Izbrannye stat'i*, 2d ed. (Leningrad: Muzyka, 1985), pp. 310–19, esp. p. 314.

10. "Ob osnovakh kino" (1927), in Iu. N. Tynianov, *Poetika. Istoriia literatury. Kino* (Moscow: Nauka, 1977), pp. 326–45, esp. pp. 342–43. Tynianov's point is that even impossible plots can be domesticated and made representable through style—we accept that nose in the hot roll because the characters in the story must accept it—and that film language is just beginning to acquire the vocabulary and stylistic registers long available to verbal language.

11. In his discussion of the emotionally based "tonal order," for example, Eisenstein speaks of "optical light vibrations (varying degrees of 'haze' and 'luminosity')" as a phenomenon identical "with a minor harmony in music." See "Methods of Montage" (1929),

in Sergei Eisenstein, *Film Form: Essays in Film Theory*, ed. and trans. Jay Leyda (New York: Harcourt Brace & World, 1963), pp. 72–83, esp. p. 76.

12. "Kino—Slovo—Muzyka" (1924), in Tynianov, *Poetika. Istoriia literatury. Kino*, pp. 320–22, esp. p. 321.

13. S. Khentova, *Shostakovich: Zhizn' i tvorchestvo*, vol. 1 (Leningrad: Sovetskii kompozitor, 1985), pp. 198–99.

14. D. Shostakovich, "K prem'ere Nosa," *Rabochii i teatr* 24 (16 June 1929): 12.

15. Gerard McBurney, "Whose Shostakovich?" in *A Shostakovich Casebook*, ed. Malcolm Hamrick Brown (Bloomington, Ind.: Indiana University Press, 2004), pp. 292, 290.

16. Sheinberg, *Irony*, p. 4. Page references henceforth are given in parentheses in the text.

17. I paraphrase here from Sheinberg's chapter 1, "The Concept of Irony: Philosophical Background," esp. pp. 33–40. In successive parts, she discusses satire, techniques of parody, the grotesque, and existential irony, illustrating each with literary examples and their musical analogues.

18. D. Shostakovich, "Pochemu 'Nos'?" prefacing *NOS. Polnyi tekst opery* (Leningrad: Teakinopechat', 1930), pp. 3–4. esp. p. 3. This final paragraph is omitted in the reprint of the preface in D. Shostakovich, *O vremeni i o sebe: 1926–1975* (Moscow: Sovetskii kompozitor, 1980), pp. 23–34, esp. p. 24. The sentiment is embroidered upon, albeit rather flatly, by Solomon Volkov in his *Testimony: The Memoirs of Dmitri Shostakovich as related to and edited by Solomon Volkov*, trans. Antonina W. Bouis (New York: Harper & Row, 1979), p. 208: "I didn't want to write a satirical opera; I'm not completely sure what that is. . . . I just find it boring; you're constantly aware of the composer's attempts at being funny, and it's not funny at all. People find satire and grotesquerie in *The Nose*, but I wrote totally serious music, there's no parody or joking in it. . . . Really, when you think about it, what's so funny about a man losing his nose [etc.]."

19. Shostakovich, "Pochemu 'Nos'?" p. 4.

20. Alexander N. Tumanov, "Correspondence of Literary Text and Musical Phraseology in Shostakovich's Opera *The Nose* and Gogol's Fantastic Tale," *The Russian Review* 52 (July 1993): 397–414, esp. 403–4.

21. A. Bretanitskaia, *"Nos" D. D. Shostakovicha* (Moscow: Muzyka, 1983), p. 17.

22. D. Shostakovich, *Nos* (score arranged for voice and piano by the author), *Sobranie sochinenii*, vol. 19 (Moscow: Muzyka, 1981), pp. 104–6.

23. F. M. Dostoevskii, *Brat'ia Karamazovy*, knigi 1–X, in *Polnoe sobranie sochinenii v 30-i tomakh* (Leningrad: Nauka, 1976), pp. 203–4. In English see Fyodor Dostoevsky, *The Brothers Karamazov*, trans. Richard Pevear and Larissa Volokhonsky (New York: Vintage Books, 1991), pp. 222–26. Translation of the song adjusted to a more literal rendition.

24. See Yury Tynianov, "Dostoevsky and Gogol: Towards a Theory of Parody. Part One: Stylization and Parody" (1921), in *Dostoevsky and Gogol: Texts and Criticism*, ed. Priscilla Meyer and Stephen Rudy (Ann Arbor, Mich.: Ardis, 1979), p. 104.

25. A Gozenpud, *Dostoevskii i muzykal'no-teatral'noe iskusstvo* (Leningrad: Sovetskii kompozitor, 1981), p. 190.

26. See Bretanitskaia, *"Nos" D. D. Shostakovicha*, pp. 28–41, and her "O muzykal'noi dramaturgii opery 'Nos,'" in *Sovetskaia muzyka* 9 (1974): 47–53, esp. 48.

27. Boris Eichenbaum (Eikhenbaum), "How Gogol's 'Overcoat' is Made," in *Gogol from the Twentieth Century: Eleven Essays*, ed. Robert A. Maguire (Princeton, N.J.: Princeton University Press, 1974), pp. 269–91, esp. pp. 284–85.

28. Tumanov argues for a personal relationship based on Shostakovich's apparent knowledge of Eikhenbaum's scholarly edition of Gogol's Petersburg Tales, at the time already prepared for publication but not yet published; see "Correspondence of Literary Text," p. 406 n. 19.

29. Ibid., pp. 411–12; p. 409. A huge gap in pitch "pumps in the emotion of fear," Tumanov claims, creating a "*vocal* image" that is both comic (because it is distorted beyond the conventional diapason) and terrifying. This piercing vocal line is employed almost as a weapon, and the audience senses it as such.

30. A book-length explication of this scandal, based on recently released archival documents, classifies it as a "cultural revolution" motivated largely by intrabureaucratic rivalry in the agitprop and art wings of the Party establishment—*not* by any particular sins on the part of Shostakovich, who was simply a convenient (because visible and accommodating) target to terrorize. See L. V. Maksimenkov, *Sumbur vmesto muzyki: Stalinskaia kul'turnaia revoliutsiia, 1936–1938.* (Moscow: Iuridicheskaia kniga, 1997), esp. pp. 73–87.

31. "Tragediia-satira," Shostakovich's article on his opera in progress, appeared in *Sovetskoe iskusstvo* on 16 October 1932 (excerpted in *O vremeni i o sebe*, p. 31). In it the composer discusses the distinction between Leskov's story and the libretto, his warm sympathy for the heroine, his special use of "satirical," and his departures in musical dramaturgy from *The Nose.* In English, see the discussion in Laurel E. Fay, *Shostakovich: A Life* (New York: Oxford University Press, 2000), p. 69.

32. D. D. Shostakovich, "'Ekaterina Izmailova': Avtor ob opere," *Sovetskoe iskusstvo* (14 December 1933), as cited in *O vremeni i o sebe*, p. 35.

33. "Lady Macbeth is an energetic woman," this musician remarked after watching the rehearsal, "but it's the other way around in your opera; here is a soft, suffering woman who arouses not terror but sympathy, pity, kindly feelings." Shostakovich agreed with this assessment. D. Shostakovich, "Moe ponimanie 'Ledi Makbet,'" in *"Ledi Makbet Mtsenskogo uezda": Opera D. D. Shostakovicha* (Leningrad: Gosudarstvennyi Akademicheskii Malyi Opernyi Teatr, 1934), p. 7.

34. On this background, see Caryl Emerson, "Back to the Future: Shostakovich's Revision of Leskov's 'Lady Macbeth of Mtsensk District,'" *Cambridge Opera Journal* 1/1 (1989): 59–78.

35. Fay, *Shostakovich: A Life,* p. 13.

36. Evg. Zamiatin, "Sovremennaia russkaia literatura" (1918), published in *Grani* 32 (October–December 1956): 90–101, quotes on pp. 97 and 100. *Rus'* or *Sviataia Rus'* (Holy Russia) was the name for the Russian Orthodox lands from Kievan times (ninth century) to the end of the medieval period (Peter the Great). The term was given currency in the nineteenth century by conservative Slavophiles; when used by twentieth-century artists it evokes images of the pre-industrial Russian countryside and its traditional peasant, merchant, and priestly cultures.

37. Zamiatin provides actual metric examples of pacing changes in his sentences, which are further conditioned by breathing patterns governed by punctuation and by the ratio of vowels to consonants. "For me it is completely clear," he writes, "that the relationship between the rhythmics of verse and the rhythmics of prose is the same as the relationship between arithmetic and integral calculus." Evgenii Zamiatin, "Zakulisy" (1929?), in *Sochineniia* (Moscow: Kniga, 1988), pp. 461–72, esp. p. 468. For a brief explication in English of these principles, see Milton Ehre, "Zamyatin's Aesthetics," in *Zamyatin's WE: A Collection of Critical Essays,* ed. Gary Kern (Ann Arbor, Mich.: Ardis, 1988), pp. 130–39.

38. *Rus': Russkie tipy B. M. Kustodieva. Slovo Evg. Zamiatina* (St. Petersburg: Akvilon, 1923), pp. 7–23. The book contains twenty-four portraits by Kustodiev, of which over half play a role in Zamiatin's story. Eleven appear to be models for the central characters (two merchants, five merchants' wives, four shop assistants/young swains); there are also prototypes for secondary figures (Marfa's aunt the abbess; the cabdrivers whose drunkenness caused the death of Marfa's parents; the trunkmaker) as well as for several cameo appearances (a pilgrim, a wanderer). Some episodes are direct narrative realizations of the pictures (Marfa in the bathhouse [no. 14]; Marfa on a walk alongside a high fence, with

a male figure in the background [no. 13]; the trunkmaker Petrov reading the newspaper in the sun [no. 17]). I am grateful to my Princeton colleague Olga Peters Hasty, a specialist in Russian ornamentalist prose, for her casually offered and highly productive suggestion that Shostakovich "might have been reading Leskov through Zamiatin's version of the tale." After the present essay was completed, there came to my attention an excellent article from 1995 that also posits Zamiatin's "Rus" as intermediary between Leskov's tale and Shostakovich's opera. Its author suggests a different sequence: that Shostakovich was first attracted to the Zamiatin tale via Kustodiev and only later settled on Leskov's "Lady Macbeth." See Andrew Wachtel, "The Adventures of a Leskov Story in Soviet Russia, or the Socialist Realist Opera That Wasn't," in *O RUS! Studia litteraria slavica in honorem Hugh McLean*, ed. Simon Karlinsky, James L. Rice, and Barry P. Scherr (Berkeley, Calif.: Berkeley Slavic Specialties, 1995), pp. 358–68.

39. Evgenii Zamiatin, "Vstrechi s Kustodievym" (1927), in Zamiatin, *Sochineniia*, pp. 333–43, esp. p. 334. Other details of the same genesis quoted here can be found in Zamiatin's contribution to the 1930 anthology of Leningrad writers, *Kak my pishem* (Benson, Vt.: Chalidze Publications, 1983, repr.), pp. 29–47, esp. p. 32.

40. See Fay, *Shostakovich: A Life*, p. 68.

41. According to Goldshtein's loosely constructed reminiscences, published in French in the 1980s, Shostakovich first discussed with Zamiatin a possible ballet adaptation of Leskov's story about the steel flea ("Levsha," the Left-handed Craftsman). But "having examined several works by Leskov, they fixed their choice on 'Lady Macbeth of Mtsensk.' In order to accommodate the needs of the stage, Zamiatin proposed that the plot be transformed and dealt with more freely. Shostakovich and Preis wrote up the libretto according to the plan that he [Zamiatin] provided. In the course of working on the opera, it was necessary to deviate from this plot. But Zamiatin's plan was preserved in its essentials. . . . [Even though his situation was difficult and he was seeking permission to emigrate] Zamiatin found time to meet with Shostakovich. He continued to propose to him various solutions and his influence on this work is easy to discern. Shostakovich himself even played for him certain fragments of the future opera on the piano." Michael Goldstein, "Dmitri Chostakovitch et Evgueni Zamiatine," in *Autour de Zamiatine: Actes du Colloque Université de Lausanne* (juin 1987) suivi de *E. Zamiatine, Ecrits Oubliés*, ed. Leonid Heller (Lausanne: Edition L'Age d'Homme, 1989), pp. 113–23, esp. p. 121. Goldshtein's vague, intriguing testimony is flawed by the absence of any precise dating and by ambiguous undocumented claims elsewhere in the essay. Zamiatin's pivotal role in the opera is reaffirmed briefly in Mikhail Gol'dshtein, "Evgenii Zamiatin i muzyka," *Novoe Russkoe Slovo*, 26 June 1987.

42. *Rus': Russkie tipy B. M. Kustodieva*, p. 9. The original edition of the story differs in several stylistic and plot details from later, more accessible reprints and anthologized versions. In 1923 the heroine's name is Marfa, not Daria, Ivanovna. Significantly for our purposes, this Marfa is even more mysteriously distanced from self-serving crime. After her merchant husband Vakhrameev dies from poisoned mushrooms, Marfa remarries. But in the 1923 original, Zamiatin does not name the new bridegroom (p. 21); in later redactions, Daria explicitly marries the Sergei figure, the "coal-black gypsy eye" (see, for example, "*Rus'*," in Zamiatin, *Izbrannye proizvedeniia* [Moscow: Sovetskaia Rossiia, 1990], pp. 181–89, esp. p. 188). Further page numbers in the text refer to the 1923 edition.

43. *Piter* is an affectionate abbreviation for St. Petersburg/Petrograd/Leningrad.

44. This point is suggested by Alina Izrailevich in her essay "*Rus' Evgeniia Zamiatina*," *Russian Literature* XXI-III (April 1987): 233–42. In her view, Zamiatin's Neorealism expresses itself in this story as a "*lubochnyi skaz-pokaz*" (a folk story demonstration in the woodcut style), where folk sayings or wisdoms are bungled and where all human acts are

justified by Nature. To this end, she argues, Zamiatin employs not cause and effect to explain events but rather the reverse: effect (that is, material result) and only then cause.

45. "Katerina Izmailova. Libretto" (Leningrad, 1934), in *O vremeni i o sebe*, p. 39.

46. D. Shostakovich, "God posle 'Ledi Makbet,'" (14 January 1935), in *O vremeni i o sebe*, p. 48.

47. Sheinberg, *Irony*, pp. 251–61.

48. Taruskin's opening statement was an essay in *The New Republic*, 20 March 1989, pp. 34–40, "The Opera and the Dictator: The Peculiar Martyrdom of Dmitri Shostakovich," later reworked as "*Entr'acte:* The Lessons of Lady M.," in Richard Taruskin, *Defining Russia Musically* (Princeton, N.J.: Princeton University Press, 1997), pp. 498–510.

49. "Anketa po psikhologii . . . ." [question no. 4], p. 474.

50. Vadim Shakhov, "Ledi Makbet Mtsenskogo uezda Leskova i Shostakovicha," in *Shostakovich mezhdu mgnoveniem i vechnost'iu*, ed. L. Kovnatskaia (St. Petersburg: Kompozitor, 2000), pp. 243–94. Specific page references can be found in the text.

51. Boris Gasparov laid out this thesis in "Eugene Onegin in the Age of Realism," a paper delivered at the December 2000 annual conference of the American Association for the Advancement of Slavic Studies, Washington, D.C. See an expanded version in his *Five Operas and a Symphony: Word and Music in Russian Culture* (New Haven: Yale University Press, forthcoming, 2004).

52. Malcolm MacDonald, "Words and Music in Late Shostakovich," p. 139.

53. "Mat' i muzyka," in Marina Tsvetaeva, *Izbrannaia proza v dvukh tomakh 1917–1937*, vol. 2 (New York: Russica, 1979), pp. 187–88.

54. Shostakovich to Glikman, 14 August 1973, in *Story of a Friendship: The Letters of Dmitry Shostakovich to Isaak Glikman, 1941–1975*, trans. Anthony Phillips (Ithaca, N.Y.: Cornell University Press, 2001), p. 190. For the tune of *Chizhik*, see Example 6 in Gerard McBurney, "Fried Chicken in the Bird-Cherry Trees," in this volume, p. 243.

55. This song has not yet been published. See Glikman's note to the letter of 22 February 1971 in *Story of a Friendship*, p. 313. See also Fay, *Shostakovich: A Life*, p. 270.

56. *Pis'ma Dmitriia Dmitrievicha Shostakovicha Borisu Tishchenko* (St. Petersburg: Kompozitor, 1997), p. 39. Two weeks later, thanking Tishchenko for the songs, Shostakovich wrote: "The songs are your huge success. As regards me, I play and sing them for whole days at a time" (9 February 1971).

57. V. Pavlova, "Dva dara," *Muzykal'naia zhizn'* 7–8 (1992): 19–20, esp. 19.

58. Vladislav Khodasevich, review of Marina Tsvetaeva, *Remeslo. Psikhei. Romantika* (1923), in *Vladislav Khodasevich: Sobranie sochinenii v chetyrekh tomakh*, vol. 2 (Moscow: Soglasie, 1996), pp. 112–13, esp. p. 112. Khodasevich's review was by no means a rave. The verses are too rich on sound, he wrote, and too thin on coherent ideas. Her metaphors tend to spin out of control. Tsvetaeva "is not inclined to worry whether her word triggers any response in the reader—and she never thinks about whether or not she believes in what she says." Khodasevich closes on the following judgment, long disproved by time, that from every page of these collections there gazes forth "the face of a capricious woman, very gifted, but as yet no more than a capricious woman, and perhaps even an hysteric: a phenomenon accidental, personal, transitory. There are many such persons in literature, but the *history* of literature never remembers them."

59. See S. Khentova, *D. D. Shostakovich, Tridtsatiletie 1945–1975* (Leningrad: Sovetskii kompozitor, 1982), p. 318; also letter to Glikman, 14 August 1973, in *Story of a Friendship*, p. 191.

60. See especially "The Poet and Time" (1932), in *Art in the Light of Conscience: Eight Essays on Poetry by Marina Tsvetaeva*, ed. and trans. Angela Livingstone (Cambridge, Mass.: Harvard University Press, 1992), pp. 87–103.

61. Marina Tsvetaeva, "Art in the Light of Conscience," in Livingstone, p. 157; subsequent quote on same page.

62. Entry for 19 March 1928, "Shostakovich v dnevnikakh M. I. Shteinberga" (publikatsiia i kommentarii Ol'gi Dansker)," in *Shostakovich mezhdu mgnoveniem i vechnost'iu*, p. 104. About *The Nose* Shteinberg wrote in the same entry: "Mitia Shostakovich dropped by this evening, he showed me the first act of his opera 'The Nose'—like everything else he's been writing recently, it's a senseless, mechanistic heap of sounds, not devoid of a significant amount of dynamism and, at times, wit. Is this really music!"

63. MacDonald, "Words and Music in Late Shostakovich," p. 142.

64. "Poeziia Kapitana Lebiadkina" (1931), in Khodasevich, *Sobranie sochinenii* vol. 2, pp. 194–201.

65. Ksana Blank, "Korni poezii kapitana Lebiadkina," unpublished paper delivered at Harvard University, March 1988.

66. Abraam Gozenpud, "Links with Dostoevsky," article commissioned for Elizabeth Wilson, *Shostakovich: A Life Remembered* (Princeton, N.J.: Princeton University Press, 1994), pp. 458–62, esp. pp. 460 and 461. In the same letter to Gozenpud, Shostakovich complained of those simple-minded lampooners and one-way parodists who saw in Dostoevsky a "like-minded thinker."

67. Letter from Shostakovich to Glikman, 23 August 1974, in *Story of Friendship*, p. 196. Translation adjusted.

68. Letter from Shostakovich to Tishchenko, 24 August 1974, in *Pis'ma Dmitriia Dmitrievicha Shostakovicha Borisu Tishchenko*, p. 46.

69. Vladimir Ovcharek, comments commissioned for Wilson, *Shostakovich: A Life Remembered*, p. 444.

70. Dorothea Redepenning, "'And Art Made Tongue-tied by Authority': Shostakovich's Song Cycles," in *Shostakovich Studies*, ed. David Fanning (Cambridge, Eng.: Cambridge University Press, 1995), pp. 205–28.

71. Sheinberg, *Irony*, pp. 284–96. Quoted phrase on p. 291.

72. Gozenpud, "Links with Dostoevsky," p. 462.

73. Texts consulted here are: F. M. Dostoevskii, *Besy*, in *Polnoe sobranie sochinenii v tridtsati tomakh*, vol. 10 (Leningrad: Nauka, 1974), pp. 95, 106, 209–10 (for "1. The Love of Captain Lebiadkin"); p. 141 (for "2. The Cockroach"); pp. 362–63 (for "3. The Ball to Benefit the Governesses"); p. 273 (for "4. A Radiant Personality"). For these references in the best English version of the novel to date, see Fyodor Dostoevsky, *Demons*, trans. Richard Pevear and Larissa Volokhonsky (New York: Knopf, 1994), pp. 117–18, 131, 265–66 (for no. 1), p. 177 (for no. 2), p. 473 (for no. 3), p. 351 (for no. 4). Translations adjusted.

74. Gozenpud "Links with Dostoevsky," p. 462.

75. Ksana Blank (see n. 65) observes that Lebiadkin's verses parody a similar cockroach tale, "Fantasticheskaia vyskazka," by the early nineteenth-century writer I. Miatlev, which is itself a parody on the lyrics of A. I. Polezhaev, a well-known parodist.

76. See n. 5 to chap. 6 in the Pevear-Volokhonsky translation of *Demons*, p. 527.

77. MacDonald, "Words and Music in Late Shostakovich," p. 145.

Fried Chicken in the Bird-Cherry Trees

Gerard McBurney

Anyone first encountering Shostakovich in his most familiar guise as the composer of fifteen symphonies and fifteen string quartets is likely to be startled encountering some of the less well-known areas of his enormous output. From his fashionably impertinent "modernist" pieces of the late 1920s through the Stalinist kitsch of his midcareer film scores and official compositions, to the inscrutably stripped-down manner of his final songs, Shostakovich availed himself of an astonishingly varied range of styles and approaches over half a century, even by the standards of an age in which it was normal for a composer's language to undergo violent change.

It is true that many of these lesser-known works belong in the category of light music, commercial music or hackwork, but they are nonetheless interesting for that. Even when written for money or to fulfill official requirements, they are still the distinctive work of Shostakovich and have pleasures to offer in themselves, and much to reveal about the wider scale and significance of this composer's legacy. It is one of the more heartening aspects of the energetic reappraisal of Shostakovich in recent years that a number of these once forgotten compositions are now appearing more often on concert programs and in record catalogues.

Of all these less familiar works, the most unexpected is probably the 1959 operetta, *Moscow, Cheryomushki,* op. 105.[1] To the more straitlaced kind of music lover the very idea of this supposedly gloomy composer writing anything so frivolous as an operetta must seem almost incredible. Yet this ebullient song-and-dance spectacular in an unabashedly lower-middle-brow idiom is a fascinating and, paradoxically, in some sense even a typical work, and should not be, as it was for many years, more or less airbrushed from Shostakovich's list of works. Apart from anything else, it was, when it first appeared, a success, at least within the well-fortified boundaries of light entertainment in the old Soviet bloc.

It is true that it long remained unknown in the West, but—leaving the obvious barriers of politics and highbrow aesthetics aside for the moment—this might have had as much as anything to do with the steep decline in the popularity of operetta in Western countries in the postwar years and the genre's replacement by similar but newer forms such as the musical and the rock opera.

It is also true that, a few years after it was written, *Moscow, Cheryomushki* fell out of the operetta repertoire even within the Soviet bloc. But that, too, is hardly surprising. It is in the nature of such works of lighthearted musical and theatrical entertainment that they should have a short commercial shelf life, especially when they involve, as *Moscow, Cheryomushki* does, a plot and libretto (lyrics and book) hanging on contemporary social and political issues and up-to-the-minute fads of popular culture.

Up to the minute the plot certainly was. The libretto, by two well-known Soviet humorists of the day, Vladimir Mass and Mikhail Chervinsky, treats of the bittersweet social, comic, and romantic consequences of Nikita Khrushchev's energetic campaign in the late 1950s to rehouse the vastly expanding populations of Soviet cities in hastily built housing projects. Contemporary humor about this herculean undertaking can be gauged from the fact that these projects, so quickly and shoddily constructed that they soon started falling to bits again, swiftly acquired the slang name *Khrushchoby*, a punning combination of Khrushchev's name with *trushchoba*, the Russian word for "slum." Such acerbic witticisms were common at this period in the USSR, not least because there was always plenty of black humor to be derived from Khrushchev's notorious and absurdly overoptimistic predictions for the country's supposedly wondrous future in the fields of social and technological advancement. So famous were some of Khrushchev's remarks that there were jokes about them even in the West, but, naturally, an especially rich crop among the Russians, who actually had to live with the consequences of their leader's hopeful pronouncements.[2] It can be noted from a good deal of Soviet art and entertainment of this period that almost anything promoted by Khrushchev had its (more or less) funny side. His utopian housing projects were no exception.

At the same time, it would be quite wrong to interpret the text of *Moscow, Cheryomushki* as simply a satire on this housing plan. Although it has many satirical elements and, overall, the hard-edged tone of satire, it is also, simultaneously, the opposite of satire. And no wonder. Everyone in Russia at this period knew that Khrushchev had the best of reasons to attempt the quickest possible rehousing of millions of people, since the conditions in which the vast majority of them lived were frightful. As much as it was meant to be entertainingly waspish, this operetta was also, quite self-consciously, part of a nationwide campaign to talk up the new building programs. In other words, it was a work of propaganda.

It should immediately be pointed out that such propaganda about a social issue was by no means an exclusively Soviet phenomenon. From the 1950s to the 1980s politicians, town planners, and architects, not just in Russia but the world over, extolled the advantages of a brave new life in highrise tower-blocks of identical apartments, filled with refrigerators, foam-filled settees, and Formica-topped chipboard kitchen tables. Those who nowadays approach *Moscow, Cheryomushki* with a supercilious sneer should remember the great quantity of glossy Western advertising, Hollywood movies, and television comedies that treated of similar issues at the same period but in our own society. The only essential difference between "them" and "us" was that in the West the new paradise was portrayed as being available for money, whereas in the Soviet Union it was supposed to be handed down from above, like a gift from one of Aurora's fairy godmothers. Of course this is a big difference, and it is undoubtedly this particular aspect of the setting and the story of Shostakovich's operetta which is most immediately striking to anyone who sees it performed in the West today.

Cheryomushki means "little cherry trees" or, more exactly, "bird-cherry trees" and refers to those quick-growing ornamental cherries planted in the millions to decorate the sidewalks of new postwar projects the world over. It was also the popular name of a real housing development in southwest Moscow, more correctly called *Novye Cheryomushki* (New Little Cherry Trees). Novye Cheryomushki was put up in the late 1950s and, long since dilapidated, continues to exist today. Plenty of people live there now. The plot of the operetta concerns the fate of a group of friends and acquaintances who find themselves allocated new apartments on this estate, at the point when it had just been built.

Each of the many characters in *Moscow, Cheryomushki* embodies a different aspect of the housing problem. The amiable Sasha, a guide in the Museum of the History and Reconstruction of Moscow, has recently married his beloved Masha, but to their frustration the young couple cannot live together since they have no home. Masha is forced to share a room with others in a temporary hostel, while Sasha lives in a communal apartment in a tumbledown old house in another part of town. Also in Sasha's tumbledown house live one of his fellow museum guides, the well-educated but bashful Lidochka (Little Lidia), and her elderly father, Semyon Semyonovich.

Meanwhile, a rather different character with accommodation problems is the rough diamond, Boris, an explosives technician who has worked in many parts of the Soviet Union but now wishes to settle in Moscow (an extremely difficult proposition in the later Soviet period, when a special permit was required to move into the already overpopulated capital). At the beginning of the operetta, Boris accidentally meets up with an old friend, Sergei, a young Muscovite working as a driver for a high-ranking official. Sergei is in love with Liusia, a glamorous young female construction worker from the Cheryomushki building site.

In different ways, each of these seven "good" characters has an interest in the utopian project of Cheryomushki. Unfortunately, they also have three dastardly enemies to contend with, of whom the most important is Fyodor Drebednev (the giveaway root of his name is *drebeden*, meaning "trash" or "nonsense"). Drebednev is a repulsively venal bureaucrat in charge of building the new Cheryomushki apartments and allocating them to those who need rehousing. He is also the very same official for whom Sergei works as a driver. He has been married three times (a somewhat lugubrious joke at the expense of the shockingly high Soviet divorce rate after the war), but is now accompanied by a new partner, Vava, a cynical young woman on the make, who sees her affair with this otherwise unattractive older man as a means of queue-jumping her way to a smart new apartment. Drebednev's sidekick is an equally corrupt lower-rank official, the estate manager Barabashkin.[3]

In the first act of the operetta, the old house in which Sasha, Lidochka, and Semyon Semyonovich have been living collapses. As a result, Sasha and Masha as well as Lidochka and her father are offered newly completed apartments in Cheryomushki. In great excitement, they are driven to the estate by Sergei, who knows Cheryomushki because Liusia works there, and Boris, who has taken an unlikely fancy to the innocent Lidochka and wants to pursue his luck with her. Unfortunately, when they get there they discover that Barabashkin is holding back keys to many of the apartments, presumably in the expectation of bribes.

In Act 2, the ingenious Boris arranges for Lidochka and her father to be flown up the side of the building by construction crane, so they can climb through the window into the apartment which is legally theirs but to which Barabashkin refuses to give them the keys. They are just making themselves at home when a partition wall is suddenly broken open and Drebednev, Vava, and Barabashkin clamber through from the neighboring apartment. Barabashkin's true purpose is now revealed. He has held back the keys from Lidochka and her father so that his boss, Drebednev, who has allocated the next-door apartment to his girlfriend, can take illegal possession of this one, too, and knock them together to make his love nest twice the standard size. By such means the odious old lecher hopes to ensure the unreliable Vava's continuing affection toward him.

As Drebednev's heinous plan becomes clear, the good characters set about defeating it. In Act 3, Boris, ever the maverick, decides to exploit his previous relationship with Vava by making love to her when he knows Drebednev will catch them together. If he can poison the corrupt official against his mistress, there will no longer be any reason for the two apartments to be knocked together. Unfortunately, his underhand strategy offends his more idealistic friends, who seek a less realistic solution. They construct a magic garden complete with a bench which forces those who sit on it to tell the truth. As a result of this fairy-tale trick, the three bad characters confess their crimes and are punished, and the good live happily ever after.

For this lighthearted if somewhat clunky saga of everyday life in Khrushchev's USSR—curiously reminiscent in subject and manner of a modern-day television sitcom or soap opera—Shostakovich wrote what is, in sheer bulk, one of his longest compositions, running, if played complete, at around one hundred minutes of music, even without the spoken dialogue. In the course of this huge score he covers, as was always his wont in lighter pieces, a huge range of styles, from the Romantic idiom of famous Russian classical composers like Tchaikovsky and Borodin to the most vulgar popular songs. Perhaps the funniest musical moment in the whole work is his quotation of "Fried Chicken," one of the earthiest and best-known tunes at the most basic level of Russian popular culture.

The result, depending on one's point of view, is either richly amusing and delightfully unexpected, or suffocatingly vulgar and empty. One of the first to take the negative view was Shostakovich himself who, only days before the piece's premiere in the Moscow Operetta Theatre on 24 January 1959, wrote to his friend Isaak Glikman:

19 December 1958, Moscow
Dear Isaak Davydovich,
    I am behaving very properly and attending rehearsals of my operetta. I am burning with shame. If you have any thoughts of coming to the first night, I advise you to think again. It is not worth spending time to feast your eyes and ears on my disgrace. Boring, unimaginative, stupid. This is, in confidence, all I have to tell you.[4]

Mstislav Rostropovich, a frequent source of colorful anecdotes about the composer, relates that during the period when *Moscow, Cheryomushki* was first in rehearsal, he met a double bassist from the orchestra of the

Operetta Theatre walking along the street. He asked what the new piece was like and received the crisp reply: "Some bits are not bad, but the rest is just Shostakovich!"[5]

Despite such disparaging first reactions, *Moscow, Cheryomushki* was pretty well received and soon received further productions.[6] In 1962, it was even transformed, with some changes, into a sparklingly comical and notably tongue-in-cheek film under the shorter title, *Cheryomushki*.[7] In this form the operetta had a continuing life even after it ceased to be regularly produced in Soviet operetta theaters, for it remained popular in Soviet television schedules, especially during the New Year holiday period, well into the 1970s and beyond.

Despite these successes, to judge by the paucity of references in later correspondence and interviews, Shostakovich himself seems not to have significantly revised his first basically dismissive opinion. Laurel Fay notes that he "continued to regard it as one of his lesser accomplishments, chalking it up in the Socialist Realist column," a point borne out by a comment made in a letter written by Shostakovich to the composer Kara Karaev on 6 February 1960.[8] After rebuking Karaev for his worldly ambition and his fondness for official recognition and awards, he added a revealing postscript:

> P.S. Very likely, when you read this letter, you'll say: He's a one to talk. He wrote an operetta himself. . . . Well, we've pretty much all sinned in the face of Almighty God and Socialist Realism. But that doesn't give us the right not to point out each other's failings to one another as friends. And I mean "as friends." The failings of Tulikov, Novikov and Koval don't worry me. I don't even notice them. But your failings pain me. They're like a knife in my heart. Don't be angry with me.[9]

It is clear from this that Shostakovich not only felt doubts about the musical quality of *Moscow, Cheryomushki,* but had moral doubts about having taken on the project in the first place. Nonetheless, whatever reservations he had about lowering himself to writing "Soviet" operettas about the joys of "Soviet" life, he did not despise the form of operetta in itself, any more than he despised any of the other popular forms he attempted during his career (songs, theater music, film scores, pieces for jazz band, and so on). Popular music, in his mind, had as much right to exist as any other form of music, and it is obvious from the whole story of his life that he never ceased to be fascinated by the chance to move freely between the highbrow and the lowbrow, whether from piece to piece, or within the course of a single work or movement. Even his loftiest works, such as the late symphonies and string quartets, contain echoes and fragments of popular music; and many of his most vulgar and occasional pieces contain moments that remind us of his "serious" art.

This is one obvious reason why, despite the composer's reservations about this music, it is well worth looking a little more closely at *Moscow, Cheryomushki*. But there are other reasons, too.

For one thing, this operetta is a revealing and, given its mordant tone of voice, a strikingly ambiguous monument to Soviet popular and public culture of the Khrushchev period. To look at it now is to open a window onto a fascinating historical moment.

As recent revivals have proved, the piece also has (whatever the composer thought) unexpected musical charm, especially as a piece of frothy and lighthearted entertainment from a period of the composer's output more usually associated with far more sombre works like the Eleventh and Twelfth symphonies, the First Cello Concerto, and the Seventh and Eighth string quartets.[10]

It is also one of the composer's rare later products in which he can be heard looking back affectionately to his earlier involvement with the heady and experimental world of Soviet theater in the 1920s and 1930s. This connection is made more intriguing by the coincidence that one of the librettists of *Moscow, Cheryomushki* was Vladimir Mass (1896–1979). Mass, like Shostakovich himself, began as a lively figure of early Soviet modernism. Between 1921 and 1924 he was heavily involved in the so-called music hall-ization of theater, writing "witty" plays with music by the composer Matvei Blanter for Nikolai Foregger's experimental Theatre Workshop in Moscow (Mastfor).[11] In the late 1920s and early 1930s he worked, as Shostakovich also briefly did, at the Leningrad Music Hall,[12] and he subsequently achieved fame as joint author with Nikolai Erdman of the script for the evergreen Soviet musical-comedy film, "Merry Fellows" (*Veselye rebiata*).[13] It is hard to imagine that Shostakovich and he were not acquainted in that prewar period, for the circles they moved in were tightly connected. In the later 1930s Mass was imprisoned and, like others who underwent the same experience, after his release became a decidedly more conformist artist.[14]

Then there is the vexed matter of the place of *Moscow, Cheryomushki* in the context of Shostakovich's stunted career as an opera composer. After *The Nose* (1928) and *Lady Macbeth of the Mtsensk District* (1932), in the field of serious opera Shostakovich subsequently achieved only the first act of his Gogol-inspired *The Gamblers* (1942), though he continued to dream of operatic projects to the end of his life.[15] While *Moscow, Cheryomushki* might seem to some an unworthy successor to his two early operatic *tours de force,* and it is certainly not an opera, it is the only other musical drama he completed.

Finally, *Moscow, Cheryomushki* can be seen as a curious and revealing example of Shostakovich's lifelong compositional habits of imitation, parody, quotation, and self-quotation. This aspect takes on particular significance when the piece is seen in the context of other works written around the same time, including the Eleventh Symphony (1957), with its web of cross-references and quotations from old nineteenth-century prisoners' songs and revolutionary hymns; the orchestration of Musorgsky's *Khovanshchina* (1958), completed at the same time as *Moscow, Cheryomushki* and a complex attempt to re-create a nineteenth-century score that never existed in the first place; the First Cello Concerto, with its several parodic references to popular songs, not to mention its sideways glances at Musorgsky; and the Eighth String Quartet, which abounds in self-quotation.[16]

The present article is particularly concerned with the last of these many different ways of approaching *Moscow, Cheryomushki,* examining this usually neglected work for the dense web of parodies, references, and quotations it contains.

• • •

It is obvious from Shostakovich's entire output and from much he said that he was very well acquainted with the more popular forms of music, and operetta especially. There is a mass of evidence for this. To take one small example, in 1997 Zoya Tomashevskaia, daughter of the distinguished literary critic Boris Tomashevsky, recalled that immediately after the war, when she and her family were living in Moscow, she went to many musical and dramatic performances at which she met Shostakovich.[17] She was particularly struck by the fact that he was often to be encountered at the operetta theater, and on one occasion, when he noticed that she had failed to appear at a certain performance, he "severely" upbraided her the next time he saw her. This anecdote easily resonates with the composer's somewhat formal published comments around the time of the premiere of *Moscow, Cheryomushki* that he was "an ardent admirer of the gay and life-asserting genre of operetta and of the work of such wonderful masters as Offenbach, Lecocq, Johann Strauss, Kalman and Lehar [*sic*]."[18] Indeed, one of Shostakovich's most famous reported remarks was that he loved "all of music from Bach to Offenbach."

The whole score of *Moscow, Cheryomushki* abounds in touches betraying this knowledge of the operetta repertoire. One need only mention, for example, the Offenbachian cancan, "Trip Round Moscow" (no. 7); or the various Lehárian orchestral colors in the opening waltz of *Moscow,*

Cheryomushki's "Overture-Prologue." Particularly witty in this respect are the passages in "Vava and Drebednev's Duet" (no. 8, rehearsal numbers 89 and 94ff.), in which each low-down character complains vociferously about the other.[19] Shostakovich accompanies this cartoonlike vignette of the gender war with a clear reminiscence of the duet from Lehár's *The Merry Widow* in which the eponymous widow's despicable fortune-hunting suitors, Cascada and St. Brioche, discuss the same gender war in similarly complaining terms:

> There is no greater insult and nothing more painfully irritating
> Than when a lady at a ball simply takes no notice of us.
> Women have fought a long time for the same rights as men.
> Now Madame here has the right to vote and makes no use of it!

A few bars further on in the same number from Lehár's masterpiece, these two suitors send up their attempts to force the widow, Hanna, to dance with them by portraying themselves as campaigners in an election. Seizing on their same "campaigning" music, Hanna retorts scornfully that "I detest politics. / They destroy men's characters and rob us women of charm." This exchange too is picked up by Shostakovich, but at a later point in *Moscow, Cheryomushki*, when Drebednev and Barabashkin ("Couplets," no. 21) argue cynically about the necessity of "connections" to anyone who wants to get on in life.

Equally intriguing, especially from the point of view of the intended audience of *Moscow, Cheryomushki*—Soviet lovers of operetta whose tastes were middlebrow rather than lowbrow, and who could have been expected to know their *Swan Lake* as well as their *Merry Widow*—are the parodies and pastiches of those nineteenth-century composers known in the Soviet period as *russkaia klassika*: Tchaikovsky and the more familiar names from "The Mighty Handful," such as Rimsky-Korsakov and Borodin.[20]

In every case, it is the most famous manner of these composers that is the butt of Shostakovich's lighthearted humor; and, perhaps inevitably, it is Tchaikovsky who figures most. For example, in the first and third of the operetta's three extended fantasy sequences, "Pantomime" (no. 3) and "Intermezzo" (nos. 28–30), both of which were evidently written to be choreographed in the style of classical ballet, we find passing recollections of *Swan Lake* and *The Nutcracker* and some obvious references to *The Sleeping Beauty*. The most striking of these latter are the deft send-ups of the "Dances of the Pages and Young Girls" from the second number of the prologue to Tchaikovsky's ballet, the "Scène dansante," one of the most famous and beautiful of all the nineteenth-century master's waltzes.

In the "Pantomime" from Shostakovich's Act 1, it is Tchaikovsky's per-oration that is the object of the joke, with its unmistakable grandeur and the courtly skip of its repeated dotted-rhythm chords for the whole orchestra at the top of the phrase, each time preceded by an upward rush of pulsing quavers (Example 1).

Example 1. Shostakovich, *Moscow, Cheryomushki,* "Pantomime" (no. 3), Act 1, mm. 78–88, piano reduction.

Shostakovich steps up the humor by coarsely distorting the phrase structure of the original and rescoring the result, replacing the splendor of Tchaikovsky's full orchestral voicing in the skipping chords with trombone-heavy brass chords, like the playing of a lumpen town band rather than a world-class ballet orchestra. The result is more like the way we remember *The Sleeping Beauty* from innumerable bad performances than the way Tchaikovsky really intended his music to sound.

Later, in the "Intermezzo" from the end of Act 2 of *Moscow, Cheryomushki,* Shostakovich again recalls this same number from *The Sleeping Beauty.* This time he pokes fun at the high-camp elegance of Tchaikovsky's distinctive melody at the opening of the waltz and clearly mimics the charming details of Tchaikovsky's rhythm and orchestration (Example 2).

Example 2. Shostakovich, *Moscow, Cheryomushki*, "Intermezzo" (no. 28), Act 2, mm. 114–33, piano reduction.

These parodies are highly recognizable and certainly musically amusing in themselves, but it is worth noting that they also have a dramatic significance in the unfolding of the plot of *Moscow, Cheryomushki*.

In the first fantasy sequence, young Sasha and Masha, recently married and with nowhere to live together, dream of the cozy apartment that will one day be theirs, as they dance like a romantic hero and heroine around a stage that is at first empty but soon begins to fill with the objects of modern Soviet life they long for—a ZIL refrigerator (notoriously large and noisy and, in the late 1950s, the most fashionable piece of new Soviet kitchen equipment), soft furniture, and a vase of flowers. As more and more couples from the *corps de ballet* appear and join Sasha and Masha dancing across the stage, these domestic objects also begin to dance. By using Tchaikovsky's peroration at this point, Shostakovich presumably has in mind that in *The Sleeping Beauty* this music similarly accompanies the dancing of a group of young men and women with romance ahead of them, and that it immediately heralds the arrival of six fairy god-mothers who will bestow their magical gifts on the infant princess Aurora (no less preposterous than a ZIL refrigerator!).

In the third fantasy sequence, the "Intermezzo," Boris, the "rough dia-mond" explosives technician, tries to explain to the genteel museum guide Lidochka the folly of her idealistic romantic dreams (he has already, in the second fantasy sequence, made an amorous attempt on her gen-tility). In particular, Boris mocks Lidochka's conventional outlook on life and her idea that her virtuous and passive acceptance of society's rules will lead her to regain the apartment of her dreams that has been unfairly taken away from her by the corrupt Drebednev. To tease her innocence, he conjures up a parody of a classical ballet, the kind of entertainment he assumes will most impress Lidochka. The dramatic irony here is less specific than in the Sasha/Masha fantasy sequence, but it is certainly enough for Boris (and Shostakovich) to make the rather obvious point that Lidochka's dreams are the stuff of romantic nonsense.

Less direct than these balletic references are echoes in *Moscow, Cheryomushki* of Tchaikovsky's most famous operas and symphonies. Here it is often neither possible nor desirable to distinguish between actual digs at Tchaikovsky, and the use (whether we choose to hear them as tongue-in-cheek or straight-faced) of the lumbering Tchaikovskyisms that were pretty much stock in trade of the Socialist Realist grand manner by the late 1950s, especially in Soviet film scores of the "tragic" kind. One might add, in passing, that some of the apparently Tchaikovskian turns in the more romantic tunes in *Moscow, Cheryomushki* almost certainly sound that way not because they are meant to make us think consciously of Tchaikovsky, nor yet because of the Tchaikovskian demands of Socialist Realism, but because in the 1950s the general idiom of the nineteenth-century "romance" was still alive and well in Soviet popular culture in the field of sentimental song.

However, two of these other references to Tchaikovsky are worth singling out.

One is the melodramatic orchestral opening to "Vava and Drebednev's Duet" (no. 8), with its grandiose and rhetorical alternation between a recitative-like phrase on unison strings and somber brass chords. This is waspishly reminiscent of the despairing manner of Tchaikovsky's lovelorn operatic heroes like Lensky from *Eugene Onegin* or German from *The Queen of Spades,* or indeed the "hero" of the *Pathétique* Symphony.[21] In

Moscow, Cheryomushki this mock-profound gesture of operatic despair is simply preposterous as the preface to the amorous maunderings of the middle-aged Drebednev, as he simpers after the charms of the self-serving young Vava (Example 3).

Example 3. Shostakovich, *Moscow, Cheryomushki,* "Vava and Drebednev's Duet" (no. 8), Act 1, mm. 1–6, piano reduction.

The other Tchaikovsky reference, almost microscopically small, is quite different and was imposed on Shostakovich by his librettists when, in the course of the "Tenants' Ensemble" (no. 10), a group of "lads" (*parni*) introduce one another to the girls with the phrase "*Pozvol'te vam predstavit'sia: Onegin vash sosed*" (Permit me to introduce to you: Onegin, your neigh-bor).[22] This is a garbled version of a line "*Rekomenduiu vam: Onegin, moi sosed*" (I commend to you: Onegin, my neighbor) from the libretto of Tchaikovsky's opera *Eugene Onegin,* when the poet Lensky introduces his friend Onegin to the Larin family.[23] So uninterested is Shostakovich in this cumbersome joke about a literary and operatic classic that he makes merely the sketchiest attempt to follow it through musically by imitating the commonplace falling cadential figure to which Tchaikovsky set his text.[24] What he does is so vague that one might easily dismiss it as no imitation at all, were it not for the verbal memory of the parallel moment from *Eugene Onegin* that inevitably jolts any listener who knows the earlier opera into comparing what Shostakovich does with the Tchaikovsky original. In other words, Shostakovich makes no attempt to contradict the reference, so he ends up sounding like Tchaikovsky anyway.

By contrast with all these various Tchaikovskian echoes, the second of the operetta's three fantasy sequences, "Lidochka and Boris's Duet" (no. 19), takes aim at Borodin and Rimsky-Korsakov and the manner-isms of the "Mighty Handful." Boris, having smuggled Lidochka into what ought to be her apartment by flying her up the outside of the build-ing on a crane, decides to try his luck by flirting a little. Starting from the point of view that he is merely a crude modern working-class boy while she, a museum guide, is an educated girl with her head in the historical past, he embarks on a series of schoolyard parodies of "old-fashioned" approaches ("I prostrate myself before thee, fair maiden!" "Do not command me to be executed, but give me leave to speak!," etc.).[25]

The various elements of mock "ancient Russian" style in the musical introduction to the number—the pseudo-medieval melody, the bare harmony with drone-like parallel fifths in the bass, the nasal woodwind orchestration with pizzicato strings to give an added *gusli*-like feel to the sound, and the sound of a solo horn—all point toward such models of *à la russe* "medievalism" as the orchestral introduction to "Iaroslavna's arioso" from Borodin's opera *Prince Igor* (the highly distinctive scoring of this passage was actually the work of Rimsky-Korsakov) or the opening measures of the suggestively "bardic" slow movement of Borodin's Second Symphony (known to Russian audiences as the *Bogatyrskaia* or "Heroic" Symphony; Example 4).[26]

Example 4. Shostakovich, *Moscow, Cheryomushki,* "Lidochka and Boris's Duet" (no. 19), Act 2, mm. 1–8, piano reduction.

Likewise, the pacing and style of what follows—a string of contrasted songs and dances, harmonized and orchestrated with dashes of "exotic" color—also suggest an obvious model from Borodin, the "Polovtsian Dances" from Act 2 of *Prince Igor.*

All this fun at the expense of *russkaia klassika* is matched, in *Moscow, Cheryomushki,* by a good deal of equally recognizable fun at the expense of Russian popular music. Here the models include folk songs, sentimental and "urban songs," Soviet mass songs including marches and other forms, and songs by well-known Soviet composers, not least Shostakovich himself.[27]

The category, popular with Soviet ethnomusicologists, of urban songs (*gorodskie pesni*) is perhaps worth special comment. What is usually meant by this term are the various genres of street songs, whether sung by drunks and merrymakers or by city laborers. Folk songs of a kind, Russian urban songs are usually either comic or sentimental and differ from the more complex and changeable forms of Russian village music in that they tend to be tonal (rather than modal), and are often inflected with nineteenth-century clichés of chromatic "expression" (though many such songs are adapted from fairly elementary ballad tunes, some are derived from opera or drawing-room music, presumably by way of the old street culture of hurdy-gurdies and barrel organs). Most urban songs tend to be resolutely strophic (often with four-line verses) and many, as well as being catchy, have gathered to themselves a rich encrustation of alternative texts, frequently of an obscene or offensive nature.

The first thing to note is that the whole of *Moscow, Cheryomushki* is shot through with what Soviet theorists used to call the "intonations" (*intonatsii*) of such popular material, whether that material is genuine folklore (village or urban) or recently composed by Soviet popular composers; that is to say, the piece abounds with the characteristic melodic and rhythmic formulae of such cheap music which, for the operetta's intended audience, would have been both reassuringly familiar and highly amusing.

One obvious such formula is a cheeky and insistently repeated bouncing third, first encountered in the chorus of builders and new tenants in *Moscow, Cheryomushki*'s opening (unnumbered) number, "Overture-Prologue" (Example 5).

Nam khotelos' by pri vstreche lish-
    nikh slov ne govorit',
Vmesto pyshnoi dlinnoi rechi
    prosto-naprosto sprosit': . . .
	When we meet you we wouldn't
	    want to waste words,
	Instead of eloquent long speeches all
	    we want to ask you is: . . .

This tick-tock figure resurfaces at many moments, usually, as here, delivered in the sharply insistent manner characteristic of the tunes associated in Russia with *chastushki* (four-line humorous and often vulgar ditties). Often—at least, to the present writer's ears—the tick-tock suggests that the composer has in mind the most famous popular tune of all in Russian culture, "Chizhik-pyzhik" (Example 6).[28]

Example 5. Shostakovich, *Moscow, Cheryomushki*, "Overture-Prologue" Act I, mm. 119–26, piano reduction.

Example 6. "Chizhik-pyzhik."

Chizhik-pyzhik, gde ty byl?　　Siskin-piskin, where've you been?
Na Fontanke, vodku pil.　　On the Fontanka [canal], drinking
Vypil riumku, vypil dve;　　　vodka.
Zakruzhilos' v golove.　　I drank one glass, I drank two;
　　　My head started spinning.

In a personal communication, however, the St. Petersburg singer and musicologist Olga Komok was keen to rebuff this particular association:

> I doubt that the several tunes you pointed to are versions of "Chizhik"—to my mind the repetition of the third in a melody is a sort of commonplace pattern for Soviet "merry" tunes. And Shostakovich doesn't make a parody of the continuation of "Chizhik," which is no less specific for this "childish" tune.[29]

No doubt Komok is right. "Merry songs" (*veselye pesni*) were a standard feature of a certain kind of Soviet music making, especially in schools, Pioneer camps, student concerts, and the like, and may be considered exactly the appropriate model for music to be sung by the optimistic new tenants of the high-rise apartment blocks of Cheryomushki.[30] The intrinsic inanity of such merry songs hardly needed to adopt the strategy of specific parody to appear ridiculous. Nevertheless, in defense of my suggestion that Shostakovich might have had "Chizhik-pyzhik" sometimes in mind, it is perhaps worth pointing out that he includes a similar merry song, but one considerably closer to "Chizhik-pyzhik" (and also fulfilling Komok's demand that the second half of the tune be present, too), to notably aggressive effect in the first movement of his First Cello Concerto, composed only months after the completion of *Moscow, Cheryomushki* (Example 7).

Other instantly recognizable popular formulae used frequently in *Moscow, Cheryomushki* include two of a more sentimental character; a sugary phrase with a pair of rising minor sixths to give the music the "sixthiness" (*sekstovost'*) that according to Richard Taruskin "defines the idiom of the *bytovoi romans*, the Russian domestic or household romance of the early nineteenth century" and has remained the principal default position for composers and improvisers of Russian romance melodies ever since (Example 8).[31]

Example 7. Shostakovich, Cello Concerto no. 1, movement 1, mm. 96–102, piano reduction.

Example 8. Shostakovich, *Moscow, Cheryomushki*, "Overture-Prologue," Act 1, mm. 181–83, piano reduction (sixths marked with brackets).

And an even more hackneyed cadential or half-cadential turn, familiar from a thousand faceless guitar songs (Example 9):

Example 9. Shostakovich, *Moscow, Cheryomushki*, "Boris's Aria" (no. 4), Act 1, mm. 52–56, piano reduction.

All three formulae make innumerable appearances in *Moscow, Cheryomushki* and play an important part in the overall character of its sound world. But even more important than them is the role of the main theme-tune of the operetta, the "Song about Cheryomushki" (Example 10).

Example 10. Shostakovich, *Moscow, Cheryomushki*, "Song about Cheryomushki" (no. 17), Act 1 finale, mm. 1–38.

Cheremushki . . . V Cheremushkakh	Cheryomushki . . . In Cheryomushki
Cheremukha tsvetet.	Bird-cherry trees blossom,
I vse mechty sbyvaiutsia	And all dreams come true
U tekh, kto zdes' zhivet.	For those who live here.

After its initial appearance in the opening bars, this childlike melody is exploited mercilessly by the composer through almost the whole of the rest of the score, turning up in twenty-five out of the piece's forty numbers. It is reiterated unaltered in seven numbers,[32] subjected to full-scale variation in six more,[33] and surfaces in fragmentary form in yet another twelve.[34]

The entire operetta, in other words, throbs with obsessive repetition, particularly with the repetition of ideas that are either commonplace and banal, or at least extremely simple. While constant repetition of banal and simple ideas is a familiar device in many of Shostakovich's more serious works (like the Seventh, Eighth, Tenth and Eleventh symphonies)—where it functions to powerful rhetorical effect, at once unifying and alienating—a skeptical listener might be forgiven for doubting whether an operetta is necessarily the appropriate place for such a harsh musical procedure. Perhaps the composer's own negative comment ("Boring, unimaginative, stupid") may be linked to his uneasy sense, once he heard the music in rehearsal, that this aspect of the piece was, to say the least, problematic.[35]

Nonetheless, whether one appreciates what Shostakovich is trying to do with such repetition or not, as far as this operetta's theme-tune goes, there is something undeniably impressive, not to say disturbing, in the composer's untiring ability to drive so far and so furiously with so dangerously limited a musical idea. In this light, it is intriguing to find that there is a little more to this tune than first meets the eye. The "Editor's Note" to the published score of *Moscow, Cheryomushki* points out that it

> is based on a song from Shostakovich's incidental music to the film *Golden Mountains* (incidentally, its melody is related to that of the urban song "There Used to Be Merry Days").[36]

Shostakovich's score to Sergei Iutkevich's early Stalinist epic *Golden Mountains* was written in 1931, nearly three decades before *Moscow, Cheryomushki*. A sumptuous and experimental piece of writing for enormous orchestra and one of Shostakovich's most interesting pieces of film music, it accompanied the mythic tale of a country lad who moves to the city and is converted to revolutionary fervor.

Actually, as it is used in *Moscow, Cheryomushki*, it is only the refrain of this song that is drawn from "There Used to Be Merry Days" (Example 11).

Example 11. "There Used to Be Merry Days" (*Byvali dni veselye*).

Byvali dni veselye,	There used to be merry days,
Gulial ia molodets;	I wandered around like a fine fellow;
Ne znal toski-kruchinushki,	I knew no longing or little sorrows,
kak vol'nyi udalets.	I was like a free adventurer.
Byvalo, vspashesh' pashenku,	You used to plough the little field,
Loshadok uberesh',	You looked after the little horses,
A sam tropoi znakomoiu	And then on the familiar path
V zavetnyi dom poidesh'.	You yourself went off to your
	beloved home.

For the central "verse" section of his tune, Shostakovich uses another urban song, albeit one that it is curiously similar: "If I Had Golden Mountains." This tune was also used extensively by Shostakovich in his op. 30 film score and the title of that film was evidently taken from its words (Example 12).[37]

Example 12. "If I Had Golden Mountains" (*Kogda b imel zlatye gory*).

Kogda b imel zlatye gory	If I had golden mountains
I reki, polnye vina,	And rivers full of wine,
Vse otdal by za laski, vzory,	I would give them all for caresses
Chtob ty vladela mnoi odna.	and glances,
	So that you alone could possess me.

The words and sentiments of these two well-known urban songs may have been neatly matched to the character and fate of the hero of Iutkevich's 1931 film, but it takes no great effort to see that they also fit pleasingly in *Moscow, Cheryomushki*, being connected both to the general optimism of those who plan to live in the new Cheryomushki housing project and to the operetta's various romantic plots.

If the combination of these songs permeates almost the entire sound world of *Moscow, Cheryomushki,* there are also a number of sharply contrasted moments in the score when the composer deliberately shifts gear to remind his audience of popular tunes of a different kind. The most striking of these is, again, the operetta's second fantasy sequence, "Lidochka and Boris's Duet" (no. 19), musically and dramatically one of the most pleasurable and satsifying passages in the whole work.

It is this number that begins by making fun of the *à la russe* style of the Mighty Handful, so it is entirely appropriate that Shostakovich should have immediately gone on to quote, just as a real Mighty Handful composer might have done, no fewer than three well-known folk tunes (that is, village songs rather than urban ones).

After the Borodinesque opening (rehearsal nos. 165–67; see also Example 4), Boris, the explosives expert, attempts to woo Lidochka, the museum guide, by using two extremely familiar folk songs of a kind often included in school songbooks in the Soviet period (rehearsal nos. 167 and 168, respectively). To Mass and Chervinsky's words:

Bud' moei, dusha devitsa,	Be mine, fair maiden,
Khorosha tvoia svetlitsa,	How bright thy chamber,
Teremochek tvoi khorosh!	How fine thy residence!
Oi, vy gusli, zvonki gusli,	O gusli, thou honey-toned gusli,
Ia tebe da ne gozhus' li?	Am I not fitting for thee?
Ali ty drugogo zhdesh'?	Or dost thou await another?

Shostakovich adapts the song "In the Garden, in the Kitchen Garden," whose traditional words are perfectly appropriate to this moment in the drama (Example 13).

Example 13. "In the Garden, in the Kitchen Garden" (*Vo sadu li, v ogorodke*).

Vo sadu li, v ogorode	In the garden, in the kitchen
Devitsa guliala;	garden
Nevelichka, kruglolichka,	A girl was walking;
Rumianoe lichko.	Little, round-faced,
	A ruddy little face.
Za nei khodit, za nei brodit	There comes to her, there wanders
Udaloi molodchik;	to her
Za nei nosit, za nei nosit	A daring young man;
Dorogi podarki.	He brings to her, he brings to her
	Expensive presents.

Boris may well be said to have brought Lidochka "expensive presents," for he has whirled her in a crane up the side of an apartment block and enabled her to gain access to her new home.

After this, the libretto of *Moscow, Cheryomushki,* continues (as before) with a string of mock "ancient Russian" expressions:

Boris:	Boris:
Ali ia ne sokol iasnyi?	Am I not thy bright-eyed falcon?
Posadi zhe v ugol krasnyi . . .	Wilt thou not sit in my icon corner . . .
Lidochka:	Lidochka:
Eto vse odni slova!	These are but words, sir!
Boris:	Boris:
Chto zh ty khochesh'?	What wilt thou command then?
Lidochka:	Lidochka:
Slov mne malo, pokazhi sebia	I have few words, display yourself
snachala,	to start with.
Raspotesh' menia sperva!	First of all divert me!
Boris:	Boris:
Ekh!	Ekh!

Here, as the sexual tension in the plot decidedly increases, Shostakovich switches to another folk song, "The Full Moon Is Shining" (*Svetit mesiats*) (Example 14).

Example 14. "The Full Moon Is Shining" (*Svetit mesiats*).

Mne ne spitsia, ne lezhitsia   I can't sleep, I don't want to lie down
I son menia ne beret;   And sleep won't take hold of me;
Ya khodil by k Sashe v gosti,   I would like to go and visit Sasha,
Da ne znaiu, gde zhivet.   But I don't know where she lives.

Poprosil by ia tovarishcha,   I would ask my friend,
Moi tovarishch dovedet;   My friend would take me there;
Moi tovarishch luchshe, krashe,   My friend is better and more hand-
Boius', Sashu otob"et.   some than me,
                                      I'm afraid he'll steal Sasha.

This pair of songs is followed by a dance in the same style, using another well-known folk tune, "Hey There, My New Porch" (*Akh vy, seni moi, seni*) (Example 15).

Example 15. "Hey There, My New Porch" (*Akh vy, seni moi, seni*).

Akh vy, seni moi, seni,   Hey there, my new porch, my porch,
Seni novye moi,   My new porch,
Seni novye, klenovye   My new porch of maple
Reshetchatye.   With latticework.

Uzh kak znat'-to mne po senichkam	Already how well-known I am for
Ne khazhivati;	my porch
Mne mila druzhka za ruchen'ku	Even by those who don't go there.
Ne vazhivati.	Dear to me is my girlfriend beyond
	the little river
	Whom I cannot fetch.

Again, given that Boris so far seems to be making little progress in his romance with Lidochka and that he has just flown her in through the window of her new apartment, the words of this song are at least mildly appropriate.

As this "porch" dance ends, Shostakovich's score suddenly lurches with splendidly satirical effect into a highly unexpected quotation of a different kind: the closing bars of perhaps the most famous popular song ever written by a Soviet composer, "Evenings outside Moscow" (*Podmoskovnye vechera*), better known in the West as "Midnight in Moscow." This memorable lollipop, the work of Vasilii Solovev-Sedoi (1907–79), first appeared to enormous acclaim only a year or so before Shostakovich began composing *Moscow, Cheryomushki*. It was the theme song of the 1956 film *In the Days of the Sports Festival* (*V dni spartakiady*) and garnered lavish prizes later the same year at the Sixth All-World Festival of Youth and Students in Moscow. Within a short time, it was being played more or less the world over. It is nowadays most frequently heard as the signature tune of one of Moscow's main radio stations.

For the most part, "Evenings outside Moscow" is a song normally treated by its many arrangers as an atmospheric croon, complete with wobbling vibraphones and smooching strings. Shostakovich, however, takes a different approach, naughtily upping the tempo to presto and transcribing it in the noisiest orchestral manner possible, to make it sound most inappropriately like a Cossack dance. The effect is made even more ridiculous because, as he begins the tune halfway through and not at the beginning, it takes a moment or two before the audience realizes what he is doing. An asterisk marks the point in Solovev-Sedoi's melody at which Shostakovich's quotation begins (Example 16).

Example 16. Solovev-Sedoi, "Evenings outside Moscow" (*Podmoskovnye vechera*).

The hackneyed and by 1959 extremely familiar words (to Russians) for this melody are by Mikhail Matusovsky:

Ne slyshny v sadu dazhe shorokhi,
Vse zdes' zamerlo do utra.
Esli b znali vy, kak mne dorogi
Podmoskovnye vechera.

Not even rustles are to be heard in the garden,
Everything here has died away until the morning.
If only you knew how dear to me
Are evenings outside Moscow.[38]

In every way, therefore, Shostakovich's raucous outburst goes *against* the sense of Solovev-Sedoi's overplayed song. Not only is the audience taken by surprise, but Boris is as well. This sudden rush of musical modernity suggests to him that he might be losing control of the situation and, addressing the orchestra pit, he pleads, "Comrade conductor! Can we go back three hundred years, please?"

But, as this sudden intrusion of pop music has already suggested, the roles in this courtship have just been surprisingly reversed. The bashful Lidochka is now no longer so bashful, and Boris has been ambushed. As the Borodin parody begins again, it is Lidochka who takes control:

Lidochka:
Nu, a vse-taki, iasnyi sokol moi,
Ne podkhodit Bam vek semnadtsatyi.

Lidochka:
All the same, my bright-eyed falcon, the seventeenth century doesn't suit you.

Boris:
Pochemu zhe tak?

Boris:
Why so?

Lidochka:
Stil' drugoi u Vas!

Lidochka:
You have a different style.

Boris:
A kakoi drugoi?

Boris:
What different one?

Lidochka:
Pokazhu seichas:

Lidochka:
I'll show you now:

What happens next, as Lidochka whirls the astonished Boris off his feet, will be examined later in this article.

Apart from "Evenings outside Moscow," one other wildly popular song by a well-known Soviet composer also falls victim to Shostakovich's humor in *Moscow, Cheryomushki*. This is the most popular song Shostakovich himself ever wrote, the "Song of the Counterplan" (*Pesnia o vstrechnykh*), the title tune from his 1932 music for Fridrikh Ermler and Sergei Iutkevich's film *Counterplan,* the film he scored right after *Golden Mountains* (also directed by Iutkevich; Example 17).

Example 17. Shostakovich, "Song of the Counterplan."

As Laurel Fay notes in her biography of the composer, Shostakovich worked hard to compose this melody: "His labor was well rewarded; the cheery 'rise and shine' song, with a text by Boris Kornilov, scored an instant hit . . . and was soon being sung by millions."[39]

Indeed, by 1942 it was being sung and played all over the West as well, and even given English words that turned it into an anthem on behalf of the Allied war effort. In this guise, it went on to achieve the distinction of a rich and fruity reorchestration by Leopold Stokowski.

For 1959 operetta audiences in the Soviet Union, however, the response to this tune would have been more specifically conditioned by Kornilov's original lyrics being at least as familiar as the melody:

Nas utro vstrechaet prokhladoi,
Nas vetrom vstrechaet reka,
Kudriavaia, chto zh ty ne rada
Veselomu pen'iu gudka?

The morning greets us with a chill,
The river greets us with a breeze.
Curly-headed girl, why are you not pleased
By the merry sound of the factory siren?

The moment they recognized the tune as it makes its first appearance in *Moscow, Cheryomushki,* those original audiences would have been most surprised to hear these familiar words replaced by a completely new text, this time sung by the museum guide Lidochka in her bashful guise as we first meet her in Act 1 (no. 6), when she confesses to the audience her lack of social skills and her regret that she spent her youth studying rather than flirting with boys:

Ya v shkolu kogda-to khodila	Once I used to go to school
I do nochi, pomniu, poroi	And then sometimes I remember
Zubrila, zubrila, zubrila,	I would swat, swat, swat until the night
Vernuvshis' iz shkoly domoi:	When I got home from school:
Biografiiu Shekspira,	The biography of Shakespeare,
Svoistva rtuti i efira,	The properties of mercury and ether,
Klimat gornogo Pamira,	The climate of the mountains in Pamir,
Skol'ko v tonne kilogramm . . .	How many kilograms in a ton . . .[40]

There are several points to be made about this replacement text for the "Song of the Counterplan."

The first is that it is simply funny.

The second, rather more serious, is that Lidochka is clearly meant to appear more than a little ridiculous here, singing of her loneliness and absence of sophisticated romantic success to a tune which, by this stage in its history, had been rammed down the throats of whole generations of Soviet children—in school, Pioneer camp, and youth group—as they were taught the virtues of social (and socialist) conformity and collective optimism. In the easier political atmosphere of Khrushchev's post-Stalinist regime (the so-called Thaw), it was not long before the more sophisticated kind of Soviet young person began to feel the stirrings of impatience with the surrounding atmosphere of stultifying compliance. Some were even becoming aware of the rumors of new youth cultures appearing in the West. To any young (or not so young) Soviet citizens of the late 1950s with even a hint of rebelliousness in their heart, Lidochka as we first meet her in the operetta would have appeared a comical figure as a *tipich-naia pionerka* (a typical girl from the Pioneers, the official Communist children's organization in the USSR).[41]

But there is also another wider point. Both Solovev-Sedoi's "Evenings outside Moscow" and Shostakovich's "Song of the Counterplan" were small elements in the vast edifice of official Soviet youth culture as it was constantly being promoted in this period by the Soviet government. Even if Shostakovich's tune was unmistakably associated with a younger, earlier, more innocent and also more Stalinist youth culture, and Solovev-Sedoi's tune represented a newer, more romantic, already slightly more sexualized post-Stalinist youth culture, they both belong unmistakably to a world in which youth and the direction in which youth was to be directed were huge issues. These were political issues, of course, constantly and overtly surfacing in propaganda and official pronouncements. But they were also deeper and more covert issues as well, sources of often unfocused anxiety, and as a result often to be found reflected in the high and low culture of the late-1950s world to which *Moscow, Cheryomushki* so clearly belongs. The use of these two tunes in this operetta simultaneously points teasingly to that anxiety and, in a small way, actually expresses it.

All the quotations and cross-references so far identified in *Moscow, Cheryomushki* may be considered obvious and intended to be recognized by any halfway attentive audience in the Moscow Operetta Theatre in January 1959. Shostakovich's score also includes, however, a number of other self-quotations, several of which would have been almost completely obscure to everyone at that time except the composer.

Some of these self-quotations may be even more complicated than that, for they come from *Antiformalist Rayok,* Shostakovich's private and savagely scatological caricature of the way he was treated in 1948 during the Zhdanov-led campaign against formalism in music, of which the chief event was the First All-Union Congress of Soviet Composers. As Laurel Fay notes, this work "surfaced in 1989 and has been the object of continued controversy ever since, chiefly over the dates of composition and the authorship of the sung libretto."[42] The dating controversy essentially concerns whether the bulk of the work was written immediately after the First All-Union Congress in 1948 or in connection with the Second All-Union Congress of Soviet Composers in 1957. For present purposes, this uncertainty is relatively unimportant since both dates precede the completion of *Moscow, Cheryomushki,* though it is worth noting that as early as March 1957, "news that Shostakovich was at work on his first operetta . . . spread around the globe."[43] However, the remaining dating issue with *Antiformalist Rayok*—that the final section of the piece was probably composed in the 1960s—also has a bearing on the piece's connection with *Moscow, Cheryomushki*.

Antiformalist Rayok is a cartoonlike pseudo-operatic satire in which the text quotes from and exaggerates the idiocy of proceedings at the First All-Union Congress. The accompanying music is as primitive as the remarks it sets. The point is to mock the Congress participants by making them sing their own words in the hideously empty and repetitive

Socialist Realist musical style which they are so busy recommending in their speeches.

The first character to appear is the "Chairman" who portentously announces:

> This shrine of culture provides for us tonight a platform for certain speeches on the theme "Realism and Formalism in Music." We shall keep to this subject."[44]

While the music in both cases is so primitive that it might be an exaggeration to talk of quotation, there is a vigorous and obvious likeness to be found between the Chairman's music in *Antiformalist Rayok*, and some of the music of Drebednev and Barabashkin in *Moscow, Cheryomushki*. Compare, for example, the utterances of the Chairman "on the theme 'Realism and Formalism in Music'" (2 mm. before rehearsal number 3) with the bullying ravings of Drebednev and Barabashkin when they begin to fear that the angry tenants might get the better of them in the "Scene of Barabashkin and Drebednev with the Tenants" (no. 16):

Drebednev:	Drebednev:
Kto eto skazal? Kto nazval skandalom, eto ukazan'e Mossoveta?	Who said that? Who said this directive of the Moscow City Council was a scandal?
Barabashkin:	Barabashkin:
Proslezhu!	I'll find out!
Drebednev:	Drebednev:
I dolozhish'!	And you'll write a report!
Barabashkin:	Barabashkin:
Dolozhu!	I'll write a report!

At the end of his introductory speech, the Chairman in *Antiformalist Rayok* introduces his first speaker, "our music expert Number One . . . dear Comrade Edinitsyn." Edinitsyn's appearance is greeted by the loud applause from a chorus of "musical functionaries" and a commonplace fanfare or flourish (*tush*) (Example 18).

Example 18. Shostakovich, *Antiformalist Rayok*, rehearsal number 5.

Vedushchii:	Chairman:
Poprivetstvuem, tovarishchi,	Let us welcome, comrades, our
nashego dorogogo i liubimogo	dear beloved comrade
velikogo tovarishcha Edinitsyna!	Edinitsyn! Glory!
Slava!	
Muzykal'nye deiateli i deiatel'nitsy:	Musical functionaries:
Slava! Slava velikomu Edinitsynu!	Glory! Glory to the great
Slava!	Edinitsyn! Glory!

This flourish is so commonplace it is hard to distinguish from similar fanfares found elsewhere in film and theater scores by Shostakovich and other composers. However, in *Moscow, Cheryomushki* it is found almost exactly as it is used in *Antiformalist Rayok*, except that it is now transposed up a semitone. On this occasion, it forms the climax of a grotesque little dance performed by comrades Drebednev and Barabashkin after their "Couplets" (no. 21; rehearsal number 208ff.), in which, in language close to that used by the characters in *Rayok*, the pair sing a little hymn in praise of their characteristically dishonest way of dealing with the problems of Soviet life:

Bez sviazei v zhizni net puti.	Without connections you can't
Bez sviazei zhit' uzhasno slozhno.	make your way in life.
Bez sviazei sviazi zavesti	Without connections it is terribly
I to byvaet nevozmozhno.	hard to live.
	If you have no connections,
	make connections
	Or you will find things get
	impossible.

Not all the "connections" between *Antiformalist Rayok* and *Moscow, Cheryomushki* relate to music given in the operetta to the characters of Drebednev and Barabashkin. The second guest speaker in *Rayok* is Comrade Dvoikin. The object of Shostakovich's malice here is the notorious party functionary Andrei Zhdanov, as is made clear by the character's mock-operatic vocalizing (Zhdanov was supposed to have had pretensions as a singer) and by the words of his speech. Dvoikin sings a serenade-like tune to illustrate the kind of music he wishes Soviet composers to write (rehearsal number 17 to 23):

My, tovarishchi, trebuem ot	We, comrades, require music of
muzyki krasoty i iziashchestva.	beauty and elegance. Do you
Vam eto stranno? Da? Nu,	find that odd? Yes? Well, of
konechno, vam stranno eto.	course, you find it strange.

Most of this passage in *Antiformalist Rayok* is almost exactly the same as "Boris's Song-Serenade" (no. 5) in *Moscow, Cheryomushki,* where the amiable explosives technician illustrates to his friend Sergei the kind of music he thinks will attract the girls (or pretends he thinks so, for he is mocking Sergei):

Taram-param, nina, nina,	Bambam-bambam, lala, lala,
Vstrechaet menia vesna, vesna . . .	I'm being met by the spring, the
	spring . . .

Especially close to *Rayok* is Boris's deliberately idiotic refrain—*Lia, lia, lia, lia, lia, lia, lia . . .* (La, la, la, la, la, la, la . . .) (Example 19):

Example 19. Shostakovich, *Moscow, Cheryomushki*, "Boris's Song-Serenade" (no. 5), Act 1, mm. 37–44.

The final meeting point between *Antiformalist Rayok* and *Moscow, Cheryomushki* concerns the last part of *Rayok*, which is assumed to have been added in the 1960s—that is, after the completion of the operetta. The Chairman's third guest speaker is Comrade Troikin, who leads the chorus of musical functionaries in a general condemnation of their ideological enemies (Example 20).

Example 20. Shostakovich, *Antiformalist Rayok,* rehearsal number 36–37.

Velikii vozhd' nas vsekh uchil	Our great leader has taught us all
I besprestanno govoril:	And incessantly said:
Smotrite zdes', smotrite tam,	Look here, look there,
Pust' budet strashno vsem vragam.	Let things be terrible for our enemies.
Smotri tuda, smotri siuda	Look there, look here
I vykorchevyvai vraga.	And tear the enemy up by the roots.

In his 1990 foreword to *Antiformalist Rayok,* Malcolm MacDonald observes that the "frivolous" tune to which these words are set is "derived from the once-popular French operetta *Les Cloches de Corneville* by Robert Planquette (1877)."[45] This may be so, but the passage quoted above is also exceedingly close to the second half of the melody of "Masha and Bubentsov's Duet" (no. 25) in *Moscow, Cheryomushki* (which itself, perhaps, could have been derived from the Planquette tune), in which Masha and Sasha, the perfect young married couple, sing with excruciating coyness of the various meanings that bells can have—school bells, alarm clocks, telephones ringing, or whatever. (Perhaps Shostakovich had in mind the Planquette piece at this point in his operetta anyway, as it too tells a story about the unexpected significance of bells and contains, as does Shostakovich's duet, twittering orchestral *ritornelli* depicting the chiming and ringing of bells; Example 21).

Example 21. Shostakovich, *Moscow, Cheryomushki,* "Masha and Bubentsov's Duet" (no. 25), Act 2, mm. 17–22.

Sasha (imagining himself as an errant schoolboy being challenged by a severe schoolteacher to prove that he has done his homework):

You look stupidly at the ceiling.
The chalk trembles in your hand,
You're done for . . . finished . . . and suddenly the bell!

Given the frequent arguments nowadays about the interpretation of Shostakovich's music, these links between *Moscow, Cheryomushki* and *Antiformalist Rayok* are certainly thought-provoking. At the very least, they allow us to see patterns of continuity in his sense of humor.

The remaining examples of self-quotation so far identified in *Moscow, Cheryomushki* all relate to music written by Shostakovich in the prewar period; that is, at the same stage of his career as the songs already mentioned from the film scores of *Golden Mountains* (1931) and *Counterplan* (1932).

While the composer would have assumed an audience in 1959 would immediately recognize the "Song of the Counterplan" and, given its reuse of two very popular urban songs, respond quickly to the "Song about Cheryomushki," these remaining quotations are somewhat different and their significance slightly more elliptical.

A great many of Shostakovich's prewar pieces had been quite lost from the repertoire by the late 1950s and forgotten by audiences. Among the most substantial of these lost pieces were his three full-length ballets (although it should be mentioned that odd extracts from them were to be found in the four ballet suites arranged by Levon Atovmian between 1949 and 1953). *Moscow, Cheryomushki* contains two quotations from these ballets.

The first of these is from Act 1 of *The Bolt* (1931), a polka-like number entitled "The Saboteurs (Intermezzo)" (Example 22).

This is transferred from the ballet into the operetta to provide the dance of triumph by Drebednev and Barabashkin at the end of their smug little "Couplets" about "connections" (no. 21). In 1931 Shostakovich had incorporated this same movement, under the more neutral title of "Intermezzo," into his orchestral suite from the ballet, op. 27a. But, given the dramatic context in the operetta, the reuse of this music at this point presumably had also something pointed to do with the original title as it stands in the ballet score.

The second extract from a prewar ballet to turn up in *Moscow, Cheryomushki* is the "Russian Dance" from Act 1 of *The Limpid Stream* (Example 23).

In *Moscow, Cheryomushki*, this reappears transformed and simplified, as a whirlwind orchestral coda to the comical three-verse vocal patter in the

Example 22. Shostakovich, *The Bolt*, "The Saboteurs (Intermezzo)" (no. 10), Act 1, 5mm. after rehearsal number 84 to number 86.

Offenbach-style cancan, "Trip Round Moscow" (no. 7). As the orchestra erupts, a mime episode shows the six characters onstage speeding excitingly around the capital in their car. According to the stage directions:

> The wheels of the mock-up ZIM car spin around, giving the impression of swift movement. At the same time views of Moscow streets are projected onto the backdrop in rapid succession.

While hardly well-known, this particular musical idea had not been quite forgotten in the 1950s as it was reused by Levon Atovmian as the closing number of the Ballet Suite no. 1 (1949). Perhaps it was rehearing this music

Example 23. Shostakovich, *The Limpid Stream,* "Russian Dance" (no. 9), Act 1, mm. 5–24.

in this form that prompted Shostakovich to return to it at this point in his operetta.

The final quotation or borrowing in *Moscow, Cheryomushki* from Shostakovich's prewar music is somewhat odder and certainly more obscure, and appears to be unrecorded in the literature. In 1931 the composer provided the music for *Declared Dead,* a show at the Leningrad Music Hall. Most of the full score for this music is, to date, missing,[46] but many of the piano-score sketches survive, including twenty-one numbers published in 1986.[47] One of these last, entitled "Twelve Apostles," belongs to Act 3 of *Declared Dead,* which consisted as a whole of a variety performance set in Heaven, with God, the Devil, saints, angels, and demons all taking part. This particular number begins with a parody version of the "Song of the Golden Calf" from Gounod's opera, *Faust,* which dissolves into a blasphemous tango based on a church chant, and then in turn gives way to a brisk string of dances (Example 24).

Example 24. Shostakovich, *Declared Dead*, "Twelve Apostles," mm. 79–118.

Example 24 continued

Nearly thirty years after it was first composed and apparently then forgotten by everyone including its composer, this dance sequence was taken by Shostakovich almost wholesale into *Moscow, Cheryomushki* and developed and expanded to provide the enchanting pileup of dances that ends the operetta's second fantasy sequence, "Lidochka and Boris's Duet." This is the moment in the fantasy when the apparently retiring Lidochka takes command of the situation and whirls her astonished suitor into a far more exciting performance than he had anticipated (Example 25).

Two points are immediately worth noting. The first is that the music may have been reordered and some new ideas added, but there are plenty of similarities in the layout of these two piano scores, both made by the composer, and there is also the fact that the ritornello in both cases is in the same key, C minor. Given that Shostakovich had presumably not bothered to think much about *Declared Dead* in the many years since he wrote it, this would suggest that, rather than working from memory, he had the original sketches of *Declared Dead* to hand when he composed *Moscow, Cheryomushki*.

The second is that one key idea from the "Twelve Apostles" has gone missing, a tune already mentioned, "Chizhik-pyzhik" (see Example 6 above). Adapting his old music for *Moscow, Cheryomushki*, Shostakovich replaced this chestnut with what, after "Chizhik-pyzhik," must be the second most famous—and equally ridiculous—tune in the lowest of lowbrow Russian popular culture, "Fried Chicken" (*Tsyplenok zharenyi*) (Example 26, p. 268).

Example 25. Shostakovich, *Moscow, Cheryomushki,* "Lidochka and Boris's Duet" (no. 19), Act 2, mm. 164–219.

Example 25 continued

Example 26. "Fried Chicken" (*Tsyplenok zharenyi*).

There are many variants of the words to this ubiquitous song, some exceedingly indecent. One widespread version will serve to provide the general flavor:

Tsyplenok zharenyi, tsyplenok parenyi,	Fried chicken, stewed chicken,
Tsyplenki tozhe khochut zhit';	Chickens also want to live,
Ego poimali, arestovali,	They caught him, they arrested him,
Veleli pasport pred"iavit'.	They ordered him to show his passport.
Ia ne sovetskii, ia ne kadetskii,	I'm not Soviet, I'm not a Cadet [a Constitutional Democrat],
A ia kurinyi komissar.	I'm a chicken commissar.
Ia ne rasstrelival, ia ne doprashival,	I've never shot anyone, I've never interrogated anyone,
Ia mirno zernyshki kleval.	I've peacefully pecked grains.
No vlasti strogie, kozly bezrogie	But the powers are implacable; goats without horns
Ego poimali, kak v silki.	Caught him, as though in a snare.
Ego poimali, arestovali	They caught him, they arrested him
I razorvali na kuski.	And tore him in pieces.
Tsyplenok zharenyi, tsyplenok parenyi	Fried chicken, stewed chicken
Ne mog ni slova vozrazit' . . .	Couldn't say a word against this . . .
Sudei zadavlennyi, on byl zazharennyi.	Knocked down by the judge, he was fried.
Tsyplenki tozhe khochut zhit'!	Chickens also want to live![48]

However little the first audiences of *Moscow, Cheryomushki* in 1959 might have known about a long-forgotten show from 1931 called *Declared Dead,* they would have had no difficulty recognizing this particular tune. What they would have made of its surfacing at this particular moment in the score is another matter altogether.

• • •

One of the great paradoxes of Shostakovich's art is to be found in the characteristic way his music nearly always offers a thick and tempting multitude of signals, symbols, clues, and signposts, all urging us to find specific meanings in what he writes; and yet, most of the time, it still manages to remain almost entirely inscrutable and ambiguous. One result of this, especially in the last twenty years or so, has been that his output has become ever more entangled in a vast overgrowth of interpretation, which, as it becomes lusher, becomes also more contradictory, doubtful, and mysterious.

Clearly, *Moscow, Cheryomushki* is yet another of his many works ripe for "reading" in this manner. Its dense connections to other things—the popular culture of its time as well as the political and historical context in which it was written, the music of other composers as much as other pieces by Shostakovich himself—would encourage this, as would the operetta's overall musical and dramatic aura, its characteristic, almost mannerist mix of obsessively repeated commonplaces and clichés (often placed in an odd relation to one another), and its strangely divided tone of voice which, much of the time, seems so uncertainly poised between cheap pleasure and brittle scorn, between the softhearted and the hardhearted.

One aspect of the work, however, is certainly made clearer by closer inspection—and, in the present writer's case, by the experience of many live performances, in several different stagings: its irresistible spirit of play. Whatever the ambiguous *meanings* of its dense web of parodies, references, and quotations (and no doubt there remain many more to be discovered in this score), their *effect* is not ambiguous at all. What they do is make the whole score pulsate with energy.

NOTES

1. "Operetta" is the term used by Shostakovich to describe the work in contemporary interviews and articles, and in his letters. "Musical comedy" is the term found on the title page of the full score of the work; D. Shostakovich, *Sobranie sochinenii v soroka dvukh tomakh*, vol. 24, ed. K. A. Titarenko (Moscow: Muzyka, 1986). In her biography, *Shostakovich: A Life* (New York: Oxford University Press, 2000), p. 209, Laurel Fay notes that at the time there was some debate as to how the piece should be described.

2. Such jokes often take the form of parodies of Khrushchev's characteristic public declarations. One of the most frequently repeated goes something like this: "In five years every Soviet citizen will have a bicycle; in ten years every Soviet citizen will have a car; in fifteen years every Soviet citizen will have a helicopter!"

3. The librettists originally called this character Kolobashkin, from *kolobok,* meaning a small round loaf of coarse bread. His replacement name comes from *barabanit'*, meaning to "play upon the drums" or, more colloquially, to "babble" or "patter."

4. *Story of a Friendship: The Letters of Dmitry Shostakovich to Isaak Glikman, 1941–1975,* trans. Anthony Phillips (London: Faber and Faber, 2001), p. 79.

5. "*Nekotorye kuski ne plokhi . . . a ostal'noe prosto Shostakovich!*" The present author heard Rostropovich tell this story in the backstage area of the Barbican Centre, London, some time during the winter of 1994–95.

6. Fay, *Shostakovich: A Life,* pp. 208–9. See also the closing paragraphs of the Editor's Note in Shostakovich, *Sobranie sochinenii,* vol. 24 (no page number).

7. This was a Lenfilm production, directed by Gerbert Rappaport.

8. Fay, *Shostakovich: A Life,* p. 209.

9. L. Karagicheva, "'Pishete kak mozhno bol'she prekrasnoi muzyki . . .': iz pisem D. D. Shostakovicha K. A. Karaevu," *Muzykal'naia akademiia* 4 (1994): 206. Serafim Tulikov (b. 1914), Anatolii Novikov (1896–84), Marian Koval (1907–71): Tulikov and Novikov wrote operettas, Koval favored operas and ballets on revolutionary and approved subjects. All three men wrote quantities of mass songs and military music, and played important roles as functionaries within the official union structures of Soviet music.

10. A version of the piece, titled *Cheryomushki,* rescored for small dance band by the present author and with a sharply adapted English translation of the libretto by David Pountney, was premiered by Pimlico Opera on 24 October 1994 at the Lyric Theatre, Hammersmith, conducted by Wasfi Kani. Since then that version has been expanded and adapted to small orchestral proportions for a production by Opera North under the title *Paradise Moscow,* first performed on 3 May 2001 in the Grand Theatre, Leeds, conducted by Steven Sloane. There have been further productions in the United Kingdom and Germany.

11. See Konstantin Rudnitsky, *Russian and Soviet Theatre: Tradition and the Avant-garde* (London: Thames and Hudson, 1988), p. 97.

12. In 1931 Shostakovich wrote the score of *Declared Dead* (*Uslovno ubityi*) for this theater. Although Vladimir Mass was not involved in this particular show, he worked on several similar shows in the same theater at the same period.

13. Mosfilm (1934), directed by Grigorii Aleksandrov.

14. Shostakovich appears to have been unmoved by any distant connections he might have had with Mass. It is fairly clear that he was unimpressed by the libretto of *Moscow, Cheryomushki* and by its two authors (Mass and Mikhail Chervinsky), passing lukewarm comment on them and their work in letters to Isaak Glikman (*Story of a Friendship,* p. 97) and to the operetta's first conductor Grigorii Stoliarov (*Dmitrii Shostakovich v pis'makh i dokumentakh,* ed. I. A Bobykina, [Moscow: GTsMMK, 2000], p. 211).

15. See Fay, *Shostakovich: A Life,* pp. 274–75.

16. The first and last movements of this concerto make particular play with the "Trepak" movement of Musorgsky's *Songs and Dances of Death*. Compare, for example, the first movement of the concerto, from 3 mm. after rehearsal number 13, with "Trepak," from m. 21ff.

17. Interview with the author, conducted in St. Petersburg in late October 1997 under the aegis of BBC Radio 3 as part of preparation for a live broadcast from the Winter Palace, "The Night of the October Revolution."

18. Shostakovich, *Sobranie sochinenii*, vol. 24, Editor's Note, where this reference is credited to *Sovetskaia muzyka* 1 (1959).

19. Divided into three acts, five scenes, the thirty-nine musical items in Shostakovich's score after its "Overture-Prologue" are numbered sequentially. For ease of reference, the number (no.) as well as the title of each will be identified in the discussion. *Ed.*

20. It is worth noting that there are no Musorgsky parodies in *Moscow, Cheryomushki,* which is especially remarkable given that Shostakovich was working on his version of *Khovanshchina* at the same time he was writing this operetta. The reason is presumably that Musorgsky was one of the composers who mattered most to him and, though he frequently refers to Musorgsky in his serious works of this period (including the Eleventh Symphony and the First Cello Concerto), parody of such a master was unthinkable.

21. At one performance of *Moscow, Cheryomushki,* the author remembers being startled by a previously unnoticed similarity between the lumbering tango rhythm that starts up in the brass immediately after this introduction and the familiar *saltando* dance rhythm in the first movement of the *Pathétique* Symphony (m. 42ff). This only goes to show that once one starts hearing echoes of this kind, there is no controlling what one might or might not be meant to hear.

22. The line is found in the four measures preceding rehearsal number 108 and is partially repeated before number 109.

23. There is no phrase at all resembling this one in Pushkin's original novel.

24. Perhaps Shostakovich disliked being pushed into a musical joke by his librettists. At all events he seems to have agreed with the immediate response of the girls to the lads: "We've . . . got a splendid rubbish chute for such witticisms" (4 mm. after rehearsal number 108).

25. The translation of the libretto used here and afterward is based on that by Philip Taylor in the CD liner notes to Shostakovich, *Moskva, Cheremushki,* conducted by Gennady Rozhdestvensky (1997), Chandos Records CHAN 9591(2).

26. The orchestration and the vocal writing of this number in *Moscow, Cheryomushki* also sometimes suggest an older Russian model, and one that Borodin himself would have had in mind in *Prince Igor*: Glinka's *Ruslan and Liudmila,* and, specifically, the Bayan's scene from Act 1 and the introduction to Ratmir's aria from Act 3. The gusli is a Russian zither, traditionally supposed to be the instrument of the early Russian bards. Its twanging sonorities sound somewhat like a lighter version of the Hungarian cimbalom.

27. Most of these specific song quotations are identified in Shostakovich, *Sobranie sochinenii*, vol. 24, Editor's Note.

28. This seems the version of the tune most familiar today, and somewhat different from that used by Rimsky-Korsakov in Act 3 of *The Golden Cockerel.*

29. Warm thanks to Olga Komok for her comments and most especially for her hard work canvassing her friends for the most widely agreed versions of the themes and texts of the popular songs quoted in this article.

30. Dmitrii Kabalevsky (1904–87) was a master of the genre.

31. Richard Taruskin, *Defining Russia Musically* (Princeton, N.J.: Princeton University Press, 1997), pp. 55–58.

32. "Overture-Prologue" (unnumbered), followed by nos. 13, 17, 24, 27, 32, and 39.

33. Nos. 3, 10, 20, 26, 31, and 37.

34. Nos. 2, 4, 5, 15, 22, 25, 28, 29, 30, 33, 34, and 36.

35. It should be pointed out (and the author has experience of this) that in a suitably stylish and knowing production the relentless repetition of this tune can take on a powerfully sarcastic, hollow, and mocking quality. While such a quality is undoubtedly appropriate to others of Shostakovich's works, whether it was quite what he intended in *Moscow, Cheryomushki* must remain open to question.

36. Shostakovich, *Sobranie sochinenii,* vol. 24. It is worth pointing out that this song is not included in the composer's orchestral suite from *Golden Mountains,* op. 30a.

37. See remarks on op. 30a in the Editor's Note (n.p.) in Shostakovich, *Sobranie sochinenii,* vol. 41.

38. For the full flavor, it is perhaps worth recalling the popular English version of this same lyric:

> Stillness in the grove, not a rustling sound;
> Softly shines the moon, clear and bright.
> Dear, if you could know
> How I treasure so
> This most beautiful Moscow night.

39. Fay, *Shostakovich: A Life,* p. 72.

40. "But this is wall-to-wall mockery" (*No eto sploshnoe izdevatel'stvo*) was how Mark Vail, the distinguished Tashkent theater director, remembered his youthful and slightly nervous response to this episode in the operetta on occasions when he watched the film version of *Cheryomushki* broadcast on Soviet television.

41. Just as, more than twenty years earlier, Peter, in Prokofiev's *Peter and the Wolf,* would have appeared a "typical Pioneer boy."

42. Fay, *Shostakovich: A Life,* p. 165.

43. Ibid., p. 207.

44. Translation of the words of *Antiformalist Rayok* adapted from Elizabeth Wilson's version in Dmitri Shostakovich, *Anti-Formalist RAYOK*: score (London: Anglo-Soviet Music Press, 1991).

45. Ibid., no page number.

46. The autograph manucripts of the full scores of numbers 1 and 2 (out of a possible total of more than thirty) are held by the Shostakovich Archive in Moscow.

47. Shostakovich, *Sobranie sochinenii,* vol. 28, pp. 62–107.

48. The composer Dmitrii Smirnov kindly provided the author with several other versions of this song, including:

> Fried chicken, stewed chicken
> Went walking around town.
> They caught him, arrested him,
> And told him to show his passport.
> He pulled out his passport, they hit him in the face,
> Then he cried and shat in his pants,
> And went to rinse himself in the stream.
> His pants were swept away, and he with them,
> And together they drowned.

Shostakovich and His Pupils

David Fanning

In the post-Beethoven era composers have generally had three options, other than inherited wealth or private patronage, for keeping body and soul together: performance, commissions for stage and screen, and teaching. Obviously each of these may feed back into the central activity of composition, at any level from individual musical ideas to broad attitudes to communication. In the case of teaching it is not hard to conceive of the influence of pedagogue on pupil. Yet the more interesting topics are surely the pupil's resistance to influence and the teacher's susceptibility to it. And it seems plausible, at least, that even the most individualistic and self-sufficient of composer-pedagogues, such as Schoenberg and Messiaen, may have derived creative stimulation from pupils as gifted as Berg and Webern, or Boulez and Stockhausen.[1] In the case of Shostakovich, there are two or three clearly documented examples of the influence of his pupils on his works. Besides these, a number of prima facie cases have been identified, and a number more will be proposed in this article. In addition, the impact of teaching activities on Shostakovich's artistic development in general, though hard to gauge with any precision, may well have been greater than is generally realized.[2]

Before taking a closer look at these specifics and generalities, it may be helpful to gather the threads of available information on Shostakovich's teaching, since they are dispersed in so many sources and are for the most part untranslated. The most detailed overview remains that of Sofia Khentova in her two-volume life-and-works study, and she also published several of her interviews with Shostakovich's pupils, on which much of that overview is based.[3] Various other published reminiscences and studies supplement her account. A recent concise but authoritative summary may be found in Laurel Fay's biography.[4]

Shostakovich as Teacher

Shostakovich's official activity as a teacher occupied three main periods in his life: from 1937–41 (Leningrad Conservatory), 1943–48 (Moscow Conservatory, with roughly six weekly trips to Leningrad, where he was reregistered as professor on 1 February 1947, after the death of his own former composition teacher, Maksimilian Shteinberg), and 1962–66 (Leningrad, a monthly class for graduate students, for which he traveled from his Moscow home).[5] The breaks in this activity were due, respectively, to his wartime evacuation from besieged Leningrad (from 1 October 1941), to the antiformalist clampdown in January 1948 (leading to Shostakovich's dismissal from both his Moscow and his Leningrad posts by September), and to his recuperation from his first heart attack (in May 1966). During and outside his main periods of teaching he offered more or less informal advice to a large number of aspiring composers other than his official pupils: notably to Veniamin Basner (1925–96), Mieczysław Weinberg (Moisei Vainberg, 1919–96), Edison Denisov (1929–96), and Nikolai Martynov (b. 1938).[6] In the 1937–41 and 1943–48 periods he also taught classes in orchestration, during which he also advised on compositional matters. An official orchestration student such as Mstislav Rostropovich could bring his compositions for scrutiny, and class members would routinely be encouraged to orchestrate their own music.[7] Students in the orchestration class are accordingly included in Table 1, but not those composers who regarded Shostakovich as a mentor, or those he regarded as his pupils, without their being officially enrolled.

Iurii Levitin has claimed that the initiative for Shostakovich's appointment at the Leningrad Conservatory in 1937 came from himself, supported by a number of other students.[8] Documentary evidence suggests, however, that in the first instance it was Shostakovich's own wish, recorded by Shteinberg in January 1937, on the grounds that his composing was "not working out" at the time.[9] This statement was surely a euphemism for the parlous situation in which Shostakovich found himself after the *Pravda* denunciations of January and February 1936 and his enforced withdrawal of the Fourth Symphony in December of that year, and before his full rehabilitation with the premiere of the Fifth Symphony in November 1937. With commissions drying up and the need to provide material support for his family becoming ever more pressing (his daughter Galina was born 30 May 1936), the restoration of his professional and financial stability had become a matter of urgency. It would become all the more so as the Great Purge of 1937 began to sweep the country, gathering several of Shostakovich's family members and professional associates in its tide of arrests. At this time it may be that the head of the Leningrad Conservatory, Boris Zagursky, saw an opportunity to strengthen the ranks of his institution, while offering some kind of haven to embattled or potentially embattled musicians; among other new-blood appointments in 1936–37 were Shostakovich's closest artistic friend and ally, Ivan Sollertinsky, and his former co-student in Leonid Nikolaev's piano class, the celebrated Vladimir Sofronitsky.

Table 1. Shostakovich's Official Pupils		
1937–41	**1943–48**	**1961–66**
Boldyrev, Igor (1912–80)	Berlinson, R.[11]	Belov, Gennadii (b. 1939)
Dobry, Iosif (b. 1905)	Bunin, Revol (1924–76)	Bibergan, Vadim (b. 1937)
Evlakhov, Orest (1912–73)	Aleksandr Chugaev (1924–90)[12]	Mnatsakanian, Aleksandr (b. 1936)
Fleishman, Veniamin (1913–41)	Gadzhiev, Akhmed (b. 1917)	Nagovitsyn, Viacheslav (b. 1939)
Katsnelson, Moisei (b. 1912)	Galynin, German (1922–66)	Okunev, German (1931–73)
Leviev, Minasai (b. 1912)	Karaev, Kara (1918–82)	Tishchenko, Boris (b. 1939)
Levitin, Iurii (1912–93)	Khachaturian, Karen (b. 1920)	Uspensky, Vladislav (b. 1937)
Lobkovsky, Abram (1912–85)	Makarov, Evgenii (1912–85)	
Sviridov, Georgii (1915–98)	Nazirova, Elmira (b. 1928)	
Tolmachev, Boris	Rostropovich, Mstislav (b. 1927)	
Tolstoy, Dmitrii (1923–2003)[10]	Saliutrinskaia, T.[13]	
Ustvolskaya, Galina (b. 1919)	Sarian, Lazar (1920–98)	
	Smirnov, Kuzma (1917–63)	
	Tchaikovsky, Boris (1925–96)	

Shostakovich began teaching orchestration at the conservatory soon after making his approach to Shteinberg.[14] He took on a composition class later in the year. More or less an unknown quantity as a pedagogue—as a graduate student he had done a couple of months of music theory teaching at Leningrad's Choreographic Tekhnikum in 1929—the thirty-year-old composer now joined a faculty that already included Shteinberg, Mikhail Gnesin, Boris Kushnarev, Pyotr Riazanov, Mikhail Iudin, Boris Asafiev, and Vladimir Shcherbachev. Since Riazanov was on leave at the time, he recommended that his pupils Georgii Sviridov and Orest Evlakhov should go to Shostakovich.[15] Sviridov was destined to become one of the most successful composers of vocal and choral music in the Soviet era; Evlakhov would become Chair of Composition at the Leningrad Conservatory and would persuade Shostakovich to go back to teaching in December 1961, after a thirteen-year hiatus during which he refused to return to official duties, without explanation.[16] These two pupils were soon joined by the others listed in the first column of Table 1, among whom the most significant are Veniamin Fleishman (who died at the battlefront in 1941 and whose opera *Rothschild's Violin* Shostakovich completed and orchestrated), Levitin and Ustvolskaya (the most independent-minded of Shostakovich's pupils, whose stark yet spiritually charged music only began to receive its deserved international recognition in the 1990s).

Shostakovich taught in two stints of five to seven hours per week, in room 36 of the Leningrad Conservatory, where Rimsky-Korsakov had taught before him.[17] He observed an old-fashioned, almost pedantic precision of manners, using the polite you form (*Vy*) to address his pupils, making a point of arriving first to the class, and appearing punctually at nine in the morning even on the day after the historic premiere of his Fifth Symphony, when his students found him playing through the score of Glazunov's ballet *Raimonda*.[18] Although he was insistent on the value of counterpoint and analysis of the classics, and intolerant of amateurism or laziness, he made no use of textbooks or courses of instruction; in all the copious reminiscences of his pupils there is not a single reference to Fux, Bellermann, Riemann, Asafiev, Yavorsky, or any other theoretical or pedagogic text. This may reflect a conscious attempt on Shostakovich's part to steer clear of the authoritarian approaches of his own former teachers, in particular Ignatii Gliasser and Shteinberg. But it is not to say that his classes were in any way relaxed or unfocused, even if they did on occasion extend to discussion of broad artistic and ethical issues.[19] Rather, he strove to instill the habits that experience taught him were essential to a professional composer. First and foremost was the active engagement with the established repertoire through piano duet performance, ideally as a daily ritual. At their very first lesson Sviridov and Evlakhov found themselves sight-reading a Mozart symphony, and Shostakovich himself often took part in such readings, usually playing the bass part; from 1939 to 1941 his composition assistant Izrail Finkelshtein (a former composition student with Gnesin) generally took the treble.[20] Works played and discussed in this way included "symphonies by Mozart, Tchaikovsky, Brahms, Schumann, Beethoven, Mahler, Borodin, Taneev, symphonic poems by Richard Strauss . . . Prokofiev Piano Concertos, Glinka's orchestral works, and Verdi's *Otello*."[21] Where no four-hand version existed of a particularly interesting score, such as those relayed to him by musicologist Pavel Lamm, Shostakovich would occasionally make his own, as in the famous example of Stravinsky's *Symphony of Psalms*.[22] In his 1960s classes, when his piano playing was suffering because of illness, the emphasis shifted away from duet playing toward listening to contemporary scores on LP or taped recordings, such as Sviridov's *Kursk Songs,* Weinberg's Sixth Symphony, and Britten's *The Turn of the Screw* and *A War Requiem*.[23] At this time it seems that a particular feature of Shostakovich's classes was his citing of favorite poets and commendations of particular writings.[24]

Such lists already give snapshots of Shostakovich's musical preferences at various points in his life, adding details to the already well-stocked database of his likes and dislikes. These reminiscences may be more or less tinged by the predilections of the reminiscer or by fear of disapproval, as when Levitin notes that Shostakovich "insistently and repeatedly cautioned his pupils against the exaggeration of external effects, against deliberate garishness and any kind of hysterics."[25] Nevertheless there is a good deal of consistency in pupils' assessments of Shostakovich's tastes. He extolled Verdi's vocal music over Wagner's, calling *Lohengrin* "Unteroffizier music"; he loved Berg but not Schoenberg (except for the latter's Second String Quartet); and he liked most of Stravinsky, with reservations over *The Firebird* and *The Rite of Spring* and with more enthusiasm for Stravinsky's coloristic sense than for his formal or melodic gifts.[26] Notwithstanding that, his general antipathy toward merely coloristic music was intense. Hence impressionism was for him virtually a term of abuse, though he did express admiration for certain Debussy *Préludes*. Similarly he was often scathing about any suspicion of the "salon-like" in song-setting, and his particular dislike for Rachmaninoff has been recorded.[27] Evgenii Makarov reports a succession of Shostakovich's negative opinions—on Miaskovsky's Twelfth Symphony, Tchaikovsky's *Manfred,* and Prokofiev's *War and Peace* ("gentlemanly music") and *Ode on the End of the War*.[28] Dmitrii Tolstoy recalls an incident in 1934 or 1935 that he considers to have been important for the development of his teacher's personal dislike of Prokofiev, when the latter reacted coolly to Shostakovich's recently completed First Piano Concerto.[29]

Four-hand score-playing and subsequent comment was preceded by discussion of pupils' own scores, again normally at the piano (official conservatory examinations for composers would often be based on piano or piano-duet performances of ensemble or orchestral scores). Shostakovich would insist on complete pieces being brought to each session, or at least complete sections of more extended movements, so that his comments could embrace matters of form as well as detail. Such remarks were often preceded by a laconic "this is good" or "this is bad," though it is not surprising to learn that the intonation used was as important as the words.[30] Other ways for Shostakovich to express non-approval were to comment on the high quality of the manuscript paper, or to step into the corridor for regular cigarettes.[31] An overriding aim was to foster self-criticism, professionalism, and regular daily work. He was intolerant of sloppiness, once evicting a student from class for writing impossible chords and harmonics for violins.[32] On the positive side, he could even take the trouble of sending his pupils lists of proofreading-type corrections.[33] Kara Karaev stresses his flexibility by saying that he had as many principles as he had talented students, but he goes on to list Shostakovich's hatred of amateurism, "commonplace ideas and padding, surface luxuriance and decorativeness."[34] In a similar vein, Dmitrii Tolstoy noted his teacher's intolerance for luxuriant texture, banal turns of phrase, bombastic and pathetic harmonies à la Wagner, and sentimentalism à la Varlamov or Gurilev (minor contemporaries of Glinka, best known for their domestic songs).[35] Concision was a watchword, and his pupils' reminiscences are full of his advice to cut out superfluous material.[36] These were clearly principles Shostakovich sought to live by in his own work, and he was quite prepared to lead by example and to discuss his own experience as a composer, routinely bringing his own works to class—from his national anthem entries to a modernist masterpiece like *The Nose,* at a time when it was languishing, unpassed for performance—and getting his pupils to sit in on open rehearsals. He would occasionally carry out the same instrumentation or composition tasks he set, sometimes even during the course of a class.[37] He would point to alternative possibilities for themes, on one occasion even composing a development section for string quartet to given themes, when the composers themselves had claimed that this could not be done.[38] He would refer to Tchaikovsky as a source for solving his own compositional problems, though Dmitrii Tolstoy claims that Shostakovich found Tchaikovsky's music in general disappointing, and he admitted that returning to the piano to improvise could occasionally

get him over moments of writer's block.[39] Although in later years especially he was perfectly capable of self-deprecation, he was not comfortable
with others casting aspersions, even on his weakest works.[40]

Outside the classroom, Shostakovich's kindness to his pupils was legendary. He provided financial support for Evlakhov's recuperation from
illness, without the latter being aware of it at the time.[41] He helped
Fleishman to get into the Composers' Union and secretly protected
Martynov from exclusion from it.[42] He donated the royalties for his work
on Fleishman's *Rothschild's Violin* to the composer's widow.[43] He was
unstinting in his support for pupils whose work he felt justified it, lob-
bying for performances and recordings and publishing appreciations
of their work.[44] Abram Lobkovsky suggests that he got this generosity
from the example of Glazunov.[45] On the other hand, he was not entirely
uncritical of his weaker students, even in public arenas. For example, he
was prepared to go against a recommendation for Lobkovsky and Boris
Tolmachev to receive scholarships, and he introduced a performance of
Igor Boldyrev's symphony with the frank comment that the composer
had not yet found his own musical language.[46] Almost from the start he
organized an annual concert featuring his pupils' compositions, and later
in his career he encouraged concerts of their music, such as one in 1957
for Gadzhiev, Galynin, and Sviridov and the 1964 Gorky event where
works by Okunev, Uspensky, Belov, and Tishchenko were played.[47] Not
content with that, he also encouraged joint sessions of the conservatory
and the Composers' Union, from which reports of detailed criticism
of works such as Fleishman's opera have been retained.[48] On the lighter
side, he also arranged a men-only gathering at the end of each academic
year in his apartment, refereeing ball games played between the two
main rooms.[49]

Podrazhatel'stvo

For all his willingness to discuss his own music and to encourage his
pupils to engage with it, Shostakovich was intolerant of imitativeness
(*podrazhatel'stvo*).[50] Nevertheless, *podrazhatel'stvo* was hard for his students
to resist, and when they were guilty of it, it did not go unnoticed, either
by their teacher or by outsiders. It was an accusation Iosif Dobry had to
defend himself against, as did Sviridov, whose String Symphony (1940)
was noted as having been written under the spell of his master's Fifth
Symphony, just as his Piano Trio of 1945 closely shadows Shostakovich's
of the previous year.[51]

On occasions, the urge to imitate reached almost laughable proportions. The relationship between model and imitation in Example 1 is unmistakable. The imitation uses essentially the same motives, the same texture and scoring, even the same harmonic progression, and it continues long past the few bars cited. The composer-imitator is Akhmed Dvezhdet Gadzhiev, who came from Azerbaijan to study with Shostakovich in Moscow after the Second World War, then returned to Baku and taught at the conservatory there, serving as rector for twelve years. The work in question is his Fourth Symphony, composed in 1952–56 and dedicated to the memory of Lenin.

How to describe such parasitic music? It is not quotation, certainly not in the way Boris Tishchenko quotes Shostakovich's Eighth Symphony in his Fifth (1976) as an overt and reverent homage (one of many such works composed just after Shostakovich's death). Nor does it seem to be an allusion made with an allegorical subtext in mind. Rather, it is surely a straightforward case of plagiarism, or something very close to that. In fact, it seems to have been not unusual for Gadzhiev to borrow his teacher's themes—and indeed those of other luminaries—then stretch them out, add little ethnic twiddles à la Khachaturian, and pass the results off as his own work. The second movement of his Fourth Symphony is a gloss

Example 1a. Gadzhiev, Symphony no. 4, first movement, mm. 29–38, first and second violins and violas.

Example 1b. Shostakovich, Symphony no. 8, first movement, mm. 18–22, first and second violins and violas.

on the sword-fight music from Prokofiev's *Romeo and Juliet*; the third movement draws heavily on Shostakovich's *Leningrad* Symphony, and the finale echoes corresponding passages in both that work and Shostakovich's Fifth. Gadzhiev was certainly not exaggerating when he declared, "The symphonic output of my teacher and mentor D. D. Shostakovich has always been the brightest example for me."[52]

The story goes that Gadzhiev was actually accused of plagiarism and ran off to Shostakovich and came back with a written testimonial: "This is to certify that the works of A. D. Gadzhiev have nothing in common with mine." Evidently Shostakovich could turn a deaf ear to *podrazhatel'stvo* when he chose. But he was certainly not unaware of Gadzhiev's limitations, as an unpublished passage in a letter of 6 June 1947 to Karaev indicates: "He's a capable fellow, but without much individuality as a composer. There's a lot of imitativeness in his music. We must hope that this will disappear as the years go by."[53] Why then might he have written in his pupil's defense? Was the nurturing instinct so unconditional? Perhaps he was merely mindful of his own reputation as a teacher. At any rate, the supposed testimonial seems not to survive, and it may be that the details of the story have become exaggerated in the retelling. But it has found its way into print, courtesy of the cultural historian Mikhail Gasparov.[54] It also makes a nice musical illustration for a well-known cartoon, published in *Sovetskaia muzyka* in 1948, a year after Gadzhiev's graduation from Shostakovich's class. This may be seen on the dust jacket of Rosamund Bartlett's *Shostakovich in Context* and in the text of Laurel Fay's *Shostakovich: A Life*, where the caption is nicely translated: "Year after year these glorious portals / Disgorge a stream of inglorious mortals. / They keep on coming—in vain one bemoans / All the Shostakovich clones!"[55]

The devotion of Shostakovich's pupils to him was evidently as consistent as his to them, and it extended beyond musical matters. More than one memoirist has used the word "worship" to describe their attitude.[56] Dmitrii Tolstoy reports that in prewar years Shostakovich could be seen walking the corridors of the Leningrad Conservatory with his students in front and behind.[57] Mikhail Meerovich, one of many composers who benefited from consultations with Shostakovich without ever being a formal pupil, has left a colorful impression of this phenomenon: "You could tell a Shostakovich pupil a mile off; they all wore glasses, both those who needed them and those who didn't. They imitated his jerky movements and stuttering manner of speech. They all seemed to look like him."[58] There is a certain amount of photographic evidence to support Meerovich's apparently implausible assertion—in particular in portraits of Revol Bunin, who studied with Shostakovich at the same time as Gadzhiev. Whatever his

Который год из этих славных стен
Идет чреда бесславных смен.
Идут, идут —
Хоть караул кричи!
Всё маленькие шостаковичи!

Figure 1. "Pedagogical humor," by A. Kostomolotsky, in *Sovetskaia muzyka* 4 (1948).

inclination to adopt Shostakovichian spectacles and tonsure, as a composer Bunin was no mere imitator. He was a more than respectable craftsman. So too was Karen Khachaturian, even though we are told by Denisov—a composer with something of a modernist ax to grind—that Shostakovich did not take him, or indeed Levitin, seriously.[59] Like other, better-known Shostakovich pupils such as Sviridov, Boris Tchaikovsky, and Tishchenko, these composers were obviously profoundly influenced by their master,

and echoes of his work ripple through theirs. But again, imitators or pla-
giarists they are not, at least not in their mature work. Rather, their confident,
characterful music is an impressive testimonial to Shostakovich's qualities
as a teacher. Some of it has come back into circulation thanks to the CD,
but much remains obscure and unpublished. It would therefore seem premature to attempt evaluation at this stage and not especially enlightening
to point to obvious instances of Shostakovich's style informing theirs.

The Teacher as Learner

Of rather more interest may be what Shostakovich learned from his pupils
and from his teaching activities in general, since this leads back to the familiar Shostakovichian issues of quotation, influence, and symbolic meaning
(or rather the speculative interpretation thereof, since documentation is
generally lacking).

Like Rimsky-Korsakov back in the 1870s, Shostakovich initially felt
underqualified for the job. Although he had enjoyed a far more thorough
training than had his grand-teacher, he must have had to do a fair amount
of homework in preparation, or at least give fresh thought to the traditional repertoires of concert music. How crucial that was in his enforced
stylistic retrenchment we can never know for sure, but it was certainly
not the only factor. After all, as a performer Shostakovich had never lost
touch with traditional forms and genres, even though his own music
between 1927 and 1937 shows little sign of it other than in the cello
sonata of 1934. The fact remains that his compositional reengagement
with tradition in the years following his denunciation in *Pravda* went
hand in hand with the day-to-day activity of teaching, and the parallel
phenomena invite comment. In 1937 he had yet to compose a string
quartet, for instance, despite having talked about the importance of Soviet
composers not neglecting chamber music; his First Quartet came in the
following year, and in places it gives the impression of the sort of speed-
writing exercise he would carry out in the presence of his students.

Two specific instances of the impact of Shostakovich's pupils on his development are well-known. There is strong circumstantial evidence that
Fleishman's *Rothschild's Violin,* orchestrated and completed by his teacher after
the composer's death at the battlefront, gave Shostakovich significant impetus toward his adoption of Jewish dance idioms from the Second Piano Trio
on.[60] Also familiar is the Ustvolskaya connection—in particular that
Shostakovich quoted a theme from her 1949 Trio for Clarinet, Violin and
Piano, both in his Fifth String Quartet (1952) and much later in his *Suite on*

Texts of Michelangelo Buonarroti (1974), plus that he proposed marriage to her following the death of his first wife in 1954. Ustvolskaya turned him down. But when her first husband died in 1960, at a time when Shostakovich's second marriage had recently broken up, he again proposed a relationship and was again rebuffed.[61] Further details of the Shostakovich-Ustvolskaya connection, though widely speculated upon, are hard to pin down, largely because she, still alive at the time of writing, is an intensely private person. That has not stopped her voicing, and agreeing with, trenchant rejections of Shostakovich's musical language and ethics.[62] She claims never to have been close to him, either personally or as a composer, and to have destroyed all of his letters to her.[63] But the quotation in Shostakovich's Fifth Quartet does invite further comment, since its ramifications—both programmatic and structural—have been little explored.

The theme from Ustvolskaya's Trio, with its characteristic psalm-like repeated notes and minor third descents, is quoted in the first movement

Example 2a. Ustvolskaya, Trio for Clarinet, Violin and Piano, third movement, mm. 60–66.

of Shostakovich's quartet, at the high-point of an intensely worked-out development section where it tussles with material from the first subject in the viola and cello (see Example 2).

The invitation to programmatic interpretation at this point is clear enough, not only because of the quotation and the biographical connection, but because this new theme so strikingly infringes on our expectations of a sonata form retransition. In structural terms it is a startling incursion. The hysterical tone in which the quotation is initially couched—the insistent dynamics and stratospheric tessitura—is easy to relate to Shostakovich's real-life passionate affection. The same theme will be wistfully recalled in the same movement's coda, and when it comes back in the third movement, again at a point of retransition in the (sonata-rondo) structure, the suggestiveness of the scenario, if we choose to read it as such, develops. Equally significant as the Ustvolskaya theme here is the motif Shostakovich splices on to it (the repeated-note anapest pizzicato chords in Example 3). It is hardly original to propose that this gesture

Example 2b. Shostakovich, String Quartet no. 5, first movement, mm. 261–66.

may be read as a Shostakovich fingerprint. But Russian musicologist Aleksei Vulfson has gone further, relating it to the composer's pet name, Mitenka, the affectionate double diminutive of Dmitrii by which his mother would have called him and whose natural speech rhythm is a beginning-accented anapest. On that basis Vulfson's colleague Arkadii Klimovitsky has suggested upgrading it to the status of a rhythmic counterpart to the DSCH signature.[64] If we bring to mind other prominent appearances of the repeated-note anapest gesture—in the third movement of the Tenth Symphony or in the fourth movement of the Eighth Quartet, the very works in which the DSCH signature also figures most prominently—then the signature hypothesis begins to feel rather persuasive. Klimovitsky's article does not mention the Fifth Quartet, where strictly speaking the figure in question is not beginning-accented (though no one but a score reader would guess as much). But if those striking pizzicato chords in the finale do in some way stand for the composer—whether as signature or fingerprint—then it is worth considering their appearance in light of the Ustvolskaya connection and pushing the hypothetical autobiographical scenario a stage further. The lead into the "signature" chords consists of the Ustvolskaya theme descending from its "unattainable" heights into the female then the male vocal register. As soon as it arrives there—as it were within reach—the anapest chords lunge impulsively at it. There is no consummation, however, and pretty soon the wishfulfillment scenario dissolves (Example 3).

Pushed this far, interpretation approaches the banal and the vulgar, if it has not already crossed the line. Shostakovich's music need not fear such accusations, however, because the passages in question, for all their emotional intensity and apparent transgression of norms, are so thoroughly integrated into the broader musical flow. Admittedly, it would be perverse to argue that there can be no relationship between Shostakovich's personal feelings about his pupil and the music on the page, just as it would be to ignore the self-portraying function of the DSCH motif. But the degree of literalism involved will always be a matter of interpretation. The question remains: whatever the extra-musical dimension may be, what is its relationship with the musical? Which supports which, and which supported which in the composer's mind? Are these discrete or overlapping aspects of meaning? There are no definitive answers here, partly because the extra-musical aspect is itself speculative, partly because the questions touch on fundamental issues of musical aesthetics.[65] But as so often, Shostakovich's music brings the issues to the surface with particular force.

To balance out the above speculative programmatic interpretation it is worth stressing the structural role of the Ustvolskaya quotation. This

Example 3. Shostakovich, String Quartet no. 5, third movement, mm. 337–43.

is partly a matter of forging a cyclic connection between the outer movements (the kind of possibility Shostakovich routinely pointed out to his pupils when they presented him with themes for extended pieces). But it goes further than that. These passages expand the structure from within, by giving exceptional bulk and profile to the retransition phase. By convention, the retransition would be, along with the coda, almost the last place in a sonata form structure where a new theme would be appropriate. By introducing such a theme at this point, in the highly suggestive form of a quotation, Shostakovich both opens up interpretive space and enables his movement to fill an exceptionally broad canvas. This in turn helps to explain why the overall layout should comprise three rather than four movements (these being almost equivalent in overall length to the five movements of his Third Quartet). The first movement of the Fifth Quartet thereby becomes one of the most ambitious, perhaps even *the* most ambitious, of Shostakovich's first movement allegros, in terms of range of expression and density of incident. It is this design, expressed in all its myriad detail, that we respond to, indeed that we are forced to respond to if we know nothing of the Ustvolskaya connection. Knowing about an extra-musical connection, or in this case positing one, surely does not obliterate that response but merely enriches it, just as the documented programmatic elements in Janáček's two quartets and Berg's *Lyric Suite* do. In short, the personal program (whatever we take it to be) serves the musical structure, rather than the other way round. It enables the composer both to discover new shades of musical rhetoric and to devise structures in which to contain and enhance them. Looked at this way it seems that with the help of his pupil-muse Shostakovich not only created a remarkable large-scale musical design but also enhanced his compositional resources as a whole.

The same applies to a rather better-known example of a pupil-cum-muse embodied in Shostakovich's music. The work in question is the third movement of his Tenth Symphony, composed the year after the Fifth Quartet. Here the atmosphere of the coda is especially suggestive. Emblematically speaking, the Elmira Nazirova theme on the horn in Example 4 stands for another unattainable female muse, who happens to be another pupil (the notes EAEDA stand for E–La–MI–Re–A).[66] As a tailpiece comes DSCH on the flute and piccolo. Here, near the end of the movement, the two characters, presented in isolation earlier on, are at last together in time, yet still apart in registral space. Again the metaphor can easily be elaborated and indeed tipped into vulgarity if confined to literalism. To broaden the focus somewhat, then: the simultaneous sense of proximity and distance is both intensified and generalized by the harmonic reference (C major with added sixth) to the end of "Der Abschied" from Shostakovich's favorite Mahler score, *Das Lied von der Erde*. In this environment it feels that the horn motif has finally come home, while the flute/piccolo line is still disembodied. This is a wonderful way of balancing out the tensions of a movement whose role in the overall symphonic scheme is subtle and profound (it follows a massive, moderately paced, thoughtful first movement and a manic, hard-boiled scherzo, and precedes a deceptively upbeat finale). Once again the personal and the musical are mutually supportive.

Could these passages from the Fifth Quartet and Tenth Symphony have come about at all without the stimulus from Shostakovich's pupil-muses? In general atmospheric terms perhaps yes, but they obviously would not have been articulated in the same specific ways. And in his later

Example 4. Shostakovich, Symphony no. 10, third movement, mm. 492–97.

works the basic intervallic cells of the Ustvolskaya and Nazirova motives develop into near-obsessions. It is possible to argue that their symbolic role recedes as their musical potential develops (though symbolism of some kind surely lies behind the quotation of the full Ustvolskaya theme four times over in Shostakovich's *Michelangelo Suite*).[67] It is also true that these motivic cells are not unprecedented in Shostakovich's output—the second half of the Ustvolskaya theme is prefigured in the First String Quartet (first movement, from rehearsal number 8 in the second violin), as are the oscillating fourths of the Elmira monogram in the coda to the first movement of the Fourth Symphony (from rehearsal number 107 on cor anglais) or, less prominently but at the "Elmira" pitch level, in the Third Symphony (between rehearsal numbers 6 and 7 on horn). The motivic elements in themselves are musically self-sufficient and in no need of decoding. Incongruity and the consequent provocation toward programmatic interpretation exist only when Shostakovich creates them contextually, as he does in the Fifth Quartet (by the impropriety of a new theme at points of retransition) and in the Tenth Symphony (by means of motivic unrelatedness to the rest of the work and timbral distinctiveness). All the same, once the association of the muse had become attached to the motives in these works, it is hard to imagine that it disappeared entirely from Shostakovich's mind when he deployed the core motivic elements in later life, as he did so often and so prominently. This may even be the reason why they forced themselves to the surface: they demanded from him a nurturing in art that he was not able to offer to their associated muses in life.

If the history of these highly charged motives is intimately bound up with his pupils, what about the most symbolic of them all, the DSCH monogram? Elena Silina is surely right to say that its disguised, transposed appearance at the beginning of Fleishman's *Rothschild's Violin* is coincidental.[68] Rather more striking is a passage from the piano concerto of 1946 by German Galynin (another Shostakovich pupil in the immediate postwar era, who died young from complications associated with schizophrenia). Perhaps the prominent but transposed DSCH motives in Example 5 are merely another coincidence. But Shostakovich was just about to embark on his First Violin Concerto, with its own prominent near-miss DSCH signatures in the second movement and cadenza, and there is nothing in his previous works that so suggestively prefigures the DSCH motif. In the absence of documentation this may be as far as we can go. Speculating on the ancestry of the DSCH motif is a cottage industry all its own—rather as trying to identify Elgar's "Enigma" theme has been in Britain. No one knows its origins in Shostakovich's mind, and probably no one ever will. Shostakovich's thoughts on Galynin's first movement in class focused on his concern that the exposition was too "abbreviated."[69] The finale was evidently composed earlier, while Galynin was still studying with Miaskovsky, and Shostakovich found it talented if "somewhat superficial."[70] After the first performance in 1955, he was much more complimentary, in a letter to the ailing composer's wife.[71] So pending the unlikely appearance of documentary corroboration, the Galynin example merely confirms that the DSCH motif was in the air before Shostakovich finally netted it and pinned it to the page in his Tenth Symphony.[72]

Example 5. Galynin, Piano Concerto, third movement, mm. 88–92.

There is at least one other instance of his quoting directly from a pupil, which is the appearance of a theme from Sviridov's 1951 musical comedy *Ogon'ki* (roughly translated, "Rays of hope") in the finale of the Eleventh Symphony (Example 6). In Sviridov's original this theme is a kind of leitmotif for the revolutionary spirit of factory workers around the time of the 1905 unrest. It appears first in the overture; in the action of the musical comedy it is printed on an agit-leaflet and sung to the words:

> Boldly, friends, do not lose your courage in the unequal struggle
> Save our mother country, our honor and freedom
> If we are to die in prisons and damp pits
> Then our blood, our death will echo in generations of the living.

The general cut of Sviridov's theme is similar to that of the authentic revolutionary songs that run through Shostakovich's Eleventh Symphony. So its quotation there may simply be a *jeu d'esprit,* given that the operetta is set around the same time as the events of Bloody Sunday, ostensibly commemorated in the symphony, and given that the story had been proposed to Shostakovich in the 1940s before eventually passing to Sviridov for setting.[73]

In matters of overall design and technical/aesthetic principles, as much as of the small-scale motives and themes considered so far, Shostakovich probably got more ideas from his pupils than they have been given credit for, particularly in his later years. And it may be that an individual work reflects the stimulus of more than one pupil.

Example 6a. Sviridov, *Ogon'ki,* no. 6, mm. 23–30.

Example 6b. Shostakovich, Symphony no. 11, fourth movement, mm. 347–54.

For instance, in terms of genre the Thirteenth Symphony may seem to come out of the blue, given that the Soviet vocal/choral symphony virtually went into cold storage in the mid-1930s. But of course the Socialist Realist oratorio had been absolutely standard, especially in the post-1948 era, and it may well be that the Thirteenth Symphony is in part a "creative response" to such conformist pieces, not least to Sviridov's *Oratorio Pathétique* of 1959, just as it may be to his own Twelfth Symphony.[74] But there is also the splendidly isolated case of Ustvolskaya's First Symphony of 1955 to consider, with its eight settings of poems by the Italian author-journalist Gianni Rodari, sung by two child soloists. Those texts are all about the "poverty of capitalism." Yet their resonances are wide-ranging. Take the fourth poem, "The Boy from Modena," with lines such as "Yesterday you were happy; today they shot our fathers." Suddenly it seems no great leap to Shostakovich's Thirteenth.

Ustvolskaya's First Symphony was not performed until the late 1960s, but she has said that Shostakovich knew all her music at the time it was composed.[75] In any case her two vocal soloists, the gloomy poems, and the austere, pared-down musical language take us closer still to Shostakovich's Fourteenth Symphony of 1969. And there are two more links in this particular chain. The first is supplied by Mieczysław Weinberg— not an official pupil of Shostakovich, it should be remembered, but in his own eyes very much a disciple. The configuration of his Sixth Symphony of 1963 with children's choir, and of his Eighth of 1964 with its ten movements, tenor solo, and mixed choir, may have lent support to Shostakovich's reengagement with the subgenre of vocal symphony. Like Shostakovich's Thirteenth, Weinberg's Sixth is in five movements with the last three linked; like Ustvolskaya's First its texts deal with childhood innocence and its violation. This was a work Shostakovich particularly admired and which he recommended to his pupils for listening.[76] Weinberg's second movement directly prefigures the corresponding movement of Shostakovich's Fourteenth (compare the violin writing especially). The other link is via Karaev's Third Symphony of 1964, which makes a feature of twelve-tone row construction. This was by no means the first Soviet symphony to do so—there had been a flurry of such works the previous year—and Shostakovich himself had already independently approached the brink of twelve-tone thematic construction. Nor would the examples of twelve-tone writing in works he admired by Berg and Britten have escaped his attention. But given the debates that had raged on dodecaphony in the Soviet Union, and given Shostakovich's influential official position, it was a significant decision for him whether or not he should take the leap himself. His high opinion of Karaev's symphony is documented in a letter to the composer of 17 May 1965.[77] In his conscious and deliberate use of twelve-tone themes from 1968 onwards (most consequentially of all in the Fourteenth Symphony), he may well have taken heart from the example of his pupil.[78]

Roughly the same may be said of the quotation game in the Fifteenth Symphony, especially at the opening of the finale, with its tantalizing crypto-symbolic suggestiveness. The Wagner references at this point are at once more public (thanks to the familiarity of the originals) than the Ustvolskaya quotations in the Fifth Quartet, and yet more resistant to interpretation than those instances or than the locus classicus of Shostakovichian quotation, the Eighth Quartet. In this instance the significant forerunner is Boris Tchaikovsky, another pupil of Shostakovich in the postwar years. In the late stages of the first movement of his masterly Second Symphony (from rehearsal number 113, interrupting the recapitulation), completed in 1967, Tchaikovsky strings together a medley of themes from Mozart's Clarinet Quintet; Beethoven's String Quartet, op. 18, no. 4; Bach's *St. Matthew Passion,* the alto aria "Erbarme dich, mein Gott"; and Schumann's "Des Abends" with brief interconnecting passages. I have not seen any attempts to "decode" this passage, and I am certainly not going to offer one here, despite the obvious temptation.[79] Because the crucial similarity with the finale of Shostakovich's Fifteenth Symphony is precisely the unexplained quality of the quotations—their impression of something disembodied taking over the music.[80] Real-world time stops and we enter the realm of ghosts. Of course, from a global perspective these are anything but isolated cases, pastiche and collage having been symptoms of incipient postmodernism in the West throughout the 1960s. Both in atmosphere and technique, the Tchaikovsky passage is strikingly prophetic of Luciano Berio's Schubert homage, *Rendering*, of 1989–90. But it is the way in which the Tchaikovsky and Shostakovich quotations resist interpretation that declares their mutual affinity. And the way in which their contexts, as it were, sustain the suspension of time and physicality in favor of out-of-body experience places them in a particular regional tradition that stretches forward to Schnittke and Silvestrov, but perhaps not backward. The very fact that Shostakovich's quotations have provoked such intense curiosity suggests the lack of clear historical precedents.

Like so many tempting parallels, this one has (as yet) no documentary support. Even when corroboration apparently exists, it needs to be handled carefully. For instance, Khentova reports that Shostakovich composed the six slow movements of his Fifteenth Quartet under the impression of Boris Tchaikovsky's Third Quartet (1967), "in which all the movements are slow."[81] Her comment has been echoed in the West.[82] But Tchaikovsky's Quartet is by no means uniformly slow; its six movements are headed moderato, andante marcato, andante, allegro moderato, allegretto, and andante—not an adagio in sight. The composer was unsurprisingly skeptical about the connection:

> About the Third Quartet, for example, Dmitrii Dmitrievich said: "It's all quiet, not a single loud sound in it." That's not right; there are many loud passages. But Shostakovich, who liked the Third Quartet very much, took the measure of it as a whole from the fact that the music arises out of silence and that this is the basic mood of the Quartet. There is crescendo and forte, but they are not defining aspects.[83]

So we do not need to dismiss the notion of influence as a myth in this instance, nor should we seek to confine it to what is supported by hearsay evidence. Like Shostakovich's Fifteenth Quartet, Tchaikovsky's Third is in six movements, all of them played attacca, and saturated with Shostakovichian gestures. This may indicate his response to his former teacher's seven-movement Eleventh Quartet, composed the previous year. A further stimulus toward Shostakovich's last quartet, surely, were the opening bars of Tishchenko's 1963 Cello Concerto no. 1, which supply the initial motif. Here again it seems he sensed in the work of former pupils possibilities that he might never have discovered of his own accord, or at least that he might never have exploited in quite the same way. It was this concerto, incidentally, whose orchestration Shostakovich had advised his pupil to revise, since he feared that Tishchenko's seventeen brass and woodwind, percussion, and harmonium were likely to drown out the soloist; in 1969 Shostakovich himself made a complete reorchestration in which he cut down on the woodwind and eliminated the brass altogether, and which he presented to the composer on his thirtieth birthday.[84]

There are many other details to be added to this picture: the example of Tishchenko provoking Shostakovich's engagement with the poetry of Marina Tsvetaeva, for instance, or the conclusion of Ustvolskaya's violin sonata of 1952, whose ghostly percussive tappings on the body of the violin are echoed eighteen years later in the fast central section of Shostakovich's Thirteenth Quartet.[85] A comprehensive survey of his pupils' works might well be able to extend the list a good deal further. And the personal and musical significance in each case identified above can doubtless be viewed in other ways than I have suggested. But one important lesson here seems to be that Shostakovich's uniqueness has not so much to do with the invention of unprecedented themes or gestures as with the way in which he embodies them in the broader musical-dramatic flow. That is of course a truism applicable to any composer whose music has lasting value. But it is one too easily forgotten in Shostakovich's case, thanks to the vividness of his gestural language and the temptation to relate it to his painful experiences in the outside world.

If closer examination of his pupils' music apparently downgrades the uniqueness of Shostakovich's gestures, reflection on his teaching activity in general may encourage an appreciation of his mastery of continuity and structure. His ability to make music flow in broad channels, to derive more drama from less material, deepened appreciably at the time he began teaching. All the lessons he absorbed from Bach, Beethoven, Verdi, Wagner, Offenbach, Pyotr Tchaikovsky, Mahler, Stravinsky, Prokofiev, Hindemith, Britten, and indeed from his own teachers back in the 1920s, no doubt played their part in forming his style at various points in his career. Where he would have gone without the experience of teaching is as imponderable as the kind of music he might have composed without political intervention. That intervention took place, and for good or ill it shaped his maturity. So too did his teaching.

Quite apart from its role as an enabling force in Shostakovich's path to artistic maturity, teaching was evidently one of his coping strategies, especially in the early phases. It confirmed his commitment to the system, as an insider rather than a maverick; it filled the gap left by dwindling commissions and performances; it was a boost to his self-esteem; and it provided him with a cohort of loyal supporters. As his published letters to Glikman, Denisov, and others attest, he would periodically complain of creative impotence, isolation, and disappointment with himself, and various of his pupils confirm these moods.[86] So it should be no surprise that he valued their presence in his life, both for moral support and for musical stimulation.

For all the heated disagreements about where Shostakovich's music comes from—ideologically, culturally, and aesthetically—the forces that nourished his creativity in a practical way also deserve consideration. His activity as a teacher was one such force, and one that should not be underestimated. He was, in more ways than we have perhaps recognized, a pupil of his pupils, and a pupil of his teaching.

NOTES

This article originated as a paper for the conference "Shostakovich: Twenty-five Years On," University of Glasgow, October 2000. I am grateful to Laurel Fay for her comments on two draft versions and for copies of a number of the Russian sources cited; also to Igor Prokhorov for guiding me to the reminiscences of Boris Tchaikovsky.

1. An exception would be Schoenberg's famous prefatory remark to his *Harmonielehre*: "This book I have learned from my pupils"; Arnold Schoenberg, *Theory of Harmony*, trans. Roy Carter (London: Faber, 1978), p. 1. Later in his preface, following thoughts on the nature of education in what he regarded as the comfort-obsessed early 1900s, Schoenberg elaborated on his aphorism: "It should be clear, then, that the teacher's first task is to shake up the pupil thoroughly. When the resultant tumult subsides, everything will have presumably found its proper place. Or it will never happen! The activity which in such manner emanates from the teacher comes back again to him. In this sense also I have learned this book from my pupils" (p. 3).

2. A hint at the general influence of Shostakovich's pupils on his own work comes from Veniamin Basner, in Sof'ia Khentova, *V mire Shostakovicha* (Moscow: Kompozitor, 1996), p. 191; more specific instances are pointed out in Khentova, *Shostakovich*, vol. 2 (Leningrad: Sovetskii kompozitor, 1986), pp. 292, 330, 387, 522, 556–57.

3. Sof'ia Khentova, *Shostakovich*, vol. 1 (Leningrad: Sovetskii kompozitor, 1985), pp. 467–82; *Shostakovich*, vol. 2, pp. 381–87. Khentova's 1996 revision of these volumes is hard to come by and contains no substantive revision to her work on Shostakovich as a teacher.

Khentova's interviews with Shostakovich's pupils are in *V mire Shostakovicha*: Levitin, pp. 165–68; Lobkovsky, pp. 168–71; Ustvolskaya, pp. 171–75; Peiko, pp. 175–77; Okunev, pp. 177–78; Nagovitsyn, p. 343; Katsnelson, pp. 343–45; Evlakhov, pp. 345–46; Tishchenko, pp. 354–61.

4. Laurel E. Fay, *Shostakovich: A Life* (New York: Oxford University Press, 2000), pp. 97, 108–9, 226–27.

5. Date of 1947 reregistering is according to Shostakovich's personnel file at the St. Petersburg Conservatory (my thanks to Laurel Fay for this information).

6. In October 1963 Shostakovich himself compiled a list of his composition pupils for possible inclusion in concerts during the Gorky festival devoted to his music the following

February. Here he left out a few of the less significant figures, such as Tolmachev, Tolstoy, Berlinson, and Saliutrinskaia (Bibergan and Nagovitsyn were enrolled after this date), and included several names outside the official roster, such as Sultan Gadzhibekov, Boris Kliuzner, Margarita Kuss, Albert Leman, David Lvov-Kompaneets, Vladimir Maklakov, Mikhail Matveev, and Vartan Tigranian (Khentova, *V mire Shostakovicha*, p. 320). Orest Evlakhov added the names of Boris Golts, T. Oganesian, and Vadim Salmanov to the list of class members, "Klass kompozitsii D. D. Shostakovicha," in *Leningradskaia konservatoriia v vospominaniiakh*, vol. 1, ed. G. G. Tigranov (Leningrad: Muzyka, 1987), p. 172. The majority of these "extras" were officially students of Mikhail Gnesin. Shostakovich's comments on the free interchange of students between his class and that of Gnesin can be found in Shostakovich, "K 50-letiiu G.V. Sviridova," *Sovetskaia muzyka* 12 (1965): 21. This open arrangement presumably accounts for Galina Ustvolskaya's reference to joining a class of thirty students (Khentova, *V mire Shostakovicha*, p. 172). Also not to be confused with Shostakovich's pupils are the various assistant teachers attached to his classes in the prewar and wartime years, including Vasilii Kopansky for instrumentation, Izrail Finkelshtein, and Nikolai Peiko.

7. Evlakhov, "Klass kompozitsii D. D. Shostakovicha," p. 174.

8. Khentova, *V mire Shostakovicha*, p. 165, and, without mention of Levitin, Khentova, *Shostakovich*, vol. 1, p. 467.

9. Elena Silina,"Veniamin Fleishman, uchenik Shostakovicha," in *Shostakovich: mezhdu mgnoveniem i vechnost'iu*, ed. Liudmila Kovnatskaia (St. Petersburg: Kompozitor, 2000), p. 346. For a complete citation of this source, see p. 118 in this same volume.

10. Son of the well-known Soviet writer Aleksei Nikolaevich Tolstoy, Dmitrii was briefly in Shostakovich's orchestration class in 1937, then informally attended his composition class from 1943.

11. Berlinson is a shadowy figure, mentioned by Nikolai Peiko as having moved to Poland. Khentova, *V mire Shostakovicha*, p. 175.

12. According to the recollection of Karen Khachaturian, "Ob uchitele," in *Shostakovichu posviashchaetsia: sbornik statei k 90-letiiu kompozitora (1906–1996)*, ed. Elena Dolinskaia (Moscow: Kompozitor. 1997), p. 167.

13. Saliutrinskaia is another obscure figure, mentioned in Khentova, *V mire Shostakovicha*, p. 175.

14. Fay, *Shostakovich: A Life*, pp. 97, 307 n. 46.

15. According to Georgii Sviridov, Riazanov had been summoned to Moscow to work for the recently established Committee for Artistic Affairs. "Korotko o godakh ucheniia," in *Leningradskaia konservatoriia v vospominaniiakh*, vol. 1, ed. G. G. Tigranov (Leningrad: Muzyka, 1987), p. 170. However, Evlakhov suggests that Riazanov had been called away for teaching duties in Tbilisi ("Klass kompozitsii D. D. Shostakovicha," p. 171).

16. Khentova, *V mire Shostakovicha*, p. 166.

17. Ibid., p. 170.

18. Khentova , *Shostakovich*, vol. 1, p. 476.

19. Ibid., p. 470.

20. Regarding the Mozart symphony, see Evlakhov, "Klass kompozitsii D. D. Shostakovicha," p. 171.

21. Ibid., p. 173.

22. Scheduled for publication as vol. 114 of the *New Collected Works* (Moscow: DSCH Publishers); vol. 115 will contain four-hand arrangements of Honegger's *Symphonie Liturgique* and part of Mahler's Tenth Symphony, which were presumably also made for pedagogic use.

23. Regarding his illness and duet playing, see Nikolai Martynov, "Uroki Shostakovicha; Stunden von Schostakowitsch," in *Internationales Dmitri-Schostakowitsch-Symposion Köln*

1985, ed. Klaus Wolfgang Niemöller (Regensburg: Gustav Bosse, 1986), pp. 87, 97; regarding his listening habits, see Boris Tishchenko, "Etiud k portretu," in *Dmitrii Shostakovich: stat'i i materialy*, ed. Grigorii Shneerson (Moscow: Sovetskii kompozitor, 1976), p. 102.

24. Tishchenko, "Etiud k portretu," pp. 103–4; Martynov, "Uroki Shostakovicha; Stunden von Schostakowitsch," pp. 88, 99.

25. Iurii Levitin, "Uchitel'," in *Dmitrii Shostakovich: stat'i i materialy*, ed. Grigorii Shneerson (Moscow: Sovetskii kompozitor, 1976), p. 83.

26. Regarding Wagner and Verdi, see Dmitrii Tolstoi, *Dlia chego vse eto bylo* (St. Petersburg: Bibliopolis, 1995), p. 147; regarding Stravinsky, see Tishchenko, "Etiud k portretu," p. 103; regarding Stravinsky's coloristic sense, see Evgenii Makarov, *Dnevnik: vospominaniia o moem uchitele D. D. Shostakoviche* (Moscow: Kompozitor, 1998), p. 20.

27. On the "salon-like," see Liudmila Karagicheva, "'Pishete kak mozhno bol'she prekrasnoi muzyki . . . ': iz pisem D. D. Shostakovicha K. A. Karaevu," *Muzykal'naia akademiia* 4(1997): 204; on Rachmaninoff, see Tishchenko, "Etiud k portretu," p. 102.

28. Makarov, *Dnevnik: vospominaniia o moem uchitele D. D. Shostakoviche*, pp. 30–32.

29. Tolstoi, *Dlia chego vse eto bylo*, pp. 103–6.

30. On laconic remarks: Khentova, *V mire Shostakovicha*, pp. 170, 179; on intonation: Makarov, *Dnevnik: vospominaniia o moem uchitele D. D. Shostakoviche*, p. 17.

31. Comments on manuscript paper: Vladislav Uspenskii, "Pis'ma uchitelia," in *Shostakovich: mezhdu mgnoveniem i vechnost'iu*, ed. Liudmila Kovnatskaia (St. Petersburg: Kompozitor, 2000), p. 511; on having a cigarette: Levitin, "Uchitel'," pp. 84–85.

32. Kara Karaev, "D. D. Shostakovichu—60!," *Sovetskaia muzyka* 9 (1966): 10.

33. Uspenskii, "Pis'ma uchitelia," p. 512.

34. Karaev, "D. D. Shostakovichu—60!," p. 10.

35. Tolstoi, *Dlia chego vse eto bylo*, p. 145.

36. Makarov, *Dnevnik: vospominaniia o moem uchitele D. D. Shostakoviche*, pp. 6–7, 11; Tolstoi, *Dlia chego vse eto bylo*, p. 145.

37. Evlakhov, "Klass kompozitsii D. D. Shostakovicha," pp. 172–73; Levitin "Uchitel'," p. 83; Aleksandr Livshits, *Zhizn' za rodinu svoiu: ocherki o kompozitorakh i muzykovedakh pogibshikh v Velikuiu Otechestvennuiu voinu* [on Fleishman] (Moscow: Muzyka, 1964), p. 299.

38. Karaev, "D. D. Shostakovichu—60!," p. 10.

39. On Tchaikovsky as source: Evlakhov, "Klass kompozitsii D. D. Shostakovicha," p. 174; Tchaikovsky's music as disappointing: Tolstoi, *Dlia chego vse eto bylo*, p. 147; on writer's block: Makarov, *Dnevnik: vospominaniia o moem uchitele D. D. Shostakoviche*, p. 10.

40. Khentova, *V mire Shostakovicha*, p. 168.

41. Ibid., p. 345.

42. On helping Fleishman: Silina, "Veniamin Fleishman, uchenik Shostakovicha," p. 363; Nikolai Martynov's account of Shostakovich's protection in "Pis'ma Shostakovicha: Stranitsy iz zapisnoi knizhki," in *D. D. Shostakovich: sbornik statei k 90-letiiu so dnia rozhdeniia*, ed. Liudmila Kovnatskaia (St. Petersburg: Kompozitor, 1996), p. 292.

43. Silina, "Veniamin Fleishman, uchenik Shostakovicha," p. 384.

44. Shostakovich, "K 50-letiiu G.V. Sviridova," pp. 20–21; "Vospitannik konservatorii," in *German Galynin*, ed. A. Ortenberg (Moscow: Sovetskii kompozitor, 1979) (orig. pub. in *Sovetskoe isskustvo*, 1 January 1948), pp. 207–10.

45. Khentova, *V mire Shostakovicha*, p. 168.

46. On scholarships, see Khentova, *Shostakovich*, vol. 1, p. 478; on Boldyrev, see Silina "Veniamin Fleishman, uchenik Shostakovicha," p. 372.

47. On 1957 concert: Karagicheva, "'Pishete kak mozhno bol'she prekrasnoi muzyki . . . , '" p. 209; on 1964 Gorky event: Uspenskii, "Pis'ma uchitelia," p. 524.

48. Khentova, *Shostakovich*, vol. 1, pp. 478–80.

49. Ibid., p. 478.

50. Khentova, *V mire Shostakovicha*, pp. 180, 183; Tolstoi, *Dlia chego vse eto bylo*, pp. 145–46.

51. Silina, "Veniamin Fleishman, uchenik Shostakovicha," pp. 371, 381–82.

52. Khentova, *Shostakovich*, vol. 2, p. 552.

53. I am grateful to Laurel Fay for this reference.

54. Mikhail Gasparov, *Zapisi i vypiski* (Moscow: Novoe literaturnoe obozrenie, 2000), p. 303.

55. *Shostakovich in Context*, ed. Rosamund Bartlett (Oxford, Eng.: Oxford University Press, 2000); Fay, *Shostakovich: A Life*, p. 163.

56. Khentova, *V mire Shostakovicha*, p. 166; Genadii Belov, "Zagadochnyi Shostakovich," *Muzykal'naia akademiia* 4 (1997): 225.

57. Tolstoi, *Dlia chego vse eto bylo*, p. 146.

58. Elizabeth Wilson, *Shostakovich: A Life Remembered* (London: Faber, 1994), p. 190.

59. Ibid., p. 302.

60. Silina, "Veniamin Fleishman, uchenik Shostakovicha," pp. 407–8; also numerous citations in *Dmitri Schostakowitsch und das jüdische musikalische Erbe*, ed. Ernst Kuhn, Andreas Wehrmeyer, and Günter Wolter, (Berlin: Verlag Ernst Kuhn, 2001).

61. Khentova, *Udivitel'nii Shostakovich* (Leningrad: Variant, 1993), pp. 153, 155, 161.

62. Olga Gladkova, *Galina Ustvol'skaia* (St. Petersburg: Muzyka, 1999) pp. 39–53.

63. Khentova, *V mire Shostakovicha*, p. 175.

64. The DSCH motif is a musical representation of the composer's initials—the Cyrillic letters ДШ—in their German transliteration D-SCH (the German spelling of his surname being Schostakowitsch). In German, S by convention stands for "Es," or E♭, and H is the English B♮. Hence the notes of the signature-motif: D-E♭-C-B. Arkadii Klimovitskii, "Eshche raz o teme-monogramme *D-Es-C-H*," in *D. D. Shostakovich: sbornik statei k 90-letiiu so dnia rozhdeniia*, ed. Liudmila Kovnatskaia (St. Petersburg: Kompozitor, 1996), p. 265.

65. For a recent overview of musicological debates in this area see Nicholas Cook, "Theorizing Musical Meaning," *Music Theory Spectrum* 23 (2001): 170–95.

66. See Nelly Kravetz, "A New Insight into the Tenth Symphony of Dmitry Shostakovich," in *Shostakovich in Context*, p. 161.

67.The text with which the Ustvolskaya theme appears is a famous real-life exchange between Michelangelo and his admirer Giovanni di Carlo Strozzi. Contemplating Michelangelo's *Night*—the sculpture of a reclining female nude—Strozzi writes:

So this is Night, so peacefully sleeping
before us, the creation of an angel.
She is of stone, but there is breath in her.
Just wake her and she will speak.

And Michelangelo replies,

Sleep is sweet for me, but more so to be of stone,
when all around is shame and crime:
not to feel, not to see, is a relief.
So be silent, my friend, why wake me?

Concerning Shostakovich's use of the Ustvolskaya theme in his setting of these words, a range of possible symbolic meanings opens up, including her "stoniness" and her (admired?) withdrawal from society.

68. Silina, "Veniamin Fleishman, uchenik Shostakovicha," p. 403.

69. Makarov, *Dnevnik: vospominaniia o moem uchitele D. D. Shostakoviche*, p. 36.

70. Shostakovich, "Vospitannik konservatorii," p. 208.

71. Ibid., p. 210.

72. Of course it was by no means only Shostakovich's pupils who supplied him with his favorite motives. Quite apart from his routine drawing on the stock of European

mainstream musical literature, he received two such motives from his richly talented near-contemporary Gavriil Popov. From the finale of Popov's First Symphony comes the coda motif of Shostakovich's Fifth and from his Suite for Two Pianos comes the main first movement motif of the Tenth Symphony.

73. Khentova, *Shostakovich,* vol. 2, p. 330.

74. For Denisov's report of Shostakovich's contempt for this piece and his distress at Sviridov's betrayal of his own talent by writing "for the licensed officials," see Wilson, *Shostakovich: A Life Remembered,* p. 302.

75. Khentova, *V mire Shostakovicha,* p. 174.

76. Tishchenko, "Etiud k portretu," p. 102.

77. Karagicheva, "'Pishete kak mozhno bol'she prekrasnoi muzyki . . . ,'" p. 206.

78. That the issue of Soviet twelve-tone music was still contentious as late as 1966 may be judged from the report of the Theoretical Conference, Composers' Union Plenum, December 1965, in *Sovetskaia muzyka* 5 (1966): 22–33; *Sovetskaia muzyka* 6 (1966): 23–31.

79. While acknowledging the suggestiveness of the quotations, the composer himself called the work "obviously non-programmatic." K. T. Korganov, *Boris Chaikovskii: lichnost' i tvorchestvo* (Moscow: Kompozitor, 2001), p. 66.

80. The obvious, but surely far too glib, explanation in the case of Shostakovich's finale is a direct invoking of Siegfried's Funeral Music from *Götterdämmerung* (not, *pace* many commentators, the "Todesverkündigung" from *Die Walküre*) to express his own sense of impending death.

81. Khentova, *Shostakovich,* vol. 2, p. 522.

82. "He may have been inspired to write a cycle consisting only of slow movements by the third quartet of his pupil Boris Tchaikovsky, likewise made up of slow movements alone." Dorothea Redepenning, "The Shostakovich String Quartets," booklet essay to CD recordings by the Brodsky Quartet, Teldec 9031-717-2 (1992).

83. Korganov, *Boris Chaikovskii,* p. 67.

84. Boris Tishchenko, *Pis'ma Dmitriia Dmitrievicha Shostakovicha Borisu Tishchenko* (St. Petersburg: Kompozitor, 1997), pp. 21, 34–35.

85. On engagement with Tsvetaeva's poetry, see Fay, *Shostakovich: A Life,* p. 277.

86. Regarding 1945: Makarov, *Dnevnik: vospominaniia o moem uchitele D. D. Shostakoviche,* p. 29; regarding 1955: Karagicheva, "'Pishete kak mozhno bol'she prekrasnoi muzyki . . . ,'" p. 208; regarding 1967: Belov, "Zagadochnyi Shostakovich," p. 224.

Shostakovich's "Twelve-Tone" Compositions and the Politics and Practice of Soviet Serialism

Peter J. Schmelz

Throughout the 1950s and well into the 1960s, Shostakovich's public pronouncements on twelve-tone music were predictably and doggedly negative, wholly in keeping with the official Soviet line on dodecaphony. Such was the case with the comments he made to a Polish journalist after attending the Warsaw Autumn Festival in September 1959 as a member of the Soviet delegation.[1] While it is unclear which concerts Shostakovich attended, he certainly presided over the several performances of his own compositions on the program: his First Piano Concerto was performed at the opening concert of the 1959 Festival on 12 September, and his Fifth and Sixth Quartets were performed by the Beethoven Quartet at the penultimate concert on 19 September. The Festival also included the Polish premieres of Boulez's Second Piano Sonata and Sonatine, Berio's *Sequenza I*, Xenakis's *Diamorphoses*, Penderecki's *Strofy*, Nono's *Composizione per orchestra no. 1*, Webern's op. 6 and op. 21, and Stravinsky's Symphony in Three Movements, among other compositions. Reacting to these works by most of the leading Darmstadt figures[2] as well as those by younger Polish composers like Penderecki and Lutosławski, he declared, "Dodecaphony not only has no future, it doesn't even have a present. It is just a 'fad' that is already passing."[3] Later attacks on twelve-tone music that Shostakovich made in the 1960s included the following gem: "Dodecaphony, serial, pointillist and other kinds of music are one of the greatest evils of twentieth-century music . . . [They] came into existence fifty years ago and yet I cannot name *a single* work in this vein which lives and has an influence on the public to this day."[4] Such negative Soviet reactions to the twelve-tone system were hardly unusual in the late 1950s and early 1960s, the height of the Khrushchev Thaw, for this was just the time that dodecaphony was beginning to infiltrate the USSR. Shostakovich may have been reacting to the experiments of the European and Polish avant-gardists, but his words (whether actually his or those of his ghostwriters) were targeted at a far different constituency: the small group of young Soviet composers just beginning to experiment with twelve-tone music.

By the Warsaw Autumn Festival of September 1965, these young composers were beginning to rise to prominence. The festival again featured a number of Shostakovich's own works (though he himself was not in attendance), and the rest of the program that year included a typically mixed bag of Eastern and Western European composers, among them the Darmstadt figures that had been so evident at the 1959 festival.[5] This time, however, alongside the compositions of Lutosławski, Górecki, Ligeti, and Stockhausen, the festival also offered important performances of two seminal works by young Soviet composers, including the world premiere of Alfred Schnittke's integrally serial *Music for Piano and Chamber Orchestra* (1964), and the first Polish performance of the Estonian Arvo Pärt's serial *Perpetuum Mobile* for full orchestra (1963).[6]

As these two compositions demonstrated, between the Warsaw Autumn Festivals of 1959 and 1965 much had changed in Soviet music, most noticeably in the music of its younger generation. Though these works, and especially Schnittke's intricately constructed opus, were in some ways the limit points of Soviet serialism, they were by no means the only examples of Soviet dodecaphony. During the 1950s and early 1960s the young Soviets slowly gained access to previously forbidden scores by composers from Schoenberg and Webern to Krenek and Boulez. They also heard new music from visiting foreigners as diverse as Glenn Gould, Igor Stravinsky, and Luigi Nono.[7] Andrei Volkonsky (b. 1933) had been the first of the "young composers," as they were labeled in official publications, to apply twelve-tone techniques, doing so in a 1956 piano composition with the loaded title of *Musica Stricta*. Volkonsky was also the first to be rebuked for doing so. Yet the other young Soviets, including Pärt, Schnittke, Edison Denisov, and Nikolai Karetnikov among others, were not far behind. They consistently explored serialism well into the 1960s. Many strictly applied twelve-tone techniques, and several serialized multiple parameters within their compositions, as Schnittke did in both his *Music for Piano and Chamber Orchestra* and his other 1964 composition, *Music for Chamber Orchestra*.

As pianist Mariia Yudina's important 1961 Moscow and Leningrad premieres of Volkonsky's *Musica Stricta* had demonstrated, performances of the young composers' twelve-tone compositions became a form of resistance for the small Soviet audiences that were able to hear them in small, out-of-the-way locations.[8] These concerts took place in private apartments or smaller official venues like the Small Hall at the Moscow Conservatory.

Some even occurred at very official venues where those in charge chose to look the other way, as was the case with the concert series at high-powered scientific research facilities like Moscow's Kurchatov Institute and FIAN—the Physics Institute of the Academy of Sciences.[9] This "unofficial" concert subculture grew in size and importance as the decade progressed, allied in many cases with the unofficial art culture that had also developed in the Soviet Union around painters like those in the Lianozovo group, among many others. It was this subversive societal threat associated with and represented by twelve-tone techniques, still only an ominous possibility in 1959, that in large part inspired the heated rhetoric against dodecaphony by Soviet officials, of which Shostakovich's statements were but a small, relatively restrained example.

During his momentous 1962 return visit to Russia, Igor Stravinsky made a prophecy about twelve-tone music to Tikhon Khrennikov, the head of the USSR Union of Composers: "You, too, Tikhon Nikolayich, will be trying it soon."[10] And, as we shall see, in a decade this Cassandra-like utterance would come true. But little could Stravinsky have predicted how pervasive twelve-tone music would eventually become in the Soviet Union. By the mid-1960s it had filtered to nearly all levels of Soviet musical life, official and unofficial alike. Shostakovich's very personal adoption of the technique in the late 1960s was but the tip of the iceberg.

While not of the epochal significance of Stravinsky's earlier apparent about-face, Shostakovich's application of twelve-tone rows in his late works reflects important Soviet musical trends of the late 1960s and early 1970s. Shostakovich's "twelve-tone" writing has been rarely discussed, and it has never been positioned against its proper backdrop: the broader Soviet engagement with twelve-tone music in the second half of the 1960s.[11] While in a strict sense Shostakovich's twelve-tone music is only just that, it also bears close resemblance to other Soviet twelve-tone compositions from the period, most notably that of the young composers he was hectoring in his 1959 statements. This essay will explore the worlds of official and unofficial Soviet dodecaphony in the 1960s, both of which informed the composition and interpretation of Shostakovich's later music. An examination of Shostakovich's twelve-tone scores and representative Soviet twelve-tone works, together with a discussion of the official Soviet debates regarding twelve-tone music that led to its begrudged acceptance at the end of the decade, will provide a fuller understanding of Shostakovich's own "twelve-tone" compositions.

Shostakovich first applied twelve-tone rows in two compositions from 1967: Seven Verses of Aleksandr Blok, op. 127, and the Second Violin Concerto, op. 129 (see Table 1 at end of chapter).[12] In the Blok Songs, written for cellist Mstislav Rostropovich and his wife, soprano Galina Vishnevskaya, the twelve-tone rows appear only in the aptly titled sixth movement, "Mysterious Signs" (*Tainye znaki*). The unclear harmonic language of the work reflects the apocalyptic text of the poem, which presents images that are part nocturnal hallucination, part ecstatic vision ("gold and red poppies," "sky-blue chimeras," and the "golden braid of a maiden") that culminate in an omen: "My preordained end is near/And war, and fire—are ahead."[13] The song begins with a twelve-tone row in the solo cello that ends on F♯ before leaping to B and then hovering around and alternating between these two pitches. The cello opening prepares the first vocal entrance in the soprano (F♯-B-F♯) while also introducing F♯ as a key pitch for the remainder of the highly chromatic, tonally unstable composition (a position it shares with G♯; see Example 1a).

Later iterations of the row (e.g., measure 24 in the violin, and, near the ending, in canon between the cello and violin; Example 1b), are always at the same transposition level; the "row" retains its identity as a

Example 1a. Shostakovich, Seven Verses of A. Blok, no. 6, "Mysterious Signs," mm. 1–9.

Example 1b. Shostakovich, Seven Verses of A. Blok, no. 6, "Mysterious Signs," m. 82 to end.

single, unchanging melodic figure, not at all consistent with "traditional" Schoenbergian twelve-tone writing (and only rarely would Shostakovich use his rows harmonically).[14] This song presents one aspect of Shostakovich's use of twelve-tone rows: as a catalyst of harmonic instability and atonality.

In the third movement of the Second Violin Concerto Shostakovich distilled this idea—twelve-tone rows as a means for the creation of harmonic ambiguity—into a twelve-tone row that in and of itself became a condensed representative of harmonic instability or atonality. In the concerto, he employed brief twelve-tone sequences to create a hazy opening from which the clarity of the main movement only slowly emerges. Twelve-tone rows were no longer the agents of extended atonal sections, but lone signifiers of atonality that needed to be, and were, quickly "resolved." In the concerto the beginning is "exactly like a temporary fogging over with the goal of a succeeding clarification," as Soviet critic Daniel Zhitomirsky wrote in 1976 of the later Twelfth String Quartet.[15] The concerto's third movement begins with two nearly identical twelve-tone sequences, both of which trace a step-wise ascending figure starting on A♮ (after an initial held A♭) before each leaps off course (Example 2). These ambiguous melodic lines introduce the antiphonal minor seconds

Example 2. Shostakovich, Violin Concerto no. 2, third movement, mm. 1–14.

that echo back and forth between the violinist and the horns at rehearsal number 67, and which eventually lead into a typical Shostakovich scherzo finale ending in D-flat major.

Subsequent works would continue this practice of clearly resolving a single twelve-note row (or a short succession of rows) into more tonally stable material, but others of Shostakovich's later compositions created lengthier, more intricate twelve-tone passages. In his 1968 Violin Sonata, Shostakovich again used multiple rows in conjunction with wandering chromatic melodies to create an effect of long-term shifting instability, only occasionally landing on semi-stable ground. This is most evident at the beginning of the first movement, where a sequence of two rows is repeated in the piano, above which the violin enters with a chromatic melody typical of Shostakovich's late style. While harmonic centers emerge later in the movement—especially D, G, and E—the overall effect is one of an unstable, extended chromaticism, of which the twelve-tone rows are an integral component. But it was in other late works like the Twelfth String Quartet and the Fourteenth Symphony that Shostakovich most extensively used his twelve-note rows to blur the line between tonality and atonality, as he had first done in the Blok songs.

At first, the Twelfth Quartet appears to herald back to his earliest attempts, announcing its intentions up front with an enigmatic, wandering row, stated initially in the solo cello as in the earlier Blok song. The quartet flounders in a brief blurred world before landing on D♭ (Example 3a).

Yet the number of rows in this quartet becomes much more extensive, as twelve-tone sequences appear throughout the first and second movements. In the first movement they usually appear at moments of transition (as at 1 measure before rehearsal number 4, or at rehearsal number 8—a permutation of the opening cello row—at rehearsal number 10, and at 1 measure before rehearsal number 12), a function similar to that used at the opening of the work (Example 3b).[16] As Laurel Fay has noted, there are points of intervallic similarity between the many rows throughout the quartet, but these are the result of motivic transformations, not traditional dodecaphonic manipulations.[17] Certain rows recur verbatim at structurally significant points, like the opening cello row which comes back near the end of the first movement (rehearsal number 16). There are also instances of row transposition, as in the viola row at rehearsal number 8, which is heard again a half-step lower at rehearsal number 10. But no retrogrades or inversions appear. Instead, all are distinct rows, with distant family resemblances.[18]

In the second movement of the Twelfth Quartet the function of the rows shifts as the line between tonal and "twelve-tone" becomes blurred.

Example 3a. Shostakovich, String Quartet no. 12, first movement, mm. 1–4.

As in the Blok song and the violin sonata, the rows become crucial to creating harmonically unstable sections. Soviet musicologist Viktor Bobrovsky (1906–79) called the beginning section of the quartet's second movement (from rehearsal number 17 to rehearsal number 42) "atonal."[19] And while one might quibble with his interpretation of the work's formal divisions, the label of "atonal" best describes the ambiguous harmonic language that results from the juxtaposing and superpositioning of twelve-tone rows with the more familiar rhetoric of Shostakovich's late style and its wandering, chromatic counterpoint.[20] For example, note the section from rehearsal number 33–34, where the three bottom voices imitatively treat the same row, starting on different pitches, but the resulting layered repetition of each line creates a cacophonic wash of chromaticism above which sound the passing, aching dissonances of the first violin's double-stops (Example 4).

Example 3b. Rows in Shostakovich, String Quartet no. 12, first movement: 1 m. before rehearsal number 4; rehearsal number 8; rehearsal number 10; 1 m. before rehearsal number 12.

This in turn flows into a reprise of the movement's trilled twelve-tone opening at rehearsal number 34. In the Twelfth Quartet, twelve-tone rows had become a more integral aspect of Shostakovich's vocabulary, both as a clear, condensed opposition to tonal writing and, in an expanded sense, as a means for fleshing out lengthier, highly chromatic sections.[21]

The Fourteenth Symphony has points of twelve-tone use as extensive as any in the Twelfth Quartet.[22] Near the end of its third movement, "Lorelei," to a poem by Guillaume Apollinaire, Shostakovich used layers of successively changing twelve-tone rows to create a wash of sound, more akin to the noise experiments of the Polish avant-garde, termed *sonorika* by the Soviets, than to anything twelve-tone (Example 5, pp. 314–16).[23] (This is not unlike the layers of generally chromatic twelve-tone rows at rehearsal number 33 in the second movement of the Twelfth Quartet.)

The seventh movement, "In the Santé Jail," also to an Apollinaire text, contains examples of this practice as well. Here a twelve-tone canon from rehearsal number 91–97 consisting of eight successive twelve-tone rows, each different though clearly derived from the previous rows (especially in their emphases on B♭), is stated successively in the bass (P-0, the untransposed prime form), cello (P-7, the prime form transposed up seven half

Example 4. Shostakovich, String Quartet no. 12, first movement, rehearsal number 33–34.

Example 4 continued

steps), viola (P-6, up six half steps, etc.), violin 1–2 (P-5), and violin 1 (P-1), creating "pure serial dodecaphony" as Bobrovsky called it (Example 6, pp. 317–18).[24] The polyphony that results sounds, as we will see, like many of the other twelve-tone fugues that characterized the music of the young generation of Soviet composers from Volkonsky's *Musica Stricta* to Arvo Pärt's First Symphony.

Shostakovich's taut, strained Thirteenth Quartet (1970) continued to employ sections of "twelve-toneness" (as later Russian theorists would term this phenomenon). At the beginning of the quartet a lone row in the solo viola slides into the full ensemble's intonation of a mournful passage in D-flat (a previously unidentified quotation of no. 67, "Lament" [*Plach'*] from Shostakovich's 1970 film music to Kozintsev's *King Lear*, op. 134). At other moments, the rows contribute to a suspension of tonality, as in the section starting at rehearsal number 10 that reaches its climax in the strained chromatic chords between rehearsal numbers 17 and 18 and the very "twelve-tonish" pointillistic transition that follows at rehearsal number 19 (Example 7, pp. 319–20).

These moments of "twelve-toneness" even spill over into the few points of tonality in the quartet, both in the central *danse macabre,* where the cello provides a twelve-tone ostinato support to the general B-flat minor of the upper strings; and in the final pages, where as Fay aptly notes, instead of resolving into the quartet's key of B-flat minor, the viola actually obscures the harmony of the conclusion.[25]

On the other hand, in the second movement, "Serenade," of the Fifteenth String Quartet (1974), the rows present isolated moments of dissonance that shatter the overall calm. In a similar fashion, the brief introductory twelve-tone rows in the voice and piano at the start of the first of

Example 5. Shostakovich, Symphony no. 14, third movement, "Lorelei," 3 mm. before rehearsal number 46 to end (example continues onto pp. 315–16).

Shostakovich's Six Verses to Texts of Marina Tsvetaeva (1973) mark a return to the practice of the openings to both the Blok songs and the Twelfth Quartet. In the Fifteenth Symphony, isolated rows in the solo cello and violin provide moments of sparse, ruminative monologue that link the brass chorales in the second movement's introduction. In the symphony's third movement the initial melody is also based on twelve-tone rows. In these later works, the rows provide only brief departures from the tonality or quasi-tonality of the rest of the composition in which they appear. Shostakovich no longer used his rows as extensively as he had in the Twelfth Quartet or the Fourteenth Symphony.

Example 5 continued

The earliest Soviet analyses of Shostakovich's twelve-tone rows were mainly descriptive and tended to downplay their importance, or rather emphasized their dependence on the overall tonality of the works in question. Typical is the following passage from a 1968 essay by Bobrovsky, one of the Twelfth Quartet's first Russian reviewers:

Themes and melodic formulas at times even appear as their own type of twelve-tone rows. However, the composer either takes them to a clear tonic, or, the opposite, begins from them, moving further to a mid-tonal instability (as also usually happened in the classics of the previous [nineteenth] century). . . . It is as if the melody goes around the periphery of the tonal center, exciting all its functional reserves, and in the end this tonality is outlined sufficiently clearly.[26]

Example 5 continued

Bobrovsky went further in a later article and, in typical Soviet fashion, interpreted the programmatic significance of the opposition in the quartet: "A staging of the most difficult, one would think, insoluble problems (atonality) and their complete resolution, connected with the highest spiritual joy of understanding (tonality)."[27]

A similar review of Shostakovich's late style by musicologist Daniel Zhitomirsky appeared in the September 1976 *Sovetskaia muzyka*. It simultaneously defended Shostakovich's twelve-tone usage while attacking twelve-tone composition in general and the postwar Darmstadt avant-garde in particular.[28] Like Bobrovsky, Zhitomirsky emphasized the "indissoluble connection between the tonal and atonal moments in Shostakovich's music," and the fact that his twelve-tone themes

Example 6. Shostakovich, Symphony no. 14, seventh movement, "In the Santé Jail," rehearsal number 91 to 2 mm. after number 93.

Example 6 continued

create the optimal conditions for the expulsion (*vytesneniia*) of a tonal center. It is not difficult to notice, however, that in Shostakovich those conditions do not always lead directly to such a result. In the majority of cases they only aid the creation of a highly strained "strong pole." The tonal beginning in them, as is correct, does not vanish, although frequently it is as if already hanging by a thread.[29]

According to the sympathetic Zhitomirsky, Shostakovich only used twelve-tone devices for specific emotional effects; his twelve-tone themes were but an example of "melodic intensity" of a type that had existed in music since the nineteenth century.[30]

Early critics in the West were more perplexed by Shostakovich's new vocabulary and played up its twelve-tone aspects, if only to accuse him of lagging behind the times. As critic Hans Keller summarized: "The incomprehension the Shostakovich quartet has encountered—in the guise, needless to add, of knowledgeable rejection—is the opposite [to that of contemporary rejections of Beethoven's *Grosse Fuge*]: why does he do so many outdated things? What's worse, why does he do things which perhaps were never legitimate in the first place?"[31] Despite Keller's obsession with arguing that the Twelfth Quartet is modeled on Schoenberg's First Chamber Symphony, he actually formulated a compelling, albeit lengthy, description of the twelve-tone rows' function in the composition:

Example 7. Shostakovich, String Quartet no. 13, 3 mm. before rehearsal number 18 to number 20.

Example 7 continued

What Shostakovich is interested in fundamentally is the motivic role of both a tone-row and its segments; any other aspects of dodecaphony he simply disregards. . . . By placing his twelve-tone rows . . . within a pronouncedly tonal context, Shostakovich lends them a novel function. Not only is their motivic significance thrown into relief, but the manifold interrelations between them emerge with crystalline clarity—which is really why he can afford to use a whole bunch of them: they inevitably impress themselves intensely upon the aural attention whenever they occur. Paradoxically, moreover, Shostakovich thus succeeds in turning the abstract concept of "the twelve-tone row" itself (any twelve-tone row as distinct from a specific one) into a concrete musical thought: when, in such a tonal context, where melodies and phrases and motives are, in essence, triadically determined, you suddenly hear a twelve-tone row, and then again another, not only do you immediately recognize each as a row of twelve notes, but you identify the two as belonging to the same expressive area, having the same, or similar structural functions—acting as each other's deputies, as it were, within a well-defined edifice of contrasting (diatonic and dodecaphonic) styles where, once there is dodecaphony, not only can all twelve notes be equal, but all twelve-tone rows are too![32]

In this breathless description, Keller reacted to the same basic opposition between tonality and atonality as Bobrovsky and Zhitomirsky, emphasizing the general tonal context even as he focused on the interdependence of the twelve-tone rows. Yet neither Zhitomirsky nor Keller mentioned the extended stretches of atonality that Bobrovsky comfortably acknowledged in his later survey of Shostakovich's 1960s works (published in two halves from 1973 to 1975).[33] Shostakovich's late language was not always as "pronouncedly tonal" as Keller would have it.[34]

A more valuable perspective on the compositional language of Shostakovich's later works and specifically on the Twelfth Quartet—arguably the most extensive of his twelve-tone compositions—existed, but Bobrovsky, Zhitomirsky, and Keller missed it. Many techniques bearing a close resemblance to Shostakovich's later rows were audible at the 1965 Warsaw Autumn Festival, and they were not the Darmstadt compositions that Zhitomirsky inveighed against. In addition to the undeniable impact of the Polish school, those very composers Shostakovich was ostensibly condemning in 1959, the influences on the Twelfth Quartet and Shostakovich's other "twelve-tone" compositions lay closer to home and came from two sides: official and unofficial.[35]

It is common to discuss the influence of Shostakovich on the succeeding generations of Russian composers, including his students Kara Karaev, Karen Khachaturian, and Georgii Sviridov, as well as members of the younger generation like Mikhail Marutaev, Aleksei Nikolaev, Schnittke, Denisov, and Sofia Gubaidulina. On my trips to Moscow in the late 1990s, nearly every one of my informants emphasized their debt to Shostakovich. Shostakovich corresponded with Denisov and gave him advice when he was unsuccessful in his first application to the Moscow Conservatory.[36] And Gubaidulina remarked, in an oft-cited statement, that Shostakovich encouraged her to "continue on her own 'incorrect' path."[37] While Shostakovich's influence on the younger composers is assumed, what needs to be considered is the possible influence that the younger generation had on Shostakovich, particularly with regard to his late and idiosyncratic adoption of twelve-tone techniques. The compositions of the younger generation, in at least this regard, offer a revealing vantage point on this aspect of Shostakovich's late style.

By the mid-1960s, despite the best intentions of the Soviet authorities, twelve-tone music seemingly appeared everywhere. Young composer Edison Denisov discussed the pervasiveness of dodecaphonic music in his 1965 lecture, "For Objectivity and Justice in the Judging of Contemporary Music."[38] This lecture addressed many of the broader concerns listed by Denisov in an earlier essay (written in 1962, published in 1969), "Dodecaphony and the Problems of Contemporary Compositional Techniques,"[39] but focused more polemically on the "catastrophic break between the actual situation of the musical world and that fictitious picture which is often drawn by our musical critics."[40] Without dwelling on the same technical issues that he had in the lengthier article, Denisov blasted the inaccuracies and one-sidedness of the arguments that had surrounded all discussions of twelve-tone music in the Soviet Union: "Perhaps no other technical idea has been entangled in such a stream of verbal garbage as that technique."[41] He also noted that the campaign of misinformation launched by the cultural establishment had only succeeded in increasing the interest of Soviet musicians and composers in dodecaphony.[42] After all, as he asserted, twelve-tone techniques allowed for a wide range of expressive possibilities. By way of example he proudly cited the large number of Soviet composers who had tried using twelve-tone techniques by 1965:

> In the Soviet Union in the last years serial techniques found application in the music of composers of such varied individuality as: A. Volkonsky, V. Salmanov, A. Pärt, R. Shchedrin, S. Slonimsky, Kara Karaev, B. Tishchenko, V. Geviksman, N. Peiko, N. Karetnikov, K. Sink, A. Babadzhanian, A. Schnittke, J. Rääts, S. Gubaidulina, R. Grinblat, M. Meerovich, L. Grabovsky [Hrabovsky], N. Mamisashvili and many others.[43]

Several of the more obscure names (Geviksman, Meerovich) may have been added as padding, but it is undeniable that by the middle of the 1960s, dodecaphonic techniques had filtered into the more official levels of Soviet composition. Denisov drew particular attention to Armenian composer Arno Babadzhanian, both in his 1962/69 article and in this lecture, where he claimed that his was the first dodecaphonic work by a Soviet composer to be recorded and released.[44] These pieces were the *Six Pictures* (1965), where the second movement "Folk" (*Narodnaia*) employs rudimentary twelve-tone techniques as do the "Intermezzo" (movement 4), the "Chorale" (movement 5), and the final movement, "Sasunsky Dance" (*Sasunskii tanets*).[45]

More important, Denisov called attention to the double standard that affected official pronouncements on twelve-tone music, quoting an earlier comment that theorist Lev Mazel made before the Moscow Branch of the Union of Composers: "When Schnittke or Volkonsky use this technique it is called 'Dodecaphony' and calls forth severe criticism, but when anyone from the Secretariat [of the Union of Composers] uses it, it is called 'new materials' and welcomed with all the official stamps of approval."[46] This increasingly apparent double standard was one of the major transformations of Soviet music of the mid-1960s. Just as some of the young unofficial composers became more frequently chastised and censured, their official brethren, including Shchedrin, Peiko, Salmanov, Karaev, Babadzhanian (all composers named by Denisov in his list), and, of course, Shostakovich, began to use the very same techniques while suffering fewer repercussions. Yet Shostakovich's own usage resembled not the more official composers but that of the younger unofficial Soviets, especially Andrei Volkonsky, Arvo Pärt, and Alfred Schnittke. In fact, the more official composers, like Salmanov and Karaev, would actually go further than Shostakovich in their application of twelve-tone devices.

As always in the Soviet Union the boundary between official and unofficial remained fluid and variable, depending not only on the position of the individual employing the techniques but also on the context in which they were heard. The unofficial composers were not only younger, but politically and musically set apart from other Soviet composers. "Unofficial" is not only a generational distinction, but a political, social, and stylistic one. The unofficial composers were performed in different venues, often outside or at the margins of the official system, and their adoption of the taboo, and hence attractive, sounds of twelve-tone music drew a different, self-consciously rebellious, audience. Yet because of the close interaction and interrelationship of the official and unofficial Soviet musical worlds, both unofficial and official twelve-tone compositions contributed to the composition and reception of Shostakovich's own twelve-tone works. We begin with those by the first "unofficial" composer, Andrei Volkonsky, whose works help introduce the uneasy ambiguities of the theory and practice of Soviet dodecaphony.

In his first twelve-tone compositions, Andrei Volkonsky applied an idea of twelve-tone music drawn from his personal study and interpretation of Schoenberg and Webern, resulting in a curious and novel blend of intuition and orthodoxy. Volkonsky's twelve-tone usage in *Musica Stricta,* while literal and thorough, also demonstrated the liberties and idiosyncrasies with which many of the young unofficial composers initially treated twelve-tone composition. Shostakovich knew of Volkonsky and might have heard or seen a score of *Musica Stricta* either by way of Yudina or through other channels afforded by his official position.[47] Whether or not it directly influenced him, in many passages *Musica Stricta* shows an approach to composing with twelve tones similar to Shostakovich's. Such a moment occurs between mm. 19 and 23 in the first movement of *Musica Stricta,* where the clear unfolding of the four pitch *grundgestalt,* reminiscent of Schoenberg's technique in his early atonal piano pieces, is interrupted by a profusion of different twelve-tone rows. This "twelve-toneness" provides a contrasting

Example 8. Volkonsky, *Musica Stricta*, movement 1, mm. 19–23.

middle section to the work before it returns to permutations of the original tetrachord (Example 8). A similar multiplicity of twelve-tone rows occurs
in the second movement's fugue, in which the episodes are marked by
three rows, while the fugue subject and countersubject each have their
own, different rows (Example 9).

While most analysts might have a difficult time categorizing the profusion of twelve-tone rows at these moments in Volkonsky's score, there
is a Russian term for the phenomenon. This term is the "technique of
rows" (*tekhnika riadov*), following the lead of Russian theorist Iurii Kholopov,
who penned the articles on "dodecaphony," "serial music," and "row" in

the *Musical Encyclopedic Dictionary* in the 1970s and 1980s and was one of the most well-versed Russian theoreticians of twelve-tone music. Kholopov was one of the first to actually theorize twelve-tone music instead of only describing it as earlier theorists like Mazel, Mikhail Tarakanov, and Denisov were by necessity forced to do.[48]

According to Kholopov's interpretation, which has since become disseminated by his many students to become the dominant Russian thinking on the topic, the "technique of rows" uses "twelve-tone rows" (*dvenatsatitonovye riady*) while the "technique of series" (*tekhnika serii*) uses a series.[49] There are additional complications however, for as Stravinsky's gradual serial development most prominently taught the world, serial music does not necessarily have to use rows of twelve different pitches. Thus there is also music constructed with a "dodecaphonic row" (*dodekafonnyi riad*), music that in the English-speaking world is normally called twelve-tone. To further muddy the waters, there is atonal music that sounds twelve-tone, leading Kholopov to coin the useful term *dvenadtsatitonovost'*, or "twelve-toneness" to describe works of this nature, specifically sections of Volkonsky's *Musica Stricta*.[50] The easiest way to visualize the hierarchy imag-

Example 9. Volkonsky, *Musica Stricta,* movement 2, mm. 1–6.

ined by Kholopov is as a series of concentric circles: atonal music ("twelve-tonish" music) is the largest, followed by twelve-tone music (that uses multiple twelve-tone rows that do not determine every note in a composition), a subset of which is serial music (that uses a row of ordered pitches that governs an entire piece, but does not necessarily consist of twelve pitches), a subset of which is dodecaphonic music (that uses a row of twelve pitches that governs the entire piece).[51]

Now, the Anglophone reader might express some confusion regarding the distinction between a twelve-tone row and a dodecaphonic row, terms that are synonymous in English. But according to Russian thinking, tutored by the example of Volkonsky and Shostakovich among others, there was an important distinction. Only in Russia was there a pervasive tendency to construct pieces with multiple twelve-tone rows that in fact obeyed none of the traditional Schoenbergian "laws" of twelve-tone music (or if they did, did so only selectively). Thus two separate terms needed to be applied to these alternatives: music constructed with rows of notes that include all twelve pitches of the chromatic scale (something more specific than simply chromatic or atonal music) and music constructed with a twelve-tone row that determined the entire fabric of a piece. In theorist Svetlana Kurbatskaia's definition of the "technique of twelve-tone rows" (*tekhnika 12-tonovykh riadov*) she writes, "A row is a horizontal succession of non-repeated pitches (or with a minimum of repetition), which is used like a melodic construction and is not the single source of the sonic fabric."[52] Kurbatskaia's examples include the last of Berg's op. 4 songs, no. 16 from Shchedrin's *Polyphonic Notebook*, and Shostakovich's Fourteenth Symphony (movement 7, "At the Santè Jail," rehearsal number 91; see Example 6 above), but her technique of rows also describes the way that Shostakovich applied his rows in the sixth Blok song and the Twelfth Quartet and Volkonsky applied his rows in *Musica Stricta*. It also matches the usage of Pärt and Schnittke in several of their compositions.

Because of the techniques that Volkonsky used and the audiences he drew, Khrushchev himself condemned him, especially during the artistic crackdown that followed the infamous Manezh exhibition of 1963.[53] But Volkonsky was not the only young composer to use the technique of rows, or to be criticized by the regime for doing so. Arvo Pärt also experimented with twelve-tone rows in the early 1960s, and, as a result, both Volkonsky and Pärt were the two young Soviets most frequently chastised by officialdom during the last years of Khrushchev's reign.

Like Volkonsky, Pärt applied multiple rows in his early 1960 composition *Obituary* (*Nekrolog*). At measure 19, the beginning of the first major section of the piece, Pärt starts gradually developing and piling up rows, until by measure 66 five different rows are in play. Starting from the bottom they are: bass, piano, and contrabassoon (measure 71); cello and bass clarinet (measure 68); viola and clarinet (measure 66); and second violin and flute (measure 68; see Example 10).

The fifth row, which is to become one of the two central rows of the piece, is introduced in the solo first violins in measure 66 as the culmination of this section. Each of these rows, it should be noted, is different, though they are clearly derived from one another, much like the rows in Shostakovich's Twelfth Quartet or the rows in the first movement of *Musica Stricta*. Nor does any one of them appear in other than its prime form. Amid the resulting chaos, the individual characteristics of each row count less than the chromatic, pointillistic wash it produces in combination with the other three. The only row that stands out is the violin row, because it

Example 10. Pärt, *Obituary*, mm. 66–73.

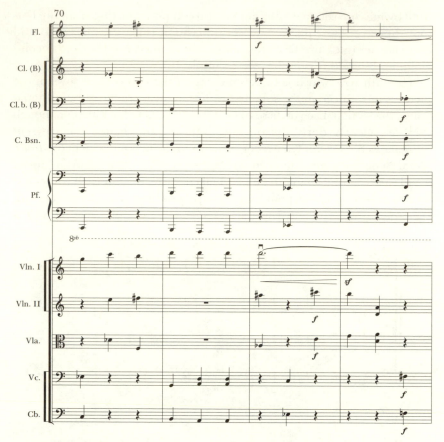

Example 10 continued

is the first true melody in the work. It is also the only one of these rows to be used in the remainder of the composition (in conjunction with a new row introduced in the oboe in measure 153). Only in the broadest sense is *Obituary* a serial work. Though it includes twelve-tone rows, the language of *Obituary* is freely atonal, or more accurately, "twelve-tonish." Despite the aural similarities between its first section and the canon in the seventh movement of Shostakovich's Fourteenth Symphony, the majority of the work sounds like a typically bombastic Socialist Realist composition.

Schooled by the example of Volkonsky's *Musica Stricta* (an influence on the Soviets as strong as Schoenberg's or Webern's), many young composers were attracted by the fugal or canonic possibilities of twelve-tone writing. In his First Symphony, Pärt applied twelve-tone rows in a polyphonic framework, which if not in substance at least in style resembled Shostakovich's occasional polyphonic application of twelve-tone rows. Many of the twelve-tone constructions that Pärt employed in this work, and specifically the vertical arrangement of hexachords that he used from rehearsal number 37 through 38, are far more complicated and detailed than any Shostakovich used, but there are two moments that bear some resemblance to Shostakovich's approach.[54] In the first movement of Pärt's Symphony, subtitled "Canon," the first true canon begins in the strings in measures 105–109 (Example 11a) and is similar to the canonic section at rehearsal number 33 of the Twelfth Quartet's second movement (see Example 4).

The final "Fugue" of Pärt's second movement ("Prelude and Fugue") also shows an interest in twelve-tone *sonorika* like that in the "Lorelei" movement of Shostakovich's Fourteenth Symphony. Starting in measure 75 the violas establish a fixed rhythm, repeated verbatim in each instrumental entrance that follows. Each entrance, however, is on successive pitches of

Example 11a. Pärt, Symphony no. 1, first movement, mm. 105–109.

a row form, in this case, R-0, then R-1 after measure 101 (rehearsal number 46). The serial patterning quickly loses significance in the driving, obsessive buildup that follows (see the climax in mm. 134–39, Example 11b). Indeed, by the end of the piece the row has lost its importance, *sonorika* predominates, and the "twelve-toneness," while audible, is subsumed by the sharpness of the harmonies and rhythm.

As Pärt's First Symphony suggests, over the course of the 1960s many of the young composers grew dissatisfied with a strict application of twelve-tone principles. For these composers, twelve-tone music gradually acquired a more abstracted character. Twelve-tone music began to represent simply another style of music that could be evoked with a single twelve-tone row, much as Shostakovich had done at the beginning of compositions like the Twelfth Quartet or the sixth of the Blok songs. At the end of the decade, Schnittke and Pärt began to follow this logic in their music as they explored diverse techniques and diverse styles and attempted to get around the roadblocks of Socialist Realism to find expressive means suitable to their shifting internal and external situations. Pärt, for one, ended his Second Symphony by pitting *sonorika* built of twelve-tone rows against a quotation from Tchaikovsky, as occurs at rehearsal number 36, where the unremitting dissonances of the preceding movements (and the preceding section) give way to Tchaikovsky's "Sweet Daydream" (*Sladkaia greza*), no. 21 from the 1878 album of children's piano pieces, op. 39.

Pärt's next composition, *Pro et Contra* for cello and ensemble, continued this tearing up of genres and styles. The first of the composition's three movements opens with two gestures in opposition, the first a D-major chord, the second a *sonorika* chord—aleatoric blocks in the winds, brass, vibraphone, and marimba, with the mallet instruments both cycling through the same twelve-tone row while the strings hold a cluster. These were the two forces at battle in Pärt's creative conscious—tonality contra aleatory and serialism, tradition versus the avant-garde. Ultimately in his 1968 *Credo* for chorus, orchestra, and piano solo, Pärt pledged his faith in Bach as represented by the C-major prelude from Book I of *The Well-Tempered Clavier*, opposing it to noisy layers of twelve-tone rows—*sonorika*, in other words—representing a rejection of the experimental language of his recent works. In his Second Violin Concerto, a literal musical depiction of the Passion, Schnittke had provided another allegorical meaning to the opposition, using twelve-tone rows to represent biblical law, while applying atonality to represent the "opponents" to the soloist, that is, Christ.[55] Pärt and Schnittke were not alone in this stylized abstraction of dodecaphony. And this is where they departed from Volkonsky's first

Example 11b. Pärt, Symphony no. 1, second movement, mm. 134–39.

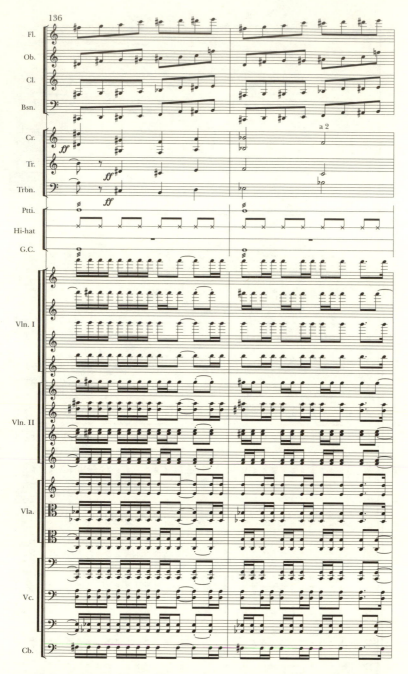

Example 11b continued

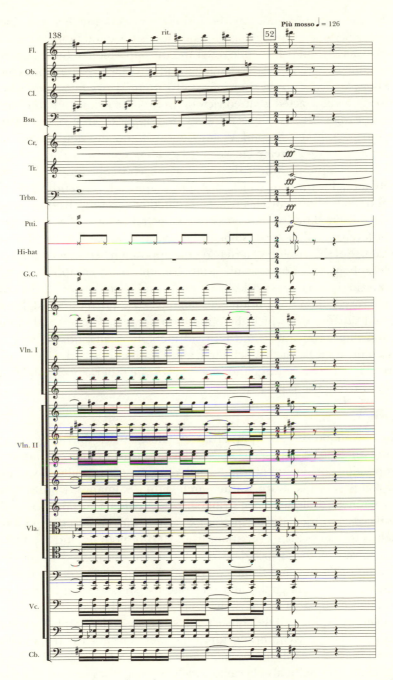

Example 11b continued

twelve-tone composition. For these two composers tonality and dodecaphony became abstracted as C-major scales (or quotations of familiar tonal material) and twelve-tone rows, and the opposition of these elements in a composition reflected the clashing worldviews each system represented.

Shostakovich's application of "twelve-tone" rows falls somewhere between this abstracted, stylized view of twelve-tone writing and the "technique of rows." It lies between the stylized application of rows in Pärt's *Credo* or Schnittke's Second Violin Concerto and the dense layers the "technique of rows" created in Volkonsky's *Musica Stricta* or Pärt's *Obituary* and First Symphony, where the rows comfortably contribute to the generally atonal setting in which they are employed. Depending on the composition, Shostakovich's rows alternated between twelve-tone music as a signifier and twelve-tone music as an integral element of a highly chromatic (even atonal) texture, sometimes appearing as both, as they do over the course of the Twelfth Quartet. Yet the opposition between tonality and dodecaphony was not as symbolically fraught in his compositions as it became in those crucial works of Schnittke and Pärt, despite the fact that he too relied upon the tension between the two languages. Shostakovich created situations in which the opposition between tonality and atonality was important and could be read metaphorically, but he had not passed the limit point that Schnittke and Pärt had reached, where, as in Pärt's *Pro et Contra*, it was either one style or the other. For Shostakovich things were not so clear-cut.

The "technique of rows" employed by Shostakovich and many of the young unofficial composers stood in stark contrast to the contemporary compositions of several official Soviet composers. Ironically, it was official composers like Kara Karaev and Vadim Salmanov who adopted twelve-tone techniques more stringently than either Shostakovich or the unofficial composers did in anything but their very earliest compositions (such as Denisov's Piano Variations from 1961 or both his and Schnittke's violin sonatas, both of which date from 1963). The official twelve-tone compositions of Karaev and Salmanov reveal the growing acceptance of the technique in official circles and illustrate its pervasiveness by the time Shostakovich made his own twelve-tone forays in the late 1960s.

A perfect example of the "official" school of Soviet dodecaphony is Kara Karaev's Third Symphony for Chamber Orchestra from 1965. Shostakovich knew this composition and even wrote to Karaev of it in May of 1965.[56] The piece also became widely known as a result of the scandal it encountered when it was to have been awarded the prestigious

Lenin Prize in the jubilee year of 1967 (the fiftieth anniversary of the October Revolution). When the committee was informed that the piece used twelve-tone techniques, it was recommended that another work be chosen to replace it, his ballet *Path of Thunder* (*Tropoiu groma*).[57] Such a prestigious award indicates the very official level upon which Karaev was operating. None of the younger composers would have been eligible in the first place.

Unlike Shostakovich's twelve-tone compositions, Karaev's academic symphony is very traditional and thorough-going in its application of both twelve-tone methods and symphonic form. It even includes the conventional four movements: I. Allegro Moderato, II. Scherzo, III. Andante, IV. Allegro. In the first pages of the symphony one gets a sense of Karaev's approach to dodecaphonic writing, as within its first fourteen measures the piece uses the prime, retrograde, inversion, and retrograde inversion, all at the original transposition level. Only once, at rehearsal number 2, does the P-1 version occur in the first violins (Example 12). All the movements of this extensive symphony are based on the same row, and transpositions are rarely used.[58]

Official works like Karaev's Symphony did not share the same unofficial cachet and have the same resistant air that the works of Volkonsky, Denisov, and the other young composers had acquired. Apparently many Soviet listeners either by choice or by ignorance denied that compositions like Karaev's were twelve-tone at all, as Bobrovsky and Zhitomirsky had done in downplaying the twelve-tone tendencies in Shostakovich's works. At a "discussion and evaluation" of Karaev's symphony that took place on 24 March 1967 before the Commission of Musical Critics (*Komissiia muzykal'noi kritiki*) of the USSR Union of Composers, Lev Vasilevich Danilevich (1912–80), a lecturer at the Moscow Conservatory, apologized for the symphony's use of twelve-tone techniques.[59] Danilevich began by stating that the symphony was only

> comparatively serial. A rather large number of our composers use serial techniques. Moreover I am convinced that serialism is used among us entirely differently than in the West. If you take Pärt's symphony [no. 1], and compare it with Webern's symphony, then it will be sufficiently clear that they are different musical works. It is possible to critique Pärt's symphony in various ways, consider it successful or unsuccessful, but it is not the same as what we hear in the works of Schoenberg and Webern. Among us the devices of serial techniques are used differently, in accordance with the world-view of the Soviet composer.[60]

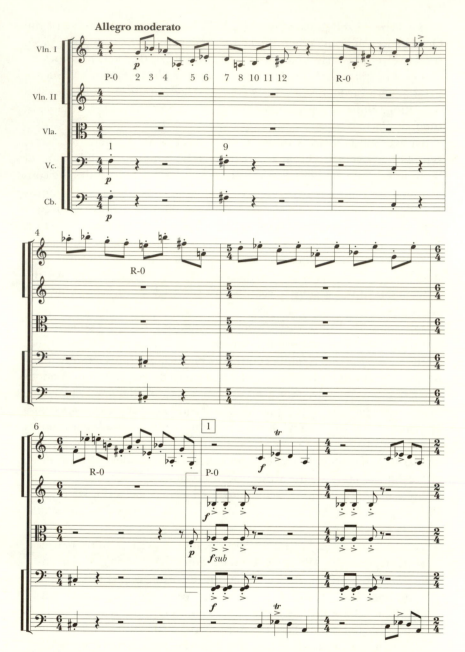

Example 12. Karaev, Symphony no. 3, first movement, mm. 1–16.

Example 12 continued

These comments reveal the shift that had taken place in official attitudes toward twelve-tone music since the beginning of the 1960s. In 1962 Pärt's notorious *Obituary* had drawn criticism from high levels of the Soviet musical bureaucracy as an example of a "bourgeois style . . . ideologically foreign to Soviet music."[61] Now Pärt had become a model of Soviet serialism. Now Danilevich could even float the previously unthinkable opinion that serial techniques could be used "in accordance with the worldview of the Soviet composer."

Danilevich next turned to the serial techniques at work in Karaev's symphony, demonstrating his own skill in aurally analyzing a twelve-tone composition:

> As regards Kara Karaev's symphony, in the first and second movements I did not notice any serialism—it is not there. Elements of serialism appear in the third and fourth movements. Insofar as I could notice, that serialism is not dogmatic and, of course, not total. It is used like an element of the whole, and I propose that it is impossible to object to this or that technical method if it is not used dogmatically by the composer, but is used as a certain part of the whole.[62]

Serialism then, could be used by established Soviet composers as long as it was not applied "dogmatically." The criteria were still vague, but a chink in the armor had been exposed.

Of course, Danilevich was wrong in his aural analysis. As already mentioned, the entire first movement is serial, as are the succeeding three movements. Whether Danilevich really did not hear this or was merely obfuscating in favor of his colleague is unclear. In any case, none of the commentators at the session actually criticized the work for the serial techniques that it used. Instead, most of the listeners were overwhelmingly supportive.[63] This seemed to be the shift that was occurring. It did not matter if serial techniques were used, at least by an official composer. It also helped to be established and to have been a former student of Shostakovich's.[64] Of course Karaev's work was heavily promoted and recorded, and he continued to compose twelve-tone pieces like his violin concerto from 1968.[65]

Karaev was not the only member of the old guard to try more orthodox twelve-tone techniques. Vadim Nikolaevich Salmanov (1912–78), a former student of Mikhail Gnesin and professor at the Leningrad Conservatory (where Shostakovich knew him), also used twelve-tone writing in his own Third Symphony (1964) in addition to several other compositions from the 1960s, including his earlier Third String Quartet from 1960. On 3 May 1962, Salmanov had spoken about the usefulness of twelve-tone methods in a paper presented to the Composition Faculty at the Leningrad Conservatory, "On Tonal Serial Techniques." In this paper he had argued in favor of the advantages that serial techniques provided the composer: "Those dodecaphonic techniques may be used which in my eyes provide unusually interesting results. But for that it is initially necessary to reject the first postulate of dodecaphonic construction—the principle of atonality."[66] As he writes, a row is tonal "if in the tone row exists even a hint of harmonic definition."[67] His own practice proved how small this "hint" needed to be.

Example 13. Salmanov, String Quartet no. 3, first movement, mm. 1–13.

Example 13 continued

Salmanov's Third Quartet begins with the solo first violin playing P-0, undergirded by chords drawn from the final tetrachord of the row, an opening gesture akin to Shostakovich's later Twelfth Quartet. Yet whereas Shostakovich's introduction had immediately swerved to diatonicism, Salmanov remains resolutely twelve-tone, as the first page indicates (Example 13). The whole quartet was made palatable and acceptable by its almost Bartókian style, especially the evocative "night music" of the second movement.

Salmanov's Third Symphony exhibited the same consistent twelve-tone writing. At the very beginning of the symphony the trumpets repeat a twelve-tone row twice, as if to underscore the point, before the entire orchestra enters at rehearsal number 1 with their own statement of this prime form of the row, which leads at 6 mm. after rehearsal number 1 to a statement of the inversion of the row in the horns (Example 14).

Each of the succeeding three movements is based on a new row. In character, however, the rest of the symphony, together with Karaev's Third, could constitute a new genre of socialist serial symphonism, combining the optimistic, overheated rhetoric of the Socialist Realist symphony with the traditional features of twelve-tone writing. The stylistic exteriors of these compositions, together with their composers' official positions, saved them from the criticism their technical constructions would have been expected to evoke. But what is most interesting about these more academic, conservative twelve-tone pieces was how orthodox their treatment of twelve-tone music was. Absent here is any of the "twelve-toneness," "technique of rows," the stylized symbolic rows, or the general experimentation that characterized both the early works of the young

Example 14. Salmanov, Symphony no. 3, first movement, mm. 1–25.

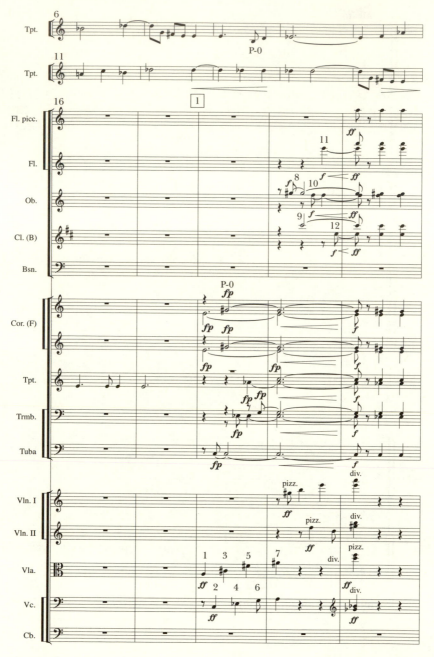

Example 14 continued

Example 14 continued

"unofficial" composers and that of Shostakovich himself. Though rudimentary, here everything is by the book.

Official composer Grigorii Frid (b. 1915), best known as the founder and guiding spirit behind the Moscow Youth Musical Club (*Moskovskii molodezhnyi muzykal'nyi klub*; abbreviated as MMMK) an important staging ground for the unofficial composers and their eager audiences, also experimented with twelve-tone music in some of his pieces from the late 1960s.[68] He began to apply dodecaphony in 1966 or 1967 with his violin sonata and the second and third movements of his trombone concerto, because it was "interesting to me."[69] Frid also used twelve-tone themes in his operas the *Diary of Anne Frank* (1969) and *Letters of Van Gogh* (1975). He no doubt saw his colleagues trying it and wanted to find out for himself what all the fuss was about. Frid was significantly older than the young composers, and as he explained to me, "Because of my age it wasn't the main direction. I didn't feel as close to it as Schnittke did . . . Schnittke was born in 1934 and I was born in 1915. For him it was a natural process, I came to it with difficulty."[70]

Shostakovich apparently did not share Frid's difficulty. He became familiar with the scores of Schoenberg and Berg in the 1920s, and therefore, unlike Frid or the younger composers, was not overwhelmed by their novelty in the 1960s. He never tried to apply dodecaphony dogmatically, instead used it as a logical extension of his already chromatic language, as many have noted and as he himself blandly told American interviewer (now film music scholar) Royal S. Brown on his last trip to America.[71] When asked about his use of twelve-tone rows in the Twelfth Quartet and the Violin Sonata, Shostakovich replied:

> I did use some elements of dodecaphony in these works. Of course, if you take a theory and use solely this theory, I have a very negative attitude towards this kind of approach. But if a composer feels that he needs this or that technique, he can take whatever is available and use it as he sees fit. It is his right to do so. But if you take one technique, whether it is aleatory or dodecaphonic, and use nothing but that technique, then it is wrong. There needs to be a mélange.[72]

Mélange is the best description of the music by the young composers in the mid-1960s. It also aptly describes Shostakovich's "technique of rows," and his late style in general.

No matter how official or pervasive twelve-tone music had become in the Soviet Union by the end of the 1960s, there were always going to be detractors, one of the most vocal of whom was, predictably, the conservative Dmitrii Kabalevsky. At a meeting of Frid's Moscow Youth Musical Club he raised the issue in a debate with Frid, where Frid took the role of the "dodecaphonist" and Kabalevsky was the "normal composer." According to Kabalevsky's rules in the demonstration, he, the normal composer, and Frid were to compose a piece, but Kabalevsky could pick any note from the twelve notes of the chromatic scale whereas Frid, the dodecaphonist, could select only from those he had not already chosen. As the exercise progressed, Kabalevsky chose to repeat several pitches whereas each time Frid, of course, was left with an ever-dwindling selection. At the end Kabalevsky was triumphant because he could pick any pitch he wanted, while Frid was left with only one. This was all the evidence that Kabalevsky needed to proclaim that "Dodecaphony is on the decline [*ushcherbnyi*] and limited [*ogranichen*], while I compose freely [*no ia sochinaiu svobodno*]."[73] Frid said that unlike nearly everyone in the hall he remained unconvinced. This "debate" certainly reveals both the generally primitive level of the discussions regarding dodecaphony at the time and the entrenched opinions that all composers of twelve-tone music were fighting, no matter how orthodox their handling of the system.

Though in reality the tacit official acceptance of dodecaphony had begun around 1965, as demonstrated by the increased official publications about dodecaphony and the increase in both official and quasi-official performances, only later was this shift officially acknowledged. One of the signals was the Second Congress of the RSFSR Union of Composers from 14–16 May 1968.[74] At that Congress a resolution was passed that read:

> Mastery of new expressive means sometimes moves forward into the quality of an end in and of itself, becoming the first principle of a plan to create a basis for the penetration of *avant-garde and other foreign influences* in our art [author's italics].[75]

There was reportedly much debate as to the exact phrasing of the italicized section above.[76] But the first part of this statement, together with other speeches by Andrei Petrov (b. 1930), as well as Sergei Balansanian (1902–82) and Iurii Keldysh, seemed to open the door for "authorized" composers to begin writing using expanded techniques, among them dodecaphony, as long as these did not become an "end in and of themselves."

Moscow composer Aleksandr Baltin (b. 1931) believed that the 1968 congress marked a new sanctioning of dodecaphony, aleatory, and *sonorika*, though he added that in actuality it did not really change anything, which was certainly true for the young composers.[77] Young Leningrad composer Sergei Slonimsky saw the earlier 1966 plenum of the USSR Union of Composers as the turning point: "After [the plenum] it became possible . . . to print and even perform pieces using those new techniques . . . even though they had just rushed at me."[78] He characteristically declared this to be an unfair and unequal treatment of his compositions; a month after criticizing him for using them, they had approved his techniques. But by that time such arbitrariness from the Union of Composers was hardly unexpected.

The official decrees reflected the fact that by the middle of the 1960s twelve-tone music had begun to lose its edge. It was no longer at the fore-front of the avant-garde. True, it could still be used as a pretense for preventing works from being performed, but by the late 1960s the unofficial list of composers who were off-limits was already well in place. Everyone already knew who the "difficult" composers were. The belated resolution (*tezis*) from the Second Congress of 1968 merely gave an opening to composers not on that unwritten, yet commonly understood, list to begin experimenting with "new expressive means." For their part, the young unofficial composers began to abandon twelve-tone techniques; only a few, like Denisov and Karetnikov, continued to write strictly serial music. As these shifts began to take place, a wider number of other Soviet composers began to wonder what all the controversy was about and tried their own hand at the method. It should come as little surprise that Shostakovich was among their ranks.

Even the head of the Soviet Union of Composers, Tikhon Khrennikov, wrote "twelve-tone" music at the beginning of the 1970s, as if belatedly fulfilling Stravinsky's 1962 pronouncement. The official acceptance of dodecaphonic music in the Soviet Union can be convincingly dated to 1972 and the first bars of Khrennikov's Second Piano Concerto, a statement of policy if ever there was one (Example 15).

This piece might also be heard as a musical thumbing of the nose, an indication that serialism is not difficult, everyone and anyone can do it. Perhaps Khrennikov thought that by appropriating twelve-tone music he would make it official and hence unpalatable to both the young composers and the older official ones. But the twelve-tone section of this piece does not last much beyond the first page. Khrennikov's preemptive strike was too late. By 1971 few of the young composers were still writing twelve-tone music, and Shostakovich had also ceased using his own rows.

The point at which Shostakovich began to apply his own "technique of rows" fits into the broader acceptance of twelve-tone music in Soviet musical life. Although he never strictly employed twelve-tone techniques, Shostakovich was indebted to the several specifically and idiosyncratically Soviet strands of twelve-tone writing that had begun to develop at

Example 15. Khrennikov, Piano Concerto no. 2, first movement, mm. 1–27.

Example 15 continued

the end of the 1950s and were flourishing by the end of the 1960s, specifically the "technique of rows" and a stylized evocation of dodecaphony.
Like many other composers, Shostakovich had been given tacit permission to try his hand, as long as it fulfilled the dramatic functions belatedly
permitted by the 1968 resolution. But then again, Shostakovich did not
need any permission; his official standing at this point was enough to excuse
him. If Karaev's Third Symphony and Salmanov's Third Quartet and Third
Symphony were passable, then Shostakovich's dodecaphonic works were
as well, as proven by the sympathetic readings of Soviet theorists like
Zhitomirsky and Bobrovsky. In this respect the younger generation
revealed its more precarious, leading position. They would continue to
draw fire for their experiments and the unofficial social role that their
music played; Shostakovich would not.

Table 1. Shostakovich's Compositions with Twelve-Tone Rows

Year	Composition
1967	Seven Verses of A. Blok, op. 127
1967	Violin Concerto no. 2 in C-sharp Minor, op. 129
1968	String Quartet no. 12 in D-flat Major, op. 133
1968	Sonata for Violin and Piano, op. 134
1969	Symphony no. 14, for soprano, bass, string orchestra, and percussion, op. 135
1970	String Quartet no. 13 in B-flat Minor, op. 138
1971	Symphony no. 15 in A Major, op. 141
1973	Six Verses of Marina Tsvetaeva, op. 143
1974	String Quartet no. 15 in E-flat Minor, op. 144

NOTES

This essay is dedicated to the memory of Iurii Nikolaevich Kholopov, who passed away while I was at work revising it for the present publication. I am forever indebted to the advice and support he provided when I was in Moscow from 2000 to 2001.

1. All performance details are taken from *Warszawska Jesień/Warsaw Autumn,* ed. Tadeusz Kaczyński and Andrzej Zborski (Poland: Polskie Wydawnictwo Muzyczne, 1983), pp. 273–74.

2. After World War II Darmstadt, or more specifically the Darmstadt Summer Courses or *Ferienkurse für Neue Musik,* became a center for avant-garde and, at least initially, serial music experimentation. Started by Wolfgang Steinecke in 1946, by the early 1950s they were one of the leading venues for young European composers like Pierre Boulez, Karlheinz Stockhausen, Luigi Nono, and Luciano Berio, who were interested in exploring and applying the most modern of compositional devices. For more information, see *Von Kranichstein zur Gegenwart: 50 Jahre Darmstädter Ferienkurse, 1946–1996,* ed. R. Stephan et al. (Stuttgart, 1996).

3. The translation cited is from Laurel E. Fay, *Shostakovich: A Life* (New York: Oxford University Press, 2000), p. 214. (Unless otherwise noted all translations are mine.) See also Fay's discussion of Shostakovich's attacks on dodecaphony after the Warsaw Autumn festival when in October and November 1959 he toured America with a Soviet delegation on a U.S. State Department–sponsored exchange program, pp. 214–15.

4. See Laurel Elizabeth Fay, "The Last Quartets of Dmitrii Shostakovich: A Stylistic Investigation" (Ph.D. diss., Cornell University, 1978), p. 64.

5. The most prominent performance came on 30 September, the last date of the festival, when Shostakovich's *Katerina Izmailova,* the reworking of his earlier controversial opera *Lady Macbeth of the Mtsensk District,* was presented. His other works had been performed earlier in the Festival and included the Sixth Symphony (23 September), and the First and Fourth String Quartets (24 September). The other notable performances that particular year included the Polish premieres of Ligeti's *Apparitions,* Lutosławski's String Quartet, Stravinsky's *Agon*; Carter's Double Concerto; Messiaen's *Chronochromie,* Stockhausen's *Kontakte,* Penderecki's Sonata for Cello and Orchestra, and a new version of Nono's *Diario polacco '58.* Other concerts included Gorecki's *Elementi* for three strings, Boulez's *Structures,* book II (parts 1 and 2), and a whole evening devoted to the music of Berg. Kaczyński and Zborski, eds., *Warszawska Jesień,* pp. 285–87.

6. Ibid.

7. Gould visited Moscow and Leningrad in May 1957, Stravinsky in October 1962, Nono beginning in 1962.

8. Though *Musica Stricta* was most likely performed in private following its completion sometime in 1956 or 1957, its first public performance was at a concert at the Gnesin Institute in Moscow, 6 May 1961, with Yudina performing. Yudina played it again on 11 May in Leningrad at the concert hall near the Finland Station. An anonymous negative review appeared in *Sovetskaia muzyka* in July 1961. See Peter J. Schmelz, "Listening, Memory, and the Thaw: Unofficial Music and Society in the Soviet Union, 1956–1974" (Ph.D. diss., University of California, Berkeley, 2002), pp. 94–99.

9. Ibid., pp. 350–55.

10. Igor Stravinsky and Robert Craft, *Dialogues and a Diary* (Garden City, N.Y.: Doubleday, 1963), pp. 257–58.

11. A notable exception was Laurel Fay's 1978 dissertation on Shostakovich's late string quartets. Fay was the first American to give a detailed consideration to the application of

dodecaphonic techniques in Shostakovich's late quartets and in his late style in general. See Fay, "The Last Quartets of Dmitrii Shostakovich," especially pp. 17–30 and 64–91. A recent German-language volume on Shostakovich's late style that delves into a detailed analysis of Shostakovich's twelve-tone language in the Fourteenth Symphony is Sebastian Klemm, *Dmitri Schostakowitsch: Das zeitlose Spätwerk,* Studia Slavica musicologica/ Schostakowitsch-Studien, Band 4 (Berlin: Verlag Ernst Kuhn, 2001). However, in its emphasis on both German twelve-tone theorizing (Schoenberg, Adorno, and Dahlhaus) and its reliance on the one-sided, "official" perspective of secondary literature like Boris Schwarz's *Music and Musical Life in Soviet Russia: Enlarged Edition, 1917–1981* (Bloomington, Ind.: Indiana University Press, 1983), Klemm's work misses out on the specifically Soviet nature of Shostakovich's "twelve-tone" technique (see, for example, pp. 69–76).

12. In a recent article, Levon Hakobian alleges that Shostakovich first applied "quasi-serial themes" in the fourth movement, "Fears," from his Thirteenth Symphony. This labeling reveals the loose standard that many Russian analysts still maintain for dubbing a work "serial," as the work does not feature serial structuring in any recognizable sense. There are no twelve-tone rows, nor do series of pitches recur, other than in a general manner typical of Shostakovich's melodic writing at this stage in his life. See Levon Akopian, "'Khudozhestvennye otkrytiia' Chetyrnadtsatoi simfonii," *Muzykal'naia akademiia* 4 (1997): 186.

13. The translation is from Tim Langen and Jesse Langen, "Music and Poetry: The Case of Shostakovich and Blok," in *Intersections and Transpositions: Russian Music, Literature, and Society,* ed. Andrew Baruch Wachtel (Evanston, Ill.: Northwestern University Press, 1998), pp. 154–58. They translate the title as "Secret (Mysterious) Signs" and indicate that in the original, Blok did not give the poem a title.

14. This would remain consistent throughout Shostakovich's late style. As Laurel Fay has pointed out, only rarely were twelve-tone rows presented chordally, as in sections of the Thirteenth and Fifteenth Quartets. Fay, "The Last Quartets of Dmitrii Shostakovich," pp. 67–68.

15. D. Zhitomirskii, "Iz razmyshlenii o stile Shostakovicha," *Sovetskaia muzyka* 9 (1976): 60.

16. The rows also continue to appear at important transitions in the second movement: at rehearsal number 45 the cello introduces the funeral march that begins at rehearsal number 46, and at rehearsal number 51 the first violin starts a building moderato passage that reaches its climax after rehearsal number 57.

17. Fay ably discussed the similarities between the rows in the Twelfth Quartet in her dissertation. See Fay, "The Last Quartets of Dmitrii Shostakovich," pp. 19–20. In a contemporary review of the quartet, Hans Keller also pointed out the similarities between rows and their function at "structural articulation points." See Hans Keller, "Shostakovich's Twelfth Quartet," *Tempo* 94 (Autumn 1970): 12–13. He also makes brief mention of the characteristics of this row in an earlier article: see Hans Keller, "Shostakovich Discovers Schoenberg," *The Listener,* 8 October 1970, p. 494.

18. Eric Roseberry has commented: "In Shostakovich's works twelve-note 'themes' are as likely to assume an improvisatory character that changes shape, yields new continuations in the course of their ritornello-like recurrence, as assume the identity of an *idée fixe.*" See Eric Roseberry, "A Debt Repaid? Some Observations on Shostakovich and His Late-Period Recognition of Britten," in *Shostakovich Studies,* ed. David Fanning (Cambridge, Eng.: Cambridge University Press, 1995), p. 247.

19. For Bobrovsky this was a "secondary part," the second theme of the larger sonata form that he saw the two movements as fulfilling—before the recapitulation of the main part at rehearsal 61 and the return to D-flat major. Viktor Bobrovskii, "O nekotorykh chertakh stilia Shostakovicha shestidesiatykh godov," part 2, *Muzyka i sovremennost'* 9 (1975): 46.

20. Fay was the first Western commentator to note the "outright atonality . . . in extended sections of the second movement." See Fay, "The Last Quartets of Dmitrii Shostakovich," p. 20. In the section on the Twelfth Quartet in the published version of his dissertation, Eric Roseberry concentrates only on the tonal areas of the quartet. See Eric Roseberry, *Ideology, Style, Content, and Thematic Process in the Symphonies, Cello Concertos, and String Quartets of Shostakovich*, Outstanding Dissertations in Music from British Universities (New York and London: Garland Publishing, Inc., 1989), p. 486.

21. Klemm is getting at something similar when he summarizes: "Twelve-tone constructions in Shostakovich are either a distinct contrast to a central tonality or are integrated so organically into an extended tonality that they blend into it." Klemm, *Dmitri Schostakowitsch: Das zeitlose Spätwerk*, p. 124.

22. Klemm delves into a detailed analysis of the work, looking at each movement through an "analytic 'twelve-tone filter'" (*Zwölftönigkeitsfilter*): Ibid., p. 77. The result is occasionally illuminating, but the goal of looking at everything in this work from a twelve-tone perspective leads to some wrongheaded assertions, as in his analysis of the row rotation at the beginning of the "Lorelei" movement (pp. 94–97, especially his Example 11).

23. A similar effect is achieved in the eighth movement of the Fourteenth Symphony, "The Reply of the Zaporozhian Cossacks to the Sultan of Constantinople," from rehearsal number 115 to the end where the divisi strings fill out the total chromatic, each successive violin (reading down the staff) playing the same figuration a half step lower.

24. Bobrovskii, "O nekotorykh chertakh stilia Shostakovicha shestidesiatykh godov," part 2, p. 60. See Klemm, *Dmitri Schostakowitsch: Das zeitlose Spätwerk*, pp. 113–16 for a more detailed discussion of this section.

25. Fay, "The Last Quartets of Dmitrii Shostakovich," p. 72.

26. Viktor Bobrovskii, "Pobeda chelovecheskogo dukha," *Sovetskaia muzyka* 9 (1968): 33. He makes a similar statement in a later article: "In the opening cello recitative the tonality of D-flat major is born before our eyes. The tonic, now found, draws into itself all of the instability accumulated in that brief instant and sounds especially triumphantly assertive, but the development that arises later becomes stable to a greater degree" ("O nekotorykh chertakh stilia Shostakovicha shestidesiatykh godov," part 2, p. 74).

27. In his later article Bobrovsky emphasized both the tonal and atonal possibilities afforded by Shostakovich's twelve-tone rows, as well as the different "intonational" (in the Asafievian sense) opportunities they allowed, still emphasizing the programmatic interpretation of the rows. Bobrovskii, "O nekotorykh chertakh stilia Shostakovicha shestidesiatykh godov," part 2, p. 47. See also p. 74.

28. Zhitomirskii, "Iz razmyshlenii o stile Shostakovicha," pp. 55–62. Zhitomirsky also enlists Adorno and Hindemith in his criticism, taking on the postwar avant-garde and its relationship to the war. As he wrote, "The postwar 'avant-garde'—if we look truth in the eye—is one of the ruins left by the Second World War. There was the destruction of cities, the destruction of families, the crippling of people. There were also devastated souls. Devastation by lack of faith, skepticism, etc. . . . Such it seems to me are the historical and psychological foundations of the new 'avant-garde'" (pp. 61–62).

29. Ibid., p. 61, pp. 55–56.

30. Ibid., p. 57. This was typical of many Soviet analyses that attempted to defend twelve-tone techniques by finding precedents in music from the distant past, from Renaissance polyphony to Bach and Mozart, always culminating in nineteenth-century extended tonality. A prime example of this is Lev Mazel's self-consciously monumental three-part survey from 1965 called "Regarding the Course of Development of the Language of Contemporary Music" (*O putiakh razvitiia iazyka sovremennoi muzyki*), *Sovetskaia muzyka* 4, 5, 6 (1965). Though it concentrates on nineteenth-century precedents, Edison Denisov's essay, "Dodecaphony and the Problems of Contemporary Compositional

Techniques," is another example. Edison Denisov, "Dodekafoniia i problemy sovremennoi kompozitorskoi tekhniki," *Muzyka i sovremennost'* 6 (1969): 478–525.

31. Keller, "Shostakovich's Twelfth Quartet," p. 7.

32. Ibid., p. 9.

33. In his later, more detailed study of Shostakovich's compositions from the 1960s, beginning with *The Execution of Stepan Razin* and ending with the Thirteenth String Quartet, Bobrovsky more readily acknowledged the atonal nature of passages in the Twelfth Quartet and the Fourteenth Symphony. ("O nekotorykh chertakh stilia Shostakovicha shestidesiatykh godov," part 2, pp. 46–47, pp. 56–61).

34. Keller did acknowledge at least one moment in the Twelfth Quartet when "tonality is at a low ebb" ("Shostakovich's Twelfth Quartet," p. 14). And in his earlier article for the BBC's *The Listener,* Keller wrote: "But not all is tonal in Shostakovich's world. When we come to the scherzo section that opens the second of the work's two movements . . . his dodecaphony becomes almost as anti-tonal as 'proper' 12-tone music" ("Shostakovich Discovers Schoenberg," p. 494).

35. Benjamin Britten's own idiosyncratic twelve-tone style is another potential influence. Yet in emphasizing Britten at least, scholars like Eric Roseberry have overlooked the possible Soviet influences. Roseberry, "A Debt Repaid?," pp. 245–48.

36. See their correspondence as reprinted in Iurii Kholopov and Valeriia Tsenova, *Edison Denisov* (Moscow: Kompozitor, 1993), pp. 172–83. In French as Edison Denisov and Jean-Pierre Armengaud, *Entretiens avec Denisov: Un compositeur sous le régime soviétique* (Paris: Editions Plume, 1993), pp. 273–77.

37. Gubaidulina's full statement: "Sometimes a person pronounces only one word, but it turns out to be defining and lights the way for [your] entire future life. I will never forget the moment when he told me 'I want you to continue along your "incorrect" path.' From that moment I have felt endless gratitude to him." Valentina Kholopova and Enzo Restan'o, *Sofiia Gubaidulina* (Moscow: Kompozitor, 1996), p. 16; this is a re-translation from the Italian of *Gubajdulina,* ed. Enzo Restagno (Turin: E.D.T., 1991), p. 12.

38. This lecture is reprinted in its entirety in Edison Denisov, "Za ob"ektivnost' i spravedlivost' v otsenke sovremennoi muzyki," in *Svet-dobro-vechnost': pamiati Edisona Denisova, stat'i, vospominaniia, materialy,* ed. Valeriia Tsenova (Moscow: Moskovskaia gosudarstvennaia konservatoriia im. P. I. Chaikovskogo, 1999), pp. 22–32.

39. See note 30.

40. Denisov, "Za ob"ektivnost' i spravedlivost' v otsenke sovremennoi muzyki," p. 22.

41. Ibid., p. 27.

42. Ibid., p. 26.

43. Ibid., p. 28.

44. Ibid., p. 28.

45. For an early, generally positive, reception of Babadzhanian's composition see Iuliia Evdokimova, "'Shest' kartin' Arno Babadzhaniana," *Sovetskaia muzyka* 2 (1967): 20–24.

46. Denisov, "Za ob"ektivnost' i spravedlivost' v otsenke sovremennoi muzyki," p. 27.

47. According to Laurel Fay there is a document at RGALI (Russian State Archive of Literature and Art) that includes a petition sent in March of 1957 from Shostakovich to Molotov on Volkonsky's behalf asking for an extension of his parents' temporary residence permit in Moscow. RGALI f. 2048, op. 2, ed. khr. 99. Yudina frequently performed *Musica Stricta* through the 1960s; conversation with Anatolii Mikhailovich Kuznetsov, Moscow, 19 October 2000.

48. See, for example, Lev Mazel', "O putiakh razvitiia iazyka sovremennoi muzyki: dodekafoniia i pozdneishie avangardistskie techeniia," *Sovetskaia muzyka* 6 (1965): 6–20; and Mikhail Tarakanov, "Novye obrazy, novye sredstva," *Sovetskaia muzyka* 1 (1965): 9–16; and 2 (1965): 5–12.

49. See also Svetlana Kurbatskaia, *Seriinaia muzyka: voprosy istorii, teorii, estetiki* (Moscow: Sfera, 1996). This was the first book completely devoted to the topic in Russia. See pp. 32–40, chapter 2, "On the System of Terminology." Here Kurbatskaia defines twelve different types of "twelve-toneness" (*dvenadtsatitonovost'*): 1) Free atonality (*svobodnaia atonal'nost'*), 2) Technique of tone centers (*tekhnika zvukovogo tsentra*), 3) technique of synthetic chords (*tekhnika sintetakkordov*), 4) twelve-tone chords (*12-zvukovye akkordy*), 5) technique of twelve-tone rows (*tekhnika 12-tonovykh riadov*), 6) technique of twelve-tone fields (*tekhnika 12-tonovykh polei*), 7) technique of tropes (*tekhnika tropov*), from Hauer's system, 8) serial techniques (*seriinaia tekhnika*), 9) dodecaphony (*dodekafoniia*), 10) microseries (*mikroseriinost'*), 11) total serialism (*serializm—serial'naia tekhnika*), 12) serialism (*seriinost'*), used in a more over-arching than numbers 8 or 11. In this classification system Kurbatskaia appears to be using "twelve-toneness" in a broader sense than Kholopov does.

50. Iurii Kholopov, "Initsiator: O zhizni i muzyke Andreia Volkonskogo," in *Muzyka iz byvshego SSSR*, vol. 1, ed. Valeriia Tsenova (Moscow: Kompozitor, 1994), p. 10. In English as *Underground Music from the Former U.S.S.R.*, ed. Valeria Tsenova (Amsterdam: Harwood Academic Publishers, 1997).

51. This entire discussion is indebted to the author's multiple conversations at the Moscow Conservatory with Iurii Kholopov on this topic, particularly those on 25 October and 29 November 2000.

52. Kurbatskaia, *Seriinaia muzyka: voprosy istorii, teorii, estetiki*, pp. 34–35.

53. See Schmelz, "Listening, Memory, and the Thaw," pp. 173–75.

54. Ibid., pp. 235–36.

55. Ibid., pp. 481–93.

56. Liudmila Karagicheva, *Kara Karaev: stat'i, pis'ma, vyskazyvaniia* (Moscow: Kompozitor, 1978), p. 57.

57. See Tsenova, *Svet-dobro-vechnost'*, p. 33.

58. Some liberties are taken in the second movement, where hexachordal segments of the row and its permutations are used, as Denisov, for one, had done in his 1964 song cycle *Sun of the Incas*. Karaev also repeats notes (see measure 5 of the first movement, with the repeated Eb, Example 12) and takes some liberties with pitch order, especially when presenting the row chordally, as at rehearsal number 4—apparently a loose iteration of the I-0 form of the row.

59. RGALI f. 2077, op. 1, ed. khr. 2607.

60. Ibid., l. 16.

61. The quotation comes from a report dated 5 February 1962 by the USSR Union of Composers RGALI f. 2329, op. 3, ed. khr. 1186. At the Third All-Union Composers' Congress, held in Moscow, 26–31 March 1962, Tikhon Khrennikov had also declared, "A work like Pärt's *Obituary* makes it quite clear that the twelve-tone experiment is unten-able. This composition is dedicated to the memory of the victims of Fascism, but it bears the characteristics of the productions of foreign 'avant-gardists': ultra-expressionistic, purely naturalistic depiction of the state of fear, terror, despair, and dejection." Schwarz, *Music and Musical Life in Soviet Russia*, p. 346.

62. RGALI f. 2077, op. 1, ed. khr. 2607, l. 16.

63. Ibid., l. 6.

64. Composer Sergei Slonimsky lamented this fact, complaining, "My friendship [with the composers in Moscow] was stronger than with my colleagues in Leningrad. Because all of them, although I myself am for Shostakovich, all of them were protected too much, therefore they could allow themselves a lot—they always had a 'roof.' And it was as if they were always under the roof and I was always in the rain." Here Slonimsky significantly used the Russian term for Mafia protection, "*krysha*." From an interview with Sergei Slonimsky by this author, Moscow, 6 December 2000. Denisov also recalled that [Shostakovich]

"usually didn't help composers who had not been his pupils." See Edison Denisov in Elizabeth Wilson, *Shostakovich: A Life Remembered* (Princeton, N.J.: Princeton University Press, 1994), p. 304.

65. Karaev's Violin Concerto was reviewed by Tarakanov in *Sovetskaia Muzyka* 10 (1968): 31–37. See also Boris Schwarz, *Music and Musical Life in Soviet Russia,* pp. 461–62. The extent of the promotion of Karaev's work is indicated by RGALI lists of works recommended for performance and promotion from the early to mid-1960s. See Schmelz, "Listening, Memory, and the Thaw," pp. 337–42.

66. Vadim Salmanov, "O tonal'noi seriinoi tekhnike (fragment)," in *V. N. Salmanov: materialy, issledovaniia, vospominaniia,* ed. S. Salmanova and G. Belov (Leningrad: Sovetskii kompozitor, 1982), p. 37.

67. Ibid.

68. The club was founded in 1965. See Schmelz, "Listening, Memory, and the Thaw," pp. 365–74.

69. Grigorii Frid, interview with the author, Moscow, 21 September 1999.

70. Ibid.

71. See, for example, Fay, *Shostakovich: A Life,* pp. 257–58, and Francis Maes, *A History of Russian Music: From Kamarinskaya to Babi Yar* (Berkeley and Los Angeles: University of California Press, 2002), p. 372.

72. Royal S. Brown, "An Interview with Shostakovich," *High Fidelity* 23, no. 10 (October 1973): 89.

73. Grigorii Frid, interview with the author, Moscow, 21 September 1999.

74. See *Soiuz kompozitorov Rossii. 40 let,* ed. E. Vlasova and D. Daragan (Moscow: Kompozitor, 2000), pp. 41–57.

75. Ibid., p. 57.

76. Ibid., pp. 57–58.

77. Aleksandr Baltin, interview with the author, Moscow, 2 October 2000.

78. Sergei Slonimsky, interview with the author, Moscow, 6 December 2000.

Listening to Shostakovich

Leon Botstein

I.

In Jörg Steiner's Gogol-like novella *Wer tanzt schon zu Musik von Schostakowitsch,* the protagonist and his companion (who is "musical") confess that they like most of all to listen together to Shostakovich on a summer night, on records (not CDs), at full blast, with the windows wide open. It is a sort of ritual. Once, at midnight, two uniformed policemen arrive. A neighbor complains. As one officer points to the amplifier, the other asks that the music be turned down and inquires as to what is playing. "Shostakovich, a Russian" is the answer. The officer turns to his partner and says, "Did you catch that—a Russian, and aren't you a socialist anyway?" The officers then decide to stay. They drink wine, take off their jackets, and even agree to turn up the volume. At 3 AM they leave in good cheer, one having given away his jacket and the other singing as he takes the wheel of the car. The next day, the protagonist apologizes to his neighbors, who confess that, actually, it was not the loudness of the music that disturbed them, but the balancing act the two maintained sitting on the edge of the window over the terrace.[1]

In this metaphorical nutshell of fiction Steiner, writing almost a decade after the collapse of the Soviet Union, captures many patterns and paradoxes in contemporary attitudes toward Shostakovich. The music is immediately engaging; it demands a wide audience. It compels both the connoisseur and the novice listener. The music generates quickly a sense of community among individuals from divergent social groups. A clear association persists between the composer (and his music) and both Russia and socialism, particularly Russian state socialism of the Soviet era. The music's qualities—the temporal frame, the sonority, the accessible surface, and the spacious and hard-edged features—require that it be loud, like pop music. The music is memorable. But at the same time, at first hearing it does not seem particularly problematic or disturbing. Shostakovich's music inspires extraordinary, if not facile popularity among listeners both untutored and sophisticated, without apparent controversy.

Although derision of the sort directed at Shostakovich by modernists in the 1940s and 1950s persists (and this itself is worthy of consideration), it has become strikingly muted, as befitting the current pluralistic and eclectic context of new music today.[2] Few would challenge the notion that the best of Shostakovich's music is, on first encounter, impressive, even startling. We acknowledge that the composer and his music are inextricably linked to the ideologies and events of Soviet Russia. If there is controversy about Shostakovich, it is about the relationship of the composer and his music to politics during the composer's career. Nonetheless, the radical political changes of the 1990s have left the allure of Shostakovich undiminished—in fact, that allure has increased. The historical context in which Shostakovich's music was composed and performed, its substance (considered normatively as music apart from issues of intentions and origins), and its growing popularity all invite us to consider the question of how music, particularly music of the very recent past, is heard in the present as possessing meaning. Indeed, who still "dances" to the music of Shostakovich, and why?[3]

As the eminent scholar Richard Taruskin has persuasively argued, no other music so powerfully illuminates the fact that the meaning of music, particularly instrumental music without words or images, is not "immanent" in the text nor controlled by authorial intention, even if that can be pinpointed and defined. Rather, its meaning—or as Taruskin terms it, "interpretation"—is a transaction between the objective and the subjective, between a sounding text and the listener. There is a perpetual instability in the construction of meaning, even though subjectivity must take into account the irreducible commonality represented by the object, however minimally construed.[4] That object, however, contains a secondary but powerful variable of instability—shared, of course, with all music but particularly pronounced in the case of Shostakovich—the specific character of the performance and the context of performance. Realizations of a musical text in a studio for recording or at "live" performances are different experiences, each influencing differently what the intended listener may consider the object and its substance to be. Agreement regarding the object may even be hard to establish among the elite who believe, in the spirit of Roger Sessions, that the best performance is the one they can create in their heads silently reading the text, the score.

In the case of Shostakovich the instabilities regarding the musical object, text, or performance are matched by particularly notorious parallel difficulties in the subjective sphere: the disparate preconceptions and wishes brought to bear on playing and listening to Shostakovich by musicians and audiences. Many contemporary musicians, notably string players and conductors, have been influenced by the volume *Testimony* and its defenders.[5] They think that by advocating the music Shostakovich wrote after the mid-1930s, they are not peddling the work of a propagandist or collaborator with Soviet tyranny, but are assisting in an ethically noble cause. They are revealing hidden resistance to Stalin, the sufferings and inner emigration of a great artist. They are helping to underscore, through the communication of empathy in listening, the horror and evil of the system that produced and maintained the Gulag. The notion that resistance to tyranny was embedded in the music, judging from Sir Michael Tippett's 1980 review of *Testimony,* was not created by or contingent on *Testimony*. *Testimony* popularized and sought to legitimate a viewpoint that held that Shostakovich, despite his well-known public status as a patriotic Soviet artist, used music intentionally as "doublespeak" to express dissent and resistance, finding a way through music to evade censorship and elude imprisonment and execution.[6]

One's view of the political or ethical intentions of the composer can influence a performer's interpretive intent and perhaps the sounding results. Whether a performance designed to highlight the alleged "dissidence" in the music achieves its goal with an audience (and gains its echo or its reverse, its mirror image) depends on the so-called "extra" musical preconceptions within that audience. Consider the differences between performing the Shostakovich Fifth Symphony in Israel in 2004 with an orchestra consisting of almost 50 percent Russian émigrés before an audience with comparable demographics (or in New York, where a critical mass of Russian musicians and audience members resides), and doing the same work in St. Petersburg or in a city without many Russian musicians and residents. On both sides of the musical experience, on the stage and in the audience, there are often individuals who possess an autobiographical relationship to the music. Not that there is agreement among Russians about Shostakovich. On the contrary, the debate inside Russia over meaning and authorial intention is frequently sharper, deepened by personal remembrances (depending on the age of the protagonists). These may include recollections of performances of Shostakovich in the Soviet era, under Mravinsky, Barshai, Svetlanov, and Rakhlin, and by Oborin, Oistrakh, and Rostropovich (and for a very few, by the composer himself), in the presence of an audience for whom most of the music was written. Add to these quite contrasting contexts our unparalleled access to the historical record of past performances. We now can listen to recordings from the Soviet era, to Eastern European accounts from between 1945 and 1989, and readings by Russian émigrés to the West from before 1989. We have access to performances in the West from the early 1940s and during the Cold War (for example, Bernstein's legendary Fifth and Stokowski's rendition of the Sixth Symphony). Each of these contexts can be said to have widely divergent implicit, if not explicit, determinants of meaning and significance. In the case of post–Cold War Germany, the embrace of Shostakovich and his music as admirable because of the composer's presumed struggle and success in finding a way to articulate and communicate resistance under dictatorship has a special source. There, coming to terms with Shostakovich becomes an admirable and sympathetic model for the sorting out of German behavior under Hitler, particularly among artists.

The contemporary enthusiasm among performers and audiences for Shostakovich outside of Russia is propelled, however, by more than the overtly political. The shift away from midcentury modernism, the cultural residues of a new conservatism, the revival of religion, the influence of popular visual and musical art forms that thrive on sophisticated technology, immediacy, and repetition—all can be said to have contributed. The revival of interest in the music of twentieth-century composers once considered conservative, including Shostakovich, nonetheless possesses political overtones. During Shostakovich's lifetime he was viewed, in aesthetic terms, as being on the periphery. Well into the mid-1970s, radical and experimental breaks with past musical practice were deemed the preferred response to post-1945 modernity and the evils of European fascism. This connection between radically new music and progressive politics was particularly strong in Europe, as the cases of Boulez, Nono, and Stockhausen reveal. The substance of politics and the connections between art and politics have now shifted sufficiently to place Shostakovich in the center. In our post–Cold War world it is no random coincidence that Shostakovich's popularity in the West has been supported by a warm embrace of the belief that the music was and remains inherently resistant to and subversive of dictatorship, oppression, and terror.[7] Puncturing the surface of Shostakovich's overt and explicit loyalty to the regime would have been politically sensitive toward the end of the composer's lifetime, in the reactionary era of Brezhnev, precisely because of the presence of dissidents and defectors. Now that the Soviet Union is gone and there is no need to sustain "peaceful coexistence" or "détente," there are no barriers to idealizing Shostakovich as a spiritual opponent to the radical evil of the last century embodied by Stalin as well as Hitler. We can imagine the same process of revision in interpretation continuing in succeeding generations of Russian performers and listeners, as the memory of the complex relationship between the composer and the Soviet regime fades. Whatever the historical claims, Shostakovich's music, as Taruskin has rightly observed, will continue to survive and command our attention. It breaks out of its context of origin as powerful and significant—even if one, however reluctantly, considers it not to have been written as an act of secret dissidence or resistance to tyranny with coded meanings.

Shostakovich was, as Taruskin noted, "the one and only Soviet artist to be claimed equally by the official culture and the dissident culture."[8] No "official" music written in the Nazi era, not even Carl Orff's ever popular *Carmina Burana,* is comparable to Shostakovich in terms of ambiguity or merit. With the possible, although not comparable, exception of the music Richard Strauss wrote between 1933 and 1945, no music of such quality emerged from Nazi Germany after 1934 that was susceptible to interpretation as both affirmative and resistant. It needs to be remembered that official sanction was indispensable for the performance of music under both regimes. Under Stalin and Hitler, no composer revealing dissidence or resistance could remain in the public arena and survive, much less flourish, as did Shostakovich. Despite his undeniable sufferings, one cannot proclaim him a non-collaborator. Karl Amadeus Hartmann, for example, wrote music that was clearly dissident, critical, and resistant to Nazism in Germany during the 1930s and 1940s. But none of it was published or performed. He wrote in private, if not in secret. He withdrew from public life and had no career. No one is in doubt about his intentions, as some are vis-à-vis Shostakovich. But neither did Hartmann court risk by communicating to a public living under tyranny. His music was not designed as a "civic" act either supportive or subversive—or both—of the regime. Hartmann did not write music in a manner that exploited the inherent ambiguity of meaning that music possesses in regard to censors, dictators, and political operatives, for it had no public face and presence. His was a genuine case of "inner emigration."[9]

But that fact does not necessarily lend Hartmann some higher status in the realm of "moral judgment." If in his public life as a composer Shostakovich indeed communicated ambiguity, providing the opportunity for his public to express the intense emotions of fear, loss, and loathing without evident risk to themselves in the uniquely privileged space of concert life, then he in fact undertook a heroic and nerve-racking task, as his admirers and friends have argued. That music can play a special role in times of dictatorship is not new to the twentieth century. Composers using genres of classic and romantic composition, writing under conditions of tyranny, have exploited music's capacity to generate multiple and contradictory meanings—including nothing irreducibly concrete—

since well before Shostakovich's time. The music of Beethoven and Schubert from the years after 1815 can be interpreted in this light.[10] Franz Grillparzer, the long-suffering and still underestimated nineteenth-century Austrian writer, openly envied composers operating under the censorship of dictatorship. Well-trained professional authorities, even those who operated under Stalin, routinely have more difficulty locating the subversive in music than they do in the arts that require natural language or visual imagery and symbols. Unfortunately for Grillparzer, the literature (particularly on the stage) that flourished under Metternich (clearly no match for Stalin in terms of evil and brutality) was fantasy and farce laced with surface triviality, satire, irony, mysticism, the grotesque and the exotic—not the realistic or the tragic.[11]

There is, as the cliché has it, no easy music. In Shostakovich's case, the barriers to fashioning a convincing basis for interpretation and ascribing meaning to Shostakovich and his music are higher than those usually encountered in thinking about music, because of the historical context (the Soviet Union). But the sorts of complexities to which we are accustomed in thinking about Beethoven or Mahler derive largely from judgments about depth, originality, and greatness we believe located in the musical texts and revealed by analysis. Debates about intentions with respect to a "message" or meaning are augmented by historical and biographical research. All this is compounded in the case of Shostakovich. A straightforward reliance on music analysis alone, in defense of the autonomy of the artwork, seems inadequate in the case of Shostakovich. The formal aspects of the music, the materials and strategies, demand consideration not only as part of the evolution of twentieth-century concert music, but also within the framework of Soviet history. Shostakovich's enduring and growing popularity among professionals and the lay audience requires us to try to take into account not only the analysis of musical texts, but the music's context of origin, the performance history, and our contemporary biases.

As new research and publication make us ever more aware of the brutality of the Soviet era, finding a way to understand sympathetically music written and performed under Soviet patronage is not an easy task.[12] The process of critical engagement with Soviet art and culture in the West has been unusually contradictory, contentious, unreliable, and unstable from the early 1920s. The fall of the Soviet Union has now given us the opportunity gradually to forget the whole issue. One can deny or forget the link between Orff and the Nazis, but that is because one can just as easily dispense entirely with Orff's music.[13] With Shostakovich these two straightforward strategies (just play the music and enjoy it, or banish it from the stage) won't do. The music is just too compelling. Furthermore, the twentieth-century political contexts surrounding the making of music are hard to banish in general, whether one is considering the generations from Pfitzner and Schoenberg to Britten, Dallapiccola, Copland, Sessions, Harris, or on to Nono, Boulez, and Stockhausen.

And the Soviet Union needs to be considered a case apart. After all, more of the music repertory from the Soviet era than Shostakovich's is at stake. A good deal of officially sanctioned music written between the mid-1920s and the early 1980s merits performance and a place in the repertory as more than a historical curiosity: there is Miaskovsky, Shcherbachev, Gnesin, Khachaturian, and Prokofiev, as well as composers born later—Denisov, Sviridov, Ustvolskaya, Weinberg, Tishchenko, Schnittke—even Boris Tchaikovsky. A better grasp of how to confront the tension in Shostakovich between degrees of cooperation (consonant with official approval) and resistance (covert critical responses to dictatorship) may help build a bridge to the music of his contemporaries in comparable circumstances. The benefits will go well beyond the music of Prokofiev written after his return to Russia.[14]

II.

The question of how one might read texts produced in times of persecution and lack of freedom was addressed brilliantly by the philosopher Leo Strauss. The utility of Strauss's analysis in the case of Shostakovich has been dismissed, largely on the basis of a critique of Strauss by Hans-Georg Gadamer.[15] However, it is not clear that this dismissal is warranted. Strauss's argument makes several useful points. Since Strauss's topic was philosophy, he made the crucial observation that the writing of philosophy, particularly in times of persecution, involved a challenge to orthodoxy cast in the plausible and eloquent defense of that orthodoxy. Routinely, then, philosophers divided their audience into a "class" of philosophers and the rest, all non-philosophers. Furthermore, even in cases where there was an esoteric meaning hidden and locatable only with the systematic use of counterintuitive clues by a few philosophers, the surface orthodox arguments, however undermined, were not rendered trivial. Particularly in matters of religion, Strauss argued that caution and patience were needed to argue against false official doctrine: "The replacement of the accepted opinions could not be gradual, if it were not accompanied by a provisional acceptance of the accepted opinions."[16] The ordinary reader could embrace the orthodox surface text without any sense of missing anything. Precisely because censors and authorities included an elite of readers (including orthodox philosophers), no reductive or obvious contrast between accepted opinion and its undermining would work. Strauss understood this well.

However, the essential difficulty that must be solved in Strauss's approach is how to verify the esoteric heretical meaning underneath a surface of orthodox argument. The surface of orthodoxy itself must be convincing, even to the well-trained reader. Just to assert a hidden meaning is not enough. It must at once be found and nearly impossible to find. Without some compelling evidence, all suggestions of a deeper "hidden" truth would be equal. A defensible and systematic way of locating the esoteric is required. A philosopher working in a context of persecution and unfreedom who seeks to say something in opposition to the authorities must do two things: generate a powerful affirmative case and conceal its opposite. If the affirmation is not effective, the professionals (in Shostakovich's case, distinguished composers and musicologists eager to serve the state, such as Khrennikov, Kabalevsky, and Asafiev) might have detected the subversion, even if the general public did not. Music, like the philosophy Strauss wrote about, was subject to official "supervision" during Shostakovich's lifetime.[17] Lenin and Stalin had many willing "thoughtful men" who were "careful readers" working for them.[18] As a result, in a work such as the Fifth Symphony, Shostakovich made the "acceptance of accepted opinions" plausible and convincing.[19]

Our subject is music and not philosophy. What follows is an effort to apply Strauss's reasoning (he never discussed music) to the case of Shostakovich. One adaptation of Strauss's observation is to assert that Shostakovich himself may have been profoundly ambivalent and inconsistent in his attitude to the regime and its authorities. Perhaps there was no explicit intent, in contrast to the cases of Farabi, Judah Halevi, or Maimonides, to present a contradictory argument of a "private character" in a manner that assured "its inner freedom from supervision." If that was the case, then it should come as no surprise that in the music of Shostakovich written after 1936 there seems to be an intertwining of otherwise mutually exclusive arguments—an intimate rhetorical connection between the affirmative and its opposite. In such music, even the best of philosophers (and therefore the Party apologists among the composer's colleagues) cannot locate the heresy. They should not even sense its presence. When hidden resistance is being communicated in such works, the assertion of the existence and nature of esoteric meaning becomes arcane, controversial, and even doubtful, precisely because the exoteric—the surface—is so brilliant, engaging, and overwhelming. If there is an integral ambivalence on the author's part, the affirmation of orthodoxy may be even more dominant, as perhaps was the case with Shostakovich. The exoteric convinces the listener. Writers on religion and composers of music writing in an age of persecution share the need to deal with orthodoxy effectively; if they are ambivalent or even unclear about that orthodoxy, all the more reason for readers and listeners to take the exoteric orthodoxy seriously.

One piece of evidence supporting the notion of an intention to generate multiple and perhaps coded or hidden meaning comes from Shostakovich himself. Much in the spirit of Strauss's distinctions, he was aware of the differentiations within his intended audience. He understood how subtle, yet ultimately clear, one had to be to a select few in telling the truth—saying what one wishes—through music. In a letter to Isaak Glikman from 8 May 1966, concerning "a singer of intellectual pretensions" who sought to perform his "Humoresques" from *Krokodil* (the "Five Romances on Texts from *Krokodil* Magazine," op. 121), Shostakovich described his response to the singer's questions. To the query about meaning the composer answered, "Nowadays, audiences are ready and willing to play an active part in looking and listening. . . . True, it took a little while for the intellectual singer to see my point. It seems to me that as distinct from singer-philosophers there do exist readers who have a true understanding of what is good and what is bad."[20]

Shostakovich, as Strauss's logic encourages us to speculate, knew that even under Stalin, to whose brutality the arbitrary nature of persecution was integral, the burden of proof lay with Soviet officialdom. In 1936 and in 1948, it was these officials who had to make some sort of argument against him. In the absence of such an argument, "active" listeners who possessed the capacity to discriminate the true from the false were free to perceive the "true" nature of his works. Nonetheless, the integration of hidden truth would have had to be placed into the larger frame of convincing "falsehood." Shostakovich, in Strauss's words, needed to combine "understanding with caution." However, since Shostakovich shared the view that the "gulf" separating those few who could really understand the truth from everyone else was wide, it was not reasonable to tell "lies" to the many—the broad Soviet public—who might not be able to pick out hidden meanings. Shostakovich was a patriot and believer in the future of the potential of a socialist Soviet social order perhaps until the very end, after the so-called Thaw and the negative reaction to the Thirteenth Symphony. But even in the last symphony, the Fifteenth, one can argue that there can be no "lies," even on the surface. As in his previous works that are now understood to have both exoteric and esoteric meaning, e.g., the Tenth Symphony, there was "a popular teaching with an edifying character" in the foreground, even if there was, in addition, "a philosophic teaching concerning the most important subject, which is indicated between the lines."[21]

This suggests that in the works after 1936 that gained the most popularity and official praise, notably the Fifth and Seventh symphonies, the foreground of affirmation was for the composer both edifying and truthful. Perhaps he expected his fellow listeners, those "readers who have a true understanding," to grasp "teachings" about the most important subject, which may have been the inhumanity of the regime. This mix of popular affirmation and hidden criticism carefully constructed within musical structure and form that exploits the inherent instability and ambiguities of instrumental composition does not, however, make Shostakovich a dissident or a hero; it does not diminish the extent of his cooperation with the regime, since his music is explicitly designed to win the assent of censors and authorities.

III.

The question remains whether we can locate the hidden teaching in some nonarbitrary and therefore reasonable manner. The subject, after all, is not philosophy, but music, and methods specific to reading between lines in philosophy are not transferable. One possible and powerful answer lies in a habit of listening from the history of music associated with the seventeenth and eighteenth centuries: the cultivation of the sensibility of "sympathy."[22] Instead of looking for semantic representations in the music of resistance or dissidence (for example, the use of satire, irony, parody, and the grotesque, as recently argued by Esti Sheinberg), one can suggest that the composer, knowing his community of "active" listeners, understood how to use musical time and expression specifically with them in mind.[23] Despite the effort to locate meaning through an analysis of formal structures and procedures, the argument that supports the presence of some stable propositions, even reciprocal meta-messages, is dependent on what Ludwig Wittgenstein and Friedrich Waismann described as "the inclination to search for words to go with music." This inclination derives from the fact that we tend to see music as a "prolongation" of language, even though, in truth, music shows us that which "would no longer be called language."[24]

By using the notion of sympathy—which then is given linguistic forms by the listener in response to what the listener feels—we move away from looking for clues in the texts. The issue becomes not what was "in" the music (so to speak) or about links between compositional usage and so-called extramusical meaning. The argument shifts away from an analogy to language and propositions in texts. Meaning would be in a range of responses determined by the specific expectations, characteristics, and habits of the audience. In the case of Shostakovich, listeners would be responding sympathetically using expectations regarding the historic tradition of multi-movement instrumental genres (symphony, quartet, and chamber music with strings) specific to the musical culture of key cities (Leningrad and Moscow) and Russia itself. The habits of active listening in these settings were mediated by the audience's awareness of the official ideology regarding art. Therefore adaptations of models in musical practice defined by particular traditions of composition and performance took on specific local meanings.

Sympathy does not necessarily arise from an identifiable system of syntactic or semantic usage that transcends the local and the temporal moment, or of structural parallelisms between the use of sound and images and language. The composer's discovery of how to evoke sympathetic sensibilities by manipulating and inventing is contingent on the experience of music shared by a particular musical community.[25] These could then disappear with the passage of time and the changes in the venues of listening. This by no means excludes the possibility that for today's listener an elaborate and identifiable arsenal of musical techniques that deliver "a far more general satirical message condemning human stupidity and cruelty," evident beyond a specific audience, can be said to exist in Shostakovich. But here again Strauss's analysis of the conditions and consequences of persecution is relevant. If Shostakovich employed "referential expression" with "strong ethical connotations" (being "first and foremost an artist"), and revealed human nature as both "repellent and cruel" and simultaneously "cowardly and loving, humorous and courageous" and was therefore clearly "a humanist," by implication he was also, in some implausible manner, practically denying the intelligence and brutality of Stalin and his operatives.[26]

Those who hear today a "compound" message of existential irony as the composer's "meta-message" may not be wrong to do so. That this may have been the composer's intention and that it can be located today quite directly—audible through gestures and patterns or tone painting, however subtle—does not mean it could have been so located in Stalin's day, when to do so would have placed Shostakovich and his family in even greater danger than he was. There is more than a merely rhetorical difference between the claim that a meta-message is semantically locatable within the syntax and structure of composition through fixed variables representing parody, satire, irony, and the grotesque—all categories of visual and literary argument—and the suggestion that in the context of persecution such a propositional meaning can be generated by the listener, privately, through a far more ambiguous process permitting the evocation of sympathy.[27] In the Fifth and Seventh symphonies (and even the more controversial subsequent symphonies), the composer, in the opinion of local listeners and the authorities, successfully justified official ideology. The sophisticated ears of his rivals, supporters, and critics responded to the music as possessing convincing ideological conformity and affirmation. Under the reality of persecution and terror, such affirmation could not easily be negated: at one and the same time, the listeners had to be able to locate in their experience of the music sympathy with their own ambiguities. A truthful and edifying overt message as well as the suggestion of its contradiction were encountered simultaneously. For the most part, listeners in the Soviet era (even Party officials) maintained an ambiguous relationship with the regime, as did the composer. What strikes us now as evidently ironic, or satirical, or as parody and grotesque, can only be a small part of the story.[28] As Strauss's argument inspires us to think, perhaps Shostakovich wished to be (and was) successful in communicating, both to the general public and to his trained colleagues, a powerful and convincing message on behalf of the regime that could not be discounted, let alone negated, by a competitive sense of existential irony.[29]

This demarcates the difference between Gustav Mahler and Shostakovich. Mahler's music contains important clues to understanding Shostakovich. First, beginning with the Fifth Symphony (notably in the second movement, the Scherzo) there are innumerable points of musical comparison that have long been audible to performers and listeners. Second, as will be discussed later in this essay, Shostakovich in the 1930s turned to Mahler as a model. In Gustav Mahler's career there was no cause for fear and there was no regime to serve. The composer was free from state persecution. What he chose to communicate through music to his audience was motivated by factors other than fear for his life and the need to accommodate or further a political system and its ideas. Shostakovich was forced to find a way to reach an audience with seemingly contradictory needs: those expecting music to encourage patriotic and ideological enthusiasm and those suffering under the weight of oppression who sought, in the experience of music, some emotional resonance with their own despair, hope, fear, and resignation. Unfortunately, too much of the claim now being made on behalf of Shostakovich's command of humanist semantics and existential irony (including his embrace of Jewish musical materials and idioms) conveniently overlooks that Shostakovich successfully and intentionally served the Soviet regime. He inspired its loyalists, not all of whom were stupid and insensitive, without an evident undermining subtext of irony, parody, and satire. Shostakovich did more than tell "of the ironical acceptance of the despicable, the ridiculous and the beauty of human existence."[30] If individuals in the late 1930s heard this in his music, many others of equal intelligence, education, and musicality heard at the same time a direct and convincing affirmation of Stalin's tastes and Soviet ideology.

This articulates the unique paradox and achievement of Shostakovich: in the foreground a massive edifying popular surface; beneath it—quite hidden and framed by the kind of caution and ambiguity not always compatible with that which we now hear as satire, irony, and parody—signs of opposition to the foreground. Indeed, Shostakovich's turn to Mahler as a model in the mid-1930s, encouraged by Ivan Sollertinsky, may hold a clue; the composer may have found in Mahlerian procedures strategies that could function, sympathetically, to convey coherently affirmation along with despair and doubt. Perhaps Shostakovich adapted the elaboration of the Western symphonic tradition by Mahler, the last great "petit bourgeois" exponent of the "heroic symphony," for a new purpose—the expression of coded opposition, and did so precisely because of Mahler's appeal (and relative novelty) in providing a musical framework that allowed for the expression of various if not contradictory emotional states.[31] Shostakovich's choice, if it was motivated by that purpose, may convince us today about what the composer's "most important subject" was.

IV.

What then might have been the "the most important subject," beyond the official and the affirmative? The answer lies in the crisis of 1936. Taruskin's description of Shostakovich as a "civic" composer is indeed apt. As Leo Strauss argued in the case of philosophers, Shostakovich wanted to serve the socialist state constructively, despite his criticism of it. The question, then, was how to do so successfully, particularly under Stalin, without lying. The difficulty cannot be underestimated. It is a tribute to Shostakovich's genius that he succeeded without ending up writing forgettable music. But it needs to be remembered that the basis of his current popularity may not derive exclusively from the meta-message of "inner emigration," resistance, and existential irony found by contemporary writers. Indeed, the accessible foreground of joy, heroism, epic illustration and celebration—the unabashed self-revelatory intimacy bereft of any hint of irony—may have as much to do with the composer's success today as it did after the premiere of the Fifth Symphony. Perhaps even today we respond to the way he articulated in music a kind of celebration of the individual in community in Soviet culture.

The critical cultural events regarding meaning in Shostakovich occurred in 1932, and particularly after the 1936 *Pravda* editorial against *Lady Macbeth of the Mtsensk District*.[32] Issues of multiple or hidden meaning, of "extra" musical intentions, and the intent and character of the composer's choices of genre and style abound in works after the Fourth Symphony, beginning with the triumphant Fifth. Until the end of the 1920s, the Soviet regime under Lenin and Anatolii Lunacharsky held a favorable attitude toward what in the West were progressive modernist aesthetic developments. Until 1932 Soviet ideology favored futurism in music as in literature, theater, and architecture. It did so in the spirit of a new age of Communism and a radical break with the past. In April 1932 the Communist Central Committee ordered the reorganization of literary and artistic organizations that carried with it an official signal of a change in aesthetic objectives. The pre-1932 approach combined a vision of modernism that broke with the past, creating a style that appeared compatible with an internationalist egalitarianism. Such an aesthetic favored abstraction, rationalist, even mechanistic experimentation, and functionalism that suggested universals. In the 1920s an aesthetics of autonomy, a version of art for art's sake, was viewed as a worthy parallel to the true nature of socialism. In the 1920s "the complete blending of art with life" encouraged the nonfigurative in the visual arts and architecture (consider, for example, the competition and ultimate design by A. Shchusev for Lenin's Tomb; it is juxtaposed against the architecture of the Kremlin, St. Basil's Cathedral, and the historicist, nineteenth-century facade of the former GUM in Red Square). Therefore, "the affirmation of the right of art to speak in its own language" was underscored.[33] This ideology would later be condemned in both music and architecture as formalism.[34]

Political idealism and competing factionalism regarding what sort of art and culture a new socialist utopia should develop was flourishing in the 1920s when Shostakovich made his sensational entrance onto the Russian and international scene. The modern abstract idealism of art of the early 1920s was deemed nearly scientifically true, in the sense of Marxism itself. Its integration with life eschewed mimetic realism and favored a utopian celebration of the new. A superficial definition of realism toward the figurative and illustrative, as in the Socialist Realism of the late 1930s, was rejected in favor of underlying universal "formal" conceptions. A non-cynical and radical partisanship on these issues, including a rival reductive advocacy of "proletarian" populism, engaged most of Shostakovich's immediate contemporaries and was visible within conservatories and institutions of music.[35] Even in 1930 the sense of persecution from above was less powerful than that of disillusionment and the search for new responses to the challenge of creating a social-ist utopia.

Beginning with Stalin's accumulation of power, particularly after the reor-ganization of artistic life implemented in 1932, tyranny and fear gradually came to dominate artistic life. They gathered momentum through the 1930s and would remain in place despite the sense of common purpose and patriotism of the war years between 1941 and 1944, which only per-sisted until victory was plainly in view. After that, the conditions of insecurity and brutality were stark and evident to all until the death of Stalin and the subsequent Thaw. Yet even in the late 1930s—despite the Hitler-Stalin Pact—the serious voluntary, non-cynical reconsideration of the premises of the relationship between art and society that had flourished in the 1920s continued. In other words, not all apologists for Stalin were pup-pets, and not all those who had second thoughts about formalism were simply towing a Party line. Although the post-1932 ideology was certainly spearheaded by Stalin, it also involved a substantive reversal, as Vladimir Paperny has argued, in how art might serve the socialist vision of Russia. An obsession with history replaced futurism. Traditionalism took the place of experimentation. A sense of hierarchy and localism replaced an inter-est in progressive international-style uniformity.

A revised and antimodernist definition of a "realism" appropriate to socialism emerged victorious. It claimed to celebrate the sense of the human, of the emotional living person (therefore giving rise to the seem-ingly ludicrous emphasis on easily identifiable "melody"). It responded to the objection that artists in the 1920s were too elitist and concerned with the counterintuitively rational and mechanical. A progressive mod-ernist universalism was replaced by suspicion of the West. The purpose of art in the public arena, after 1932, was increasingly construed as help-ing the masses live a life enhanced by the aesthetic, to see "the world artistically."[36] Given the historicism of the Stalinist era, this meant cam-ouflaging the industrial and functional, and encouraging a symbolic and nostalgic return to ornament and decoration. At the same time there was a demand, in Paperny's formulation, for the "truthful reflection of life from the artist. The formalist found this approach foreign. Formalism pulled the artist away from life, away from reality, to forms dissimilar to life."[37] Paperny's use of the word "formalism" is itself intentionally ironic, for the artists of the 1920s did not use that term; it became, however, the primary and endlessly repeated epithet in the vocabulary of Stalinist criticism. After 1932, official culture demanded an idealized and stylized realism bordering on the mythological and heroic that permitted the public to identify, through art, with a monumental and historicized but recognizable ideal of the real. No better example of this amalgam exists than the major large-scale Stalinist building projects that still dominate Moscow's skyline.

The musical manifesto calling for a shift in Soviet music away from the currents of the 1920s was the January 1936 *Pravda* editorial "Muddle Instead of Music." Its force was augmented by responses, including Boris Asafiev's important 1936 article in *Sovetskaia muzyka*. Open discussions in the Leningrad and Moscow meetings of the Composers' Union were held to discuss the *Pravda* editorial.[38] The criticism leveled at Shostakovich and *Lady Macbeth* has been extensively discussed and documented. However, it is more useful and enlightening to take the criticism seriously than to condemn the critics and the criticism. Richard Taruskin has done this in part with respect to the ethical implications of the way Nikolai Leskov's story was set to music.[39] But equally interesting is the critique of originality in Asafiev's comments, his plea to return to history, and the repeated praise of Shostakovich's potential and talent.

We can easily dismiss the comments of those who participated in these discussions as motivated by fear or cowardice. But what if one takes seriously the rejection of what *Lady Macbeth*, with its imitation of models of originality prevalent in the West, appeared to represent: the mere "striving for modernity," arrogant "subjectivism"? As Maksimilian Shteinberg noted, siding with the great piano pedagogue Heinrich Neuhaus, the call in the *Pravda* editorial for music that could be more directly understood and appreciated by "the broad masses" need not require a vulgar "simplification." So long as the distinction between "artistic economy" and "mere simplification" could be preserved, the ideals of the *Pravda* criticism were not in themselves inappropriate.

It should be noted, however, that the tone of the editorial was intended to be unmistakably personal and harsh. Shostakovich's music was used as an explicit example of errors that others would be well advised to avoid. The "Muddle" editorial was followed in February 1936 by a second attack on Shostakovich's music, "Balletic Falsehood."[40] And *Pravda* did not let up, publishing further editorials in the same vein. But it was the argument of the "Muddle" editorial that dominated the debate among musicians. Most interesting, perhaps, was the contribution to the debate by Sollertinsky, himself subject to criticism and a close friend of Shostakovich. As with Shostakovich, Sollertinsky's career flourished, despite the 1936 controversy, until his untimely death in 1944. Sollertinsky predicted that the composer would respond to the criticism not with arguments, but with "creative deeds" that would respond to the main purpose of the *Pravda* article: to achieve "a truly proper orientation for the whole of Soviet music."[41] His overt and courageous warning was not against "self-criticism," but against the use of fear as opposed to open argument.

The direction Shostakovich's response might take was outlined by Sollertinsky. "Naturally," he wrote, "the true way lies in the language of heroic representations and the language of Soviet monumental art." If Shostakovich was to develop a "true connection" to the Soviet public, he would have to utilize a "Soviet thematic" and find "a new intonation." His failing up to that point, in the opinion of Sollertinksky, one of the composer's closest friends (whose judgment the composer trusted and relied on), was that he "lacked the true heroic pathos." Indeed, much opportunity stood before him, particularly in the genre of the "heroic symphony." Sollertinsky predicted, "I see his ultimate field of endeavor in the genre of Soviet musical tragedy and the Soviet heroic symphony." Shostakovich's subsequent output can be regarded as following quite closely this direction (with the exception of the field of opera, which Sollertinsky hoped he would pursue).

The 1948 debate, in contrast, would be hard to consider as worthy of substantive analysis. It followed the notorious Central Committee resolution of February 1948 in response to Vano Muradeli's opera, *The Great Friendship,* and called for a radical, simplistic, melodic Socialist Realism in music. It condemned the music of Shostakovich, Prokofiev, Miaskovsky, Khachaturian, Popov, and Shebalin as catering to a clique of aesthetes, ignoring national character and pursuing an "illusory" innovation, once again condemned as "formalism."[42] The appropriateness of taking the articulate embrace of the 1936 *Pravda* criticism seriously and not merely as a form of coded doublespeak, even on the part of Sollertinsky and other allies, is suggested by the period. In 1936, the full extent of Stalin's brutality was not entirely evident. Both in Russia and the West, idealism persisted about reconsidering the possible connections between the high art traditions and a more just and socialist society. Was there not a chance that the masses could be moved and reached, could become part of the public for art? The shift from the music of *Lady Macbeth* and the Fourth Symphony to the style of the Fifth and subsequent works of the late 1930s and early 1940s may therefore reflect a genuine desire on the part of the composer to achieve the goals set forward in the *Pravda* editorials, particularly as interpreted by Sollertinsky. There is an irony, however, in all this. *Lady Macbeth* had been enormously popular during its initial two years of performances, which is why it became the focus of attack. The unperformed Fourth Symphony and the opera *The Nose,* were, in musical terms, the more adventuresome and less evidently comprehensible on first hearing.

Another indication that this might be so comes from Sollertinsky's 1932 Mahler monograph. Sollertinsky's advocacy of Mahler and conception of Mahler's achievement were important influences on Shostakovich. Written at the beginning of the official shift in cultural policy that began with literature, the book was not republished and allowed to disappear. Ironically, however, its argument regarding the significance of Mahler to the future of Soviet music was entirely compatible with the direction suggested by the *Pravda* editorial. Mahler, more than musical "Impressionism or Constructivism," more than Debussy, Stravinsky, Richard Strauss, or Hindemith, was relevant to the "task of creating a Soviet symphonic tradition." That task required "a grand societal idea" that provided the philosophical underpinnings of the symphony. Only Soviet society could furnish that basis. Mahler was the model that pointed the way to achieving in Soviet music the next stage in the future of Soviet symphonic music. Mahler's example indicated the utility of applying four criteria:

1) great philosophical-ethical Pathos,
2) grounding the symphony on song,
3) linking expression at all costs to a distinctive emotional character in the music, owing to the need to create the largest possible collective of listeners, and
4) an exceptional command of the apparatus of the orchestra and the human voice.[43]

Were it not for two suggestive parallelisms, one might be inclined to dismiss Sollertinsky's rhetoric from both 1932 and 1936 as either required ideological boilerplate or possessed of some hidden contradictory meaning. First, Shostakovich can be understood to have adjusted his compositional strategies in ways that correspond to Sollertinsky's writings. This is evident not only when comparing the Fourth Symphony to Shostakovich's subsequent efforts in the genre, but by considering the uniqueness of the opening movement of the Symphony no. 2 from 1927. This movement, with its striking and daring use of sonorities, was clearly in the line of Sollertinsky's "Impressionism and Constructivism." Further, and more importantly: similar sentiments, if not second thoughts about the musical modernisms of the 1920s, were being voiced outside of the Soviet Union. Both in Russia and the West, the motivation behind these second thoughts about the relationship of music to socialist politics was comparable, even if outside Russia the context did not involve a life-threatening command structure from above. The place of Mahler's music in this post-1920s search for a path different from both the models of Stravinsky and Schoenberg was significant. During the 1930s Benjamin Britten (who would become Shostakovich's closest and most admired Western colleague) confessed that he began "a great crusade among my friends on behalf of my new God" (with "average success"): Mahler—who had been, during his youth, the object of derision among American and English musicians.[44]

Another early advocate of Mahler was Aaron Copland, who reported that he had studied Mahler's orchestrations with Nadia Boulanger.[45] Early in his career Copland defended Mahler against the dismissive attitude of New York critics.[46] Furthermore, around the time Copland was working on *Statements for Orchestra* in Minnesota, he found himself drawn into politics, even giving a speech to an assembly of farmers in the summer of 1934. Inspired in part by progressive politics and his encounters with a different segment of the American population in the heartland of the country, Copland shifted his style, convinced that "the American people could be reached by good music." It was only fair, he thought, that the contemporary composer "meet his audience partway." Copland's new ambitions were in the direction urged by the *Pravda* editorial in 1936. His output after *Statements* includes his most popular works, among them *Appalachian Spring*, the Third Symphony, the *Lincoln Portrait, El Salón México,* and the ballet score *Rodeo*. These works can be understood as running parallel to the shift called for by official Soviet aesthetics toward a heroic, nearly mythic realism. They can be set alongside the trajectory of Shostakovich's development. Copland made the same observation as Shostakovich's teacher Shteinberg that "the challenge was to find a way without sacrificing musical values." In 1936 Copland wrote, "to compose music of 'socialist realism' has stumped even so naturally gifted a man as Shostakovitch."[47] However, by emulating Mahler—something Copland, despite his admiration, never did—Shostakovich did not remain "stumped" for long.

The search for an anti-formalist way of reconciling modernism with populism in the 1930s, particularly in America, extended to the visual arts. The search for a uniquely American approach to the notion of "good" art for the masses was inspired in part by a close reading of Walt Whitman and extended to the circle of leading painters and photographers around Alfred Stieglitz.[48] The dilemma of how to make new art—particularly music—from within the traditions of high art without alienating the mass of fellow citizens led other contemporaries of

Shostakovich's in the West to abandon the highly aestheticized, formalist, and complex progressive developments of the several modernisms of
the 1920s. Ferruccio Busoni's student Kurt Weill and Schoenberg's student
Hanns Eisler are the two most prominent cases; the direction taken by
the young Austrian composer Marcel Rubin (who, as a Jew, was forced
to emigrate to Mexico in 1938) is another less well-known example.[49] In
terms of ideology and aesthetics, Arthur Honegger can also be considered part of this evolution. He broke with the Communists only after
attending the infamous 1949 conference hosted by Zhdanov in Prague.[50]
In all of these four cases the resulting music can be said to parallel urg-
ings not too different from the infamous *Pravda* 1936 editorial and the
ideological prejudices of Stalin with respect to music and art.

One can therefore consider the music of Shostakovich after 1936 as
an honest civic attempt to generate a more powerful Soviet art. There
may be no intentional "subtext" to either the Fifth or the Seventh
Symphony. It was the peculiar genius of Shostakovich to be able to quickly
compose—in response to public criticism and Sollertinsky's influence—
works in traditional genres whose mix of accessibility and complexity
permitted the plausibility of differential readings then and now. By the
time he wrote the Tenth Symphony, the contradictions created by a sincere desire to maintain his status within the official culture may have
driven the composer more in the direction of intentionally using techniques to communicate a sense of irony, despair, and self-loathing—the
price extracted by the need to sustain both his public role and his sense
of human integrity.[51] But even in the presence of a subtext, understanding Shostakovich's music through its affirmative voice may be one
crucial key to grasping even the late music's power and appeal. The com-
patibility of surface with imputed subversive undercurrents suggest that
Shostakovich's most "important" objective was the evocation, with sympathy, of the predicaments of everyday life; the compromises, the suffering,
and the tragic consequences, not only for any artist of conscience in the
public eye, but for the ordinary listener.

V.

The case of Shostakovich is one of the artist who found a way not only
to survive but to thrive in the public realm under brutality and tyranny.
His achievement has managed to outstrip the historical circumstances of
its creation so that it appeals to subsequent generations long after the political circumstances we readily condemn have vanished. These truths may

lead to the conclusion that it is not necessary to reconfigure the composer's biography: Shostakovich may attract us precisely because he was not a hero, not a dissident. His nonheroic accessibility and careerist ordinariness (in ethical terms) may actually reflect an admirable willingness to take responsibility for compromise, for adjusting to life. The techniques he used, particularly his approach to speech making and writing, strike us as befitting the special character of Soviet life.[52] But in music, Shostakovich's struggle to keep on writing something he could defend as music while maintaining his family and career ought to ring familiar. His actions are, after all, not so different from any successful individual's routine participation in, avoidance, and observation of evil done to adjust to the structures of power in all twentieth-century political contexts. There is, for example, room for comparison between Shostakovich and his political context (including censorship and patronage) and Beethoven during the process of composition and dedication of the *Eroica* Symphony. Both tried to reconcile personal beliefs with the shifting directions of political power from above.[53] Sympathetically, through music, Shostakovich reminds his listeners of ordinary life. The "most important thought" may be the human need to come to terms with ethical compromise, with a troubling mix of sensitivity and insensitivity, idealism and selfishness, sensuality and asceticism, cooperation, indifference and resentment within the world. This demand for compromise was and remains required of music's listeners, of educated individuals with careers.

Certainly, we are drawn in Shostakovich's case to the severity of the conflict and compromise between conscience and ambition. We are also drawn by the capacity of his achievement to transcend the historical era from which it emerged, including its evils. In this sense Shostakovich's place in the history of music becomes a moral equivalent of that of Galileo in the history of science. The suggestion of a comparison with Galileo makes sense simply on account of the comparable greatness of the individuals in question and the severity of the power that could and was exerted in both cases. It is therefore interesting to note that the Galileo case makes an appearance in the poetic text of the last movement of the Thirteenth Symphony. There the issue of the conscience of the artist is set in a musical context that has been termed "cheerful" if not "lightly ironic."[54] Furthermore, Shostakovich permitted Iurii Liubimov to use the *Hamlet* music he had written in 1932 for a 1966 Moscow production of Bertolt Brecht's play.[55] The composer, writing to Isaak Glikman in February 1967, commented, "I did not really like either the play or the production."[56]

The treatment of Galileo by Brecht stands in stark contrast to Evgenii Yevtushenko's handling of the Italian astronomer in his "A Career." The

Russian poet indulges in too obvious a form of moralizing, self-pity, and loathing, as Boris Tishchenko (Shostakovich's student) once noted.[57] But Tishchenko was, after all, responding to Shostakovich's allegiance to poetry based primarily on its political and moral significance. Indeed, the citation of Galileo by Yevtushenko was, as Laurel Fay has noted, entirely "didactic."[58] But Brecht's treatment is not. His use of the Galileo case is far more ambiguous. The play may have annoyed Shostakovich precisely because it fails to judge; it avoids a simple confessional and a reductive moral assessment. The comparison between Shostakovich's predicament and Galileo's, in Brecht's elaboration, becomes even more alluring when one considers that Brecht began the play in 1938 and worked on it for more than a decade, tinkering with it and revising it in two languages. More than any other single work, it dominated his career. He wrote it as a Communist who was the editor of the journal *Das Wort* (published in Moscow), as an artist voluntarily in accord with the ideological shifts toward historicism and a "new aesthetic traditionalism" put forward by Moscow. But even for Brecht, the contradictions that the late 1930s made plain were hard to deny. Brecht was disturbed by the fate of Vsevolod Meyerhold, the rigidity of the new aesthetic criteria, the fall of Czechoslovakia, and, ultimately, the Hitler-Stalin Pact.[59] The play underwent revisions as Brecht fled Germany and passed through Russia en route to America.

Shostakovich worked under the oppression of Stalin. Brecht worked on *Galileo* as a refugee, displaced and ultimately unwanted in the United States. Brecht's play, despite significant divergences between versions, highlights aspects of Galileo that make one think of Shostakovich's predicament. Does Galileo recant in order to continue to work and to think in secret? Or is he driven by the ordinary desire to live and enjoy a career and the pleasures of life? As Galileo notes sarcastically in the beginning of the play, as he pens a particularly fawning appeal to those in power, "A man like me can only get a halfway decent job by crawling on his belly. And you know what I think of people whose brains aren't capable of filling their stomachs."[60] Galileo's profound awareness of his own cowardice, expressed in scene 14, reminds one of the periodic explosions of self-criticism and disgust expressed by Shostakovich to close friends. Brecht presents Galileo with ambivalence and sympathy, as a scientist who recognizes the validity of the modern scientific credo (to seek the truth and defend it against arbitrary power and lies), but who also seeks to escape the privileged sphere of scientist (or artist) cut off from humanity.

This task of reaching out and communicating to the broader public places the obvious contradictions of conscience themselves into a problematic context. "I taught you science and I denied the truth," Galileo observes. The consequences of cowardice do not remain private. Galileo's deft understanding of and respect for his masters' knowledge and cunning are revealed, laying bare the exact nature of Galileo's compromise. Likewise, as Brecht himself observed, one feels "disillusionment" watching the "old" authorities win time and time again over the new and the true. The composer watching the play in 1967 could not have escaped this feeling. Brecht's judgment of Galileo is a mixture of "praise" and "condemnation." There is no real vindication or facile reconciliation. In the scientist's case, the criterion of truth in the judgment of history overwhelms the weaknesses of his character, even though the ultimate historical triumph of the "truth" for Brecht had the consequence of separating science from society and making the morally ambiguous atomic age possible. The consequences of Galileo's ultimate vindication are therefore contradictory.

For the composer, the consequences of his behavior and his work—both as regards the truth and the betterment of the condition of others—were equally uncertain. As Brecht's Galileo observes, "Better stained than empty. Sound realistic. Sounds like me. New science, new ethics." Brecht's close, realistic, and less reductive characterization, in contrast to Yevtushenko's facile sentimentality and the straightforward message the poet's verses communicated to the composer, is what provides the closest analog to Shostakovich's predicament. After all, Galileo muses at the end of the play: "Had I stood firm the scientists could have developed something like the doctors' Hippocratic oath, a vow to use their knowledge exclusively for mankind's benefit. . . . What's more. . . . I have come to the conclusion that I was never in any real danger. . . . And I handed my knowledge to those in power for them to use, fail to use, misuse—whatever best suited their objectives. . . . I betrayed my profession."[61]

VI.

Perhaps the toughest challenge facing contemporary musicians and audiences is to find a way to step away from looking back into the past, passing judgment, and finding redemption in the case of Shostakovich. Where audiences once heard a plea for progressive left-wing politics in the music of Copland, today we seem only to hear a patriotic evocation of a mythic America. This is so much the case that since the 1976 Bicentennial, Copland's music from the 1940s has become the sonic emblem of flag-waving boosterism. What if the need to respond critically to the grim realities of Soviet daily life may not have been Shostakovich's dominant motive? Perhaps we should be content to sense either the heroic and epic narrative or the personal and intimate without any hint of politics.[62] We can just as well choose to sense irony, bittersweet humor, and detached resignation.

Whatever the case may be, Shostakovich continues to succeed in fashioning a musical community of active listeners. The framework of past utopian politics gone awry has vanished. In its place may be a world in which listeners are consciously detached from any politics but keenly aware of the moral ambiguities of ordinary life and the ethical costs of simply seeking to keep going. Ironically, the powerful and accessible surface of affirmation—the framing narratives of Shostakovich's music—are to us both engaging and susceptible to contradictory personal appropriation. We are attracted to an epic and grand heroic narrative with the same sense of depoliticized loss and nostalgia with which we respond to Copland. Indeed, Shostakovich after 1936 succeeded in writing music that reached a broader public. Perhaps he can be most provocatively compared to Mendelssohn, whose conscious use of his prodigious talents was to write music that affirmed a set of spiritual and ethical values. Mendelssohn cultivated accessibility and directness, and by so doing captured the affections of the nineteenth-century educated middle classes of Europe and America. In the late twentieth and early twenty-first, Shostakovich appeals, with Mendelssohnian directness and accessibility, to the jaded if not cynical successors of nineteenth-century listeners, to a public that finds unqualified utopian expectations no longer reasonable. If we respond to Shostakovich as somehow more intense, personal, and profound, it is because in our time the capacity for the optimism, generosity, tolerance, and trust that Mendelssohn so keenly sought to deepen through the experience of music seems hard to muster. We therefore may prefer to subordinate or depoliticize the power and directness of the affirmative brilliance in Shostakovich's music.

NOTES

1. Jörg Steiner, *Wer tanzt schon zu Musik von Schostakowitsch* (Frankfurt/Main: Suhrkamp, 2000), pp. 80–81.

2. See, for example, Arthur Berger's review of the Sixth Symphony from 1944 and his memory of Stravinsky's views in 1940, in Arthur Berger, *Reflections of an American Composer* (Berkeley, Calif.: University of California Press, 2002), pp. 232, 221. See also the brief discussion of Shostakovich, mostly about politics, which also speaks of a "retrenchment" in style, in Robert P. Morgan, *Twentieth Century Music* (New York: W. W. Norton, 1991), p. 246.

3. The range and depth of scholarly and polemical literature on Shostakovich, particularly since his death and after 1989, mirror the broader public enthusiasm. The debates over the composer and his music have, from time to time, become stridently partisan and even assumed a bitter and intense tone. An example from the crucial year 1989 is Malcolm Barry's essay "Ideology and Form: Shostakovich East and West," in the collection *Music and the Politics of Culture,* ed. Christopher Norris (New York: St. Martin's Press, 1989), pp. 172–86. It is at least reassuring that music still seems to matter so much. As a non-expert observer in the field, I am indebted to Laurel E. Fay and her indispensable biography, *Shostakovich: A Life* (New York: Oxford University Press, 2000). Readers are encouraged to consult it and Elizabeth Wilson's *Shostakovich: A Life Remembered* (Princeton, N.J.: Princeton University Press, 1994) and the following English-language collections that represent the range and character of the debate: *Shostakovich Reconsidered,* ed. Allan B. Ho and Dmitry Feofanov (London: Toccata Press, 1998); *A Shostakovich Casebook,* ed. Malcolm Hamrick Brown (Bloomington, Ind.: Indiana University Press, 2004); *Shostakovich in Context,* ed. Rosamund Bartlett (Oxford: Oxford University Press, 2000); *Shostakovich Studies,* ed. David Fanning (Cambridge, Eng.: Cambridge University Press, 1995). See also the several collections of essays published in German by Verlag Ernst Kuhn as part of the Studia Slavica Musicologia series. Mention should also be made of the controversial biography by Ian MacDonald, *The New Shostakovich* (Boston: Northeastern University Press, 1990) that argues a Volkov-like position.

4. Richard Taruskin, *Defining Russia Musically* (Princeton, N.J.: Princeton University Press, 1997), pp. 475–77.

5. *Testimony: The Memoirs of Dmitri Shostakovich As Related to and Edited by Solomon Volkov,* trans. Antonina W. Bouis (New York: Limelight, 2000). On the controversy, see Laurel E. Fay, "Shostakovich versus Volkov: Whose Testimony?" *Russian Review* 39, no. 4 (1980): 484–93; and Ho and Feofanov's response, which occupies the first 300 pages of their edited volume, as well as Fay's update, "Volkov's *Testimony* Reconsidered (2002)," in *A Shostakovich Casebook,* pp. 22–66.

6. See David Fanning, "The Language of Doublespeak," in his excellent monograph *The Breath of the Symphonist: Shostakovich's Tenth* (London: Royal Musical Association, 1989). Fanning deals with the issue of ambivalence in Shostakovich. On dissent and resistance, see Michael Tippett, *Tippett on Music,* ed. Meiron Bowen (Oxford: Oxford University Press, 1995), pp. 81–82. Tippett invokes the reading of the Eleventh Symphony as not about the pre-Soviet past, 1905, but the present, that is, the mid-1950s, years that included the suppression of the 1956 Hungarian Revolution. On this interpretation, see Fay, *Shostakovich: A Life,* pp. 202–3; see also a 1986 German-language account (reissued in 2002), Bernd Feuchtner, *Dimitri Schostakowitsch: "Und Kunst geknebelt von der groben Macht":
Künstlerische Identität und staatliche Repression* (Kassel: Bärenreiter, 2002) that puts forward a post-Volkov argument about dissident "hidden claims."

7. See the fine recent accounts, including readings of the Tenth Symphony and the Third Quartet in Arnold Whittall, *Musical Composition in the Twentieth Century* (Cambridge,

Eng.: Cambridge University Press, 1999), pp. 150–56, and his *Exploring Twentieth-Century Music: Tradition and Innovation* (Cambridge, Eng.: Cambridge University Press, 2003), pp.108–13; for earlier treatments of modernism in the twentieth century, see H. H. Stuckenschmidt, *Neue Musik* (Frankfurt/Main: Suhrkamp, 1981), pp. 215–21, and Ulrich Dibelius, *Moderne Musik nach 1945* (Munich: Piper, 1998), where there is no discussion of Shostakovich. See also the essays by Manuel Gervink, "Schostakowitsch aus der Sicht der deutsch-österreichischen Moderne," and Jelena Poldjajewa, "Zur historischen Kategorisierung und ästhetischen Bewertung des Shaffens von Dimitri Schostakowitsch aus dem Blickwinkel der Avantgarde der 50er Jahre," in *Schostakowitsch in Deutschland,* ed. Hilmar Schmalenberg, Schostakowitsch-Studien, vol. 1 (Berlin: Verlag Ernst Kuhn, 1998), pp. 1–44.

8. Richard Taruskin, "Shostakovich and Us," in *Shostakovich in Context,* p. 13.

9. See Andrew D. McCredie, "Zur Biographie Karl Amadeus Hartmanns," in *Karl Amadeus Hartmann,* ed. Ulrich Dibelius et al., Komponisten in Bayern, vol. 27 (Tutzing: Hans Schneider, 1995), pp. 33–47.

10. See Leon Botstein, "Realism Transformed: Franz Schubert and Vienna," in *The Cambridge Companion to Schubert,* ed. Christopher H. Gibbs (Cambridge, Eng.: Cambridge University Press, 1997), pp. 15–35; see also Alice M. Hanson, *Musical Life in Biedermeier Vienna* (Cambridge, Eng.: Cambridge University Press, 1985), pp. 34–60; and, on the Beethoven Ninth Symphony, see Lewis Lockwood, *Beethoven: The Music and the Life* (New York: W. W. Norton, 2002), pp. 414–25; and Esteban Buch, *Beethoven's Ninth: A Political History,* trans. Richard Miller (Chicago: University of Chicago Press, 2003).

11. See Roger Bauer, *La Réalité Royaume de Dieu: Etudes sur l'originalité du théâtre viennois dans la première moitié du XIXe siècle* (Munich: Max Hueber, 1965); Grillparzer's play *Der Traum ein Leben* from the 1830s, on which he had worked since 1817, is a masterpiece but a powerful example of how difficult delivering coded meanings, even in the context of a comic, albeit philosophical fantasy, can be under strict censorship.

12. See, for example, Anne Applebaum, *Gulag: A History* (New York: Doubleday, 2003). Applebaum estimates that more than 28 million people went through the Gulag in the years of Shostakovich's maturity.

13. On Orff, see Michael Kater, *Composers of the Nazi Era* (New York: Oxford University Press, 2000), pp. 111–43.

14. On the repertoire, see Levon Hakobian, *Music of the Soviet Age, 1917–1987* (Stockholm: Melos, 1998).

15. Taruskin, *Defining Russia Musically,* p. 478.

16. Leo Strauss, *Persecution and the Art of Writing* (Chicago: University of Chicago Press, 1980), p. 17.

17. See Boris Schwarz, *Music and Musical Life in Soviet Russia, 1917–1970* (New York: W. W. Norton, 1972), and Strauss, *Persecution,* p. 21.

18. Strauss, *Persecution,* p. 25.

19. On the Fifth Symphony, see Richard Taruskin, "Public Lies and Unspeakable Truth: Interpreting Shostakovich's Fifth Symphony," in *Shostakovich Studies,* pp. 17–56; also in his *Defining Russia Musically,* pp. 511–44.

20. *Story of a Friendship: The Letters of Dmitry Shostakovich to Isaak Glikman, 1941–1975,* with a commentary by Isaak Glikman, trans. Anthony Phillips (Ithaca, N.Y.: Cornell University Press, 2001), p. 131. The Russian term Shostakovich uses is *pevets-myslitel'* or "singer-thinker," which might be understood as even more satirical than the Phillips translation suggests. Furthermore, the Russian for "true understanding" is more colloquial: "those who understand very well what's good and what's bad." See *Pis'ma k drugu Dmitrii Shostakovich-Isaaku Glikmanu,* comp. I. D. Glikman (Moscow/St. Petersburg: DSCH/Kompozitor, 1993), pp. 215–16.

21. Strauss, *Persecution,* p. 25. See the argument, relevant to the discussion following, that there was a coded message in the Fifth Symphony directed at its first audiences,
in Inna Barsova, "Between 'Social Demands' and the 'Music of Grand Passions': The Years
1934–1937 in the Life of Dmitry Shostakovich," in *Shostakovich in Context,* pp. 88–98.

22. I am indebted in this regard to Ruth HaCohen, "The Music of Sympathy in the
Arts of the Baroque, Or, The Use of Difference to Overcome Indifference," *Poetics Today*
22, no. 3 (Fall 2001): 607–50.

23. Esti Sheinberg, *Irony, Satire, Parody and the Grotesque in the Music of Shostakovich:
A Theory of Musical Incongruities* (Aldershot: Ashgate, 2000). For Sheinberg, Shostakovich
conveys "in his music . . . . the correlative of existential irony, i.e. *the referential idea of existential irony*" (p. 318); see also the Preface and pp. 3–4. The discussion that follows is in
no way understood as a criticism of Sheinberg's admirable and ingenious work. Problems
with her analysis and conclusion arise not when one considers Shostakovich today but
only when one seeks to apply them back into the historical moment, confronting life under
Stalin, during the crucial years in Shostakovich's career. The plausibility of her views becomes
stronger beginning after 1956, even during the reactionary years under Brezhnev, when
the composer's age, illness, and stature make the argument of a stance of existential
irony and detachment more plausible, thereby contextualizing a ritualistic, if not cyncial,
continuing collaboration with the regime, including joining the Party. See the discussion
of Sheinberg's book in Richard Taruskin, "Double Trouble," *The New Republic,* 24 December
2001.

24. Ludwig Wittgenstein und Friedrich Waismann, *The Voices of Wittgenstein: The Vienna
Circle,* ed. Gordon Baker (London and New York: Routledge, 2003), p. 395.

25. See Joseph P. Swain, *Musical Languages* (New York: W. W. Norton, 1997), pp.
68–70, 162–67, 170–76.

26. Sheinberg, *Irony,* pp. 318–19.

27. A word on the issue of Shostakovich's relationship to Jews, the fate of the Jews
in Soviet Russia, particularly between 1945 and 1953, and his use of Jewish musical materials. Shostakovich's positive attitude toward the Jews and the claim of a close identification
with their plight has been used to bolster the notion of the composer's inner resistance to
the Soviet regime, particularly after 1945. For all of the elaborate and extensive writing
on this subject, it is perhaps appropriate to strike a note of caution in using this line of
argument. As victims of a variety of forms of persecution, from discrimination in social
relations and employment to harassment, imprisonment, and extermination, the Jewish
response extends beyond the cultivation of eloquent means of communicating humor,
irony, satire, and suffering. There were also visible in Shostakovich's time in Soviet Russia
the disfiguring costs of dehumanization, denial, the struggle to accommodate, to assimilate, to please the masters, revulsion at powerlessness, and the necessity of showing what
could otherwise be deemed as cowardice. The pariah status of the Jew and the brutal denial
of the Jew's humanity resulted in the full range of responses, from the noble techniques
of "inner emigration" or "laughing through tears" to collaboration with evil. See Timothy
Jackson, "Dmitry Shostakovich: The Composer as Jew," in *Shostakovich Reconsidered,* pp.
597–642; Richard Taruskin's contrasting portraits of Stravinsky and Shostakovich in their
attitude to Jews in *Defining Russia Musically,* pp. 448–76, and the essays (including one by
Jackson) in *Dmitri Schostakowitsch und das jüdische musikalische Erbe,* ed. Ernst Kuhn, Andreas
Wehrmeyer, and Günter Wolter, Schostakowitsch-Studien, vol. 3 (Berlin: Verlag Ernst Kuhn,
2001). On Stalin's anti-Semitism and particularly his designs to eliminate the Jews after
1945, see Yaakov Aizenstat, *A Potkovtok'e Stalinim Genozida E'vre'ev* (Jerusalem, 1994).

28. See the recollection of a member of the Leningrad Philharmonic, Yakov Milkis,
in Wilson's *Shostakovich: A Life Remembered,* regarding the hidden "message" notion, particularly in the Fifth Symphony, pp. 314–15. Not only is the local context crucial, but the

active desire on the part of Shostakovich's colleagues and listeners to use his music to locate, articulate, and complete coded meanings of "registering a protest" and "mocking the Soviet regime."

29. The skill Shostakovich displayed in generating a plausible surface of musical experience consonant with the aesthetic orthodoxy put forward in 1936 in the criticism of his earlier works is notable in the Fifth Symphony. Consider, for example, not only the directness and economy of the thematic materials but the control of harmonic change. In the first movement, the transitions from D major at rehearsal number 39, through a variety of tonalities, ranging from C major, E-flat minor finally to E minor and ultimately to D minor are in audible, well-paced blocks. The same can be said for the eloquent section of the last movement, beginning at rehearsal number 113. Likewise, a sophisticated listener versed in the symphonic tradition need not deem the final section of the symphony, the D major at rehearsal 131, as anything but convincingly celebratory, given how it is prepared from rehearsal number 126 on.

30. Sheinberg, *Irony*, p. 319.

31. Iwan Sollertinski, *Gustav Mahler: Der Schrei ins Leere*, Studia Slavica Musicologica, vol. 8 (Berlin: Verlag Ernst Kuhn, 1996), pp. 10 and 70. On Mahler and Shostakovich, see Krzysztof Meyer, "Mahler und Shostakovich," in *Gustav Mahler: Sinfonie und Wirklichkeit*, ed. Otto Kolleritsch (Graz: Universal Edition, 1977), pp. 118–32. On Mahler and the imputation of emotion and psychological narratives in the reception of the music, see Leon Botstein, "Whose Gustav Mahler?: Reception, Interpretation, and History" in *Mahler and His World*, ed. Karen Painter (Princeton, N.J.: Princeton University Press, 2002), pp. 1–54.

32. See Larry Sitsky, *Music of the Repressed Russian Avant-Garde, 1900–1929* (Westport, Conn.: Greenwood Press, 1994), pp. 1–9, and Boris Schwarz, *Music and Musical Life*, pp. 88–140.

33. I am following the provocative account of the contrast between "Culture One," before 1932, and "Culture Two" after 1932, in the era of Stalin in architecture—a narrative that is useful in understanding the context of Shostakovich's career—in Vladimir Paperny, *Architecture in the Age of Stalin: Culture Two*, trans. John Hill and Roann Barris (Cambridge, Eng.: Cambridge University Press, 2002), p. 207.

34. See the essays (and the attendant illustrations) on architecture, politics, and aesthetics in this period in the Soviet Union by Olga Postnikowa, Eduard Sadiraka, Uwe Schögl, Otakar Macel, and Galina N. Jakowelka in *Kunst und Diktatur: Architektur, Bildhauerei und Malerie in Österreich, Deutschland, Italien und der Sowjetunion, 1922–1956*, ed. Jan Tibor, vol. 2 (Baden: Grasl, 1994), pp. 760–836.

35. Schwarz, *Music and Musical Life*, pp. 88–105.

36. Paperny, *Architecture in the Age of Stalin*, p. 218.

37. From a 1934 critique of literature, quoted in Paperny, *Architecture in the Age of Stalin*, p. 232.

38. *"Volksfeind Dmitri Schostakowitsch": Eine Dokumentation der öffentlichen Angriffe gegen den Komponisten in der ehemaligen Sowjetunion*, ed. Ernst Kuhn (Berlin: Verlag Ernst Kuhn, 1997), pp. 4–49. On Asafiev and Shostakovich, see Laurel E. Fay, "Shostakovich, LASM, and Asafiev," in *Shostakovich in Context*, pp. 51– 66.

39. See the chapter *"Entr'acte*: The Lessons of Lady M," in Taruskin's *Defining Russia Musically*, p. 498–510.

40. Reprinted in *"Volksfeind Dmitri Schostakowitsch,"* pp. 7–10. This article focused less on the supposed "flight into hocus-pocus and wild, unusual sounds" or allegedly incomprehensible modernism but on Shostakovich's failure to authentically represent through music the collective farm as a character of peasant culture. Shostakovich was accused of demonstrating "absolute indifference" to his presumed subject, the collective farm, in his ballet "The Limpid Stream" (p. 10). See also Leonid Maksimenkov, *Sumbur vmesto muzyki:*

Stalinskaia kul'turnaia revoliutsiia, 1936–1938 (Moscow: Iuridicheskaia kniga, 1997). Stalin himself commented on the validity of the "Muddle" argument for film music. I thank Laurel Fay for bringing Maximenkov's book to my attention.

41. In his 1936 defense of himself and Shostakovich, Sollertinsky explicitly left Gavriil Popov, whose remarkable Symphony no. 1 suffered from the shifting ideological premises of Soviet artistic policy in the 1930s, defenseless. His symphony, first performed in 1935, was ultimately suppressed after 1936. It was initially attacked, then defended and rehabilitated, only to be banned. Indeed, unlike Shostakovich, Popov seems to have been truly broken by the experience of the 1930s, despite winning the Stalin Prize in the 1940s and sustaining a career as composer and teacher. See *"Volksfeind Dmitri Schostakowitsch,"* pp. 24 and 31. On Popov, see Hakobian, *Music of the Soviet Age,* pp. 129–33, and Sitsky, *Music of the Repressed Russian Avant-Garde,* pp. 310–17.

42. See Fay, *Shostakovich: A Life,* pp. 155–58, and *"Volksfeind Dmitri Schostakowitsch,"* pp. 105–11.

43. These are Sollertinsky's four criteria, in his words, in *Gustav Mahler,* p. 74. On Sollertinsky, see Lyudmilla Mikheyevna-Sollertinskaya, "Shostakovich as Reflected in his Letters to Ivan Sollertinsky," in *Shostakovich in Context,* pp. 66–77, and Nicolai Malko, *A Certain Art* (New York: Morrow, 1966), pp. 196–97.

44. Benjamin Britten, "On Behalf of Gustav Mahler (1942)," in *Britten on Music,* ed. Paul Kildea (Oxford: Oxford University Press, 2003), pp. 38–39.

45. Aaron Copland and Vivian Perlis, *Copland: 1900 Through 1949* (New York: St. Martin's Press, 1984), pp. 63–64. On Copland's output from the 1930s and early 1940s and, as in the case of Shostakovich, its shifting ideological readings, confirming the notion of "instability" of meaning, see Elizabeth B. Crist, "Aaron Copland and the Popular Front," *Journal of the American Musicological Society* 56, no. 2 (Summer 2003): 409–66.

46. See Copland's letter dated April 2 to the *New York Times,* 5 April 1925.

47. Copland and Perlis, *Copland: 1900 Through 1949,* p. 230.

48. See Celeste Connor, *Democratic Visions: Art and Theory of the Stieglitz Circle, 1924–1934* (Berkeley, Calif.: University of California Press, 2001). One can also think of Roy Harris, particularly his Third Symphony in this regard; see Berger, *Reflections,* pp. 22–23.

49. See Hartmut Krones, *Marcel Rubin* (Vienna: Lafite, 1975/1989) pp. 74–77. There are similarities between Rubin's use of orchestra and symphonic strategies and Shostakovich's. More telling in terms of the parallelisms in the years from 1936 to the end of the 1940s is the admiration Shostakovich had for Arthur Honegger's Symphony no. 3, "Liturgique," written in 1945 and 1946. The work has much in common with Shostakovich's structures and sonorities and Shostakovich made a four-hand transcription; see Derek C. Hulme, *Dmitri Shostakovich: A Catalogue, Bibliography, and Discography,* 3d ed. (Lanham, Md.: Scarecrow Press, 2002), p. 102.

50. Harry Halbreich, *Arthur Honegger,* trans. Roger Nichols (Portland, Ore.: Amadeus Press, 1999), pp. 201–2.

51. Consider Lev Lebedinsky's description of the contradictions in Shostakovich, particularly around his joining the Party and his signing of the "official slander" of Sakharov and Solzhenitsyn in the Brezhnev era, in Wilson, *Shostakovich: A Life Remembered,* pp. 336–38.

52. See Svetlana Savenko, "Shostakovich's Literary Style," in *Shostakovich in Context,* pp. 43–49. See also Isaak Glikman's frequent references to writing for the composer and the composer's deadpan delivery in *Story of a Friendship.*

53. See, for example, the discussion of Beethoven's dedication and relationship to Napoleon in the context of shifting Austrian-French relationships in Thomas Sipe, *Beethoven: Eroica Symphony,* Cambridge Music Handbooks (Cambridge, Eng.: Cambridge University Press 1998) p. 30–53.

54. Krzysztof Meyer, *Dmitri Schostakowitsch: Sein Leben, sein Werk, seine Zeit* (Mainz: Atlantis, 1998), pp. 451–52.

55. Wilson, *Shostakovich: A Life Remembered,* p. 434; see also *Materialen zu Brechts "Leben des Galilei,"* ed. Werner Hecht (Frankfurt/Main: Suhrkamp, 1969), p. 191.

56. *Story of a Friendship,* p. 141.

57. Fay, *Shostakovich: A Life,* p. 229.

58. Personal communication from Laurel Fay, 8 February 2004.

59. Bertolt Brecht, *Life of Galileo,* ed. John Willett and Ralph Mannheim, trans. John Willett (New York: Arcade, 1994), p. vii. Citations are from this edition.

60. Brecht, *Life of Galileo,* p. 32.

61. Ibid., p. 109. Compare these lines to the self-criticism the composer subjected himself to in a letter to Glikman just two weeks before seeing Brecht's play; see *Story of a Friendship,* p. 140.

62. See two contemporary analyses of Shostakovich. "On the Eighth Quartet," by Lawrence Kramer in his *Musical Meaning: Toward a Critical History* (Berkeley, Calif.: University of California Press, 2002), pp. 232–41; and Gregory Karl and Jenefer Robinson, "Shostakovich's Tenth Symphony and the Musical Expression of Cognitively Complex Emotions," in *Music and Meaning,* ed. Jenefer Robinson (Ithaca, N.Y.: Cornell University Press, 1997), pp. 154–78, which makes the case for the communication of hope and, indeed, false hope in the work.

INDEX

Index

General Index

CONTRIBUTORS

Notes on the Contributors

Leon Botstein is President and Leon Levy Professor in the Arts and Humanities at Bard College. He is the author of *Judentum und Modernität* (Vienna, 1991) and *Jefferson's Children: Education and the Promise of American Culture* (New York, 1997). He is the editor of *The Compleat Brahms* (New York, 1999) and *The Musical Quarterly*, as well as coeditor, with Werner Hanak, of *Vienna: Jews and the City of Music, 1870–1938* (Vienna and New York, 2004). The music director of the American and the Jerusalem Symphony Orchestras, he has recorded works by, among others, Szymanowski, Hartmann, Bruch, Toch, Dohnányi, Bruckner, Richard Strauss, Mendelssohn, and Liszt for Telarc, CRI, Koch, Arabesque, and New World Records.

Malcolm Hamrick Brown is Professor Emeritus of Music (Musicology) at Indiana University, Bloomington. Founding editor of the series "Russian Music Studies," he recently compiled and edited *A Shostakovich Casebook* for the series (Indiana University Press, 2004).

Caryl Emerson is A. Watson Armour III University Professor of Slavic Languages and Literatures at Princeton University, where she chairs the Slavic Department with a co-appointment in Comparative Literature. She is a translator and critic of the Russian literary critic and philosopher Mikhail Bakhtin, and has published widely on nineteenth-century Russian literature (Pushkin, Tolstoy, Dostoevsky), on the history of literary criticism in the Slavic world, and on Russian opera and vocal music. Recent publications include *The Life of Musorgsky* (Cambridge University Press, 1999) for the series "Musical Lives." Her current research interests center around Russian philosophers as readers of Russian literature and their philosophies of the creative act.

David Fanning is Reader in Music and Departmental Chair at the University of Manchester, an active pianist (principally with the Lindsay String Quartet), broadcaster and critic, and author of books and articles on Shostakovich and Nielsen, including a forthcoming study of Shostakovich's Eighth String Quartet for Ashgate Publishing.

Laurel E. Fay is an independent scholar and author of *Shostakovich: A Life* (Oxford University Press, 2000), which won the Otto Kinkeldey Award of the American Musicological Society. She has written and lectured extensively on Russian and Soviet music.

Christopher H. Gibbs is James H. Ottaway Jr. Professor of Music at Bard College and Co-Artistic Director of the Bard Music Festival. He edited *The Cambridge Companion to Schubert* and is author of *The Life of Schubert* (Cambridge University Press, 2000). Since 2000 he has served as musicological consultant and Program Annotator for the Philadelphia Orchestra.

Levon Hakobian, a Senior Researcher at the Moscow State Institute for Art Studies, is the author of studies on medieval Armenian sacred hymnography, general music theory, and music of the twentieth century, including *Music of the Soviet Age, 1917–1987* (Stockholm, 1998) and *Dmitrii Shostakovich: opyt fenomenologii tvorchestva* (Shostakovich: An essay in the phenomenology of his work) (St. Petersburg, 2004). The compiler of the Russian edition of the Concise Grove Dictionary, he is currently working on an encyclopedia of twentieth-century music.

Leonid Maximenkov, historian and archivist, is an independent scholar who divides his time between Toronto and Moscow. Author of *Sumbur vmesto muzyki: Stalinskaia kul'turnaia revoliutsiia, 1936–1938* (Muddle instead of music: The Stalinist cultural revolution, 1936–1938) (Moscow, 1997), he is currently working on its continuation: *Muzyka vmesto sumbura: Stalinskaia kul'turnaia kontrevoliutsiia, 1946–1948* (Music instead of muddle: The Stalinist cultural counterrevolution, 1946–1948).

Gerard McBurney lives in London, working as a freelance composer, arranger, teacher, writer, and broadcaster. His arrangements and reconstructions of lesser-known or fragmentary works by Shostakovich have been widely played, and include a rescoring for dance-band of the operetta *Moscow, Cheryomushki*, op. 105.

Simon Morrison is Assistant Professor of Music at Princeton University, where he teaches courses on nineteenth- and twentieth-century music, especially that of Russia and France. The author of *Russian Opera and the Symbolist Movement* (University of California Press, 2002), he is currently working on a collection of essays entitled *Ballet Imagined*.

Rolanda Norton is a freelance translator specializing in the arts. Her previous clients include BBC Radio 3. She is married with a young family and lives in Essex, UK.

Rosa Salmanovna Sadykhova, a theater historian, is Chief of the Exhibition Department of the St. Petersburg State Museum of Theatre and Music. She has curated many international exhibitions, including *Dmitrii Shostakovich: Life and Works, Man and Culture* (Germany, 1984); *Boris Anisfeld* (USA, 1994); *Tchaikovsky in Petersburg* (Italy, 1997); *One Hundred Years of Russian Theatrical Design* (USA, 1999); and *Verdi in Russia* (Italy, 2001).

Peter J. Schmelz is an Assistant Professor of Musicology at the State University of New York at Buffalo. He is currently at work on *Listening, Memory, and the Thaw*, a book that explores the social and political meanings of the unofficial Soviet music of the 1960s.

Dimitri Shapovalov is a senior graduate student at Cornell University whose scholarly interests include literary aesthetics of early twentieth-century Russia, poetics of Russian Symbolism, and musical analysis. His dissertation, "The Russian Solo Song from Rimsky-Korsakov to Prokofiev: Aesthetic and Analytical Perspectives," explores the interaction of irony and lyricism in this diverse body of works and investigates the genre's relationship to the aesthetics of Russian modernism.